INQUISITION

Edward Peters

THE FREE PRESS
A Division of Macmillan, Inc.
NEW YORK

Collier Macmillan Publishers
LONDON

C

The Free Press
A Division of Macmillan, Inc.
866 Third Avenue, New York, N.Y. 10022

Collier Macmillan Canada, Inc.

Printed in the United States of America

printing number
1   2   3   4   5   6   7   8   9   10

Library of Congress Cataloging-in-Publication Data

Peters, Edward murray, 1936–
  Inquisition.

  Bibliography: p.
  Includes index.
    1. Inquisition.   2. Inquisition in art.
  3. Inquisition in literature.   I. Title.
BX1712. P48   1988   272'.2   87–33194
  ISBN 0–02–924980–5

Illustration Credits

Map: Gustav Henningsen
Plates 1–14, 16–27: Henry Charles Lea Library and Special Collections, Van Pelt Library, University of Pennsylvania
Plate 15: Trustees of the British Museum

Contents

Acknowledgments

All books owe many debts, and this book owes two in particular. The first is to those scholars upon whose original research so much of it depends, and the second is to the Van Pelt Library of the University of Pennsylvania and to its generous staff, particularly that of the Rare Book Collection, and also to its Curator of Special Collections, Dr. Daniel H. Traister, all of whom have been unfailingly and characteristically cooperative in my research.

Years ago, Professor Antonio Márquez extended to me the courtesy of considering me an inquisition historian long before I became one and provided me with many valuable bibliographical references. Professors Angel Alcalá, Stephen Haliczer, and John Tedeschi have invited me to scholarly conferences at which I was able to speak with other historians and learn the results of their research. Gustav Henningsen, Research Director of the Danish Folklore Archives, has always been extremely helpful with bibliographical and other scholarly advice.

Several colleagues at the University of Pennsylvania have also been extremely helpful. John Ahtes very generously read the early drafts of several chapters and provided extensive bibliographical assistance. Alan Kors greatly improved the present Chapter 6 with a critical reading. Elliott Mossman has kindly advised me concerning Dostoievsky's library. Jeffrey Sturcio kindly read and advised me on the material concerning Bruno and Galileo in Chapter 8. A generous grant from the History Department's Rosengarten Fund greatly assisted with the preparation of the illustrations. I am grateful to my chair, Alfred J. Rieber, for this assistance. Ethel Cooley and Joan Plonski combined to produce an orderly and readable manuscript on a variety of electric and electronic machines.

Over the years, conversations and exchanges with many colleagues here and in Europe have gone into this book. Joyce Seltzer deftly and patiently edited a large and vagrant manuscript into the present volume.

Introduction

"A thing . . . burdenous to the world"

I

Between the twelfth and the sixteenth centuries in western Europe, the Latin Christian Church adapted certain elements of Roman legal procedure and charged papally appointed clergy to employ them in order to preserve orthodox religious beliefs from the attacks of heretics. Between the sixteenth and the nineteenth centuries, chiefly in Mediterranean Europe, these procedures and personnel were transformed into institutional tribunals called inquisitions charged with the protection of orthodox beliefs and the maintenance of ecclesiastical discipline in the Latin Christian community. Between the sixteenth and the twentieth centuries, largely as a result of the division within the Latin Church into Roman Catholic and Reformed (or Protestant) confessions, these procedures, personnel, and institutions were transformed by polemic and fiction into a myth, the myth of *The Inquisition*. The institutions and the myth lived—and developed—in western Europe and the New World until the early nineteenth century, when most of the inquisitions were abolished, and the myth itself was universalized in a series of great artistic works into an indictment, by a modern world, of an earlier Europe for its crushing of the human spirit.

Although the inquisitions disappeared, *The Inquisition* did not. The myth was originally devised to serve variously the political purposes of a number of early modern political regimes, as well as Protestant Reformers, proponents of religious and civil toleration, philosophical enemies of the civil power of organized religions, and progressive modernists; but the myth remained durable, widely adaptable, and useful, so that

1

in time it came to be woven tightly into the fabric of modern consciousness. So tight is its place in that weave that the myth has been revived
in the twentieth century and applied, not chiefly to religious institutions
or disciplinary techniques, but to the perceived excesses of some secular
governments, and to those twentieth-century states that appear to seek
endless, detailed information about the lives and thoughts of their citizens.

There has never been an account of this history and this myth. Yet
an account of both provides an illuminating perspective on much early
and recent history, not least as an account of the ways by which the
changing value systems of a historical culture have perceived, defined,
and acted upon the problem of dissent. The problem of the self-definition
of societies in history is central to historical understanding; one way of
measuring such self-definition is to consider both the history of a culture
and the myths by which a culture perceives its own movement through
time. In the late nineteenth and twentieth centuries it has become possible
to do this for a great many cultures over long periods of the past. All
cultures have immediate uses for the past, but until recently few cultures
have distinguished between—and lived with—a mythical *and* a historical
past. Side by side with the myth of *The Inquisition*, there has also grown
up a history of inquisitorial procedures, personnel, and institutions, one
that can illuminate important aspects of the past and measure the myth
as well. Although myths compete with histories, myths themselves have
histories, and the history of myth is a valid part of history.

Any history that deals with a part of the past once preempted by
myth ought to be an account of both the history and the myth, and it
should also explain how the history emerged from a past preempted by
myth, how that history became possible and how it displaced—or attempted to displace—the myth.

This book proposes to tell three such histories. The first is that of
the legal procedures, personnel, and institutions that shaped the inquisitorial tribunals of early modern Europe. The second is the history of the
myth of *The Inquisition*, from its shaping in the hands of anti-Hispanists
and religious reformers in the sixteenth century to its universalization
in a series of great artistic works in the nineteenth century. The third
is the history of how a history of the inquisitions emerged out of myths
of *The Inquisition*.

The ecclesiastical courts that were technically called inquisitions, and
were later mythologized into *The Inquisition*, had their origins in several
procedural changes in Roman law that occurred no later than the late
first century B.C. Inquisitorial *procedure* existed first in Roman and then
in canon law, long before there were inquisitors. From the thirteenth

century on, popes appointed individuals to the *function* of inquisitor
long before later popes and other rulers established *institutional inquisitions.* There was never, except in polemic and fiction, *The Inquisition,*
a single all-powerful, horrific tribunal, whose agents worked everywhere
to thwart religious truth, intellectual freedom, and political liberty, until
it was overthrown sometime in the nineteenth century—*The Inquisition*
of modern folklore.

The origins of the myth can now be traced back through the history
of early inquisitorial procedure, personnel, and institutions. The emergence of inquisitorial procedure in Roman criminal and civil law around
the beginning of the Common Era shaped the Empire that was Christianized in the fourth century, and in turn influenced the organization of
ecclesiastical offices and the character of ecclesiastical discipline. Papally
appointed inquisitors appeared from the thirteenth to the fifteenth centuries, and from 1478 on there appeared a series of institutionalized standing
inquisitions in several parts of Catholic Europe, notably Spain, Portugal,
Rome, and Venice. Most of these tribunals were abolished between
1798 and 1820; only that of Rome survived through various metamor-
phoses into the twentieth century as The Congregation for the Doctrine
of the Faith.

Laws and institutions live in cultural and historical contexts. The
inquisitorial procedures and personnel of medieval Europe operated in
a culture in which a particular set of religious beliefs not only touched
the daily lives and thoughts of all its members, but also defined and
limited what are now recognized as such virtually independent fields as
economics and politics. One way of looking at the confessional revolutions
of the sixteenth century is to see them as a great debate about the nature
of the Christian, and hence European, life. As part of that debate,
each side of the confessional war defined itself and also defined its opponents in language that dated back to the early centuries of Christianity
itself. As the theme of ecclesiastical discipline and religious persecution
became central to these debates, and as a number of political regimes—
notably that of Spain—entered the struggle as the champions of Roman
Catholicism, opponents of both used the language of martyrology, the
concept of a hidden, persecuted, true Church, and the Satanic depravity
of their enemies to depict the inquisitions as instruments used by cynical
rulers and clergy to suppress the light of the true Gospel through religious
repression, and to corrupt the legitimate power of civil authorities.

Later in the sixteenth century, as the confessional revolution took
on a necessary political dimension, *The Inquisition* came to represent
the enemy of political liberty, the ultimate symbol of the unnatural

alliance of Throne and Altar. By the eighteenth century, when *The Inquisition* was also charged with intellectual repression, the myth had grown to such proportions that it served virtually all proponents of a particular vision of modernity as a convenient target for everything that had seemed wrong with the entire culture of the recent and remote past. It also served as a warning about giving too much power to religious authorities.

To recount the history without dealing with the myth is to tell only part of a fascinating story; to treat the myth without the history is to deprive the myth of the only thing by which it can be measured and understood. This book deals with both the history and the myth. The research of many historians over the past century has made the history possible, and a new interest in the mythologies by which cultures live has suggested that the myth, too, is a valid component of those histories.

II

When similar processes are studied in the twentieth century, they are called political mythology. As Leonard Thompson has defined it:

> By a political myth I mean a tale told about the past to legitimize or discredit a regime; and by a political mythology, a cluster of such myths that reinforce one another and jointly constitute the historical element in the ideology of the regime or its rival.

Although social groups within a state may possess their own myths, political mythology is assumed to be characteristic of the twentieth century because states are the most powerful forces in the twentieth-century world, capable of shaping public consciousness in both subtle and direct ways. But in earlier European history, some religious and philosophical causes were more important than states, and these causes too used mythologies, but as yet these have had no name. Perhaps we are still too close to the religious conflicts of the Reformation and their aftermath—and perhaps we are also too ecumenical—to term them "religious mythology." Perhaps we have too much respect for the intellectual achievements of seventeenth- and eighteenth-century philosophers to term them "philosophical mythology." In the case of *The Inquisition*, we are certainly dealing with a mythology of history, since a major component of the myth was the assertion that *The Inquisition* was so essential a component of Roman Catholicism that it had always—potentially or actually—existed, and that its sixteenth-, seventeenth-, and eighteenth-century manifestations were an unchanging continuation of its earliest existence.

Historians are not always comfortable with historical mythologies. The last work of the major twentieth-century philosopher and historian Ernst Cassirer was *The Myth of the State*, published in 1946. In it Cassirer, while recognizing the mythical component in all human life, pointed out the unique vulnerability of modern societies to state-fabricated and state-sponsored myths, and the errors of those who fail to recognize the power and the danger that these represent:

> Myth itself has not been really vanquished and subjugated. It is always there, lurking in the dark and waiting for its hour and opportunity. This hour comes as soon as the other binding forces of man's social life, for one reason or another, lose their strength and are no longer able to combat the demonic mythical powers.

But Cassirer was considering the most hideous manifestations of political mythology that the modern world had ever seen, and, as some historians have pointed out, it is an as yet unheard of society that has no myths at all, including our own, although not all of them function the same way that Cassirer saw the myth of the State functioning in the middle of the twentieth century.

In some cases, "the other binding forces of man's social life" have yet to be developed. The ideals of the twentieth century cannot be used as a norm by which to measure the social cohesiveness of past societies and other cultures without seriously misunderstanding the unique social bonds and myths of those societies and cultures. Myth, then, in this sense is simply the broadest way that any society or culture *uses* its past or present. It may be ferocious mythology of the kind Cassirer had in mind, or it may be what the Czech historian František Graus has called *lebendige Vergangenheit*, the "living past" which is the instrumental use of the past in a culture's mentality. In this sense, while myth may serve destructive ends, it may just as often serve as a substitute for as yet non-existent social bonds that will render it marginal or picturesque.

What Cassirer and Thompson call political mythology has in earlier European history also been the myth of the Church or the myth of the *Volk*—the people before it acquires a State. Leonard Thompson's own discussion of political mythology occurs in his valuable study, *The Political Mythology of Apartheid*, some elements of which derive from non-political areas, notably religion. Leon Poliakov has written of *The Aryan Myth*, the large tradition of shaped belief from which Nazis derived much of the rationalization for their policies of racial purity and violent antisemitism.

In these instances, Graus's "living past" turns deadly. But myths are not always destructive, and in many cases they may also serve to prop up a culture until that culture has devised other means of defining itself. Even when some myths serve self-definition by attacking an enemy, they serve to reinforce social and cultural bonds that may not be adequately served by institutions. Myths change as the circumstances that created and sustained them change; they serve a constant *now* by asserting that as things now are, so they have always been. They may be challenged by history, but history does not always triumph over them. The best way of understanding them is historical. In our case, we will consider what the inquisitions actually were, as formal historical research has made this possible; and we shall also consider what, for five centuries, *The Inquisition* was asserted to be.

III

This book, then, is an essay in several different kinds of intellectual history as well as a study of certain strands in legal, ecclesiastical, and political history. It is centrally a history of a myth just as much as it is a history of an institution or an idea. And it imposes some rules, chiefly concerning normally elusive and often ideological terminology.

Part of the legacy of historical myth is the history and use of historical terminology. In this book I have made some specific decisions about historical terminology that require some explanation. In describing the institutions of Christian Europe before the mid-sixteenth century, I have used the terms Greek Church or Greek Christianity for the religious world of eastern Europe and its culture. I have used the terms Latin Church and Latin Christianity to designate the religion and culture of western Europe and, after the fifteenth century, to its presence in the New World, measured in its relation to the Bishop of Rome. I have not used the term Roman Catholicism until describing events pertinent in the Latin Church from the middle of the sixteenth century on, and I occasionally use the term Roman Church for the same period. Thus, in referring to what Roman Catholics and others today refer to as the Roman Catholic Church before 1550, I use the term Latin Church or Latin Christianity. I use that term for the very same institution and culture that Protestants until recently used to designate as the False or Popish Church. I use the terms Protestant and Protestantism partly in a general sense to describe opposition to Roman Catholicism (or Latin Christianity) on the part of people in the four centuries before the present who would have agreed on very little else, or as a general term implying opposition to Rome and the manifestations of Roman Catholicism in the different regions of Catholic Europe.

When I use the term inquisition (lower case), I address the function of institutions that were so called, as historical research has described them. When I use the term Inquisition (upper case) I always refer in shorthand to a particularly constituted, specific institution (such as the Spanish Inquisition or the Venetian Inquisition). When I use the term *The Inquisition*, I am referring in one form or another to an image, legend, or myth, usually in polemic. These decisions will not satisfy everyone, but they at least make an honest attempt to remove some of the dangerous presuppositions that often creep into even the most even-handed attempts at historical neutrality.

For the convenience of readers I have not used footnotes, but at the end of the book I have appended a substantial bibliographical essay that is arranged according to the flow of each chapter and chapter section. For all works not originally written in English, the translations are mine, except where noted, and all citations are identified in the bibliographical essay.

IV

In 1659 Francis Howgill caused to be printed in London a book with the furious title,

> The popish inquisition newly erected in New-England, whereby their church is manifested to be a daughter of mysterie Babylon, which did drink the blood of the saints who bears the express image of her mother, demonsttated [sic] by her fruits. . . .

The title goes on for another paragraph. Neither Howgill's language nor his idea of "the popish inquisition" is at all uncharacteristic of the confessional polemic of the seventeenth century, in England or elsewhere. But Howgill is not really interested in the Roman Church, nor in any historical inquisition. He wrote to protest the persecution of Quakers in New England, particularly in Boston, by the Massachusetts religious authorities, none of whom remotely resembled a Roman Catholic. But Howgill desperately wanted to define his persecutors in a common language of persecution that anyone—whether friendly to Quakers or not—would instantly recognize and abhor. Howgill, as had others, found that common language of persecution in *The Inquisition*.

One of the most widely read accounts of inquisitorial activity of the sixteenth century had described the Spanish Inquisition as "a thing . . . burdenous to the world." A century later, Howgill certainly recognized it as such and expected his readers to recognize it as well. So did Voltaire a century after Howgill, but with a very different agenda. So did Verdi and Dostoievsky a century after Voltaire. Early in the eighteenth century a historian who made his own contributions to the myth of *The Inquisition* observed that:

> The Inquisition is a Subject of so particular a Nature, that any one who attempts to write upon it with Impartiality, will find that he has undertaken a very difficult Province.

As anyone who has ever worked on inquisition history knows, he was right. He was right partly because myth and history in this case are closely intertwined, and to extricate one from the other is to touch something that still resonates in modern consciousness and emotion; it also raises the charge that the historian is simply creating an uncomfortable new myth to replace the old.

Even the most competent of modern historians sometimes express the fear that no writer, however critical in methodology and terminology, can ever be so free of his or her own world view, mentality, ideology, or religious confession as not to impose new myths in place of those just exposed. At its most cynical or idealistic, this fear translates into what Alan Ryan has termed the assumption that "the nicer class of historian should put in circulation a better class of myth." On the other hand, some historians assert that their work really does deal in pure historical truth. Since, however, the matters dealt with in this book are still matters of powerful emotive resonance to a great many people, including some who have no confessional stake in their history, something must be said about myth and truth.

In a collection of source materials in English translation on the history of heresy and authority in medieval Europe, I once insisted that I had made the collection and edited it "coherently and deliberately, but not ideologically, argumentatively, or least of all confessionally." No reviewer of that collection said that I had not done so. I would like to think that I have made this book in the same spirit. If I have not, some generous critic will be sure to point this out to unwary readers, and even to some wary ones. What we have in common with people in the past is that, like them, we live in time, but, unlike them, we can observe people living in time in ways that we cannot always use to observe ourselves. Every modern historian knows that it is possible to be historically critical and even to adopt a relativist or historicist stance in estimating the moral character of data that have been discovered and written up, and that at the same time the historian as culture-bound citizen is under an equal obligation to make judgments about his or her own time, since the historian is in it and must do something about it, must act as a political and cultural citizen. If the historian separates the judgmental process about contemporary events and discards the judgmental language about contemporary events in historical analysis and description, it should be possible to reach an adequate, if not perfect, level of objectivity without falling into the trap that Ryan describes as "an overdose of detachment [boring] everyone to death." If I have gone to considerable trouble in handling some volatile materials to present them in as objective a way as possible, I have at least also been aware of the danger of boring everyone to death, and therefore trivializing an inherently fascinating story.

Granted, the cautionary remarks expressed above work better for historical questions that are more remote from our interests in the present than for those that are recent or passionately felt. It is barely possible, a century later, to find general agreement about the U.S. Civil War and the issues that precipitated it, it is far easier to find considerable disagreement, even among professional historians. Contemporary issues of race and gender extend backwards in time, even though the language in which we have finally formulated and identified them is the language of twentieth-century consciousness. How far should we take the language into historical description and analysis? It is language that serves the ends of policy and ideology as much as it may serve the ends of history. On the other hand, can history have its own clear language that is so distinct from other manifestations of consciousness that there is no bridge between the two? Does the necessity of that bridge mean that history can only be at best "a nicer sort of myth"?

Historians have gone to a great deal of trouble to be able to profess that what they produce is a legitimate kind of truth. The rigors of historical method produce work that can be challenged more effectively on grounds of method than on grounds of ideology. Truth of this kind may fit some myths better than it fits others, but it should not be criticized on the grounds of myth if it has not been produced originally in their service. Myth may accept or reject history, but, because it is myth, it cannot refute history on any grounds other than comparable historical criticism. This is a book of history and is submitted as history, both

the history of part of the past and the history of myths about part of
the past.

It is a useful rule that in the writing of history one ought to begin
with that of the earliest components of one's subject. The oldest component of both the history and myth of inquisitions is that of inquisitorial
legal procedure, which appeared in the law of the Romans and in their
courts late in the first century B.C.

Chapter One

The Law of Rome and the Latin Christian Church

From the beginning to the end of the Roman peace the culture and institutions of the Roman Empire shaped a complex imperial society, ruled by an intricate and largely autonomous legal system. Roman law, like Roman government, touched the lives of all those inside the Empire, and many of those outside it, and changes in the law, even relatively small ones, could have considerable impact, often far more widely than their designers intended.

During the first century B.C. one such change in Roman civil law began a process by which, over several centuries, the entire criminal law of Rome was changed, the disciplinary capacities of early Christian communities were shaped, and a procedure and an institution were created that became by the seventeenth and eighteenth centuries a byword for both religious intolerance and the unnatural use of force in matters of conscience. A great deal of history begins with small changes.

Long before the Christian Church possessed any judicial apparatus at all, long, in fact, before it even became a legally recognized part of the religions of the Roman world, Roman law had devised the inquisitorial procedure that later, adapted to different historical periods and problems, shaped the ecclesiastical and secular inquisitions of medieval and early modern Europe and of later European mythology. How that civil procedure emerged in Rome and how it came to be used in Roman criminal law, and then in Christian discipline, is a story that is often neglected when the later inquisitorial procedures and institutions are studied, but history begins with beginnings, however remote or inconvenient they may be. Our first history begins here.

The Emergence of Inquisitorial Procedure in Roman Law

In general Latin usage from Plautus to Quintilian the word *inquisitio* possessed a number of related meanings, some of which pertained to legal procedure, and some of which did not. Its earliest meaning, and long a common one, simply described the act of looking for something, to make a search. By the first century B.C. Cicero and other writers used the term somewhat more narrowly in the sense of inquiring into specific matters; here, *inquisitio* was often a synonym for *investigatio*, but still without a specifically legal connotation. Cicero also used the term, and the verb *inquirere* from which it was originally derived, in the more technical sense of searching for evidence in matters under litigation. Since plaintiffs in Roman law were expected to provide adequate evidence to support their charges against defendants, *inquirere* and *inquisitio* came to designate that formal stage of legal procedure in which evidence to support a charge against someone was sought by whoever had brought the charge in the first place.

The substantive *inquisitor* had a similar semantic history. The word first designated anyone who searched, and then more specifically, someone who searched for proofs or evidence to support a charge leveled against someone else. Both the *inquisitor* and the *inquisitio* were private persons and actions: neither the performer nor the act was considered a religious or public affair, nor was *inquisitio* in any sense a public act. Moreover, whether in civil or criminal cases, the evidence sought for by an *inquisitor* during an *inquisitio* was always for acts committed or omitted, or for the existence of a right, status, or obligation, and never for beliefs or opinions.

In the history of Roman legal procedure historians recognize three stages of development: that of the *legis actio*, that of the *formula*, and that of *cognitio extraordinaria*. Only in the last and latest of these did *inquisitio* take on its later meaning of the intense and detailed investigation by a magistrate who controlled the procedure of a legal dispute, whether civil or criminal, from its beginning to its end. In order to understand the importance of *cognitio extraordinaria* in the history of inquisitorial procedure, however, something must be said about the two earlier types of procedure, *legis actio* and *formula*.

The *legis actio* is among the earliest forms of Roman legal procedure. According to it, a citizen (Roman law made other arrangements for non-citizens and for disputes between a citizen and a non-citizen) with a claim against another citizen sought the advice of an amateur legal expert, who advised him about appealing to a magistrate for a remedy.

The magistrate, generally known as the *praetor*, decided whether a legal action existed, whether the claim would fit, and whether the form of action requested by the plaintiff was legitimate and appropriate. If he decided that a legitimate action did apply in the form in which the plaintiff had put the charge, the *praetor* consulted the *album iudicum*, a list of eligible persons before whom a trial might be held, and selected one person from that list, usually with the agreement of the two parties involved, as a judge or arbitrator, *iudex* or *arbiter*. The judge was also a private individual; his only public authority was that given him by the *praetor* to try a single case. The *legis actio* itself was the name given to the specific verbal formulas that the plaintiff invoked before the *praetor*, which the *praetor* recognized or did not recognize as warranting the appointment of a *iudex* or *arbiter* to hear evidence and try the case. The procedure is characterized by great formality, exact adherence to verbal rules for framing the charge, and considerable restrictions on the discretion of the *praetor* to accept or refuse the remedy sought by the plaintiff.

At some point in the procedure, evidence on both sides was searched for (the original meaning of *inquisitio*), aired, and considered, and elaborate pleadings on both sides, usually by professional orators, were allowed. The final decision was made by the judge alone, strictly according to the charge issued by the *praetor* and the judge's estimation of the evidence and the arguments of both parties.

In the *formula* system, which began to displace the *legis actio* procedure in the second century B.C., the *praetor* was no longer bound by strict verbal formulas, but was permitted to use his own discretion in choosing the form in which the charge would be submitted to the *iudex*, whom he still appointed. The *praetor* selected a *formula* (a charge agreed to by him and by both parties which was written down and might contain both specifics and programs of allowable defense) and sent both parties and the *formula* to the *iudex* for the trial. The chief features of the *formula* procedure were the greatly increased discretion and authority of the *praetor* and the written character of the *formula*, which enabled successive *praetores* to issue at the beginning of their terms lists of the cases they chose to deal with and formulas they would follow. The accumulation of material from *praetor* to *praetor* and the repetition in the edict of one *praetor* of material from his predecessors led to the written collection of praetors' edicts which was formalized by the emperor Hadrian around 125 A.D.

Both the *legis actio* and the *formula* procedures dealt with claims of one citizen against another—what would now be called civil procedure.

The nature of that procedure was accusatorial; that is, a private individual laid a charge, applied for and received either a *legis actio* or a *formula* from the *praetor*, assembled the necessary evidence, and often brought the defendant personally before the *iudex* who decided the case. In many respects, early Roman criminal law was also accusatorial. From the mid-second century B.C. Roman practice had instituted individual courts (*quaestiones perpetuae*) to try different types of criminal offenses. Even here, however, a private individual had to bring a criminal charge before the proper court against another private citizen: in this sense, criminal procedure too was accusatorial. When the accuser made a formal accusation before the proper *quaesitor* (the chairman of the individual court) and the *quaesitor* accepted it, the latter enrolled the name of the accused in the register of those scheduled to face criminal trial. The accuser had to swear that he was not making his accusation out of malice (*iuramentum calumniae*). The individual *quaestiones perpetuae* consisted of varying numbers of jurors, some of which were established by the same laws which had established each *quaestio* in the first place. Thus, the mixture of private and public actors was similar in both civil and criminal law down to the end of the first century B.C. The participation of public officials—and of private individuals appointed by public officials—was called *cognitio*, and the procedure described immediately above was called *cognitio ordinaria*.

Most of the participants in the legal procedures of the Republic—plaintiffs, defendants, *praetores*, *iudices*, and the membership of the *quaestiones perpetuae*—belonged to the middle and upper strata of Roman society. Although there is little information about the civil and criminal procedures among the least powerful and worst positioned members of Roman society, there is some evidence that procedure was much more summary and that particular officials of the city and region could administer the law in much more efficient and swifter ways. Justice also appears to have been administered by magistrates in the Roman provinces to a much greater extent than in Rome itself. Finally, in the last century of the Republic, when particular accusations did not seem to fit the established categories of offense for which different *quaestiones perpetuae* had been established, extraordinary *quaestiones* could be erected whose rules and powers may have had greater latitude than those of the earlier *quaestiones perpetuae*. These three areas of criminal procedure, about which very little is known, may have contributed something to the development of the third stage of procedure, one which encompassed both civil and criminal jurisdiction, the *cognitio extraordinaria*.

With the transformation of the Roman Republic into the Roman

Empire during the reign of Augustus (31 B.C.–14 A.D.), an enormous number of powers came into the hands of the emperor, and the structure of the Republic was transformed. Although most of the contents of Augustus's two important statutes on legal procedure—the *Leges Juliae iudiciorum publicorum et privatorum*—have been lost, it is clear that the emperor and his servants assumed more and more direct control of legal procedure, at first paralleling surviving courts and procedures, but eventually superseding them. Gradually the sources of law were narrowed down to one—the edict of the emperor. Gradually also a new mode of procedure displaced the formulary system and the trials before the *quaestiones perpetuae.*

In one instance it is possible to see the new procedure in early operation. In earlier Roman law a testator's instruction to his heir to carry out certain actions for the benefit of a third party was considered a moral rather than a legal responsibility and was designated *fideicommissum.* Under Augustus, however, a new magistrate was created, the *praetor fideicommissarius,* whose duty was to supervise the carrying out of such testatorial instructions, now deemed to have a legal bearing. The *praetor fideicommissarius* was empowered to oversee the entire procedure from start to finish, thus eliminating some of the traditional stages and figures in earlier civil law. The procedure of the *praetor fideicommissarius* was called *cognitio extra ordinem,* or *extraordinaria,* and it virtually ended the older institutions of plaintiff, *praetor, iudex, formula,* and the rest, since a single magistrate, empowered by the emperor, supervised the entire case, drawing assistance and advice when necessary from assessors who were experts in the law. In civil procedure, as the new, efficient, authoritative *cognitio extraordinaria* developed, the agreement of the parties disappeared and the general form of a civil trial began to resemble the forms of criminal trials.

The sources for the emergence of the *cognitio extraordinaria* are not entirely clear, but among them may be numbered the greater latitude of civil and criminal procedure under the governors of the provinces, the authoritarian and speedy administration of justice among the poorest of Rome's inhabitants, and the attractiveness of efficient single-magistrate procedure under a centralized government whose ambition to establish order in both civil and criminal law was great and urgent.

The terms *inquisitio* and *inquisitor* acquired new meaning under the new procedure. During the second and third centuries A.D. the term *inquisitio* came to mean the search for evidence undertaken by officials subordinate to the magistrate who tried the whole case under *cognitio extraordinaria.* Although it remained possible for a criminal charge to be made by *accusatio*, the process of magisterial supervision of the search for evidence in a criminal case transferred one more responsibility from a private party to an official of the state. Thus, under the new system of *cognitio extraordinaria* as developed during the first three centuries A.D., the magistrate presiding by virtue of the delegation of imperial authority did not require an accuser or a formal charge; he could institute proceedings on his own initiative or after information from an informer (*delator*), and he supervised the entire trial from beginning to end. Thus, alongside and often in opposition to accusatorial procedure, there emerged in the *cognitio extraordinaria* the new form of inquisitorial procedure. Originally descriptive of the role of a single magistrate throughout a case, the term came to mean the absence of a named accuser and the expanded powers of a magistrate to initiate prosecutions on his own authority, delegated from the emperor.

In the new inquisitorial procedure, which in spite of its name quickly became the ordinary procedure of criminal and of most civil law, expert jurists were now the advisers of the magistrate, who did not need to be an expert in the law. The expanded powers of the magistrate and his expanded responsibilities to inquire (*inquirere*) into the existence of crimes and the possible identities of their perpetrators removed much of the responsibility from the accuser and greatly diminished his role. The older meaning of *inquisitio*, the accuser's search for relevant evidence, gave way before the new *inquisitio* of the magistrate and his subordinate officials. The accuser's right to interrogate and bring before the *iudex* the opposing party to a suit also gave way before the power of the magistrate. The trial itself, as well as the preliminary investigation, originally conducted chiefly by the accuser, came to be conducted entirely by the magistrate. During this same period of profound procedural change in Roman law, the range of public crimes, and the subjection of the accused and, in some cases, of witnesses, to torture as a means of interrogation, began to expand upward through Roman society. Hitherto permitted only in the case of slaves, torture could be applied to free citizens in cases of treason, and from the third century on more and more crimes and more and more sorts of people were made routinely subject to it. Thus the routine criminal procedure of the Roman Empire after the second century, and perhaps earlier, came to be the old *cognitio extraordinem*, with greatly increased powers and responsibilities of interrogation on the part of the magistrate, the increased use of torture to secure confessions, and the increased use of informers in order to find and bring to trial more and more criminals. The last element of the inquisitorial process, the accusation by the state itself instead of by a private accuser, came to be used as well.

Thus, *inquisitio*, originally a routine part of judicial procedure in all Roman litigation, came to designate the central role of the magistrate in all criminal cases—the obligation of finding out the truth in criminal matters. The transformation of *inquisitio*, the parallel rise in the importance of confession, the slowly upward-spreading use of torture to elicit it, and the bureaucratizing of the legal personnel of the Empire together greatly homogenized and routinized the public prosecution of crime from the third century on. The growing division of society into the classes of *honestiores* and *humiliores* increased the differentiation among citizens, as did the increasing articulation of the doctrine of *infamia*, infamy, which imposed judicial disabilities upon certain classes of people. By the early fourth century, Roman criminal procedure may be said to have been put into place under the direction of emperors and their servants. That procedure differed greatly from the institutions and judicial theory of Republican Rome. In the hands of a single public official lay the entire process, from investigation to accusation to conviction, and that official was guided by elaborate rules of procedure which could now be termed *inquisitorial* procedure. This was the character of Roman criminal law when the Empire converted to Christianity in the fourth century, and this was the law that Christian emperors applied to heretics.

The Heretics of Old

Christianity expanded from a small group of men and women following a single teacher in a particular region in Palestine to a number of distinctive sub-communities scattered throughout the empire ruled by Rome. Originally designated "Nazarenes" (Acts 24.5), the followers of Jesus first called themselves "Christians" (Acts 11.26) in Antioch, one of the most cosmopolitan cities of the empire, in 63 A.D. With the passing of the generation which had personally known Jesus—or known those who had—the faith of Christians came to depend more on a set of texts, the common loyalty to Jesus' memory within individual communities, and the individual charisma of those who propounded them than upon the personal memory or the reported "sayings" of Jesus.

Among the problems that faced the early Christian communities, those of distinguishing themselves from Jews and then from gentile pagans were paramount. The third distinction that emerged concerned the nature of Christian identity in a world that saw rapidly divergent beliefs and practices emerge shortly after the middle of the first century. The *Acts of the Apostles* and the *Epistles* of St. Paul and others reflect a number of conflicting beliefs and practices among individual Christian communities and between different communities. St. Paul's wide travels and his consultations with different communities make both his own letters and those attributed to him and to other apostles the earliest sources attesting to the emergence of these differences.

St. Paul's warning to the young churches concerned "another Jesus, another spirit, a different gospel" (2 Cor. 11.4). It took four centuries for a sufficiently widely accepted canon of Christian scripture to be defined and accepted (modeled upon Jewish religious literature, which then came to be called by Christians the "Old" Testament), and the existence of a wide body of texts purporting to be canonical is confirmed not only by St. Paul, but by subsequent archaeological and literary discoveries. St. Paul's somewhat bleak concept of the tendency of human nature to backslide heightened his concern over divisiveness, and he therefore placed great emphasis upon uniformity of practice and the solidarity of belief within each community, and the homogeneity of both among different communities. For Paul and others, a common faith and a common manner of living and worshiping identified the authentic Christian community—*ekklesia*, "assembly"—and distinguished it from those who seemed to cause divisions within it.

The best known identification of those who seemed to divide the early Christian communities derives from two texts, one of which is attributed to St. Paul. In 1 Corinthians 11.18–19, Paul observed:

> For I hear that when you meet in congregation there are divisions (*schismata*) among you, and in part I believe it. For there must be factions (*haireseis*) so that those who are approved may be made known among you.

The Epistle to Titus (3.10–11) is somewhat harsher:

> The factious man (*haereticum hominem* in the Latin Vulgate) after the first and second correction, avoid, knowing that he is perverted and sinful and condemned by his own judgment.

The terms that Paul used, *schisma* and *hairesis*, originally had quite different meanings in Greek. *Schisma* simply meant any sort of division, and *hairesis* originally meant "choice." *Hairesis*, however, had come by the first century to mean several specific kinds of choice, most popularly the choice one made as to which philosophical school to follow. The Jewish historian Flavius Josephus (37–100 A.D.) used the term, for example, to identify different sects within the Jewish world. The writings of St. Paul and others, however, gave these terms (as they gave others, including *ekklesia*, which came to mean "Church") a distinctly religious meaning, and they applied them to people whose teachings or actions appeared to "divide" the communities whose solidarity was so essential for the preservation and dissemination of Christ's message. By the fourth century, however, although *schisma* retained its sense of simple division and disagreement, *hairesis* (Lat. *haeresis*) had come to mean specifically a difference over doctrine and belief. This was increasingly perceived as differing substantially from schism.

The first disputes over Christian unity were probably fought over practice and forms of life, and then over the acceptance of different scriptural texts and their dogmatic differences. Since the official Christian canon of scripture (including both "Old" and "New" Testaments) was not finally established until the Council of Carthage in 397, many other texts could legitimately be recognized by different communities and individuals, and some "authentic" texts could be ignored. The first generally distinctive body of "heretics" were Gnostics, who chose selectively from some Jewish and Christian texts, neglecting some later declared canonical, and adding others that were later rejected by the Christian majority. The discovery of a Gnostic "library" at Nag Hammadi in 1945 suggests how varied and distinctive such beliefs could be. Questions also arose as to how scripture was to be interpreted. Jewish exegesis depended upon the principle of *peshat*—strictly literal understanding of the Torah— while Christian interpretation divided between a literalist school, centered at Antioch, and a figurative or allegorical school, centered at Alexandria. Over several centuries, the figurative method of interpretation, particularly of the text of the "Old" Testament, became standard among Christian exegetes.

After scripture in the shaping of Christian orthodoxy came tradition *paradosis*. Christian writers, including St. Paul, placed great emphasis upon the continuity of Christian beliefs and practices, and they and later writers often attributed the key elements of tradition to the practices of the apostolic community itself, thereby validating in time doctrines that came to be accepted as orthodox.

Orthodoxy meant literally "to believe rightly." Its opposite was heterodoxy. These two terms, with *hairesis/haeresis*, came to describe the conflicts that faced the Christian communities in the second through the seventh centuries A.D. The long process of shaping orthodox Christian belief paralleled development of the concept of the institution of a universal *ekklesia/*(Lat. *ecclesia*, or "Church"), and the content of orthodoxy (consisting of a scriptural canon, tradition, ritual practices, forms of living, and a clerical hierarchy within the community of Christians), was widely understood and accepted by most Christians by the beginning of the fourth century. Orthodox belief was summed up in "rules of faith," creeds (statements of fundamental beliefs, often specifically designed to counter heterodox opinion and teaching), and the opinions of a number of individual Christian thinkers and writers whose works, from the second century on, became almost as authoritative as scripture itself. Among these, St. Irenaeus of Lyons (130–200) and St. Cyprian of Carthage (d. 258) were particularly influential and widely accepted, and there were others as well. By the fifth century, St. Vincent of Lérins could define orthodox Christian belief as "that which has been believed everywhere, always, and by everyone." Such a definition of Christian orthodoxy was accepted by a Church that was *katholikos* (universal).

As orthodox doctrine slowly took on its formal shape and content, it became the *consensus ecclesiae*, the common opinion of the Church. As structures of authority (at first intellectual and ritual) also developed, the authority of the church became part and parcel of its truth, and a great deal of that authority was shaped in battles with heterodox opinion. Elements of the defeated Gnosticism were adapted by Manichaeism, originally a heterodox form of the Persian religion of Zoroastrianism. Manichaeism plagued the orthodox communities, especially in North Africa, in the fourth and fifth centuries and elicited powerful anti-heretical statements from a number of orthodox writers, among them St. Augustine (359–430), probably the most influential writer on Christian doctrine since St. Paul. Other heterodox opinions focused upon the relations between the human and divine natures of Jesus Christ and upon the relative places of Christ and God the Father and the Holy Spirit, the other two persons of the Trinity. Still other debates focused upon the possibility of continuing revelation from God, the nature of clerical authority and character, and the problem of the "magical" powers of those to whom "secret" revelation had been granted.

Although there is not space here to list the large variety of heterodox doctrines that influenced not only the shape of orthodox belief, but the structures of authority within early Christian communities, the names of several are particularly important because they were used by writers much later to identify heterodox opinion in the eleventh, twelfth, and thirteenth centuries and therefore formed part of the influences that shaped the first ecclesiastical, or papal, inquisitors. As St. Bernard termed them in the mid-twelfth century, the later heretics were but "the heretics of old" come back to plague the medieval Latin Church. Such a view was greatly influential in the twelfth and thirteenth centuries, because it invited churchmen to reread the early Christian writers on heresy and apply their theology to twelfth- and thirteenth-century circumstances, as well as to contemporary circumstances for which the Fathers had provided no direct precedent or literary tradition.

Besides Gnosticism and Manichaeism (a term that heresiologists applied to the beliefs of the Cathars in the twelfth and thirteenth centuries), other early heterodox beliefs also lent their names to later medieval and early modern heterodoxies. Donatism, which challenged the sacramental legitimacy of acts performed by morally unsuitable clergy, troubled the communities of North Africa in the fourth and fifth centuries, and the literature against it (much of it by St. Augustine) worked its way into later canon law and was applied both to medieval heresies and to Protestant confessions in the sixteenth century and after. Arianism, which troubled particularly Alexandria and eastern Christianity in the fifth and sixth centuries, generated an enormously large literature and also influenced later interpretations of heterodox beliefs.

The debates within the Christian communities not only shaped orthodox doctrine and ecclesiastical structures of authority, but the attitudes of Christians toward Jews and pagans as well. Much of the early anti-heterodox literature attributed the tendency toward heterodoxy not only to fallen and weak human nature, but to the insidious influence of Jews and pagans (particularly philosophers) as well. Thus, the experience of the early churches, wholly outside of the changes in Roman law, shaped the concepts and definitions of orthodoxy and heterodoxy, created a large and influential literature on the subject, and developed means whereby Christian communities could identify and deal with heterodox elements in their midst.

The early churches' means of dealing with heterodox opinion varied considerably. Early Christianity possessed no civil authority—indeed, until the early fourth century it was an illegal religion itself; hence it could not litigate against heterodoxy, nor did the early Christians believe that coercion was a legitimate response. The author of the Epistle to Titus (3.10–11) had simply advised the early churches to warn "factious" co-believers twice and then to avoid them, perhaps excluding them from community worship and affairs at the same time. This text parallels the advice in the Gospel of St. Matthew (18.15):

> If your brother commits an offense, go and take the matter up with him, strictly between yourselves, and if he listens to you, you have won your brother over. If he will not listen, take one or two others with you, so that all facts may be duly established on the evidence of two or three witnesses. If he refuses to listen to them, report the matter to the whole congregation; and if he will not listen even to the congregation, you must then treat him as you would a pagan or a tax-gatherer.

These early doctrines of fraternal admonishment envisioned a "worst-case" scenario of expulsion from the community. In the light of other related Christian practices—the tendency to settle other kinds of personal dispute within the community rather than through civil litigation in Roman courts, the early development of charity and internal social services, and the handling of common community property—the integrity of the community, its internal harmony, and individual deference to community interests under the guidance of elders and clergy clearly dominated the attention of early Christians and determined their scope of action against all forms of internal disruption or division.

St. Paul's *homo haereticus*, and the troublesome "brother" of St. Matthew, may have adequately characterized the early evangelical communities of the mid- to late first-century Church, but the increasing size and range of those communities found simple exclusion not always a satisfactory solution to the problem of unity. Often, substantial segments of communities seriously disagreed with each other, and Christian travelers to other communities were scandalized by entire communal sets of customs that seemed wholly out of keeping with those of the home community. With the growth of intellectual, or doctrinal heresies, the "factious man" of St. Paul and St. Matthew's intractable "brother" ceased wholly to characterize the holder and teacher of heterodox beliefs.

There is a tendency in third- and fourth-century anti-heretical literature, also echoing St. Paul, to hold that the heretic is not simply an example of weak and stubborn human proneness to sectarianism and faction, but a person of specifically perverted intelligence and will, tempted by the Devil and his agents (chiefly Jews and pagan philosophers or magicians)—a unique *kind* of person. From this period on, in fact, the terms schismatic and heretic began to diverge sharply from their once common meaning. *The* heretic began to take on a specific form, and the founders of heresies—the heresiarchs—began to parallel Jesus and the apostles in a theologically dualistic sense.

In the rapidly changing world of the third- and fourth-century churches, the shaping of the new image of the heretic paralleled the shaping of structures of ecclesiastical authority. From the third century on, the *consensus ecclesiae*,—the "common opinion of the Church"—came to mean that of the leaders of different Christian communities acting together rather than as individual charismatic teachers. Networks of Christian communities were established, with regular communications; common positions were taken on questions of heterodoxy; and the leaders of each community were empowered to speak in the name of the whole community. Thus, the meetings of community leaders—bishops—often agreed upon the texts of creeds and rules of faith, collectively condemned hetero-dox doctrines, and stiffened the response of Christian communities to the changing figure of the old "factious man." The records of such collective actions, which came to be regularized as formal church coun-cils, became a fundamental part of Christian literature and the growing body of Christian law.

Other examples too suggest the increasing popularity of legal ideas and language among Christians. Although Christians condemned Jews for excessively literal adherence to Torah—The Law—it was hardly avoid-able for Christian communities of the second, third, and fourth centuries to adopt legal rules internally for themselves and to define universal Christianity in increasingly legal terms. The apologist Tertullian at the end of the second century published an *Injunction Against Heretics,* which was a condemnation of certain heterodox practices cast in the form of a speech in a Roman civil law court. Moreover, as bishops and other clerics came to acquire substantial legal control over community property and wealth, the legal arrangements of Christian communities became more and more important, particularly when heterodoxy chal-lenged not only orthodox belief, but also the material circumstances of the Church, community rights, and property. In North Africa, for in-stance, the Donatists retained a number of church buildings and properties for themselves and denied them to orthodox bishops. In Alexandria and elsewhere, Arian heretics did the same.

Besides the necessity of establishing more complex and effective legal practices than St. Paul's and St. Matthew's fraternal admonishment, Christian leaders also worried about the scandal that divisions within the Christian community might give to non-Christians. In the second century, the great anti-Christian philosopher Celsus held up divisions within the Christian community as a sign of its lack of truth and divine inspiration. St. Irenaeus, in the same century, attacked the validity of pagan philosophy on the grounds of disputes among philosophers, and warned Christians against following their example.

For all of these reasons, late third- and early fourth-century Christian communities had come to possess a very different concept of heterodoxy and its dangers from that of St. Paul and St. Matthew. St. Augustine, no great admirer of human nature himself, squarely represents the early fifth-century Christian view of the problem:

> No one is indeed to be compelled to embrace the faith against his will: but by the severity, or one might rather say, by the mercy of God, it is common for treachery to be chastized by the scourge of tribulation . . . for no one can do well unless he has deliberately

chosen, and unless he has loved what is in free will; but the fear of
punishment keeps the evil desire from escaping beyond the bounds of
thought.

Augustine, who admired public authority no more than he admired
human nature, nevertheless was willing to turn to public authorities
when faced with what he considered a danger to the faith and security
of the entire Christian community. Augustine's text suggests other important aspects of Christian thought on heterodoxy early in the fifth century:
conversion by coercion is illegitimate, but the disciplining of the "treacher-
ous" is not. Tribulation is God's legitimate instrument against evildoers,
and those who oppose orthodox Christians who have *freely chosen* orthodox
doctrines must be coerced, even occasionally by "godly magistrates,"
lest they pollute the entire community. Augustine's doctrines, reached
with much difficulty, did not derive exclusively from misanthropy, but
from several centuries of the problem of heterodoxy, the particular circumstances of Augustine's own experience in North Africa, and a growing
body of Christian literature and practice that dealt with a real problem.

By the beginning of the fourth century, then, the small and scattered
Christian evangelical communities of the first century had grown into
the very large churches substantially represented in all parts of the Roman
world. The earlier disciplinary injunctions of St. Paul and St. Matthew
no longer adequately addressed problems that had grown far larger and
more dangerous since the apostolic period, and that put at issue (as
they had helped to shape) the structure of the Church and the nature
of authority in it. What might have happened if, at the same time, the
emperors of Rome had not become Christian and made the forces of
the Roman state and the doctrines of Roman law available to Christian
authorities, is impossible to say. But with first the legal toleration extended
to Christians by the Emperor Constantine in the second decade of the
fourth century, and then the conversion of the whole Empire to Christianity by the end of the fourth century, the relation between heterodoxy
and orthodoxy, and between fraternal admonishment and the exercise
of an increasingly legally conceived and defined ecclesiastical authority,
opened an entirely new chapter in the history of Christianity, and indeed
in the history of the world.

Roman Law and Christian Rome

Once permitted legal status as a religion within the Roman Empire,
Christianity then encountered the conversion of the emperors themselves.

Even more troublesome was the conversion of large numbers of Romans who became Christians chiefly because the emperors had; their faith was doubtful and their opinions were often extremely heterodox. The Christians also had to work out the principles by which a Christian state should operate, a subject about which earlier Christian literature had provided remarkably little guidance. Among the most vexing questions they faced in this context was the degree to which ecclesiastical discipline might legitimately become part of Roman law.

The oldest Christian attitude toward litigation between fellow believers was that Christians should wherever possible settle their own affairs, even their own legal affairs, among themselves. This made proselytization and conversion considerably easier, and it gave Christianity a respectability that is hard to assess, but was considerable among legal-minded Romans. This new legal status of Christianity, however, made this tradition less necessary from the fourth century on.

Although the Hebrew scriptures contained a number of political doctrines and much political and constitutional history, it was not easy to conceive a Roman emperor as taking David or Solomon as his role model, although later Germanic kings of early medieval Europe found it much easier to do so. The most that could be taken from a literal reading of Christian Scripture was the well-known role of obedient subjects whose refusal to observe some Roman practices did not indicate a contempt for others, or for Rome itself. St. Paul's injunction that "the powers that be are ordained of God" (Romans 13.1–10) was interpreted by Christians traditionally to refer to all public powers. Various sayings of Jesus were also similarly interpreted, notably his remark "Render unto Caesar the things that are Caesar's" (Matthew 22.15–22). Much of early Christian apologetic literature attempted to assert the civil loyalty of Christians to the Roman Empire and dissuade imperial officials from persecuting the illegal sect.

The sense of Christian distance from the affairs of this world was heightened by other scriptural texts as well. The first Epistle of Peter reminded Christians that they were essentially *strangers and pilgrims* on earth, and in the world of Roman law the rights of strangers were few indeed. According to the Gospel of John (18.33–40), Jesus had claimed that his kingdom was not of this world. Such a view accepted toleration by the Roman Empire, but little else. Indeed, a number of fourth-century Christian writers warned Christians of becoming too comfortable in a world in which not only legitimacy, but power, had been offered them. To such thinkers—St. Augustine among them—the powers of the earth might legitimately be employed to guarantee the security and tranquility of Christian communities, but they must never be regarded as the fulfillment of any Christian social ideal. In the city of the world, Christians were to remain strangers and pilgrims. Only in Jesus' "kingdom . . . not of this world" were they to be full citizens. According to Augustine in his influential work *The City of God* (ca. 425), even the best-intentioned creations of man share in the defects of fallen human nature and cannot attain perfection. The City of God, Jesus' "kingdom . . . not of this world," merely sojourns on earth, and may use earthly powers only to protect its temporary, earthly peace.

It was largely in this sense that Augustine's reluctant urging of civil authorities to control heretics must be understood. Augustine, who, as bishop of the North African city of Hippo, conducted a great deal of legal business as a judge between Christians, was not a theoretician of coercion except in the very limited sense of guaranteeing the peace of the Christian community. His notion of the proper Christian use of civil authority was far more that of the "godly magistrate" than that of the Christian kingdom or Empire, and in no case were civil authorities to assume doctrinal authority.

Other Christian thinkers, specifically hermits and monks, fled even a rapidly Christianizing Roman world for the rough and solitary life of the desert. On occasion, individual holy men might return to the imperial world and scold public authorities, but they did so as visitors from another world who had earned their right to speak by their denial of human nature and human weakness, and they always came as critics, never as bearers of constitutions. These attitudes found much support in earlier Christian thought and literature, including that of Tertullian. The early Christian concept of apocalypse—the soon-to-come end of the world and Christ's second coming—supported this attitude.

On the other hand, a second, initially much weaker, Christian tradition allowed for greater hope from earthly society. Late in the second century Melito of Sardis pointed out that God had permitted the Romans to impose their imperial peace upon the world in order to prepare for the coming of Christ. This idea was remarkably developed by the third-century exegete Origen, who observed:

> God was preparing the nations for his teaching, that they might be under one Roman emperor, so that the unfriendly attitude of the nations towards one another (cf. Ps. 2.1) caused by the existence of a large number of kingdoms, might not make it difficult for Jesus' apostles to do what he commanded them when he said "Go and teach all nations." It is quite clear that Jesus was born during the reign of Augustus, the one who reduced to uniformity, so to speak, the many kingdoms of the earth so that he had a single empire.

In addition, the conversion of large numbers of fourth-century Romans meant that the early sharp distinction between this world and the next was blurred, particularly with the coming of official toleration.

Eusebius of Caesarea, the biographer of Constantine and historian of the liberated Church, was extremely influential in conveying the idea of the Roman emperor as a power directly appointed by God to carry out the divine will. Indeed, Constantine himself intervened in the matter of the Donatist heresy, convoked Church councils (most important, that of Nicaea in 325) on his own authority, and began the process by which the clerical orders within Christian communities were aligned with the grades of the *cursus honorum*, or civil service, of the Empire, given privileges parallel to those of corresponding civil service ranks, and legally empowered to undertake many of the legal functions of imperial officials, with full state authority.

By the late fourth century, when paganism was outlawed altogether and Judaism was permitted, but with heavier restrictions than ever before, it was virtually impossible for a Christian Roman emperor (who once held the old pagan priestly title *pontifex maximus*) not to envision his role in the Church as a dominant one, advised and counseled by church-men, but delineating power in ways that no earlier Christian literature had foreseen. Those who disturbed ecclesiastical peace were among the first to feel the presence of this new kind of power.

With the new civil status of clergy, particularly bishops, and the great legal strength that this status gave to orthodoxy, the treatment of the heterodox underwent a great change. Before the late fourth century, for example, heterodox teachers and their followers could function pub-licly within Christian communities—they did not have to be sought out by anyone. During the fourth, fifth, and sixth centuries, churchmen representing both sides of theological disputes could argue their positions clearly and loudly in councils and public debates and proclamations and propaganda wars. On occasion, theological opinions later deemed heterodox were supported by individual emperors and their servants. For a long time Arianism was favored by some of Constantine's descen-dants. The occasional imperial support of heterodox positions only strengthened the arguments of those who rejected the idea of any sort of Christian state at all, and at the same time gave even orthodox church-men the obligation to correct the opinions of an erring ruler. Thus, from the fourth century on, the role of the Christian higher clergy could and did range from full support of imperial Christian policies (Eusebius), to a combined role of priest and prophet who corrected emperors legitimately when they erred (St. Athanasius), to imperial oppo-nents who could invoke outright ecclesiastical discipline against erring emperors (St. Ambrose of Milan, and Gelasius, bishop of Rome). The vexing question that was much later labeled "the conflict of Church and State" had begun. It was not ended until the nineteenth century, and its echoes resound in the late twentieth.

For the most part, however, the fourth- and fifth-century Church entered the imperial world willingly, as it slowly did the world of imperial law. The new concept of heretics, the new problems posed by heretics, and the new power of churchmen, whether alone or in collaboration with civil authorities, greatly altered the relative status of orthodoxy and heterodoxy from the fourth century on. Beginning with Constantine's actions against the Donatists and his convoking of the Council of Nicaea, the power of the Roman state was placed at the disposal of orthodox clergy and communities.

In time, theology accepted the new status of civil authority. An example from the exegesis of St. Augustine reveals some of the theological basis of this acceptance, expounding the meaning of the parable in Luke 14.15–24, which tells of a man who prepared a great feast and sent his messengers out to inform the invited guests that it was ready. One by one, the invited guests sent their regrets, and the man then ordered his messenger to go out and bring in the poor, the halt, and the lame. When this was done, the messenger told the master that there was still room at his table:

> And the master said to the servant, "Go out into the highways and the hedges, and compel them to come in [*compelle intrare*, in the Latin Vulgate], so that my house may be filled. For I say unto you, that none of those men who were bidden shall taste of my banquet.

For Augustine, the original invited guests were the Jews, the cripples from the city were the gentiles converted to Christianity, and those who were compelled to come in at the very end were those who returned to the orthodox faith from heresy and schism. By this use of allegorical interpretation of scripture, Christian leaders forged new policies against heretics in an empire that was not only Roman, but Christian as well. And that empire was ready to turn against the heterodox the same punitive legal measures that it had employed against all Christians earlier, and all breakers of Roman law at all times.

For such prosecution to take place at the hands of the Roman state new civil laws were required, and these laws were modeled upon older laws for similar offenses. By the fourth century the standard form for the promulgation of laws was by imperial constitution, or proclamation, which immediately became law and was to be administered by the civil servants who served as magistrates in the Empire. With this change, heresy had become a criminal offense, punishable by civil authorities. Such authorities had available a number of procedures, but as we have seen the most common form of criminal procedure in the fourth century was the old *cognitio extraordinaria*, or inquisitorial procedure, investigated by a single magistrate, who functioned in modern terms as evidence collector, prosecuting attorney, and judge. The custom of professional accuser had also developed in the later empire, and professional *delatores*, or seekers-out and denouncers of criminal acts and conspiracies, continued to function, as did a large and vigorous intelligence service.

But heterodoxy was no longer, and had never exactly been, a crime against an individual. It was a crime against the ecclesiastical community, and once that community became identical with the empire, a crime against it became a crime against the empire—treason—as well. A constitution of the emperors Valentinian III and Marcian of 453 explicitly identifies pagans with those who hold imperial laws in contempt, and condemns those convicted of paganism to the confiscation of all their goods and to capital punishment. At the same time, identical penalties were imposed upon heretics. Although Roman emperors issued many other constitutions dealing with ecclesiastical affairs—indeed, by doing so they shaped the public character of the Christian clergy for more than a millennium—the imperial constitutions against heterodoxy were particularly severe and relentlessly invoked.

Partly as a result of these events, heresy no longer proclaimed itself as openly as before, except in areas and institutions (such as councils held under the authority of sympathetic emperors) where it had a chance to win. From 376 on, we find imperial constitutions forbidding the secret meetings of heretics, and from the sixth century on, the condemnation of those who do not denounce heretics. From the fourth to the sixth century, the full apparatus of Roman criminal law was brought to bear upon heterodoxy; once a council—or an emperor—had condemned a particular doctrine, the full force of the law came down upon those who held it and those who protected those who held it.

The best sources for these imperial decrees are the two collections made in 453 and 534 by imperial fiat. The *Codex Theodosianus* contains a substantial number of imperial constitutions from the reign of Constantine on, and the great *Corpus Iuris Civilis* of Justinian, issued in 534, gave a final codified and regularized form to the great mass of Roman legal rule and doctrine. By the sixth century Roman law imposed a broad range of sanctions against heretics, the same range that operated against other kinds of criminals: fines, confiscations of goods, exclusion from inheritance, exile, deportation, death; and it also invoked an impressive array of sanctions, which included extremely severe civil disabilities, against those declared legally infamous. Roman law had regularized and recognized an amazing range of civil and criminal sanctions, and for two hundred years the full weight of both was brought to bear upon heretics.

As heretics necessarily became more clandestine, old Roman fears of clandestine crime were resurrected, the same fears and myths that had once been invoked against all Christians as well as against magicians and members of other forbidden religions. Under these laws, those who were convicted were subjected to extremely aggravated sentences of death: to crucifixion, immolation, or the beasts in the arena.

Yet the uneasy collaboration between churchmen and imperial authorities introduced a new element into the administration of both ecclesiastical and temporal discipline: that of the good of those coerced. In a letter to Boniface, Roman proconsul of Africa, St. Augustine expounded his exegesis of the parable in St. Luke cited above. Augustine then went on to observe that the heretics have become enemies of God and the Church out of vanity and pride, and for this reason God has given the Church the powers of the Empire to assist it in forcibly returning the heretics to the real banquet of the Lord, which is the only remedy for the sins of pride and vanity, since it consists not only of the ritual life of the community, but of the true peace of the community as well. From such a point of view, the facts of coercion and persecution are not vindictive, but therapeutic; they are not designed to avenge wrongs committed by the heretics, but to correct the errors of the heretics out of charity. This doctrine parallels the views of St. Augustine and other early Christian writers on war, that the just war is waged not out of hate for an enemy, but out of concern for his salvation from sin. The Roman Empire, as the Church's instrument for restoring true peace, thus legitimately coerced heretics because of the greatest concern that spiritual or temporal powers could possess—concern for the heretics' salvation and their turning away from sin.

But there was no automatic transfer of ideas from Church leaders to emperors. There still was a considerable gap between the pronouncements of prelates and councils on the one hand, and imperial constitutions and procedures on the other. For the most part, the strongest denunciations of heterodoxy and the harshest penalties against it are uniformly found in the imperial legislation and in imperial judicial practice. A considerably milder set of disciplinary codes is revealed in the collections of the canons of ecclesiastical councils and letters from individual prelates that became the regional guides to the internal organization of Christian churches; however, the denunciations of the errors of heterodoxy are equally severe. For example, some of the most frequently transmitted conciliar canons are those of the Council of Laodicaea of 364, which, as some historians have noted, are aimed far more at preserving the Christian faith than at constraining heretics. Heretics are forbidden to enter orthodox churches, and orthodox Christians are forbidden to visit the meetings at which heretics assemble, to pray with them, to participate in their liturgical rituals, or to marry them.

When the higher clergy sought action, it was usually directed against well-known individual heretics rather than against heresy generally. Most of the letters in the early canonical collections show that the prelates would rather urge the civil authorities to act than prescribe action themselves. With the imperial laws and legal administration containing the most severe legal sanctions, a system of ecclesiastical—or canonical—sanctions also developed that was both milder and more articulate about the ultimate purpose of religious coercion, emphasizing as it did the ultimate charitable purpose of coercion. Much of the material in early collections of canon law urges preaching against heretical opinions and attempts to convert heretics by persuasion; heretical clerics are to be degraded, heretical monks expelled from their monastic communities, public officials to be dismissed, private individuals to be deprived of their property, or publicly beaten and permanently exiled. These canonical sanctions were preserved in legal collections that circulated, at first regionally within the Roman Empire, and, after the disappearance of imperial power and institutions in the West, in collections assembled privately, which effectively transmitted much later imperial thought and law through the troubled public order of the early medieval period, to be revised and added to from the tenth century on.

Thus, the period between the conversion of Constantine and the law code of Justinian, from 330 to 530, saw a great transformation in the concept and definition of heresy and in the two major sets of procedures designed and enacted to combat it. The old and newer criminal sanctions of Roman public and criminal law produced a large body of legislation that passed down to later periods, and the development of internal disciplinary practices and theories within the Christian community led to the early canonical collections which also were transmitted to later periods. In the case of heterodoxy, the combination of the law of Rome and the Christian community had acquired a firm foundation.

Ecclesiastical and Civil Discipline, 600–1100

The conversion of the Empire had transformed the Church, and the absorption of the Church had transformed the Empire. When the Roman Empire ceased to exist in the west after the fifth century, a number of its institutions, practices, and values survived in the Latin Christian Church, including the disciplinary practices that had emerged over two centuries of cooperation. From the fifth century on, the Empire was succeeded in the west by Germanic kingdoms, states that used secular authority far differently, and exercised it upon a differently constituted population, than had the Romans. For several centuries Roman criminal legal procedure, like other aspects of Roman law, disappeared from practice and gave way to uniquely Germanic procedures. But the practice of *inquisitio* survived as an internal doctrine of the Church, as did others, even though they were rarely invoked during a period when conversion rather than internal discipline became the chief aim of Latin Christianity. Although a great number of text collections survived the disappearance of Roman power and culture, they survived in cultures that themselves were hardly able to use them as they had been designed, and that often faced other problems for which the texts could provide very little guidance.

From the late sixth through the tenth centuries, the doctrinal heresies that had been the subject of literature and legislation from the second to the sixth centuries ceased to trouble the Latin Christian community, although a number did survive in the less disrupted Greek Christian community in the Eastern Roman Empire centered in Constantinople. From the sixth century on, the chief problems facing Latin Christian clergy were the preservation of internal discipline within the Church and the conversion of northern European pagan peoples who had never been in touch with Roman society and did not face Roman problems. It is the conversion of western Europe, the acculturation of pagans to Christianity, and the creation of a new European society that greatly preoccupied the time and the minds of most churchmen.

The period is also complex and important because of the paucity of sources of the kind that are so abundant for the fourth, fifth, and sixth centuries. The transmission and generation of literary and documentary records was largely in the hands of monastic clergy, and although the great ages of monasticism produced a vibrant, accomplished, material and intellectual culture, its great aim was the preservation of the works of the mighty Church Fathers and the imitation of their thought, rather than the precise day-to-day observation of the events of their own time. When monastic chroniclers and theologians did attend to contemporary affairs, they usually did so using the forms of discourse developed by earlier thinkers such as St. Augustine and Pope Gregory I (590–604). Thus, a great deal of the work of early heresiologists was preserved in vast collections of excerpts from patristic literature, in collections of canon law, and in newly written works of the eighth, ninth, and tenth centuries. The combination of traditional history and doctrine, the distinctive character of monastic thought and culture, and the novel social and cultural situation of Europe during these centuries gave a distinctive character to both the idea of heresy and measures taken to combat it.

The transformation is most dramatically seen in the temporal sphere. The vast governmental apparatus of the late Roman emperors was of little availability or use to the Germanic kings who succeeded them, even in provinces that had long been part of the Roman Empire. Germanic kingship, which in practice proved to be a far greater influence on later political thought and political structures than that of the Roman emperors, was not based upon an idea of authority, and did not possess either the personnel or the power in any way similar to that of the emperors. Although many early medieval rulers tried to imitate Roman rulership, their most useful sources were those of Germanic tradition, the contingencies of recent experience, the models of Old Testament rulers understood in seventh- and eighth-century terms, and the advice of churchmen who themselves had only vague notions of imperial rulership. One doctrine that did survive, perhaps strengthened by the early medieval reading of early Hebrew history, was the notion of the king as responsible to God for his subjects' spiritual welfare, although few kings could be brought to use this as an active political principle before the late eighth century. Among the most ambitious in this respect were the Visigothic kings of Spain in the sixth, seventh, and early eighth centuries, who issued wide-ranging and extremely harsh legislation against heretics and, unlike many other Germanic rulers, turned savagely against Jews. Other rulers might pay lip service to the notion, but their own limited powers and the condition of the clergy in their own kingdoms made any effective action very difficult. Under the early Merovingian rulers of the Franks in the sixth and early seventh centuries, for example, a number of church councils were called, but these ceased in the seventh century; by that time, the duties of churchmen were far less complex than they had been in Rome. The conversion of pagans, the prevention of backsliding, and the maintenance of a modicum of canonical discipline within a poorly trained clergy were the most that could be hoped for.

Aside from the efforts of individual rulers and cooperative churchmen, the first large-scale attempt to enforce a ruler's Christian duty among the Germanic kingdoms may be seen in the case of Charlemagne. The son of an ambitious and talented aristocrat who had usurped the throne of the Franks in Gaul and Rhenish Germany, Charlemagne (742–814), appreciated his father's successful cooperation with reform minded churchmen to accomplish his revolution, and he himself appears to have acknowledged a genuine personal responsibility to improve the spiritual character of his kingdom. In eighth-century Europe, improvement meant "reform," and "reform" meant a return to an idealized Christian political past. Charlemagne himself was responsible for restoring networks of communication throughout much of western Europe, including parts of Europe that he himself did not rule. Along these networks traveled not only people and goods but also books, so that a number of important canonical collections that preserved much earlier legislation and themselves transmitted it to later centuries were the products of this Carolingian "renewal" of Christian rule in Europe.

Charlemagne's actual legal reforms were greatly outnumbered by the reforms that he wanted to institute but could not. The material and political limitations on monarchy, even one as great as Charlemagne's, were substantial. Charlemagne's emphasis and insistence upon judges' obligation toward written law was overshadowed both by custom and by the reluctance of judges and litigants themselves. Above all, the accusatorial procedure of litigation in both civil and criminal cases came virtually to eliminate the inquisitorial procedure that had taken over Roman law and been introduced into the law of the Church in the fourth century. To charge anyone with any offense, public or private, once again required an accuser, and the limited institutions of social control in eighth- and ninth-century Europe made the process difficult and cumbersome. Even in the days of Charlemagne's greatest power, the administration of the law was more a matter of reaching agreeable truces between contending parties than impersonally administering a common law for all people.

The one area of concern to this book that does display some innovation lies precisely in legal procedure. Normally, even before the royal court itself, an accuser and an accusation made by one party against another were required before even the most powerful court could act. Even with these, the accusatorial procedure greatly limited the courts' discretion and its powers to investigate and find according to law. In certain cases, however, where the royal judges were aware that offenses had been committed but where no accuser stepped forth, the Franks developed the process known as the *Rügeverfahren*—perhaps best translated as censuring-procedure—in which the judges conducted an inquest on the basis of *fama*—widespread public knowledge of the offense and a suspicion of those with a sufficiently bad reputation to have committed it. *Fama*, or *mala fama* (ill-fame) had a long history in Germanic law, and although it roughly resembled the old Roman concept of *infamia* (infamy), it was probably independently derived (although later it came to be joined to it). But *Rügeverfahren* had probably better be considered as an early form of a preliminary inquest than an *inquisitio*-procedure in the Roman sense.

Independent of the *Rügeverfahren* was the actual procedure of inquest itself, apparently new with Charlemagne, and applied especially in the commands to a class of royal servants called the *missi* ("those sent"). Well aware of the great size of his kingdom and the limitations of his resources, Charlemagne designated a group of particularly trusted nobles and clergy to travel through his kingdom supervising the normal organs of governance and the operation of local courts. The charge to the *missi*, laid out in great detail in a capitulary of 802, insisted that they "inquire diligently" into the law itself and its administration, and that they are to "make diligent inquiry" into accusations of injustice; they are given extraordinary powers to carry out their tasks. Charlemagne had a passion for orderly social life, and his exceptional power permitted him to devise the *missi* and give them exceptional powers of inquiry. The *missi* technically conducted an *inquisitio* (probably a more general inquiry than a technical *cognitio extraordinaria* in Roman legal terminology). The practice appears first to have been used at the royal court itself, in cases concerning royal rights. It then seems to have been used by the *missi* in cases of property disputes, and it eventually was available to the county courts and to ecclesiastical courts generally.

Both *Rügeverfahren* and *inquisitio*, however, although they greatly enhanced the ability of courts in an age of accusatorial procedure and great social pressures on litigation, depended upon strong royal patronage and a certain legal skill which, recent research has shown, was certainly available in the age of Charlemagne. But the use of these procedures was limited, and their developments in general public law were for several centuries limited to the more general right of inquest and to ecclesiastical circles, where, for some specific reasons, they survived better than elsewhere.

One extremely important aspect of early medieval law was the doctrine of the personality of the law, that is, the rule that a free person could be judged only by the law of the people into which he was born, regardless of where or among whom he was charged with an offense. In many cases, early Germanic kings created particular legal codes for their Roman subjects, not because they admired or understood Roman law, but because Roman law was regarded as the personal law of those born Roman. Although by the seventh and eighth centuries law was becoming more territorial than personal in most of Europe, and a separate Roman law for the subjects of a Germanic king was disappearing, complaints about these differences were raised even after Charlemagne's reign; Charlemagne himself could not stop the practice. When an individual entered the Church as a cleric, however, most early medieval laws recognized him as having, in a sense, come under another personal law, and one of the early legal codes phrased this difference in clerical status nicely: *ecclesia vivit lege romana*. "The church[man] lives according to Roman [personal] law" meant that clergy were expected to abide by whatever Roman law had survived in their particular community, modified by the lack of legal science and the accident of source transmission. In many respects, at least in theory, the structure of membership and authority among the clergy made it more amenable to some Roman legal forms and doctrines than any other branch of society. Episcopal power, at least in theory, was official and sacramental; the subordination of clerics within a legally and canonically defined hierarchy was explicit, if not always meticulously observed. Clerical privileges and responsibilities were extensively defined and quite distinct from other contemporary forms, for example, of holding and transmitting property, of determining personal inquiry, of being subject to litigation, and of other aspects of full social participation. Thus, the canonical collections that transmitted the legal and canonical thought of the patristic period of late Rome applied more readily to clergy than to the laity, and the obligations of bishops, if not always or often observed, were widely known, including the bishop's responsibility for discovering heresy or schism, particularly among the clergy itself.

Canonical collections and episcopal constitutions from the ninth and tenth centuries added little to earlier theory, but they preserved and extended some important aspects of eighth- and ninth-century practice. Among these are the preservation of the *inquisitio*-procedure in ecclesiastical affairs (usually exclusively among the clergy itself or in matters involving ecclesiastical property or rights). There appeared, in the tenth-century collection of Regino of Prüm, individuals known as *testes synodales* (synodal witnesses), who appear to have been individuals of good local reputation who were expected to denounce crimes and people of bad reputation to ecclesiastical authorities. The future of synodal witnesses was considerable, and they may be regarded as representing a direction away from the strictly personal accusatorial forms toward the form later known as the *denuntiatio evangelica*, the "evangelical denunciation," which transposed the initial accusation made for private reasons into an identification of an offense and a probable wrongdoer for the sake of ecclesiastical justice.

The synodal witnesses were expected to function in the context of another tenth-century development, the episcopal visitation. In Regino's collection, among the duties of a bishop is to visit the different parts of his diocese regularly, on which occasions the synodal witnesses will have prepared a list of offenses and individuals of whom it is proper for the bishop to take cognizance by virtue of his legal rights. Genesis 18.21 was invoked to remind bishops that God did not condemn the wickedness of Sodom from afar, but went down into the city himself to discover its offenses. Bishops, like God, should investigate their flocks, if not yet by the inquisitorial procedure, then at least by the year 1000 according to a procedure that was far removed from the conventional restrictions of Germanic private law and the accusatorial procedure. This was not yet, of course, what can legitimately be called an inquisition, but it marks both the survival of older doctrines concerning heresy and ecclesiastical discipline, on the one hand, and the development of newer ideas. *Mala fama, Rügeverfahren, inquisitio, testes synodales,* and episcopal rights of visitation now constituted the shape of ecclesiastical disciplinary authority over both clergy and laity in an age when secular powers were too weak or intermittent to collaborate on anything like a regular scale.

Although the social and political circumstances of tenth- and eleventh-century Europe greatly reduced the scope of public offices and greatly narrowed the intellectual horizons of those responsible for them, the textual preservation of both patristic and Carolingian thought and practices enabled reformers to cite precedent and tradition in their criticism of contemporary abuses and to hold out the ideal of a perfectible Christian society. Thus, when clerical purity and clerical independence from lay domination became a major theme of reformers during the eleventh century, the inquiry into clerical abuses grew apace, and Regino's rules for episcopal visitation took on new meaning. But the world of clerical reform was not the only world that invited new procedures in the eleventh century. The greatly reduced power of kings and the assumption of much public authority by private territorial state-builders led to continuing friction and to the emergence of claims to lands and rights countered by other claims. Even lay authorities were faced with the necessity of investigating the basis of their own claims and those of others, as they were faced with the obligation to seek out heterodox beliefs and clerical abuses. And for all of these exercises, the term *inquisitio* was widely used.

Perhaps the best known event in which this process may be observed occurred as a result of William of Normandy's conquest of England in 1066. For nearly twenty years after the conquest, William saw the emergence of tangled claims to land and rights over it and the people on it, until, in 1085, he commanded a survey of all the land in England, its holders, and their obligations to him. The result, in 1087, was the great collection of information called Domesday Book. The accounts of the making of Domesday Book uniformly term the inquiries that produced it *inquisitiones*—that is, William's commissioners inquired concerning the extraordinary information they were obliged to produce, and they did this by visiting each shire in England and summoning witnesses to answer a prepared list of questions. The staggering scope of the commissioners' work and the great achievement that Domesday Book represents have been widely described elsewhere. Here, it is important to note merely the evidence of what the commissioners said that they were doing: they were conducting an *inquisitio* into the rights of the king and others, by a process new to English law—and extraordinary anywhere in Europe at the time—and made possible only by the extraordinary circumstances surrounding William's title to England and the force of his own ambition. Structurally, however, Domesday Book was the result of procedures that were not inherently different from those technically available to bishops or to other temporal rulers, that is, the right or obligation to seek detailed information as part of their office and status. Such a right of course, was far from the routine judicial procedure of the eleventh century, but a number of circumstances in the course of the eleventh century made this and other *inquisitio*-procedures more common.

Nor was William the Conqueror the only eleventh-century ruler to experiment with an *inquisitio*-procedure in extraordinary circumstances. Several decades before the investigations that produced Domesday Book, the young German ruler, Henry IV, actively attempting to recover in Saxony royal possessions and rights that had been usurped from royal control during his nine-year minority from 1056 to 1065, employed royally appointed judges in cases affecting his claims. These judges used the testimony of witnesses and the *inquisitio*-procedure, which was contrary to Saxon custom and traditional legal procedure. This greatly offended the Saxon nobility, which repeatedly revolted against Henry in the next two decades.

In the cases of William the Conqueror and Henry IV, unusual circumstances and the ambitious exercise of royal power combined to introduce, even briefly, the rudiments of *inquisitio*-procedure, if only in the form of inquest. In a number of other eleventh-century cases, similar claims were made by churchmen and princes alike that such procedures were preferable to traditional forms of judicial settlement. Although the use of the procedure remained unusual, and different forms of judicial inquiry survived side by side for more than a century, the occasional use made of inquisitorial inquiry; the testimony and examination of the accused and of witnesses; the increased latitude in the nature of judicial evidence; the increase in written records and written evidence, all these pointed to the advantage the *inquisitio*-procedure offered to courts that were strong enough to insist on its use and to enforce settlements reached through it. In the eleventh century and the early twelfth, such courts and such use were unusual and infrequent. But by the mid-twelfth century, the use of the procedure in other cases besides those of royal or ecclesiastical rights or particularly heinous offenses began to increase.

The textual memory of late Roman procedural law, preserved in ecclesiastical literature and occasional usage, the reforms of Charlemagne and Louis the Pious, revived in circumstances as different as those of Regino of Prüm and William the Conqueror a century and half apart, offered attractive tools to both clerical reformers and ambitious rulers in an age when the need became pressing for information that was ordinarily very difficult to acquire. In the course of the eleventh century, a new outbreak of heterodoxy and dissent, a new consciousness of clerical abuses, and a new set of relationships between spiritual and temporal powers gave great impetus to the revival of older practices and transformed the judicial face of Europe forever.

Chapter Two

Dissent, Heterodoxy, and the Medieval Inquisitorial Office

One of the great themes in medieval European history is that of the debates it witnessed concerning the proper ordering of the Christian life. During a long period that saw dramatic material growth and social change, the emergence of new forms of political and ecclesiastical organization, and a heightened consciousness of the quest for eternity, the ordering of the Christian life became a central problem for popes and clergy, kings, aristocrats, and ordinary lay people.

The Christian life was a matter of belief and behavior. Through the early Middle Ages belief had been taught by religious specialists through the use of simple creeds, and behavior had been regulated by a series of penitential regulations and by the rich liturgy performed by trained specialists. These rules had achieved the conversion of most of northern Europe to Christianity by the year 1000. They had depicted the world as a place of temptation and the prospects of salvation in it as slender. But during the course of the eleventh century a spirit of religious reform argued that the prospects of salvation in the world would be greatly increased if only the world were reformed. With the reform of the papacy itself at the end of the eleventh century the Latin Church began to devise its grand program of sanctifying the world.

The program required a greater articulation of belief and a systematic set of rules for behavior. Those who dissented from belief or behaved in a manner that was explicitly defined as un-Christian appeared no longer as erring souls in a temptation-filled world, but as subverters of the world's new course. At first, the reformed world believed that it could persuade dissenters by teaching and sermons. When these appeared to fail, ecclesiastical and lay leaders turned to coercion, and as part of that process of coercion they revived and transformed the older *inquisitio* legal procedure and created a new office, that of inquisitor.

The Emergence of Dissent and Heterodoxy

In the view of the eleventh- and twelfth-century ecclesiastical reformers the purpose of Christian society was essentially religious; there could be no separation of "religious" and "secular" spheres of identity or function. Although salvation was a matter of individual virtue, there was no salvation outside the Church, and there was no legitimate society that was not Christian. The system of belief that was developed by the new discipline of theology and taught by preachers, schools, and liturgists required universal assent, for upon it depended God's favor for the Christian world. Dissenting belief or behavior not only threatened to corrupt Christian society, but it also entailed the danger of bringing down the wrath of God upon guilty and innocent alike.

Such beliefs necessarily committed the laity as well as the clergy to viewing dissent with considerable anxiety. That anxiety led to a revival of older definitions of heresy and to their broader application to a widened spectrum of behavior and professed belief. With the appearance of dissent in the eleventh and twelfth centuries, society itself seemed to be in danger, and legitimate sources of both knowledge and power stood challenged at the heart of their own ground. In the new world of the eleventh and twelfth centuries the term "heresy" itself took on new meaning.

Old, universal terms like "heresy" were the only vocabulary often available to those who described the religious climate of the eleventh and twelfth centuries. Throughout most of this period, the term *haeresis* had acquired a loose and—to us—casual meaning. It was used for extremely abstract disputes among clerical scholars, to describe political differences, and even to indicate simple intellectual errors. By the mid-twelfth century, however, most religious dissent was increasingly labeled heresy, and the increased perception of dissent as heresy shaped the long transition from persuasion to coercion that followed.

Several decades of close textual analysis of the sources for the history of dissent and heterodoxy in the eleventh and early twelfth centuries suggest few common doctrines, and even no common set of criticisms of orthodox belief and practice. The origins and nature of this dissent have been, and still are, matters of scholarly debate. Generally, however, they may be usefully considered as offering new kinds of human associations, legitimized by shared interpretations of the Christian life, new bonds of the spirit for people who, for widely varying reasons, were becoming dissatisfied with the old and remained unimpressed with, or actively hostile to the reforms of the late eleventh century. They encountered different types of opposition: from fearful neighbors anxious over the potential contamination of a religious community, from local lay powers who saw in them a threat to God and themselves, and from representatives of the Church who, faced with the shock of dissent on a large scale, turned to the writings of the Church Fathers and later commentators, professing to see in "the heretics of old" the prototypes of contemporary dissenters. These encounters laid the groundwork for the definition of medieval heresies and the steps taken to eradicate them.

At the conclusion of one of his sermons on *The Song of Songs*, St. Bernard of Clairvaux (1090–1153), the most respected and influential churchman of the twelfth century, reminded his monastic audience of what he perceived to be the antiquity of the heretics' teachings, if not their style: "For I do not recall having heard anything new or strange in all their mouthings, numerous as they are, but that which is worn by use and long agitated by the heretics of old, and which has been well threshed and winnowed by our theologians." According to such a view, not only were contemporary twelfth-century dissenters merely the continuation of a persecution to which the Church had been subjected since the days of St. Paul, but a great many different manifestations of dissent tended to coalesce into "heresy." The earlier loose definitions of the term *haeresis* took on during the twelfth century a new precision and a specific denotation. By the early thirteenth century, the definition given by Robert Grosseteste (d. 1253) served to illustrate this process:

> Heresy is an opinion chosen by human faculties, contrary to Holy Scripture, openly taught, and pertinaciously defended. *Haeresis* in Greek, *electio* [choice] in Latin.

This definition illustrates the spectrum along which dissent became heresy. An opinion is voluntarily arrived at, but amenable to proper teaching. A heretical opinion must be the result of voluntary human choice (and not demonic inspiration), based upon an erroneous reading of Scripture (with which it must be declared in conflict), publicly taught and professed (private, personal heresies were another matter), and persisted in even after adequate and authoritative instruction. The late twelfth-century heretic was a certain *kind* of person, one whose curiosity was not disciplined by reason and revelation, whose will was stubborn, refusing to bow before superior wisdom and legitimate authority, and whose pride was so great as to require that others validate his own opinion by following him as a leader.

As the type of the heretic emerged in the literature of the twelfth century, the processes of dealing with heresy also narrowed. The concern of the Church focused upon two particularly offensive spiritual movements, Waldensianism and Catharism. Both movements seemed to attack not merely ecclesiastical authority, but the very world-view of an entire society and culture. Their opponents were not only church officials, but clergy and laity from all levels of society. Long before the inquisitorial tribunals of the thirteenth century, popular lynchings, secular judgments, and various other forms of coercion by laity of all kinds represented the "popular" side of the resistance to and fear of religious dissent. On the other hand, a number of clergy urged patience and toleration. Attacks upon the Church and the world-view it represented generated widespread anxieties across a broad spectrum of society, and the first counterattacks were not primarily the reaction of an authoritative ecclesiastical structure to challenges to its legitimacy and power.

The Cathars, influenced at various times by spiritual movements from the eastern Mediterranean and the Balkans, posited a different cosmos from that of the rest of Latin Christianity. In that cosmos, two deities, one material and evil, the other immaterial and good, struggled for the spirits of humans which were trapped in flesh and bone. Material creation was evil, the work of an evil god; man's duty was to escape from it and reject those who recognized it as good. The decentralized character of Catharism (the name refers to the designation of its adherents as *catharoi*, the Greek term meaning the "pure ones"), its broad appeal to different ranks in society, and its relentless condemnation of the Latin Church as the instrument of the evil god made it one of the major targets of the more rigorous approach to heterodoxy in the late twelfth and early thirteenth centuries.

Waldensianism, founded by the Lyonais merchant Valdes in 1173, did not disagree with orthodox theology, but with ecclesiology—the nature of the structure of the Church and the place of authority in it. The Waldensians placed much emphasis upon the use of vernacular versions of Scripture, the right of all instructed persons to preach, the requirement of apostolic poverty, and the rejection of the church as a sacramental, teaching, and legal authority.

Both Catharism and Waldensianism circulated in southern France, northern Italy, and the great urbanized regions of the Rhine Valley and southern Germany. As these two confessions became the principal targets of civil and ecclesiastical concern and the concept of heresy narrowed, other groups were swept into the category of heresies as well. Certain kinds of academic debate, of communal life and prayer, of difference from authoritative ecclesiology, divergent movements within religious orders, and finally witchcraft and magic all came under the new definition of heresy and were subjected to the new forms of persuasion and coercion.

From Persuasion to Coercion

From the earliest Christian communities to the late twelfth century, Christians placed great faith in the power of instruction to root out even the most egregious of errors. The teaching authority of the community and its leaders, the *magisterium*, was invoked again and again, from the learned debates of fourth- and fifth-century Church councils to the sermons of twelfth-century monastic and secular clergy. Since the Truth had been revealed, it could surely be demonstrated. Those who refused to accept demonstrative truth were necessarily considered either as invincibly ignorant or willfully perverse. Nevertheless, many churchmen could and did exhibit great faith in persuasion and great patience in applying that faith.

Even the disciplinary literature of the Latin Church recognized the power of *persuasio* and allowed for its operation even in the most extreme cases. But when *persuasio* failed, other disciplinary means were called for, and the twelfth century, basing its work on earlier literature, erected an elaborate disciplinary structure upon which to draw after persuasion had failed.

Such disciplinary measures were aimed more often at protecting the faith of the community rather than at explicitly punishing the heretic. A well-known letter attributed to Pope Liberius (352–366) listed the judgment of God, the anger of the emperor, the deposition of clerics, the expulsion of monks from their monasteries, the removal from office of civil servants and officials, the confiscation of the goods of private citizens—if they were nobles—or their beating and condemnation to perpetual exile if they were non-noble. Other and later texts emphasized the excommunication of heretics and the prohibition of communication with them, citing the second Epistle of John 5.10.

Collections of legal principles in the Germanic church were much more severe. Public shame, mutilation, and severe physical punishments were prescribed for those found guilty of heresy and other severe crimes. A church council held at Reims in 1157 prescribed branding the convicted heretic with a hot iron, imprisonment, and the withdrawal of the right to testify in court. The mechanism for such accusations and punishments appears to have been that of accusatory procedure, with the *testes syno-*

dales, the synodal witnesses, probably bringing the complaint. Such procedures were applied not exclusively to heretics, but to all who faced severe ecclesiastical discipline. Moreover, the disciplinary aspects of these procedures were conducted by lay authorities, since churchmen were prohibited from the shedding of blood.

The literature of the early Church was transmitted chiefly in a series of privately made collections of theology and canon law. A number of these produced in the eleventh and early twelfth centuries, notably those of Burchard of Worms, Anselm of Lucca, and Ivo of Chartres, contained extensive provisions for defining heresy and treating it, but these were purely local in scope and had no binding authority on churchmen elsewhere than in the dioceses in which they were written. Besides these private collections, a number of polemical treatises in the struggle over papal reform preserved and emphasized disciplinary measures, often considered in terms of general enemies of the Church who were described as heretics rather than against doctrinal heresies specifically. Finally, the revival of Roman legal studies at Bologna in the eleventh century brought to light the extensive discussions of heresy and ecclesiastical discipline that had been produced in the fourth, fifth, and sixth centuries by Christian Roman emperors and their Christian jurists. From Roman law came the doctrines of infamy and civil disabilities that later figured prominently in twelfth-century canon law, as well as the doctrine that heresy was analogous to treason.

Of all the private collections of the eleventh and twelfth centuries, none achieved the influence of the *Concordia discordantium canonum*, "The Concord of Discordant Canons"—or, as it became widely known later, the *Decretum*—of Master Gratian of Bologna. Gratian's collection, although unofficial, became the basis for the teaching of ecclesiastical law at Bologna and elsewhere, and it became the fundamental text— upon which jurisprudential commentary was made and to which later collections of ecclesiastical law were added—for the law of the Latin Christian Church.

The great virtue of Gratian's work was not that he uncovered unknown texts, but that he assembled a vast body of scattered texts in a format that suggested the deliberate and precise use of the words of the early Fathers, councils, emperors, popes, and rulers. Gratian's design of his excerpts, his commentary upon the texts, and his access to a large number of earlier collections made the *Decretum* the most influential direct collection of legal texts in medieval Europe.

Gratian's text accepted the traditional magisterial primacy of the Roman church, and, with the revived study of Roman law, provided substantial criminal penalties for heretical deviance. But it took several decades after 1140 for Gratian's collection to circulate widely in Europe, with a teaching commentary appended, and Gratian's texts were not everywhere and immediately adopted for dealing with heretics or indeed with other problems of ecclesiastical law.

The extensive letter collections of the eleventh and twelfth centuries indicate the extent to which bishops troubled by heretics asked their colleagues for advice, reflecting a local uncertainty that is particularly striking. The letters of Wazo of Liège illustrate the strong current of patience, instruction, and toleration that could be applied to religious dissent by a sensitive and charitable prelate. This dimension of *persuasio* is often neglected. As late as the pontificate of Pope Innocent III (1198–1216) it marked the initial response of the highest ecclesiastical levels to the problem of dissent, heresy, and challenge to ecclesiastical authority. Moreover, it obviously had substantial results. Although it is impossible to calculate the number of those brought back to orthodox belief and behavior by virtue of patience, tolerance, and instruction, the number is clearly substantial.

The route of *persuasio*, in fact, may well indicate something of the severity that ecclesiastical treatment of heretics took on from the later twelfth century. By then, those heretics that survived are said to have become more secretive, more openly rebellious to legitimate authority, and more dangerous to society as a whole. It is perfectly arguable that the more severe steps taken against heretics after 1200 were taken only after the mighty efforts at patience and persuasion had appeared to have run their course. *Persuasio* also appears to have marked the ecclesiastical advice to secular powers, and a number of churchmen restrained their more eager secular counterparts in these matters.

Twelfth-century sources inform us that excommunication, deliberation, and uncertainty characterized local response to heresy far more than did clear juridical action. The lynch mobs and severe secular judgments represented the lay response to heresy. Twelfth-century legislation by local church councils urged excommunication as the strongest penalty for heretics (as they did for practitioners of magic and witchcraft), and there was little evidence of any concerted or even purely local church effort to seek heretics out. During the eleventh and early twelfth centuries, heretics made themselves publicly known; the idea of the secret heretic who had to be inquired and sought after appeared only later in the twelfth century. Ecclesiastical discipline varied from time to time and from place to place—therefore, from bishop to bishop. A number of churchmen besides Wazo of Liège urged broad toleration and patience in dealing with heretics. Part of the reform movements of the late eleventh century dictated that a far more intensive pastoral approach should be made broadly across the Church; that is, preaching should be undertaken by bishops. Few higher churchmen were unaware of the lack of training on the part of lower churchmen, and a great many influential churchmen knew the extent to which perfectly orthodox groups of laity and clergy might seem heretical to other high churchmen who were unaware of or insensitive to the new movements of religious sensibility on the part of perfectly orthodox Christians.

In addition to the various problems of churchmen, local political struggles often prevented or delayed the application and formulation of universally valid procedures against heretics. The conflict between the popes and the emperors at the end of the eleventh century prevented the universal acceptance of such rules, particularly in the light of the wide use by papal supporters of accusations of heresy against the supporters of the emperors. In the mid-twelfth century, the conflict between the Emperor Frederick Barbarossa and Popes Adrian IV and Alexander III delayed the formulation of a universal policy during one of the periods of the most widespread growth of heretical movements and doctrines.

The tide of attempts at persuasion of dissidents may be said to have turned in 1177. In that year the reconciliation of the Emperor Frederick Barbarossa and Pope Alexander III, reflected in the Treaty of Venice, stabilized for a crucial period the relations between the two great universal authorities of the Latin European world. The Third Lateran Council of 1179 produced several canons condemning heretics—chiefly to excommunication and denial of Christian burial—and several widely circulated condemnations of heresy, with specific descriptions of heretical beliefs and practices, as well as privileges comparable to those of crusaders for those who fight against heretics and their defenders. In 1184 Pope Lucius III issued the decretal *Ad abolendam*, which confirmed the agreement of 1177. It has been called "the founding charter of the inquisition."

Ad abolendam, issued with the concurrence of Frederick Barbarossa, condemned in its opening words the "insolence" of heretics and "their attempts to promote falsehood." Here, as in some earlier sources, the defiance of authority—termed *contumacia*—constitutes a substantial part of the heretics' crime, as does their open and defiant teaching. A long list of heretical sects and a description of their points of difference from the Latin Church follows, as well as a condemnation of sympathizers and supporters of heretics. Lucius condemns heretical clergy to degradation from holy orders and submission to secular judges for condemnation; lay heretics are to be defined by proper ecclesiastical judgment and then also turned over to the temporal courts for formal punishment. In both cases, Lucius perceives the task of ecclesiastics as identifying heresy and heretics, but leaves the problems of criminal action to lay judges, who are to act within locally prescribed legal forms against them.

Lucius, however, goes considerably farther than earlier popes and Church councils. He commands that every bishop or archbishop shall visit twice a year any parish within his juridiction in which heresy has been reported. The prelate shall take an oath from three or more persons of good reputation—or, sometimes, the whole neighborhood—to the effect that they will point heretics out to the visiting prelate. The prelate will then take legal action against those so denounced and proceed against them with canonical sanctions. Lay authorities are enjoined to cooperate with the higher clergy in such matters and are to invoke against the accused the full sanctions of local secular law. Those lay authorities who refuse their cooperation are to be deprived of office themselves, excommunicated, and their lands placed under interdict. Recalcitrant cities are to be cut off from intercourse with other cities.

Ad abolendam is the most elaborate juridical statement concerning the treatment of heretics made to that date by the Latin Church. Although it does not contain new elements (the local oath-takers are very similar to the earlier *testes synodales*, for example), it coordinates earlier procedures sharply and binds lay authorities to cooperate fully with ecclesiastics. It emphasizes the obligation of the episcopal visit and mandates such visits when rumors of heresy reach the bishop. The bishop's normal canonical authority now included the right of visiting and inquiring into the spiritual life of those territories committed to his care.

Papal letters during the next decade indicate that *Ad abolendam* was not a dead letter and that both popes and emperors actively pursued information concerning the legal treatment and discovery of heretics. But in 1199 Pope Innocent III (1198–1216) issued the decretal *Vergentis in senium*, which constituted a major step in the formalization of the prosecution of heretics. Besides repeating much of *Ad abolendam*, Innocent's decretal for the first time identified heresy with the doctrine of treason as found in Roman law. The goods of heretics are to be confiscated, and their children are to be subjected to perpetual deprivation for the sins of their parents. By making the analogy between Christian society and the Roman Empire as being both the objects of *laesa majestatis*—treason—Innocent continued the conceptualization and definition of Latin Christendom as a juridically regulated society, hierarchically directed, and he linked the ideas of sin and crime as he linked the legal duties of ecclesiastical and lay authorities.

A case of reported heresy at La Charité-sur-Loire in 1197–1200 suggests an example of the procedural consequences of the period between *Ad abolendam* and *Vergentis in senium*. During an episcopal visitation, Hugh of Noyers, the bishop of Auxerre, discovered several clerics suspected of heresy at La Charité and summoned them before him. Upon their refusal to appear, Hugh informed Michel de Corbeil, Archbishop of Sens, and in 1198 the archbishop, with the bishops of Nevers, Meaux, and Auxerre, visited La Charité, appointed synodal witnesses, and took testimony which led to evidence against two prominent figures: the dean of the chapter and the abbot of St. Martin. The archbishop instituted a court consisting of himself and the bishops of Nevers and Auxerre, aided by experts in Roman and canon law acting as assessors, and, without a formal accuser, took testimony from the synodal witnesses and finally decided that the case, because of the risks involved to the accused, should be sent on to the pope. Innocent III heard the case, and decided that the most severe punishments could not be inflicted without the presence of a formal accuser, but required the accused to make extensive formal and penitential displays of orthodoxy. The case proceeded well beyond this point; however, we have seen enough to witness some of the assembling of procedural devices—rumor of heresy, synodal witnesses, episcopal visitation, expert legal advice, and removal of a case to the papal court—to estimate the treatment of heretics within an episcopal framework around 1200. Granted that the clerical status of the accused confined the procedure within ecclesiastical courts, but the procedure followed and the removal of the case to the papal court suggests the emergence of the papacy, rather than local bishops, as the only authority capable of deciding complex cases of heresy.

Although much of the activity of Innocent III was directed at reconverting those convicted or suspected of heresy, of urging clerical pastoral activities, criticizing prelates who did not appear solicitous for the spiritual condition of their people, and sponsoring devotional movements under papal patronage, the spread of heresy continued to elicit from him severe condemnations. In the decretal *Cum ex officii nostri* of 1207, he ordered:

> In order altogether to remove from the patrimony of St. Peter the defilement of heretics, we decree as a perpetual law, that whatsoever heretic, especially if he be a Patarene, shall be found therein, shall immediately be taken and delivered to the secular court to be punished according to law. All his goods also shall be sold, so that he who took him shall receive one part, another shall go to the court which convicted him, and the third shall be applied to the building of prisons in the country wherein he was taken. The house, however, in which

a heretic had been received shall be altogether destroyed, nor shall anyone presume to rebuild it; but let that which was a den of iniquity become a receptacle of filth. Moreover, their believers and defenders and favorers shall be fined one fourth part of their goods, which shall be applied to the service of the public.

With the spread of heresy in southern France and the murder of the papal legate Peter of Castelnau in 1208, Innocent convoked an army from northern France which scourged the south for twenty years in an effort to remove heretics and lords indifferent to heresy and replace them with devout rulers who would be amenable to their spiritual obligations. The severity and frequent brutality with which the northern French waged the Albigensian Crusade led to the killing of many heretics without formal trial or hearing. Most of the Crusade was entirely out of the hands of the pope, however, and the killings illustrate the continuing willingness on the part of the laity to take the most severe steps against heresy without much concern for the heretics' conversion and salvation. The complex and subtle directions of the papacy often could not control the violence and destruction which lay authorities were willing to visit upon the heretics.

Throughout his pontificate, the two great aims of Innocent III, as he himself often stated, were the reform of the Church and the reconquest of the Holy Land. In 1215 he convoked the Fourth Lateran Council, one of the most ambitious programs of reform that the Church—or any western society—has ever seen. The first canon of the Council contained an elaborate statement of the program of Christian belief; the twenty-first enjoined confession of sins at least once a year for all the Christian faithful; the third continued and articulated the procedures taken against heretics and their protectors begun by *Ad abolendam* in 1184. The consequences of the first and twenty-first canons were substantial. The publicizing of the content of belief was now readily possible and obligatory upon all those who had the care of souls; the mandating of personal confession incorporated a number of important twelfth-century ideas of conscience and its obligations; and confessions—and the art of being a confessor—became a major part of the training of specialized clergy in the thirteenth century, a psychological transformation of a penitential system that had, for the most part, been mechanical and unreflective before.

Like preaching, confession constituted a substantial part of the pastoral apparatus of which Innocent III made extensive use. With the extreme statements condemning heresy and the papal assumption of control over steps taken against heretics, the pastoral approach of *persuasio* remained the most important aspect of Innocent's pontificate. What Innocent wanted most of all was *reform*—of clergy and laity alike—not persecution or condemnation, and certainly not the devastating consequences of the Albigensian crusade.

The increased pastoral sophistication of Innocent, however, was not always or everywhere matched by that of lesser prelates. Bishops, cities, and local princes resented the intrusion into their jurisdiction of papal authority and the specialized preachers and confessors sponsored by the popes. The rights of jurisdiction were still regarded as individual privileges in the early thirteenth century, and any lessening of them, for whatever cause, was often perceived as an injustice. The popes might see the needs of Christendom as a whole and attempt to reform its ills, but this view was not always shared by those whose rights of jurisdiction appeared to be eroded.

In 1229, when the Council of Toulouse assembled to survey and regulate the results of the Albigensian Crusade, its canons reflected the severity of ecclesiastical discipline in an area in which the inability to eradicate heresy had led to profound secular and ecclesiastical consequences. The first canon of the Council insists upon the appointment of the traditional *testes synodales*, but these now have new powers of actively searching out the hiding places of heretics; condemned heretics who repent must be moved to orthodox places to live, and they must wear conspicuously colored crosses on their garments to publicly indicate their penitential status; certain professions were closed to those even suspected of heresy. In the same year the king of France, Louis IX, issued the law *Cupientes*, in which he formally committed all royal officials not only to the prosecution of accused heretics, but to the active seeking out of heretics within their jurisdictions. Moreover, during the next several decades other rulers, notably Frederick II in Sicily, wrote extremely severe laws against heretics into their own constitutions, including the death penalty.

By 1230, in spite of the continuing and active papal sponsorship of elaborate and often successful pastoral activities and ecclesiastical reform, the severity of the laws against heretics had greatly increased, and their character had borrowed greatly from parallel developments in secular law in a number of kingdoms, cities, and principalities. Not only had the balance between persuasion and coercion tilted in favor of the latter, but it did so with widespread official and popular support. Moreover, the consequences of some of the most severe actions against heretics— the Albigensian Crusade, the ferocity of lynch mobs, and the ruthlessness of individual lords and churchmen—had driven the heretics from open contempt for Christian society to concealed activity. Heretics became harder to identify and more elusive when questioned, particularly when they were questioned by incompetent or indifferent officials, clerical or lay. It had now become necessary to discover them, and, like preaching and confession, discovering them had to be undertaken by specialists. Even Innocent III often doubted the abilities of the average prelate to fulfill his extensive visitation and juridical obligations.

The slow movement from persuasion to coercion also increased the importance of investigation, of inquiry. And when no accusers came forward, or when synodal witnesses seemed unable to learn anything of heretics, those witnesses had to be given investigative powers, with new rules of evidence and a new legal procedure. The twelfth century had seen a revolution in legal procedure, and the new procedure for discovering and trying heretics borrowed much from it.

The Medieval Inquisitors, 1230–1252

By 1230 a substantial revolution in legal thought and legal procedure had taken place throughout most of western Europe. The old and localized laws and procedures were slowly being encroached upon by the centralizing legal capacities and specifically formulated procedures of cities, lords, kings, and popes. The older accusatorial procedures in criminal law— which required a specific accuser who bore the risk of reprisal if his accusation was not proved true, and placed little evidential weight upon testimony and written texts, relying instead on oath-helpers, the various forms of ordeal, and general reputation—gave way in many spheres, though not always completely, before various forms of witness testimony, documentary evidence, judicial latitude, and the inquisitorial procedure. During the thirteenth century the inquisitorial procedure became the standard form of criminal procedure throughout most of Europe. Even in those countries that did not adopt it completely—England and the Scandinavian kingdoms—it strongly influenced local legal theory and practice. As Romano-canonical procedure, it shaped European jurisprudence and legal practice until the end of the eighteenth century.

Besides various forms of inquisitorial procedure, of course, other related procedures existed. From the eleventh century on, other rulers besides William the Conqueror and Henry IV utilized different forms of inquest to discover and claim their royal rights. Even when inquest/inquisitorial procedure was not used in the final stages of a criminal process, it was often used in the preliminary stages, as Charlemagne and some of his successors had used the *Rügeverfahren* procedure in the ninth century. In England, for example, although the petty jury came to be widely used in the thirteenth century, the earlier grand jury used an inquest-type procedure to find indictments. Thus when Louis IX of France issued *Cupientes* in 1229 he was not invoking an entirely new principle in royal law.

The responsibility of the pope himself for the spiritual welfare of the whole of Christendom had by now been more explicitly spelled out and widely accepted throughout Christian Europe. More and more cases of all kinds flooded the papal court. Even when papal judges did not intrude upon the jurisdiction of bishops, bishops themselves—as in the case of La Charité—often sent difficult cases directly to the papacy. Increasingly the papal court consisted of clerics trained in the law schools of Bologna and elsewhere, and as in the case of the decretals of Lucius III and Innocent III, the content and tone of papal decisions became more and more professionally juridical. At whatever level, therefore, heresy appeared, the popes knew that they would ultimately be held responsible by God for its effects, and their actions were expected to guide the rest of Christian society.

Other legal developments during the twelfth century had enabled the popes to make their authority more immediately felt. The institution of the papal judge delegate permitted the popes to delegate to a particular individual a portion of their legal authority, often for a particular case or for a particular period of time in one area. The increasing use of papal judges delegate during the twelfth century made papal jurisdiction more effective, since not every case needed to come to Rome for a hearing. Papal judges delegate did not need to be professional lawyers, since they could seek the advice of expert assessors in legal matters, and they did not have to travel with a large entourage, since they could invoke the aid of local authorities when necessary.

Not only judges delegate, but papal legates generally carried the papal presence and authority into corners of Europe that the routine operations of the papacy could not easily have reached. The network of communications that connected Rome with different parts of Europe was large and efficient, and the ever larger collections of papal correspondence indicate the increased volume of diplomatic and legal business that occupied the popes' time and minds as the twelfth century went on. Not all papal legates, of course, succeeded—as witness the murder of Peter of Castelnau—and a great many cases were appealed from the legates to the papal court at Rome. But the formal institution of legates and judges delegate gave the popes a powerful weapon in the combat with heretics and in the routine communications with the rest of the clergy and laity of Europe.

As various forms of dealing with heresy on local ecclesiastical or lay levels came to be perceived as ineffective, the creation of specialist investigators empowered by the papacy as judges delegate came slowly to be considered a solution.

Papal legates generally came from the curia, and papal judges delegate were often local ecclesiastical authorities especially empowered by the popes. But the curia did not have enough personnel to provide a regular system of investigating judges, and local ecclesiastical personnel often proved unreliable during the late twelfth and early thirteenth centuries. In the Mendicant Orders, however, the thirteenth-century popes found ideal material for just such an office.

Founded by St. Dominic in 1220 specifically to teach doctrine and combat heresy, the Order of Preachers—popularly known as the Dominicans—demanded that its members lead lives of apostolic poverty, and undergo extensive training in preaching and theological study. Furthermore, the order derived its charter from the popes themselves. The Order of Preachers was universal, tied to no central location but divided into a number of provinces and directed by a Minister-General who was responsible only to the pope. The Order of Friars Minor—popularly known as the Franciscans—was founded by St. Francis of Assisi in 1209 as an example of the life of perfection laid down in the Gospels, and its members too were joined in an international order divided into provinces and ruled by a Minister-General responsible only to the pope. Preaching and apostolic poverty were also fundamental elements of the Franciscan mission. Somewhat later than the Dominicans, the Franciscans too turned to study and formal training in theology, confessions, and preaching. In these two orders, the popes of the thirteenth century found precisely the European-wide clergy that they required, educated and specialized in the very fields in which heresiologists needed to be, and absolutely devoted to the authority of the Church and the pope at its head.

Moreover, both Orders were unattached to the particular localities in which heresy was found. Having no local ties, members of both Orders could distance themselves from the local entanglements that often prevented local clergy, even bishops, from effective action against heretics. As preachers and confessors, Dominicans and Franciscans became widely known and respected; as outsiders, their reputations preceded them, and they were usually regarded as holier and more able than the local clergy, whose resentment they often aroused.

The use of the Mendicant Orders as papal inquisitors also overcame the problem of individual fanatic pursuers of heresy. During the decade of the 1220s, a number of unsupervised clerics and laymen undertook the discovery of heretics, particularly in the Rhine Valley. The irregular and ruthless methods of such figures as Conrad Dorso and John the One-eyed aroused great local resentment and fear, besides raising serious questions of the legitimacy of their enterprise. These were joined in 1227 by Conrad of Marburg, a Premonstratensian canon obsessed with heresy and willing to entertain any accusations in order to extirpate heresy from the Rhine Valley. Their activities led to several years of wild accusations, trials, condemnations to the stake, confiscation of goods, and cries of protest to Rome itself. Making themselves professional synodal witnesses, Conrad Dorso, John the One-Eyed, and Conrad of Marburg demonstrated that unchecked fanaticism was not acceptable either. The careers of these and other freelance discoverers of heresy underlined the need to supplement the ordinary juridical powers of bishops and lay authorities with informed, trained, and specialized investigators whose work could be supervised in order to prevent the chaos that occurred whenever unrestrained enthusiasts undertook the discovery and prosecution of heresy.

In 1231 Pope Gregory IX (1227–1241) issued the letter *Ille humani generis* to the prior of the Dominican convent in Regensburg, linking the spread of heresy directly to the malice of Satan, complaining that heretics now teach openly and contemptuously of Church authority, and declaring that he must now respond to these great evils. Gregory informs the prior of Regensburg that he is comissioning him as a judge under papal authority—that is, a judge delegate—to travel wherever he wishes, to preach, and to "seek out diligently those who are heretics or are infamed of heresy." The prior of Regensburg may appoint other Dominicans, or "other discreet people known to you," and, when heretics are found and convicted, they are to be treated as the laws, ecclesiastical and temporal, prescribe. Those who wish to recant their heresy must be investigated thoroughly. Moreover, the prior and his companions are to dissuade other sorts of preachers "from the office of preacher of this business," since this is a new task and only those now especially empowered to preach the conversion of heretics may legitimately undertake it.

Gregory IX appears to have been motivated rather by a general concern for the eradication of heresy than with the design to institute a superior kind of ecclesiastical jurisdiction. Gregory's letters to various Dominican delegations in Germany and France urge cooperation with episcopal authority and prudence. The withdrawal of several commissions indicates that the earliest years of the new papal inquisitors were full of uncertainty and irregularity.

Between 1231 and 1252 a considerable apparatus of legal theory, legislation, and practice—from the definition and identification of heresy to the final steps against convicted, relapsed, and unrepentant heretics, their followers, and descendants—made both the word "heresy" and the steps against it very different from the term and the procedures in the preceding two centuries.

Against the prevailing accusatorial system, the right and obligation of appropriate officials to proceed inquisitorially, using inquisitorial procedure, had been established. From Gratian's *Decretum* on, the dangers heresy posed both to the faith and to the common good of society were explicitly recognized. Warfare against heretics, analogous to warfare against unbelievers, was permitted; the concept of heresy as treason was recognized in canon law as it had been in Roman; and although the death penalty appeared first in secular legal systems, in time it was also recognized in ecclesiastical courts.

In spite of the stiffening of penalties and the wider employment of the new inquisitorial procedure, ecclesiastical writers still insisted that procedings against heretics be conducted, "not from a zeal for righteous vengeance, but out of love of correcting an erring brother." Even the severest denouncers of heresy freely admitted that the administration of strict justice must be tempered with mercy wherever possible. Nevertheless, from 1200 on, the secular and ecclesiastical penalties against heretics and their sympathizers and supporters piled up: condemnation by the Church, confiscation of goods, destruction of immovable property, infamy, exile, disinheritment, all of these rivaled the most severe penalties for any offense recognized anywhere in thirteenth-century law. Even the history during this period of a common phrase in the legal vocabulary of legislators and inquisitors reflects increasing severity. When popes and other churchmen spoke of punishments for heresy in the twelfth and early thirteenth centuries, they often used the phrase *animadversio debita*—"the debt of hatred"—that the unrepentant heretic had to pay for his or her offense. Until the end of the first quarter of the thirteenth century, although the phrase sometimes meant the death penalty, it usually meant whatever penalty local law provided for the offense of heresy. In the decretal *Excommunicamus* of 1231, however, Pope Gregory IX made it clear that from that date on, the *animadversio debita* was synonymous with the death penalty.

Thus, what made the inquisitors of the thirteenth century and later so formidable was not the simple introduction of Roman-inspired *inquisi-tio*-procedure—for in most respects, this would have been regarded as a modernization of legal procedure—into ecclesiastical courts. Rather, it was the simultaneous development and adoption of a number of procedures and doctrines: the increasing severity and comprehensiveness of punishments; the perceived dangers of heresy to both Church and society; the increasing degree of cooperation between ecclesiastical and lay authorities; the failure of the episcopal inquisitions; the appearance of the Mendicant Orders, well-trained and directly under the authority of the Popes; and, finally, the appointment of theological specialists in essentially judicial and investigatory roles.

At the same time, it must be pointed out that the severity and expediency of criminal law throughout Europe, including England, was drastically increasing. Although the "criminalization" of heresy is a distinct process, the widespread adoption of inquisitorial juridical procedure in secular courts, the decline of the accusatorial procedure except in "civil" suits, the introduction of stricter rules of evidence, and the concurrent introduction of torture in secular law all form a context in which the medieval inquisitors must be regarded. A good deal of inquisition history has been written as if the papal inquisitors were the only ardent pursuers of alleged wrongdoers in thirteenth-century Europe. In fact, they were always less numerous, and often less ardent than the judicial servants of secular powers.

The results of the first decade of papal inquisitorial work are summed up in the canons of the Council of Tarragona in 1242. The Council provided explicit definitions of *heretic, believer, suspects*—whether *simply, vehemently,* or *most vehemently*—*concealers, hiders, receivers, defenders,* and *favorers.* The Council also provided an explicit definition for *relapsed heretics,* those who had returned to their heretical beliefs and practices after disavowing them. The Council also took up the problem of the confessions of heretics—whether these had been made to avoid the more severe punishments following conviction—and laid out a series of penances for heretics, from distinctive costume and public penitential acts to imprisonment and the release to secular authorities for the death penalty. The canons of the Council of Tarragona summed up the legislative work of Gregory IX and constituted, in the words of the historian who knows the subject best, "a veritable directory of inquisitorial procedure." The fury and indiscriminate tactics of earlier figures like Conrad of Marburg are gone; in their place is a firmly and explicitly drawn code of procedure aimed at theological crime.

From the canons of Tarragona, inquisitorial practice proved most effective in Languedoc. A short manual for inquisitors of 1248–1249 details inquisitorial procedure from the delegation of papal authority through the final actions against convicted or relapsed heretics, provides legal formulas to be followed, and spells out in detail not only the procedures, but the theological conditions according to which they are to be carried out.

During this period the episcopal inquisitions were strengthened by the increased practice of episcopal supervision of the spiritual life of each diocese; close control over the appointment and supervision of synodal witnesses, who also acquired greater police powers; the practice of requiring a public oath of obedience to the Church and Christian doctrines from entire local populations during episcopal visitations; and the application and supervision of penances performed by convicted heretics and suspects.

With the pontificate of Innocent IV (1243–1254), the varied procedures and practices that had slowly been assembled to direct the Church's attack on heresy combined into a formalized office, that of "inquisitor of heretical depravity," which operated by formalized procedures.

Medieval Inquisitors at Work

The short manual for inquisitors in Carcassonne (ca. 1248–1249) constitutes an important literary and procedural landmark in European history: ostensibly a subdivision of the general category of treatises on pastoral or legal procedure, this work in fact instituted a long series of extremely specialized treatises on inquisitorial procedure that extended from the mid-thirteenth to the eighteenth century. Because the work of the inquisitors came to be perceived as substantially different from those of other legal personnel, the manual for inquisitors rapidly became a distinctive and original literary form, and from it and from papal letters it is possible to reconstruct the formal procedure of the inquisitors as they created an institution that derived from both theology and law and yet remained perplexingly identical to neither.

The manual begins with a letter of commission to inquisitors, sent by the Dominican provincial to two members of the order, charging them that, "for the remission of your sins,"

> You are to make inquisition of heretics and their believers, factors, receivers, and defenders, and also of persons who are defamed, in the province of Narbonne. . . .

The two inquisitors charged in the letter of commission then state that they chose a place "well suited to the purpose, from which or in which we can make inquisition of other localities." They then called the clergy and people of the area together and preached a sermon which cited their authority, urged orthodox Christians to identify known heretics or those suspected of heresy in the vicinity, and announced a "period of grace" during which voluntary confessions would be accepted without judicial consequences. During the period of grace the inquisitors would accept confessions and denunciations alike and compile a list of suspects who would have to be interrogated personally after the period of grace expired.

The manual continues with a sample citation, or summons, of someone to appear before it, specifying the reason for the summons, the limits of delay in appearance without risking the charge of contempt, and the safe places where those summoned may appear. The authors of the manual are emphatic about their points of convergence with and deviance from "established legal procedure":

> To no one do we deny a legitimate defense nor do we deviate from established legal procedure, except that we do not make public the names of witnesses. . . .

They then go to considerable length to cite their authorities for concealing the names of witnesses, citing decretals of Gregory IX and Innocent IV, as well as the substantiating opinions of several cardinals. The original reason for the concealing of the names of witnesses appears to have been the fear of local retaliation.

For those who willingly return to the Church, the inquisitors have a formulaic contract which specifies that the returned heretics are to abjure heresy, to observe and defend the faith, to pursue heretics, to assist the inquisitors in their task, and to accept whatever penance is imposed upon them. The manual also contains a form for reconciliation on these terms. On the other hand, those accused and convicted of heresy who remain obdurate are "relinquished to secular judgment" and excommunicated. For individuals who had already died and were posthumously convicted of heresy, a similar sentence was read out.

Although the procedures of the inquisitors were held *in camera*, the verdicts and sentences were read aloud in public ceremonies as elaborate as those at the first announcement of the arrival of the inquisitors and the first sermon. The final paragraph of this short manual paraphrases canon 23 of the 1243–1244 Council of Narbonne:

> We do not proceed to the condemnation of anyone without clear and evident proof or without his own confession, nor God permitting, will we do so. And all the major condemnations and penances which

we have issued and do issue, we pronounce with not only the general
but also the specific signed counsel of prelates.

The manual concludes by noting that although some of the inquisitors'
practices "cannot be easily reduced to writing" they nevertheless conform
to the letter of the law or to specific apostolic ordinances.

A specialized inquisitorial literature had grown out of the prosecution
of heretics; from the late twelfth century on it circulated the records of
papal and conciliar legislation, techniques of interrogation developed
by inquisitors, and formularies of procedure to others taking up the
inquisitorial office for the first time. Although most inquisitors were
trained theologians and preachers, and a few were legal experts (although
all had access to expert legal advice), no previous training fully qualified
anyone to be an effective inquisitor. Thus, inquisitorial literature filled
a need and was recopied throughout the fourteenth and fifteenth centuries.
Much of it was later printed to serve the same instructional purpose.

In 1323 or 1324 the inquisitor Bernard Gui (recently made rather
more sinister and notorious in Umberto Eco's novel, *The Name of the
Rose*, than he ever was historically) produced the *Practica officii inquisitionis heretice pravitatis*, an elaborate work which summed up three
quarters of a century of inquisitorial experience.

By the late fourteenth century much of this literature was summed
up in the *Directorium Inquisitorum*, written by the Aragonese inquisitor
Nicolau Eymeric, a work that was the best known manual for inquisitors
through the sixteenth and into the seventeenth century. Eymeric's manual
appears to have influenced the *Instructiones* for the Spanish Inquisition
drawn up by Tomás de Torquemada in 1484 and the *Repertorium Inquisitorum* published anonymously in Valencia in 1494. The latter is an
alphabetically arranged compendium of matters of inquisitorial interest,
from *abiuratio* ("abjuration") to *zizania* ("tares"). This literature tended
to homogenize the doctrines and procedures of inquisitors throughout
Latin Europe according to standards developed in local circumstances,
but accepted by Rome and the rest of the Church.

The doctrines and procedures of the inquisitors derived from both
theology and canon law, not only from the early works of Church Fathers
and general councils and popes, but from the systematization of these
texts from the late eleventh century on, and from the extensive development of both theology and law in the twelfth and thirteenth centuries.
By the mid-thirteenth century, much of the ambiguity and hesitation
that had characterized the attitudes toward heresy on the part of churchmen, councils, and popes was gone: in its place were the formal disciplines

of theology and law, consisting of bodies of professional knowledge applied by professional personnel trained in the new universities, expert in the relevant texts, and influential in advising those who made ecclesiastical policy; theologians and canonists provided the intellectual and technical doctrines that were applied by inquisitors.

The sources most frequently cited by both theologians and canonists were scripture and its "ordinary gloss."—the most widely accepted commentary on the text and meaning of the Bible; the *Sentences* of the twelfth-century theologian Peter Lombard and the commentaries upon it; the standard textbooks of theology; the *Decretum* of Gratian and commentaries upon it; the standard work on canon law, and subsequent collections of papal decretals and the commentaries upon them. Two texts common to both kinds of specialists are found in Gratian's *Decretum*. In C.24 q.3 c.27, St. Jerome is cited for his etymological account of the term heresy itself:

> Heresy comes from the Greek and means a choice, that is, when each person chooses for himself a doctrine which he thinks to be a better one. Whoever, therefore, understands Holy Scripture in any sense other than that given by the Holy Spirit, by whom it was written, ought to be called a heretic, even though he does not leave the Church, and he is to be considered a man whose works are of the flesh, choosing that which is worse.

Even more influential was a text from St. Augustine which focused upon the contumacious character of the heretic and probably is the single most influential text in the history of medieval heresy. In Book XVIII, chapter 51 of *The City of God*, Augustine argued that the Church had actually been strengthened by the heretics. He began the chapter with a vivid account of the Devil's great dismay at the abandonment of pagan temples ("temples of Demons," according to Augustine) and the eagerness of the human race to turn to Christ as its savior. The Devil then stirred up heretics, who professed to be Christians and remained within the Church (comparing them to the battling philosophers whose conflicting opinions are tolerated in the world, "the city of confusion"). Although Gratian did not include this account, he excerpted the text immediately following it as C.24 q.3 c.31:

> Those who conceive morbid and depraved doctrines in the Church of Christ and who, if they are corrected so as to believe healthy and proper doctrines, resist contumaciously and refuse to change their pestiferous and deadly doctrines and persist in defending them, they are heretics.

Willful erroneous choice in religious doctrine and contumacy were for both theologians and canonists the essence of the heretic.

Theologians cited these texts frequently, since *Causae* XXIII and XXIV of Gratian's *Decretum* contained a handy and systematic mine of relevant theological excerpts, largely from the Church Fathers. They also cited scripture, drawing heavily upon the wealth of scriptural commentary available to them, finding references to heretics in the lepers of Matthew 8.2 and 10.8, in the ravaging wolves of Matthew 7.15, in the turbulence of the Pharisees in Luke 12.1, in the parable of the wheat and the chaff in Matthew 13.29–30, and in the refusal by the angel of Ephesus to spare the wicked in Revelations 2.2, as well as in the epistles of St. Paul and many other scriptural texts. The weight of sophisticated theological scholarship by the time of St. Thomas Aquinas (1224/5–1274) provided an immense foundation for the theological definition of heresy and heretics and constituted one of the two major supports for inquisitorial activity, its texts and authorities frequently cited at the beginning of handbooks of inquisitorial procedure.

Just as theologians, following the standard methods of scriptural exegesis, found heretics in biblical texts, so canon lawyers found heretics in legal analogies. For them, the heretic was analogous to the sacrilegious thief, condemned to an infamous death by Roman jurisprudence, or to the traitor in Roman law. Citing some of the same texts as the theologians, canonists nevertheless drew more heavily upon the doctrines of Christian Roman law, the legislation of Church councils, and the decretals of popes to shape a juridical counterpart to the thought of the theologians, thus forming the second major support for inquisitorial activity. A striking example of the canonists' method may be found in the ordinary gloss to the *Liber Extra* of Gregory IX, the first official book of canon law, compiled by Raymund of Peñafort and issued formally in 1234. Glossing X. V.7.3. ad v. *hereticum*, the gloss enumerates seven meanings of the term:

- He is said to be a heretic who perverts the sacraments of the Church, as do simoniacs.
- So is he who separates himself from the unity of the Church.
- So is every excommunicated person.
- So is he who errs in the exposition of Sacred Scripture.
- So is he who invents a new sect or follows one.
- So is he who understands the articles of faith differently from the Roman Church.
- So is he who thinks ill of the sacraments of the Church.

A standard list of a similar kind was made by most lawyers who commented on these and similar texts, and often the lists repeated each other. In the middle of the thirteenth century the canonist Goffredo da Trani copied such a list that had originally appeared in the commentary of the canonist Tancred early in the thirteenth century:

There are six ways of identifying a heretic:

A heretic is one who either creates a false opinion in matters of faith or follows one who has.

A second way of identifying someone as a heretic is knowing that he interprets scripture differently from the sense of the Holy Spirit, by which it was written.

One may be a heretic in a third way by being separated from the sacraments of the Church or the communion of the faithful.

A fourth way is to be a perverter of sacraments.

A fifth way is to be dubious in faith, since we must believe firmly.

The sixth way is to attempt to remove the Roman Church from the summit of all the churches.

The work of theologians and canonists underlay the extensive legislation that created, sustained, and directed the work of the inquisitors. Thus, the work of the Council of Tarragona of 1242, convoked by the archbishop, Peter of Albalat, in the presence of Raymund of Peñafort himself, organized the inquisitors with the bishops of Aragón and Navarre in attendance. In a series of canons which derived from the theological and canon law views just considered, the Council carefully defined its key terms:

Heretics are those who remain obstinate in error.

Believers are those who put faith in the errors of heretics and are assimilated to them.

Those suspect of heresy are those who are present at the preaching of heretics and participate, however little, in their ceremonies.

Those simply suspected have done such things only once.

Those vehemently suspected have done this often.

Those most vehemently suspected have done this frequently.

Concealers are those who know heretics but do not denounce them.

Hiders are those who have agreed to prevent heretics being discovered.

Receivers are those who have twice received heretics on their property.

Defenders are those who knowingly defend heretics so as to prevent the Church from extirpating heretical depravity.

Favorers are all of the above to a greater or lesser degree.

Relapsed are those who return to their former heretical errors after having formally renounced them.

The canons of the Council of Tarragona are the first in a long line of accumulating directives that shaped the authority and procedure of the medieval inquisitors. Systematized in handbooks of doctrine and procedure, the work of theologians, canonists, and ecclesiastical (and often secular) legislators gave to the inquisitors their distinctive character and shaped the course of their work.

The essential purpose of the inquisitors was to save the souls of heretics and those close to them and to protect the unity of the Church. Since their work depended upon juridical theology, both elements of their task must be kept in mind. Although many of the inquisitors were not lawyers themselves, they had the assistance of expert lawyers, and they had papal authority as judges delegate. Their lack of professional expertise in the law was never flaunted, and the handbooks they consulted usually explained in great detail the reasons for the divergence of some of their procedures from those of other courts. In some instances, of course, their procedures did not diverge at all. Temporal courts in many areas, including the kingdom of France in the late thirteenth century, also refused to divulge the names of witnesses for fear of retaliation; temporal courts were also reluctant to permit counsel to defendants in many different types of cases; the standards of evidence for conviction were often more harsh in thirteenth century temporal courts than in inquisitorial courts.

In terms of evidence, for example, the precedence of temporal courts is clear. By the early thirteenth century, besides the traditional accusatorial procedure, other forms of procedure, as we have seen, also became widely used in both temporal and canon law courts such as the procedure of *denuntiatio*, in which a person of good reputation reported a crime to a magistrate without having to support the responsibility of a full accusation. In other instances, other means of informing the authorities that a crime had been committed had been developed. A magistrate's own officials might report a crime to him in a manner similar to *denuntiatio*; a magistrate might hear of a crime through *fama* (widespread public rumor or even notoriety); or he might know of it from personal experience. The judge, having been informed of a crime, had next to ascertain whether it had in fact occurred, and whether or not it was punishable. The judge would then call witnesses, hear testimony, and try to determine if anyone in particular seemed triable for the offense. These procedures were called the *inquisitio generalis*, in whatever kind of court in which they were employed.

Once the accused was identified, the *inquisitio specialis* began. The accused had to be served a written account of the charges against him; the writ of the charges also brought him to court; and before the fourteenth century, when state prosecutors appeared, it was usually said that *fama* stood in place of the accuser against him. The medieval rules of evidence recognized only full proofs and partial proofs. The only full proofs were the testimony of two eyewitnesses, catching the criminal in the act, or confession. All other evidence constituted partial proof, and no amount of partial proof could add up to full proof in cases of capital crimes. Thus, a judge who had begun to try a defendant based on results of the *inquisitio generalis* but found that he did not have full proof, could only dismiss the charge or turn to acquiring a full proof on the basis of partial proofs. If enough partial proofs were at hand, they were considered justification for the seeking of a full proof, which, in the absence of eyewitnesses or the defendant's having been caught redhanded, could only be confession.

At this point, the doctrine of torture came into play. The tradition of Roman and medieval criminal law had made torture an element in the testimony of certain classes of otherwise dubious witnesses, and a procedure that could be triggered by enough partial proofs to indicate that a full proof—a confession—was likely, and no other full proofs were available. The procedure of torture itself was guarded by a number of protocols and protections for the defendant, and its place in due process was rigorously defined by the jurists. A confession made after or under torture had to be freely repeated the next day without torture or it would have been considered invalid. Technically, therefore, torture was strictly a means of obtaining the only full proof available (and absolutely necessary in a capital crime) when a great mass of partial proofs existed and no other form of full proof was available.

In this light, far more of the procedure of the inquisition was consistent with contemporary legal values and procedures than might at first appear. In addition, the inquisitors had a different task from those of other courts. Their tasks were not only—or even primarily—to convict the contumacious heretic, but to save his soul if possible and to preserve the unity of the Church. In this their interest often ran counter to those of lay people (who simply wanted the heretic destroyed before the whole community suffered), and of judicial officers of temporal powers, who sought only to punish. Throughout the entire procedure of an inquisitorial visit to a district, from the confessions and discoveries of heretical suspects to the final disposition of all cases that came to their attention, the inquisitors were both jurists and pastors.

The elements of the procedures of inquisitorial visits described in the manual for inquisitors at Carcassonne in 1248 constituted the general form of procedures throughout the duration and activity of medieval inquisitors. The arrival of the distinctively clothed inquisitors, accompanied by a few servants and, since 1242, by a few armed retainers, was followed by the general sermon, which was followed by the period of grace. During this period, the manuals make it clear that the inquisitors had to distinguish carefully between genuine and apparent repentance, guard against envy or hostility dictating accusations by one neighbor against another, and keep open the doors of forgiveness to all who sincerely sought them. Although the trial was secret, it had to be recorded in writing in full. Although the names of witnesses had to be concealed from the accused, ostensibly to prevent retaliation, they had to be entered in full in the record and given to the assessors who advised the inquisitor. Although the accused was often permitted no defense counsel (largely, it seems, for the sake of simplifying the procedure, which was only in part judicial), inquisitors were warned in manual after manual against putting full credence in the testimony of persons who, although they might be permitted to testify in an inquisitorial trial, would not have been admitted as suitable witnesses in other courts. The accused was permitted to list his enemies, and if any of those names turned up among the witnesses against him, that witness was to be struck from the list. The recording of the trials appears to have been extremely conscientious.

As the literary genre of handbooks for inquisitors developed, it recorded the experience of many inquisitors in many situations. As the inquisitions tried more and more people accused of heresy, inquisitors acquired an idea of their own distinctive profession. The handbook of Bernard Gui contains an extensive description of the kind of person the ideal inquisitor should be and emphasizes as well the skills of heretics in evading even a skillful inquisitor's interrogation.

The sentences given out by inquisitors were also issued in the form of penance—temporal satisfaction to God after contrition and absolution had removed the actual guilt for the sin. As William of Auvergne, the early thirteenth-century theologian who was one of the first to elaborate the doctrine of Purgatory, explained, "purgatorial penalties are penalties that complete the penitential purgation begun in this life." All inquisitorial sentences proper were in this sense penitential, and they were given only to those who had shown one degree or another of repentance for their acts. These included fasting, specified penitential observations of the ecclesiastical calendar, scourging, pilgrimage, or the wearing of yellow crosses on outer garments for a specified period of time. In addition, the inquisitors appear to have been the first to develop the idea and institution of imprisonment as a penitential discipline. Inquisitorial prisons were of two types: *Murus largus* resembled life in a monastery, with physical movements greatly curtailed; *murus strictus* consisted of a single cell. All prisoners were fed a minimal diet, forbidden visitors except for spouses, and their sentences were technically for life, although often commuted to shorter periods.

In two instances, however, the inquisitors acted not as a penitential, but as a strictly judicial forum. For heretics who had repented—and for those who had not—most territorial states had derived from Roman law the doctrine that the heretics' property should be confiscated. In ecclesiastical principalities, the Church itself could confiscate. Technically, confiscation was not a penance and the inquisitors did not condemn someone to it; it was the result of temporal law. Although the inquisitors often received some of the property thus confiscated in order to maintain their staffs and themselves, confiscation itself was not usually an inquisitorial function.

Nor could the inquisitors sentence anyone to death. When faced with a convicted heretic who refused to recant, or who relapsed into heresy, the inquisitors were to turn him over to the temporal authorities— the "secular arm"—for *animadversio debita*, the punishment decreed by local law, usually burning to death. This—clearly a punishment, like confiscation, and not a penance—was governed by local criminal law, which as we have seen grew progressively more harsh from the twelfth century on.

In practice, then, except for three distinctive features, the medieval inquisitorial procedure was considerably more closely aligned with legal procedures in other canon law courts and in other temporal courts than it might seem at first glance. The three exceptions were the secrecy of the identity of witnesses, the restriction of defense counsel, and the overall penitential, rather than strictly punitive, character of the entire proceeding. These features appear less singular during the main drive against Catharism, in which the inquisitorial procedure was formed, than in subsequent dealings of inquisitors with accused heretics who were not Cathars.

Medieval Inquisition or Medieval Inquisitors?

The inquisitor could be either an official charged by a bishop to use the bishop's conventional judicial authority within a single diocese, or an individual (usually a member of a Mendicant Order) appointed a papal judge delegate either directly or through the Minister-General or Provincial of the Order) for a particular period and region. The term in the latter case was *inquisitor hereticae pravitatis*, "inquisitor (or enquirer) of heretical depravity," and the power he held in this capacity was termed the *officium inquisitionis hereticae pravitatis*, "the office of inquisition of (or of inquiring into) heretical depravity." The earliest inquisitors named by bishops and popes held individual charges, and at no time was there a centralized office or authority that may firmly and unequivocally be termed *the* Inquisition. Such organized institutions did emerge in Spain at the end of the fifteenth century, in Portugal in 1536, and in Rome after 1542, but no medieval supervisory and organizing office existed in this sense at all. Thus, it may be more accurate to speak of medieval *inquisitors* rather than a medieval *inquisition*.

On the other hand, the *practice* of inquisitorial activity, whether episcopal or papal, grew to be remarkably consistent by the first quarter of the fourteenth century. The handbook for inquisitors by Bernard Gui described techniques developed chiefly in Languedoc and Northern Italy, but it would have aided inquisitors anywhere. The *Directorium Inquisitorum* of Nicolau Eymeric was written on the basis of Eymeric's experience as an inquisitor in Aragón (and Eymeric's sixteenth-century editor, Francisco Peña, pointed out a number of local Aragonese usages in Eymeric's text), but its appeal to inquisitors elsewhere is indicated by the fact that Peña found his best manuscripts of the *Directorium* not among those used for the Barcelona printed editions of 1503 and 1536, but in the libraries of the popes, of two cardinal-inquisitors, and the Holy Office of Bologna. In this respect, it is possible to see the results of inquisitions in one period and place influencing inquisitions in others; newly appointed inquisitors may well have sought assistance from the experience of inquisitors elsewhere, or in the same locality before them, and it is not unlikely that such figures as Bernard Gui and Nicolau Eymeric wrote their handbooks with the instruction of later inquisitors in mind.

In addition, the earliest inquisitorial literature developed in areas in which heresy had been perceived as a deep-rooted, persistent, and continuing threat—in southern France and Aragón, as well as northern Italy. With the virtual extinction of Catharism by the early fourteenth century, the original impetus for the office of inquisitor had disappeared, although the office was continued for other forms of heresy, but without the sense of continuity that had developed from the later twelfth to the early fourteenth century. For instance, when Philip IV the Fair of France launched his accusations against the Order of the Knights Templar in 1310, a flurry of inquisitorial activity was launched to investigate the Order, eventually leading to its destruction at the Council of Vienne in 1312. The fear of the so-called heresy of the Free Spirit produced another increase in inquisitorial activity later in the fourteenth century, as did, especially in Italy, the papal prosecution of the Spiritual wing of the Franciscan Order at the same time.

In a number of prominent cases, the office of inquisitor also increased in prominence, but in general, outside of individual careers and particular episodes, there is no consistent pattern of inquisitorial activity in the later Middle Ages. Even the increased concern on the part of both laity and clergy with the practice of magic and witchcraft in the fourteenth and fifteenth centuries did not increase the powers of inquisitors substantially. A well-known decretal of Alexander IV of 1264 forbade the inquisitors to pursue those charged with magical practices unless these specifically savored of heresy. In the course of the fourteenth and fifteenth centuries, a number of popes, notably John XXII and Eugenius IV, acted vigorously on accusations of magic, sometimes by using inquisitors, and drew magic and heresy more closely together in identifying the one with the other; it was then the heretical character of magic that drew it into the power of the inquisitors.

In the well-known—and widely misunderstood—case of Joan of Arc in 1431, one may observe a number of features of late medieval inquisitorial practice. Captured and imprisoned by the English, Joan was tried by a tribunal of judges and assessors headed by Pierre Cauchon, bishop of Beauvais and ally of the English. Although a number of aspects of the trial were ostensibly canonical—the special powers conferred on Cauchon; the participation, however limited, of Jean Le Moine, the papal inquisitor of northern France; and the presence of theologians and canonists among the assessors—there were grave irregularities in the trial. Joan's confinement in an English military prison was strictly against inquisitorial procedure; the technical use of interrogation procedure and evidence was well below inquisitorial standards; the technicalities of Joan's conviction and turning over to the secular arm as a relapsed heretic were largely political. To see a better example of inquisitorial procedure at work in Joan's case one needs to turn to the trial of her rehabilitation in 1456. There, in the only canonical inquisitorial trial Joan ever had, she was acquitted, almost entirely by standard inquisitorial procedure. Granted that there were reasons why both the pope and the king of France wanted Joan's name cleared, the rehabilitation trial of 1456 followed strict inquisitorial procedure, and its extensive documentation informs us far better of Joan's life and activities than the original trial ever did. A simple rehabilitation by papal fiat would have been entirely possible, but the extensive procedures of the rehabilitation trial reflect late medieval inquisitorial procedure at its most characteristic.

By the late fifteenth century the shaping of the character and office of the inquisitor had been completed, as had the procedure of inquisitorial investigation. An extensive literature both described and justified them, and two centuries of inquisitorial practice lay behind them. From its origins in Roman law and continuity in ecclesiastical law, inquisitorial procedure had been adopted in a large number of courts, both lay and clerical, from the twelfth century on. The upsurge of heresy in the eleventh and twelfth centuries; the reconception of heresy in secular law, theology, and canon law; and the perceived failures of the regular episcopal jurisdictions adequately to deal with it, all had led to the office of inquisitor as a papal judge delegate. He was now usually a member of the Mendicant Orders, and his pastoral as well as judicial functions shaped the practice of inquisition and made it appear in the eyes of many as separate and distinct from other courts and other bodies of legal theory and practice. At the same time, the original impetus for the inquisitors had waned with the decline of Catharism and the withdrawal of Waldensianism to remote rural areas. The inquisitors of the late fourteenth and fifteenth centuries acted according to a routine created over a period of a century and a half, but they did not have the sense of omnipresent and threatening heresy to work against, and their activities were intermittent and occasionally non-existent.

Yet this summary does not entirely complete the history of inquisition in medieval Europe, for the term has also a linguistic dimension and a linguistic history that is also informative. Etymologically, the terms inquisition, inquire, inquiry, and inquest all are related and derive from the same Latin term. Yet their present meanings are very different, not only in English, but in other European vernaculars. Although "inquisition" still has largely a pejorative sense in most modern languages, "inquire," "inquiry," and "inquest" all possess neutral or honorific senses. To what extent does the history of inquisitorial practice play a role in the subsequent meanings of this closely related group of words?

The classical Latin terms *inquirere* and *quaerere* were shaped in vulgar Latin into the single term *inquaerere*, a participial form of which was *inquaesitio*, from which came the Old French terms *enquête*, *enquerre*, and *enquerir*. By the twelfth century, these terms translated *inquisitio* in its general juridical sense, as well as in its investigative sense for purposes of acquiring information, as in the case of the use of *inquisitio* to describe William the Conqueror's investigations for Domesday Book. With the parallel development of the inquisitorial procedure in both lay and clerical courts, *inquisitio* could routinely translate as *enquête*. With the distinctive emergence of ecclesiastical inquisitorial procedure focused exclusively upon heresy, however, *enquête* and *inquisitio* separated their meanings, the latter referring exclusively to the ecclesiastical procedure, the former referring routinely to secular aspects of inquisitorial procedure. In English, the term usually referred to intensive inquiry outside the realm of legal procedure. Thus, by the fourteenth century not only was there an office of inquisitor and a body of inquisitorial theory and practice, but there was also a distinction in a number of vernacular languages between the inquisitorial activities of the Church and other forms of inquisitorial procedure in the service of governments or lay courts. The medieval inquisitors had shaped a semantic change in Old French that influenced the usage of similar terms in English and other European vernaculars as well. Even though there may technically not have been an institution termed the medieval inquisition, the office, theory, and practice were perceived as sufficiently distinctive to govern the development of key terms in early European linguistic communities. People knew what inquisition was, and they expressed its difference from other familiar and very similar forms of inquiry in terms that have ever since maintained distinctions in different languages. Which is why today no one routinely objects to a public authority's making an inquest—except when the public objects to the purpose or methods of the inquest: it then is designated an inquisition, a transposition made possible by the semantic history of the French language in the thirteenth and fourteenth centuries as a result of the activities of the medieval inquisitors.

Maintaining Religious Uniformity in England, France, and Germany

One of the sharpest and most important distinctions between the institutional Catholicism of southern and northern Europe has been drawn by E. William Monter:

> The single most important difference within Catholic Europe after the Council of Trent was the presence or absence of an autonomous Inquisition which controlled both heretical and impious behavior, punishing both adherents of different religions and ignorant Catholics who did not properly understand their own. North of the Alps and Pyrenees, no such institutions existed during the early modern period. Here, even heretics tended to be tried in secular courts, like the *Chambre ardente* ("court of fire") created by the *Parlement* of Paris in 1549, or even the more notorious Council of Troubles created by the Duke of Alva in the Netherlands in 1567.

These features were not new to northern Europe in the mid-sixteenth century, and Monter's distinction may serve just as well to frame a discussion of the maintenance of religious uniformity in England, France, and Germany from the late fourteenth century on.

In England a number of particular circumstances shaped ecclesiastical and temporal policy and institutions in the period between the late fourteenth and early sixteenth centuries. England had been relatively free of heresy in the twelfth and thirteenth centuries, and English law evolved without that deference to inquisitorial institutions that marked the Roman common law of southern France, northern Italy, the Rhineland, and other areas in which papal inquisitorial tribunals operated from the early thirteenth century.

To be sure, the law of episcopal inquisition existed in England, as did the rest of the common law of the Latin Church. That law was supplemented in England, as elsewhere, by canons of provincial church councils, particularly those held and issued by the Archbishop of Canterbury, Thomas Arundel (1353–1414), in his campaign against Wycliffism and Lollardy in the early years of the fifteenth century. To these were occasionally added parliamentary statutes, the first of which dates from 1382, but the best known of which is the statute *De haeretico comburendo* of 1401. This statute empowered bishops to arrest suspected heretics on the basis of reputation alone, to imprison them until they abjured, and, if they did not abjure, to turn them over to secular authorities for execution. A statute of Henry V of 1414 empowered a number of secular judges to make inquest concerning heresy within their own districts, chiefly in the wake of residual Lollardy and the notorious career of Sir John Oldcastle, who was executed for heresy in 1417. This combination of ecclesiastical and secular authorities in the maintenance of religious uniformity is consistent with Monter's description of post-Tridentine northern Europe. It remained the procedure against heretics in England until 1534, when the powers and procedures of ecclesiastical courts were considerably curtailed, although at the same time the powers of secular courts were distinctly enhanced. Thus, although England possessed no "autonomous Inquisition," and the instance of heresy remained low through the fifteenth and early sixteenth centuries, the offense remained serious, and it was pursuable by both ecclesiastical and secular authorities.

The case of France between the early thirteenth and the early sixteenth centuries was somewhat different from that of England. The issuing of *Cupientes* in 1229 clearly placed the backing of the French monarchy behind ecclesiastical efforts to eradicate heresy in both southern and northern France. In the case of the Templars, prosecuted largely by Philip IV the Fair between 1307 and 1312, royal justice consistently outstripped ecclesiastical authority: Philip IV even criticized Pope Clement V for his laxity in pursuing the heresy of the Templars. Elsewhere in France, Philip permitted the ecclesiastical inquisitors a much freer hand, particularly in Languedoc, although even there he commissioned several investigations of inquisitorial activities. Clement V himself authorized similar investigations of the conduct of inquisitors and inquisitorial institutions and procedures in Languedoc and made some revisions in those parts of canon law pertaining to inquisitorial procedure. Clement's successor John XXII vigorously pursued heresy by means of inquisitorial commissions, especially in southern France. In the diocese of Pamiers, on the French side of the Pyrenees, between 1318 and 1325, the local bishop, Jacques Fournier, conducted extensive hearings about peasant Cathars in the Ariège, the results of which were deposited in the papal archives in Avignon when Fournier became Pope Benedict XII.

In northern France, however, the Mendicant inquisitions slowly gave way before royal authority and that of the *Parlement* of Paris. Although the Dominican prior of Paris was generally the inquisitor-general of France from the fourteenth century on, secular authorities increasingly advised by the faculty of theology at the University of Paris appear to have dominated the prosecution of heresy in France from the late fourteenth century. It is under these circumstances that the second trial of Joan of Arc, for example, is probably best understood, even though the first trial was clearly irregular.

In the early sixteenth century, inquisitorial tribunals in Languedoc resumed vigorous activity, initially against humanists and clerics, but after the 1530s against Lutheranism as well. Here, too, the authority and autonomy of ecclesiastical inquisitors slowly gave way before the greater power and presence of secular judges and courts.

In fourteenth- and fifteenth-century Germany, although there were equally strong and diverse motives for discovering and prosecuting heretics as elsewhere in Europe, persecution was in fact intermittent and rarely sustained. Episcopal inquisitors appear to have been more successful than papally commissioned inquisitors. Although local authorities cooperated with both, they rarely assumed the direction of investigation and trials that we have seen characteristic of northern and eventually southern France. The very absence of a directing papal institution rendered the inquisitors in Germany more autonomous but less effective than their counterparts elsewhere and helped to erect the episcopal inquisitions to a position that they had in few other localities in Europe. Although there were occasionally ferocious and brutal persecutions in later medieval Germany and Bohemia, there was no sustained presence of inquisitions comparable to those in southern France or to the new inquisitional institutions of the sixteenth century in Spain and Italy.

Thus, except for a few specific localities, the inquisitions of the thirteenth through the fifteenth centuries operated quite differently in different parts of Europe. In some cases, notably England and France, particularly the latter, there was a shift toward secular tribunals performing the inquisitorial function with the advice of inquisitors or, as in the case of France, with that of the theology faculty of the University of Paris. Elsewhere, as in Germany, papally commissioned inquisitors worked intermittently, but were not as effective as episcopal inquisitors. One of the consequences of early twelfth-century complaints about both secular authorities and bishops—that they were slow to prosecute heresy and usually incompetent when they did so,—was far less true of the late fourteenth and fifteenth centuries. By that time, both secular and episcopal authorities throughout most of Europe had come to realize and willingly undertake their responsibilities as far as religious dissent was concerned. The papally commissioned inquisitors were no longer as visible or as effective as they had been because other powers had entered the hunt for heresy and had become competent to undertake it. Not until the late fifteenth and sixteenth centuries, in the case of the *conversos* in Spain and the appearance of reformers in northern Europe and Italy, did the question of institutionalized inquisitions again arise on a large scale.

Chapter Three

The Inquisitions in Iberia and the New World

By the late fifteenth century the pursuit of heretics, an enterprise that had once required the combined resources of the entire Latin Church as articulated in theology and canon law, was undertaken by the same regional powers that had failed to accomplish it in the twelfth and thirteenth centuries. The strengthening of regional resources and the emergence of regional "styles" of Latin Christianity mark one of the main transitions from the medieval to the early modern world. It also entailed considerable strains on the cosmopolitan character of Latin Christianity. From the early fifteenth century on, for example, the papacy had to define the status and powers of the Church in many of the kingdoms of Europe by means of individual diplomatic agreements, concordats, rather than through the universal structures of ecclesiastical office and lines of communication that, in theory at least, operated everywhere in the same manner.

The regionalization of European culture tended to adapt universal doctrines about belief and behavior to increasingly powerful local conditions. Religious attitudes and sentiments took on local coloring and reflected distinctive local interests. This process blurred the universality of Latin Christianity well before the Reformation of the sixteenth century dramatically increased the identification of region and religion. It also identified local rulers as the mediators between Rome and the individual regions of Europe. The reconstruction of inquisitorial tribunals in Spain in the last half of the fifteenth century, their appearance in Portugal in 1536, and their establishment in the Spanish and Portuguese colonies in the New World constitute a spectacular example of the regionalization of Latin Christianity. They reflect both the particular religious sentiments of Spain and Portugal, and their large degree of operational autonomy from Rome. Best known and most widely discussed of the early modern inquisitions, those of Spain and Portugal also illustrate the process by which the regional pursuit of heterodoxy was identified with the pursuit of local political interests and was attacked and criticized on that basis.

Medieval Inquisitions in the Iberian Peninsula

The kingdom of Aragón, close to the centers of medieval Catharism in Languedoc, became a refuge and proselytizing center for Catharism from the 1170s on. In the first quarter of the thirteenth century, however, the kings of Aragón issued legislation subjecting heretics to stringent secular penalties, not unlike those imposed by rulers elsewhere in thirteenth-century Europe. In 1232 Pope Gregory IX offered the assistance of the Dominican Order to the Archbishop of Tarragona, and in 1233 both an episcopal and a secular inquisition were formed.

In 1236 the king of León-Castile issued equally severe laws against heretics, and in 1238 Gregory IX organized an inquisitorial tribunal in Navarre, for the region of Catalonia, assigning the Mendicant Orders to the task. At the Council of Tarragona of 1242, elaborate procedures for inquisitors were drawn up and issued upon the advice and consultation of St. Raymund of Peñafort, a canon lawyer, former papal penitentiary, former minister-general of the Dominican Order, and the most eminent churchman in the kingdom of Aragón. In 1254, at the request of Jaime II, Innocent IV organized the inquisition in the Iberian peninsula.

During the pontificate of Pope Urban IV (1261–1264) the Dominican provincial of Spain received full charge of the inquisition in Aragón, which appears to have done its work very effectively. From the late thirteenth century on, there is little trace of heresy of any kind in the Iberian peninsula, and no ecclesiastical inquisition had ever been established in Castile or Portugal.

In 1197 King Pedro II of Aragón had decreed the customary penalty of burning for convicted heretics, but in 1226 King Jaime did not mention this form of the death penalty. By the mid-thirteenth century, however, papal letters reveal that the Aragonese inquisitors and secular authorities were provided with the same instructions and directions as inquisitors and secular authorities elsewhere in Europe, and their aim was the same sort of heretic that other inquisitors were seeking out in Languedoc and elsewhere, generally the Cathar.

Elsewhere in medieval Spain, the higher clergy focused much more narrowly upon their economic and political relations with the kings and the aristocracy to take much notice of local threats to the faith or early signs of Judaizing or unorthodox religious practices. The thirteenth-century papal focus on Aragón was largely the result of its proximity to Languedoc, and not the consequence of any noticeable Iberian divergences from the faith. The kings of Castile based their authority far more on their military power and success in the *Reconquista* of Iberia from Muslim powers than upon the sanction of the Church, and Castilian higher clergy appear to have been considerably more independent of Rome than their counterparts elsewhere. Further, the popularity of the pilgrimage to Santiago da Compostela and the generally pluralist religious culture of Castile made the presence of divergent religious beliefs and practices much more routine than elsewhere in Europe. The court of Alfonso X El Sabio (1252–1284) brilliantly reflects the religious and cultural cosmopolitanism of thirteenth-century Castile, and Alfonso even called himself the king of the three religions.

From the fourteenth century on, however, a series of economic and social crises churned the political and ethnic life of Castile and gave considerably greater prominence to a different view of Castilian identity, one that emphasized Christian military nobility, Christian superiority over Jews and Muslims, and forced new legal disabilities upon non-Christians. By the end of the fourteenth century, a very different cultural climate had emerged in Castile, and it was in that climate that the Iberian inquisitions were formed.

The Inquisition and the Jews

Medieval Christian anti-Semitism expressed itself in many different forms among different levels of society. During the late eleventh and twelfth centuries popular outbursts and massacres of individual Jewish communities (particularly the attacks associated with the departure of the "Crusade of the Poor" in 1096), intermittent attempts to convert Jews to Christianity, and individual attacks on Jews and Jewish doctrines and practices were part of the ordinary expectations of any Jewish community in Europe. In spite of formal Christian expressions of limited toleration, based upon the patristic arguments that Christians were obliged to permit the existence of Jewish communities both in order to bear witness to the "Old" Testament and as destined by scripture to be converted to Christianity at the end of time, there survived both literary attacks on Judaism and intermittent popular pogroms, as well as severe legal restrictions on Jewish populations. The literary traditions consisted of Christian polemical "debates" with Jews, in which Jews were consistently depicted as blind, stubborn, rooted in the flesh, unchangeable in time; the debates preserved and echoed a common set of Christian attitudes that had developed from the fourth century on. These, with an increasingly emotional religious sensibility on the part of non-learned Christians, bore Christian anti-Semitism into the twelfth century.

In the twelfth century, however, both learned and non-learned anti-Judaism began to change. In the case of the former, the increasing identification of Christian belief with human reason added the charge of unreason to others made against Jews. In addition, increasing Christian familiarity with postbiblical Jewish literature, particularly the Talmud, led Christians to argue that the Talmud contained not only blasphemies against Christ and Christian beliefs, but heresies against biblical Judaism as well. In the case of the latter, the twelfth century witnessed the spread of what the historian Gavin Langmuir has termed "chimeric" anti-Semitism, that is, charges that Jews committed unspeakable crimes against Christians, often children; that Jews perverted Christian sacramental usages; and that Jews, in addition to the charges made against them in the learned literature, were deceitful, wicked, and dangerous to the Christian communities among which they lived. In addition, the changing economic and social culture of twelfth-century Europe intensified both popular anti-Semitism and the legal restrictions of Jewish activities in a Christian society. From these circumstances comes the image of the Jew as usurer—an exploiter, as well as a danger to all Christians. As Langmuir summarizes:

> Because of these developments, Jews, by the beginning of the thirteenth century, were no longer simply dispersed adherents of an inferior religion, but had been assigned a definite, collective, religious, legal, and social status in the organization of medieval society. They had become an institutionalized inferior minority, symbolized ecclesiastically by the distinctive clothing commanded by the Fourth Lateran Council, secularly by their legal status as serfs of secular authorities [Langmuir here refers to the status of Jews as legally the property of the princes who ruled the lands in which they lived], and socially by their prominence in money lending [an occupation to which Jews had been virtually restricted by their exclusion from others]. And now, a defenseless and institutionalized minority, Jews in northern Europe could be manipulated by the majority not only physically, but also mentally. The way was open for the development of a false, irrational conception of the Jew.

The heightened and intensified Christian anti-Semitism of the thirteenth century is reflected in an increasingly millennarian Christian sensibility, by the compulsion placed upon Jews to listen to Christian sermons, by public burnings of the Talmud from 1240 on, by evidence of Christian conversions to Judaism and of Jewish conversions to Christianity, and by the appearance of a new strand of Jewish polemic against Christianity. The last of these may be considered a Jewish response to the new tenor of Christian anti-Semitism, and a result of the demoralization of the Jewish community that also appears during the thirteenth century. This demoralization was increased by the activity of Jewish converts to Christianity who participated in the activities of anti-Jewish polemicizers.

In the late 1230s, Nicholas Donin, a former Jew, brought to the attention of Pope Gregory IX a list of accusations against the Talmud which included charges that the Talmud had replaced scripture for the Jews, that it contained blasphemies against God and Christianity, and that it engendered hostility against Christians. The result of these complaints and Gregory's response to them was a series of trials held at Paris and elsewhere through the fourteenth century in which the censuring of the Talmud was the chief aim. Although later popes arrived at a compromise by which Jewish communities were permitted to retain in their possession censored versions of the Talmud, the Talmud trials and later confiscations of Jewish books, as well as the new character of Jewish anti-Christian polemic, greatly weakened the position of the Jews in Europe by the end of the thirteenth century.

The medieval inquisitors had jurisdiction, of course, only over baptized Christians, and initially the Jews were not particularly the concern of the inquisitors. The changing attitudes of the twelfth century, however, and the new attacks of the thirteenth raised anew the question of the inquisitors' responsibilities toward the Jews. First, the inquisitors had ordinary jurisdiction over any Christian who ceased to be a Christian, whether by embracing or relapsing into heresy or becoming a Jew or a Muslim. There were a number of instances in which Jews who had been forcibly converted to Christianity had returned to Judaism, and there is some scholarly debate about the existence of a specific Jewish rite for receiving such returning converts. In addition, the inquisitors could claim jurisdiction in cases where Jews protected those hiding from the inquisitors, and there is some evidence that the "trial" of the Talmud in 1240 was a form of inquisitorial trial. The inquisitors also claimed jurisdiction over Christians who possessed Jewish books. Although the formal expulsion of the Jews from England in 1290 and from France

in 1306 was an act of royal authority, a number of Jews who had converted—or had been forced to convert—to Christianity came under the
jurisdiction of the inquisitors, as did Jewish converts to Christianity who
fled England and France in order to resume their lives as Jews among
the Jewish communities of Aragón.

Not even the argument of forced baptism protected Jews from the
inquisitors. In a trial held at Pamiers in southern France in 1320, Baruch,
a converted Jew who was accused of having relapsed into Judaism, argued
that he had been forced to submit to baptism under the threat of death.
His arguments, however, were rejected by the inquisitorial tribunal on
the grounds that Baruch had not been subjected to "absolute coercion,"
by which appears to have been meant forcible immersion in the baptismal
font accompanied by protests on the part of the defendant. Baruch's
response that he had not been forcibly held at the font and that he did
not protest at the time because he had been told that to protest meant
death did not satisfy the inquisitors, who argued that only in such circumstances as they had specified could a defense of coerced baptism be
recognized.

Thus, in spite of the restriction of inquisitorial jurisdiction to baptized
Christians, the relations between the inquisitors and the Jews became
more complex. The standard handbooks for inquisitors that circulated
from the late thirteenth century permitted inquisitors to consider Jews
subject to them in cases of Jewish blasphemy against Christians or Christian beliefs, the practice of usury, that of magic or sorcery, that of
proselytizing among Christians, and those of aiding, receiving, or otherwise helping relapsed Jewish converts to Christianity. Thus, long before
the *conversos* of Castile and Aragón came before the Spanish inquisitors
after 1478, there existed a substantial literature that spelled out all cases
in which the medieval inquisitors possessed jurisdiction over Jews. That
literature had been produced during a period of heightened anti-Jewish
emotion and argument among both lower and higher levels of Christian
society.

In 1324 a millennialist panic seized southern France. Jews were accused, with lepers, of poisoning wells and acting as a "fifth column"
whose aim was to destroy Christian society. This hysteria, coupled with
the colossal disaster of widespread fourteenth-century famine, the Black
Death of 1348–1349, and the ensuing social unrest, along with the
new anti-Semitism of the thirteenth century, helps to explain both the
rising anti-Jewish attitudes of the late fourteenth and fifteenth centuries
and the movement in Spain to take action against the *conversos*.

The Formation of the Inquisitions in Spain

The medieval Iberian kingdoms, particularly in the central and southern parts of the peninsula, ruled large populations of non-Christians: Muslims and Jews. Although these peoples suffered certain legal disabilities and were the targets of conventional intermittent Christian anti-Semitic and anti-Islamic attitudes, and were periodically subjected to attempts at large-scale conversions, their status, particularly that of the Jews, was less disabled in Iberia than in most other parts of Europe. Apart from Alfonso X's own pride at being the king of the three religions, in some royal and intellectual circles throughout Castile and Aragón a high degree of tolerance and social intercourse existed. Historians have called this *convivencia,* "living (peacefully) together." In the countryside, Jewish farmers, herders, craftsmen, and peasants lived side by side with their Christian counterparts; in the towns and cities, Jews were artisans, shop-keepers, and small merchants. They were also prominent physicians, and—because of circumstances peculiar to Castile—they were often also tax-farmers and financiers in royal service. Although Jews were barred from holding royal or other public office, they proved to be of considerable usefulness, especially in Castile, where, unlike Aragón and Navarre, they performed financial services which the Christian population was unwilling to undertake.

Financial service to the crown was not a popular role in thirteenth- and fourteenth-century Castile. The financial needs of the kings were great, and the struggle of the higher nobility to escape from royal taxation and other manifestations of royal authority tended to make the tax burden fall upon the lower ranks of Castilian society. A series of economic and natural catastrophes beginning in the mid-fourteenth century, from the Black Death of 1348–1349 on, increased widespread resentment against the tax collectors, and at the same time a more intense and widespread anti-Semitism began to circulate throughout the kingdom, sometimes fired by preachers, and often drawing upon conventional aspects of anti-Semitism increasingly popular elsewhere in Europe. From the mid-fourteenth century on, the older kinds of tolerance and cosmopol-itanism began to give way before the increasing power, wealth, and world-view of the higher aristocracy, which perceived itself chiefly as a Christian military nobility superior to Muslims and Jews, and was critical of kings who appeared to rely too heavily upon Jewish abilities and assistants. When Henry II of Trastámara overthrew and killed Pedro the Cruel of Castile (1350–1369) in 1369, he did so with the support of dissident nobles whose aid had to be rewarded and whose dislike of Pedro's reliance upon Jews was one item in their resentment against him.

By the end of the century a series of economic and natural catastrophes contributed to extensive unrest in Castilian society, not all of which was directed against the Jews. But the slow build-up of anti-Jewish feelings made the Jews the targets of a number of urban revolts and demonstrations, culminating in the terrible pogroms of 1391 in Barcelona and elsewhere, when large proportions of the Jewish populations were killed, driven into the countryside, or forced to convert to Christianity. From 1391 on there is a marked decline in Jewish wealth in Aragón and Castile, a Jewish depopulation of urban centers, and the emergence of a large group of converted Jews, the *conversos*. Although most of the conversions were forced, Christian canon law held that even a forced conversion was binding, and the *conversos*, against their will or not, were now fully privileged members of Spanish Christian society.

During the reign of Juan II of Castile (1406–1454), the sharpest anti-Semitism appears to have died down, and the new group of *conversos* appears to have succeeded greatly in occupying key roles in Castilian society, including official royal offices that, as Christians, they could now hold without legal restrictions, and they intermarried with the Old Christian nobility. As royal officials, as well as continuing to be tax collectors and financiers, the *conversos* were in a situation that was both advantageous and potentially dangerous. On the one hand, rejected by Jews, and on the other resented by the older Christian nobility as well as those on whom the burdens of taxation fell heavily, many of the *conversos* demonstrated their loyalty to their new religion but were regarded both with suspicion and with an increasing ethnic hatred that they could not control.

In 1449 in Toledo, a popular revolt with considerable Christian noble support began by attacking the houses of *converso* tax collectors and ended by assaulting the Jewish quarter of the city, causing immense bloodshed and destruction of property. During the revolt, the ruler of the town, Pedro Sarmiento, issued a harsh ordinance, the *Sentencia-Estatuto*, which professed to revive anti-Semitic laws, but extended them to *conversos* as well. Under its terms, *conversos* could never hold civil or ecclesiastical offices, nor could they act as witnesses or notaries, nor could they exercise any authority at all over Old Christians. During the troubled reign of Henry IV (1454–1474), the *Sententia-Estatuto* was not recognized by the crown and was condemned by the pope, but the king was unable to restrain the growing attitude of anti-Semitism, and the general social unrest sustained anti-Semitism as one of its aspects, as did much of the Old Christian nobility.

From the 1440s, resentment against *conversos* began to change the character of Castilian anti-Semitism. Whatever the causes of the earliest attacks on *conversos*, by this time the *conversos* were also accused of being false Christians, either continuing to Judaize or being outright atheists. Increasingly, the baptism of *conversos* came to be regarded by many Christians as invalid, or at least not sufficient to remove from *conversos* the taint of Judaism or atheism. As Christians, the *conversos* also faced a new kind of risk, for they (unlike Jews and Muslims) were now subject to ecclesiastical discipline, particularly to an inquisitor, if they were suspected of heresy.

The extant inquisitorial tribunals of the Iberian peninsula do not appear to have operated extensively in the late fourteenth and fifteenth centuries, but in 1462 Alfonso de Oropesa, prior-general of the Order of St. Jerome, urged Henry IV to establish the first Castilian inquisition with power to appoint the inquisitors vested in the crown. Henry agreed to the operation of a limited inquisition based at Toledo, whose records are sparse and whose activities appear to have been so limited that they satisfied neither Oropesa nor the fanatical theologian Alonso de Espina, whose large treatise *Fortalitium fidei* had appeared in 1460 and contained venomous attacked on Jews, Muslims, and heretics.

In 1463 Espina and others urged that Henry charge the inquisitors to look especially into heretical opinions held by *conversos*. In 1465 a group of rebels against the king published the Sentence of Medina del Campo, a program for reforming the Castilian government. Among the items of the Sentence, two provisions stand out sharply: Muslims and Jews were to be dismissed from royal service and their property confiscated, and heretical Christians, that the Sentence claimed existed in the kingdom in great numbers, should be sought out by inquisitors. Although the Sentence never went into effect, it clearly culminated five years of increased activity against Jews and Muslims, reflected the greatly increased hostility toward *conversos*, and arrived at the conclusion that an inquisition was highly desirable because heresy had now spread abroad in the land.

The troubled last decade of Henry IV's reign and the complex political maneuverings that placed his half-sister Isabella on the throne of Castile in 1474 delayed the formal establishment of an inquisition, but the events between 1440 and 1465 clearly indicated a new and more intense kind of anti-Semitism and a new hatred of *conversos*. More and more frequently, the charge that only Old Christians were sufficiently honorable and trustworthy to hold royal office and enjoy royal favor had entailed growing accusations against the *conversos*, finally shaping the charges of false Christianity and atheism and the creation of an inquisition to deal with them. Although Henry IV had agreed to the establishment of an inquisition, his actual actions appear to have entailed little more than the establishment of a panel of bishops to hear charges, with little action taken. Henry's actions were not enough for others besides Espina, however. At his death in 1474, a vast tide of anti-Semitism and anti-*converso* sentiment swept across Castile, the results of which, during the reigns of Isabella and Ferdinand, were the expulsion of all Jews from the peninsula in 1492 and the final establishment of the Spanish Inquisition.

One of the striking policies of the reign of Isabella and Ferdinand of Aragón was the discrediting of the life and reign of Henry IV. In the course of this process, Henry was described as morally and religiously lax, sexually deviant, and victim and dupe of non-Christian and false-Christian advisers, to the considerable detriment of the honor of the Church, the Old Christians, and the welfare of the kingdom. In this campaign of defamation, the results of Henry's vices and incompetence were considerably exaggerated, and the enemies of the kingdom whom he had ignored were depicted in stark features. Thus, whatever the actual circumstances of *converso* devotion, the faithlessness of the *conversos* became a leitmotif of anti-Henrician propaganda and a major item on the agenda of the new ruler. In addition, the older anti-Semitism that had focused upon Jews and ignored or even praised *conversos*, now changed into a sentiment that demanded forcible conversion or expulsion of the Jews, whose presence was increasingly said to contaminate the kingdom of Castile, but which also ceased to recognize the sincerity of Jewish conversions to Christianity. From the mid-fifteenth century on, religious anti-Semitism changed into ethnic anti-Semitism, with little difference seen between Jews and *conversos* except for the fact that *conversos* were regarded as worse than Jews because, as ostensible Christians, they had acquired privileges and positions that were denied to Jews. The result of this new ethnic anti-Semitism was the invocation of an inquisition to ferret out the false *conversos* who had, by becoming formal Christians, placed themselves under its authority.

Parallel with the new anti-Semitism there emerged a new view of the ethnic character of the Old Christians. These, it was increasingly argued, were the descendants of the Christian Visigoths, and they had heroically preserved their pure Gothic blood from contamination by the blood of inferior races that had shared the peninsula with them since the eighth century. Thus, not only did anti-Semitism assume an ethnic character that included *conversos* in its hostility, but it was now grounded in the ethnic purity of the Old Christians. In this way, the doctrine of *limpieza de sangre*, "purity of blood," became a watchword in the long internal struggle that shaped the history and society of early modern Spain.

Three years after she succeeded Henry IV as ruler of Castile, Queen Isabella visited the city of Seville, where the Dominican Alonso de Hojeda preached vigorously against the Jews and false converts to Christianity. Shortly after the Queen left the city, Hojeda professed to have uncovered a circle of Judaizing *conversos;* royally appointed investigators then charged that Judaizing *conversos* were practicing Jewish rites in secret throughout the kingdoms. Hojeda and others convinced the Queen that only an inquisition could deal with so grave and omnipresent a problem. In 1478 Isabella and Ferdinand requested a papal bull establishing an inquisition, and on November 1, 1478, Pope Sixtus IV permitted the appointment of two or three priests over forty years of age as inquisitors, their choice to be left to the crown of Castile. On September 27, 1480, royal commissions as inquisitors were issued to the Dominicans Juan de San Martin and Miguel de Morillo and to Juan Ruiz de Medina as their adviser. By mid-October, 1480, the inquisitors set to work. Although many *converso* families fled, others resisted the work of the inquisitors. When an alleged *converso* plot to take arms against the inquisitors was uncovered in Seville in 1481, the first large-scale condemnation of Judaizing *conversos* was held, along with the first public burning of condemned heretics. The public sentencing of convicted heretics came to be known as the *auto-de-fé*, the "act of faith."

The initial discoveries of the inquisitors at Seville seemed to underline the urgency of increasing the activities of the inquisition, and on February 11, 1482, a papal letter appointed seven more inquisitors, including Friar Tomás de Torquemada. New tribunals were established at Córdoba in 1482 and at Ciudad Real and Jaen in 1483. The reformed government of Isabella and Ferdinand had established a series of governmental councils, the Council of Castile, the Council of State, the Council of Finance, and the Council of Aragón. In 1483 Isabella and Ferdinand established a fifth state Council, the *Consejo de la Suprema y General Inquisición*, "the Council of the Supreme and General Inquisition," with Tomás de Torquemada as its president, and three other ecclesiastical members. Torquemada some time later assumed the title of Inquisitor-General.

In Aragón, Ferdinand began the rehabilitation of the older Aragonese inquisition, taking steps to tie it firmly to the crown of Aragón rather than to one of the Orders, to the bishops, or to the pope. In spite of a remarkable protest by Sixtus IV in 1482 against the lack of due process in the inquisition of Aragón, Ferdinand insisted upon his own control over the Aragonese inquisition, and on October 17, 1483, he appointed Torquemada as Inquisitor-General of Aragón, Valencia, and Catalonia, thus linking the Castilian and Aragonese inquisitions under a single authority whose head was a member of one of the councils that ruled the two kingdoms directly under the authority of the crown. In spite of protests from *conversos*, privileged cities and regions, and independently commissioned papal inquisitors, the monarchs' establishment of the inquisition proceeded rapidly. When the final edict expelling the Jews from Spain was issued in 1492, the Spanish Inquisition was securely in place to combat religious deviation from within the Christian community.

The Spanish Inquisition and the New Heretics

The Inquisition established throughout the Spanish kingdoms in 1478–1483 was clearly directed at the *conversos* on the grounds that they remained secret Judaizers after conversion to Christianity. But the *conversos* were not the only object of the Inquisition's activity, and the particular circumstances of the sixteenth and seventeenth centuries gave the Inquisition other work, some of which consisted of traditional inquisitorial concerns and some of which dealt with new phenomena.

Besides the early concentration on the problem of *converso* Christianity, the Spanish Inquisition encountered throughout the sixteenth century a number of other religious problems with which it had to deal. The spread of Erasmian humanism came to its attention early in the sixteenth century, and "Erasmianism" became another focus of Inquisition activity, as did that form of pietism expressed by the "Illuminists" or *alumbrados* at the same time. In the wake of the Protestant Reformation, the Inquisition also took up the problem of what it generally called "*Luteranismo,*" or Protestantism generally. In addition, the appearance of printing brought the problem of censorship to its attention. Besides these instances—all of them the result of widespread changes in European religious sensibility during the sixteenth century—the Inquisition also focused upon what might be considered the routine business of ecclesiastical inquisitions: the internal supervision of the clergy (especially concerning the problem of priestly solicitation in the confessional), the general problem of incorrect religious beliefs among Catholics, the offense of "scandalous" or "blasphemous" expressions, bigamy, various forms of "superstition," sorcery, and witchcraft, and, in the case of Aragón only, the offenses of sodomy and bestiality.

In a number of these categories of offenses, the Spanish Inquisition was not generically different from other tribunals, ecclesiastical and lay, elsewhere in Europe. Although many of these offenses were punished by secular tribunals elsewhere in Europe, they were nevertheless regarded as part of that general class of morals offenses that were the legitimate concern of spiritual and temporal courts in an age when religion, whether Catholic or Protestant, was regarded as the fundamental cultural bond and basis of all social, political, and legal structures.

The fact that in much of Mediterranean Europe these offenses were prosecuted in ecclesiastical courts, often inquisitorial tribunals, should not obscure the equally evident fact that they were prosecuted as vigorously, and usually with less care, in other tribunals throughout Christian Europe in the sixteenth and seventeenth centuries. Indeed, recent research has suggested two important features that distinguish the Spanish Inquisition from other courts that tried comparable offenses: the first is that the Spanish Inquisition, in spite of wildly inflated estimates of the numbers of its victims, acted with considerable restraint in inflicting the death penalty, far more restraint than was demonstrated in secular tribunals elsewhere in Europe that dealt with the same kinds of offenses. The best estimate is that around 3,000 death sentences were carried out in Spain by Inquisitorial verdict between 1550 and 1800, a far smaller number than that in comparable secular courts. The second is that the Spanish and Roman inquisitions were concerned to a far greater degree than other courts with the mind and will of the accused. Inquisitors, like confessors, were trained to examine the mind and the soul, and they appear to have understood their victims far better than their counterparts in secular courts. Such understanding may lead to leniency as often as to harshness.

It is one of the features of inquisitorial history that its practitioners have consistently failed to compare the Spanish Inquisition to comparable courts elsewhere in sixteenth- and seventeenth-century Europe. Its meticulous investigatory methods have produced the largest and most important body of personal data for any society in early modern Europe, particularly for levels of society that have left very few traces elsewhere. Historians have long felt uneasy about such data, since it came from the scrutinizing of consciences and beliefs, but it is only through an examination of the data that it is possible to discover exactly what it was that the Inquisition did.

Close study of large samples of the data suggests that the Spanish Inquisition devoted two major periods to pursuing Judaizing activities: from 1481 to 1530, and from 1650 to 1720. Between 1530 and 1650 it concentrated upon Protestantism and routine Christian religious offenses. From 1720 on, its activities were less clearly defined. Although the Inquisition was always a reflection of Spanish anti-Judaism, much of the rest of its role in Spanish culture depended upon its acceptance by people whose orthodox Christian beliefs were never in question. To Spaniards of all levels of society, the Inquisition "preserved the purity of the Spanish religion." If its initial activities up to 1530 reflect a distinctive Spanish problem, those for the most part after 1530 reflect a Spanish response to a European problem—the rise of Protestantism and the perceived Spanish responsibility to defeat it.

Thus, the problem of the *conversos* is one of the most important keys to understanding the development of the Spanish Inquisition until the second quarter of the sixteenth century. If the *conversos* really remained secret practicing Jews and were known to be such and therefore a danger to Spanish Christianity, the Inquisition must be regarded as a response to a real problem that could be acted upon only by means of this kind of investigation. If some, but not all *conversos* were secret Judaizers, the Inquisition faced the additional problem of distinguishing between the two, particularly in an atmosphere in which any taint of Judaism was increasingly repellent to Spanish Christians, regardless of whether or not conversions to Christianity had been genuine and sustained. If no *conversos* were secret Judaizers, then the Inquisition was the product of racial hatred and cynical politics, and it disguised in its concern for religious orthodoxy its real aim of excluding one racial group from any participation in Spanish society. To accept any of these positions is to come up with very different readings of the nature of fifteenth- and sixteenth-century Spanish society. It is also possible to interpret the Inquisition as a political instrument, the only institution common to both the Iberian peninsula and all of the Spanish possessions overseas, and therefore controlled and exploited by rulers who desperately needed its resources and powers to strengthen their own rule. Some historians have seen the Inquisition as the instrument of aristocratic clan rivalry, and others have regarded it as an attack on those who performed essential but unrespected social and economic functions by those who resented not just these activities but the people who performed them as well.

Many of these conflicting interpretations neglect the fact that there would be other means by which clan rivalry and economic resentment might more easily and efficiently be expressed. Others make extremely large and categorical assumptions about a substantial segment of the population of Spain, assumptions that are unlikely to be altogether valid. The investigative techniques of the inquisitors, the recorded evidence and testimony in their archives, and their general support among the Christian population of Spain would suggest that the most plausible interpretation is that a number of *conversos* remained crypto-Jews, that general Spanish anti-Judaism probably exaggerated their numbers, and that the detailed scrutiny of the inquisitors did not prevent false accusations from being made nor the Inquisition from becoming the vehicle for anti-Judaism, thus widening its impact and gaining it the support of many Spanish Christians.

Such an interpretation accounts for the earliest stages of inquisitorial structure and activity, and it accounts for the "inquisitorial mentality" that characterized the dealings of the later Inquisition with *alumbrados*, Protestants, and others who were not even remotely suspected of being Jews. In short, during the late fifteenth century the rulers of Aragón and Castile adapted, with papal permission, a universal judicial institution to deal with a set of uniquely Spanish conditions. Among those conditions were some features—anti-Judaism, a distinct and proud sense of Spanish Christianity, and an ignorance and fear of outsiders—that sustained the Inquisition well beyond its original purpose and adapted it to deal, wherever the power of Spain ran, in a Spanish manner with situations that were not unique to Spain at all, and to arouse enormous resentment throughout Europe for doing so.

The attitude of the Spanish Inquisition toward intellectual activity was not exclusively one of obscurantism or resistance to new thought. Its violent and rapid attacks on Lutheranism occurred in the context of the political unrest of the 1520s, the absence of the king, and the politically revolutionary movements that culminated in the revolt of the *Comuneros*. A number of scholars have argued that by 1520 the initial purpose of the Inquisition had been virtually completed and that the dangers of the new religious movements offered the Inquisition a new lease on life, one that it accepted quickly and acted upon dramatically. The scope of its activities greatly widened, and what one scholar has termed "the universe of heterodoxy" now became its chief target. The new enterprise and the new mentality that accompanied it after the 1520s transformed the earlier Spanish Inquisition into a new and more formidable institution. In 1559 it even reached out to the Archbishop of Toledo, Bartolomé Carranza, and its victims included a number of the most distinguished intellectuals of Spain, notably Juan de Vergara, Luis de León, and St. Theresa of Avila. The Inquisition's attack on *Luteranismo* enabled it to impose much farther-reaching controls on Spanish society and to establish what a number of historians have termed a "pedagogy of fear" throughout Spanish society.

Another consequence of the revived and reorganized Inquisition in the second quarter of the sixteenth century was its ruthlessness in purging internal irregularities among its own members. The trial of Diego Lucero in 1508 indicated that procedural irregularity among inquisitors (Lucero had been the inquisitor at Córdoba) had become widespread, and after the new thrust against *Luteranismo,* such misuse of inquisitorial powers was considerably curtailed. Lucero's vicious persecution of the saintly Archbishop of Granada, Hernando de Talavera, in 1506–1507 prompted outrage in the highest circles of Spanish society, and the "new" Inquisition could not afford such scandals.

The Spanish Inquisition: Organization and Procedure

Although the Spanish Inquisition dealt with an extraordinarily wide variety of offenses between 1483 and 1834, the procedure it used and the form of its organization changed very little during its lifetime. From the early eighteenth century on, the Inquisition was dramatically understaffed and underfinanced, uncertain as to its purpose and ambiguously responsive to challenges to its authority and legitimacy, but even in its last shadowy years the Inquisition retained the form of organization and procedure it had adopted at the end of the fifteenth century.

The *Consejo de la Suprema y General Inquisición,* one of the five Councils of State, consisted of an inquisitor-general and a non-specified number of other members. The inquisitor-general usually had no greater authority than the other members of the *Suprema,* and initially the *Suprema* itself had little institutional authority over other local inquisitorial tribunals. By the middle of the sixteenth century, however, the *Suprema* achieved operational and juridical superiority over all other tribunals and required an accounting of cases on an annual basis (the *relaciones de causas*) and, on some occasions, it closely supervised the operation of particular inferior tribunals.

The local tribunals were originally founded at places where a particular Judaizing community was thought to exist. When such a tribunal had finished its work, it might be moved to another location. In some cases, notably that of Ciudad Real, founded in 1483 and moved to Toledo in 1485, the tribunal was established near a larger target community (in this case, Toledo), and its operations served as a warning to a large

Plate 1. Pedro Berruguete, *St. Dominic Presiding at an Auto-de-fé* (ca. 1490).
Pictorial images of Inquisition practices were often symbolic rather than precisely
representational. This painting collapses several distinct stages of an inquisition
into a single visual event. It conveys the Spanish Inquisition's image of itself,
representing the entire Christian community restoring spiritual health to those
who have been afflicted with the sin of heresy.

Plate 2. J. B. Bertinus, *Sacratissimae Inquisitionis Rosa Virginea* (Palermo, 1662). The picture represents the Dominican rationale of the Order's mission. The Virgin and the Christ Child convey the Rosary, "the unique and singular defense against heresies," to St. Dominic, who in turn gives it to his followers who are armed with the shields of doctrine and example. The Dominicans go into battle against the figures in the lower register, representing Infidelity, Heresy, Apostasy, and Blasphemy.

A ROYAL STANDARD *of the* INQUISITION.

Pub.^d March 1810 by I. Stockdale 41 Pall Mall.

EXIGE DIE IUDICA CAVSAM TVA·:·

·EXVRGE DÑE & IVDICA C·
·EXVRGE DÑE

Plate 3. Originally printed in Lavallée's *Histoire de l'Inquisition* of 1810, reprinted here from Stockdale, *The History of the Inquisitions* (London, 1811). The banners appear to be authentic, perhaps acquired during the Bonapartist regime of 1808–1814. These banners and others like them figured in the processions at the *autos-de-fé*.

Plate 4. J. J. Stockdale, *The History of the Inquisitions* (London, 1811). The emblem of the Spanish Inquisition, displaying the cross and the emblems of mercy and justice with the motto of the Inquisition, from Psalm 73, "Arise, Oh Lord, and judge thine own cause." The banner may be seen in procession in Plate 6.

Plate 5. J. J. Stockdale, *The History of the Inquisitions* (London, 1811). This emblem, that of the Inquisition at Goa, was first printed in Charles Dellon's *Relation de l'Inquisition de Goa* in 1687 and frequently reprinted since. It shows St. Dominic with the symbols of mercy and justice (identified in the *titulus*), with the icons of the Dominican Order and the rule of the world below.

Plate 6. Philip van Limborch, *The History of the Inquisition*, English trans. Samuel Chandler (London, 1731). The procession to the *auto-de-fé* depicts the full Inquisition public display, from the banner with the Inquisition's emblem at the right to the penitents dressed in *corozas* and *sanbenitos*, followed by the effigies and coffins of the condemned absent or dead.

Plate 7. Isaac Martin, *The Tryal and Sufferings of Mr. Isaac Martin, Who was put into the Inquisition in Spain, for the Sake of the Protestant Religion* (London, 1723). The Inquisitions did not permit portrayals of the actual tribunals at work. Martin's is one of the earliest representations of an inquisitorial tribunal examining an accused.

Plate 8. Charles Dellon, *Relation de l'Inquisition de Goa* (Paris, 1709). The condemned are led out of a church to their place of penance and execution (echoing the imagery of Plate 6). This is a new addition to the Inquisition's own iconography.

Plate 9. Claude Goujet, *Histoire des Inquisitions*, Vol. II (Cologne [false imprint], 1759). The scene here resembles an *auto-de-fé* although it is a scene of execution. It, too, is an addition to the conventional Inquisition iconography, deriving from other, noninquisitorial representations of executions but redesigned to refer explicitly to inquisition executions. "Cologne" was a favorite false imprint for seventeenth- and eighteenth-century writers whose work could not be printed in France.

Representation: de ceux qui sont Condannées au feü par les Jnquisitions

Plate 10. Louis-Ellies Dupin, *Mémoires historiques pour servir à l'histoire des Inquisitions* (Cologne [false imprint], 1716). This is the earliest printing of the famous Bernard Picart engraving of an Inquisition torture chamber. It derives from other pictorial representations of torture scenes, although, like Plate 9, it has been modified explicitly to indicate inquisition techniques.

Plate 11. Modesto Rastrelli, *Fatti Attenenti all'Inquisizione* (Florence, 1783). Histories of the inquisitions depended, for much of their popularity, on the reproduction of familiar scenes and symbols. Like other writers who produced illustrated histories, Rastrelli has simply reversed the original Picart engraving. Other versions included additional varieties of torture.

and potentially resistant nearby community that its days were numbered. By the early seventeenth century there were between fifteen and twenty local inquisitorial tribunals reporting to the *Suprema*, covering the entire kingdom of Spain.

Each tribunal operated according to standard inquisitorial procedure, explicitly spelled out in a series of guides for inquisitors, called *Instrucciones*, the first of which was issued by Torquemada in 1484, and supplements to which continued to appear through the seventeenth century. A tribunal was to consist of two inquisitors, an assessor (or legal adviser), a constable, and a *fiscal*, or prosecutor, with a number of assistants. The latter, who came to comprise a large number of people, were lay servants of the Inquisition with exceptional civil privileges. Called familiars, they were expensive and troublesome, since their privileges gave them an advantaged place in Spanish society. Service in the lay staff of the Inquisition was desirable for both spiritual and material reasons. The office of familiar was sold venally—as were other offices of state in sixteenth-century Europe—and they were often inherited. The problem of the lay staffs of local tribunals became particularly great after the late sixteenth century, when the revenues of the Inquisition (never substantial, and often barely sufficient to allow it to function at all) declined at the same time as the size of its staff increased. The old argument that the Inquisition flourished upon fines and confiscations fades when its account books reveal that even in its most prosperous years—from the late sixteenth to the early seventeenth century—the Inquisition barely managed to finance itself.

Each tribunal of the Inquisition followed the procedure laid down in the *Instrucciones*. When a tribunal began its operations, it would already have had the local clergy in the district preach against heresy and describe the means of identifying heretical suspects to their congregations. Upon their arrival, the inquisitors would preach a sermon on heresy and declare an Edict of Grace, when people might voluntarily confess or identify suspects to the inquisitors. After 1500, the Edict of Faith often replaced the Edict of Grace. The Edict of Faith threatened excommunication to all who failed to denounce heretics, themselves, or others.

The Edict of Grace or of Faith proclaimed a period of from two weeks to several months for private confessions and identifications to be made and cases prepared. During this time anyone who did not confess voluntarily had to worry about the confessions of others and how he or she might have been involved in them. Fear of denunciation by others appears to have motivated a large number of individual confessions. All of the information collected in the confessions and denunciations was carefully recorded and summarized. The secrecy of testimony against others raised profound questions as to the reliability of witnesses and about the quality of testimony from witnesses who would not ordinarily be accepted because of disqualifying characteristics, including those considered infamous. Although this aspect of obtaining testimony raised serious questions about the reliability of inquisitorial evidence, there is also substantial evidence that inquisitors became relatively more skillful than others in identifying evidence or accusations given for other than pious reasons.

The evidence assembled against an individual was assessed by one or more theological consultants, and if they agreed that it seemed to indicate a case of heresy, the inquisitorial prosecutor drew up charges and issued a command of arrest, taking the accused into custody. At that moment, the goods of the accused were sequestered, his property inventoried, and the property retained by the Inquisition until the case was finally decided, when the property might formally be confiscated if the verdict went against the accused. The family of the accused was also formally notified so that it might use its power of attorney to obtain a defense for the accused.

The accused was jailed until the hearing was completed. Since inquisitorial hearings were often prolonged, this could be for a considerable time. The prisoner was supported while in prison by his own resources held by the Inquisition. Although contact with the outside world was kept to an absolute minimum and the accused was denied all sacraments while awaiting trial, the physical conditions of the Spanish Inquisitorial prisons appear to have been considerably less harsh than those of comparable holding prisons elsewhere; its later image was colored more by its secrecy than by any actual conditions of extraordinary hardship which it provided.

If sufficient evidence accumulated against an accused who did not confess, the Inquisition had torture at its disposal, as had all ecclesiastical and secular courts—except in England—since the thirteenth century. Although torture as an incident of legal procedure was permitted only when sufficient circumstantial evidence existed to indicate that a confession could be obtained, inquisitorial torture appears to have been extremely conservative and infrequently used. There is enough inquisitorial literature on torture contained in *Instrucciones* intended only for the eyes of inquisitors, for us to conclude that the Inquisition's use of torture was well under that of all contemporary secular courts in continental Europe, and even under that of other ecclesiastical tribunals. The entire procedure of torture was recorded by an official notary, and it was included in the file of the accused along with all other documents of the case.

In a trial before the Spanish Inquisition, the very fact that the accused had been charged and arrested at all indicated that sufficient evidence for guilt had already been accumulated on the basis of denunciations by others, the testimony of other tried heretics, evidence from neighbors or local clergy, or self-incriminating evidence from one's own household. But the aim of the Inquisition remained penitential rather than purely judicial. After his arrest, usually without a specific charge having been made known to him, the accused was urged several times to examine his conscience, identify the charge against him, and confess at some stage before formal proceedings began. If the accused did not, he was faced with formal charges which he had to answer immediately. After answering, the accused was permitted legal counsel and presented with the evidence against him, omitting material indicating the identity of witnesses.

Each case before a local inquisitorial tribunal or before the *Suprema* had a file, and these files constitute the vast mass of Inquisition records now being investigated by social historians. The file included not only the formal legal documents of the case, but personal materials as well. They were compiled by court notaries and included the place of the audience, the date, the type of session, the names of those present, and the subject of the audience. The prosecutor's arraignment was included after having been read to the defendant, as were the testimonies of informers and other testimony, any technical material, and the defense's questionnaire of the indicting testimony, the testimony of witnesses for the defense, and the prosecution's and defense's summations.

Each case might also take a very long time to complete, since the court might meet in several audiences over a period of years before all witnesses were heard and all evidence of the prosecution and defense was laid out. At the end of all of the audiences, the local inquisitorial tribunal formed a *consulta-de-fé*, a committee composed of the inquisitors, local theological advisers, and a representative of the bishop, to decide upon guilt or innocence. After the late seventeenth century, when all sentences were formally given by the *Suprema* itself, the *consulta-de-fé* fell into disuse. The final sentence might occasionally be issued privately to an individual in cases of guilt for minor offenses—a session known as the *auto particular* or *autillo*. For most of those convicted, however, the sentence was not issued privately, but publicly and collectively at a ceremony called the *auto-de-fé* or "act of faith." These ceremonies, publicly held and widely popular, consisted of processions of penitents, public prayers, and sermons. They served as a means of reinforcing the faith of those who observed them as much as a means of celebrating the penitence of those who participated in them.

Among the sentences which the Inquisition could issue, were included the possibility of dismissal of the charges or suspension of the case—which meant that the case might later be reopened if new evidence turned up. There was the possibility of outright acquittal as well. The majority of cases in which some form of conviction was involved, however, resulted in reconciliation with the Church, a procedure which freed the accused, but often with severe conditions attached to his freedom. He might, for example, have to wear a distinctive garment, the so-called *sanbenito*, on specified liturgical occasions for a specified number of years; or he might have to make a pilgrimage or participate penitentially in liturgical ceremonies as required. The confiscation of goods, imprisonment, exile, scourging, service in the galleys, all constituted possible sentences for those convicted, and these convictions, with reconciliations, always constituted the majority of sentences at an *auto-de-fé*.

Like the medieval inquisitions, the Spanish Inquisition was not permitted to sentence anyone to death. The formal means by which unrepentant convicted heretics or relapsed heretics were executed was the technique known as relaxation to the secular arm. As in the thirteenth century, the inquisitors formally declared the convicted heretic guilty and turned him over to public officers of the crown, who performed the burning—either in person or in effigy if the convicted heretic had fled or escaped—after the *auto-de-fé* had been completed.

The immense popularity of the *autos-de-fé* illustrates once again the place the Inquisition held in Spanish popular feeling. Since the chief purpose of the ceremony was a demonstration of faith and the reconciliation of heretics to the Church, there was no other public occasion so effective in asserting the orthodoxy of Spanish Christianity, nor was there one that received so wide a response.

After the *auto-de-fé*, when the actual sentences were carried out, those who were released upon conditions lived a life of penury (after punitive confiscations or after their substance had been exhausted for their support while in prison) and shame. The public wearing of a *sanbenito* marked out a penitent, often for life, and upon the death of a penitent, the *sanbenito*, with his name on it, was hung in the parish church, reminding his neighbors and descendants of his shame and penitence. Thus, the impact of the Inquisition did not cease once a case was completed, even if the case resulted in reconciliation. Spanish society continued to be reminded of those who had once failed in their faith by the most graphic of methods—the public character of penitence and the enduring place of the *sanbenitos* in an intimate society which knew and remembered everything about its convicted or suspected neighbors.

The investigation and trials of *conversos*, Erasmians, *alumbrados*, Protestants, Moriscos, and other kinds of ecclesiastical offenders did not exhaust the role of the Spanish Inquisition. From the late fifteenth century, ecclesiastical and intellectual reform had been a major characteristic of Spanish society, and the work of such scholars and reformers as Nebrija, Pedro de Lerma, and Cardinal Ximenes rivalled the intellectual and reform work carried out elsewhere in Europe at the time. The first Spanish printing press was set up at Valencia in 1474, and with the founding of the University of Alcalá in 1508 and the publication of the great Polyglot Bible in 1522, Spanish humanism claimed a distinguished place in European thought. The outbreak of the Reformation, however, presented the defenders of orthodoxy with a new threat, and as the Inquisition turned its attention to yet newer heretics, it looked more closely at other forms of thought and expression as well.

Beginning in the 1530s the Inquisition turned its attention to intellectual heterodoxy, and from 1558 on it launched a massive campaign against Lutheranism in Spain, which it quickly associated with Erasmianism and identified as a form of *converso*—and hence Jewish—heterodoxy. At the same time, the Spanish government restricted the activities and curriculum of university professors and students, and the first of the Indices of Prohibited Books also appeared.

The long history of early European attitudes toward secular learning is complex. From the twelfth century on, two currents appear to flow together: one argued for a kind of intellectual freedom based on the argument that learning leads to spiritual virtue; the other held secular learning as suspect and always inferior to spiritual learning. A number of different episodes in the thirteenth and fourteenth centuries strengthened the views of both sides. The condemnation in 1277 of a number of propositions said to be taught in the Faculty of Letters at the University of Paris heightened the arguments of both sides, and the increasing fear of the Averroist interpretation of Aristotle served as a similar rallying point. The rise of humanism set academics and humanists against each other, and the new fervor for purity of devotion that swept much of Europe in the late fifteenth and early sixteenth centuries—and included sporadic outbursts of public book-burnings—led to the first papal statement on censorship, the bull *Inter sollicitudines* of 1515.

Inter sollicitudines prohibited the publication of books that contained doctrinal error, attacks on the Christian faith, or defamation of individuals, and insisted that an official at Rome should screen books before publication. Since the printing press possessed the power to disseminate both good and bad books, its operation and control became one of the central targets of reformers on both sides of the argument over secular literature, and later on both sides of the dividing line created by the Reformation. From the beginning of the sixteenth century—and from 1502 in Spain—a number of cities and kingdoms ordered the censorship of books suspected of heterodox content and required an *imprimatur* before publication, fining printers who printed without one.

Throughout the early sixteenth century the works of individual authors were frequently condemned in toto, notably those of Erasmus and then of Luther. Beginning in the 1540s, however, the cities of Milan, Lucca, and Siena published Indices—lists of books that could not legally be printed or sold—and the city of Venice published a similar Index in 1549. The first Index in Spain was issued in 1547, and again in 1551, and the Inquisition issued a more complete version in 1559. During the 1540s local tribunals issued individual Indices, but the royal legislation on censorship in 1559 centralized Spanish efforts, and from that date on the censorship of books came directly and exclusively under the control of the Inquisition. The most extensive Index of Prohibited Books in Spain was that compiled by Gaspar de Quiroga in 1583, reflecting not only the hostility toward heterodoxy that characterized all of Europe at the time, but also a distinctive effort to protect Spanish Christians from non-Spanish ideas in many other fields as well.

Throughout the late sixteenth and seventeenth centuries, Spanish Indices consistently appeared, updated and carefully edited. One striking feature of these Indices, however, was the system of categorization. While some books were listed as prohibited because of forbidden author, others—(according to subject) were allowable in expurgated editions only; and still others were listed according to the anonymity of their authors. The categories of prohibition and expurgation permitted a number of important works, usually scientific, to be printed with expurgations and often a note indicating the doubtful orthodoxy of the author. The result of these Spanish categories was that a number of works that might otherwise be banned outright in Spain were permitted to be printed with selected passages expurgated.

The impact of the censorship of books in sixteenth- and seventeenth-century Spain is difficult to assess. The same period of extensive press censorship was also the golden age of Spanish vernacular literature. In this respect, the Spanish Inquisition and its activities ceased to be part of inquisition history and became a part of Spanish history itself, a very different subject from that of this book.

Unlike the medieval inquisitors, the Spanish Inquisition became and remained a uniquely Spanish institution, its theological and juridical legitimacy conferred originally by the popes, but its institutional existence and personnel dependent upon the rulers of Spain, and it functioned as much to protect a distinctive form of Spanish Christian culture as it did to protect Latin Christian orthodoxy generally. The identification of the Inquisition with Spanish culture and Spanish policies in sixteenth- and seventeenth-century Europe colored its image outside of Spain, and the image of the Inquisition that emerged colored all accounts of all inquisitions throughout history.

The Inquisition in Portugal and the New World

The Jewish population of late medieval Portugal grew larger with the immigration of Jews expelled from Spain in 1492 and with the arrival of large numbers of Spanish *conversos* who fled from the Inquisition of Spain after 1478–1483. Although Portuguese law was relatively tolerant of Jews, similar kinds of anti-semitism to those of fifteenth-century Spain were equally prominent, and the new influx of Jews and *conversos* between 1478 and 1492 heightened anti-Jewish sentiment in Portugal. In 1496 King João II ordered the expulsion of all Jews from Portugal, but a year later flatly commanded the forced conversion of all who remained. Thus, after 1497 there were no Jews left in Portugal, only native Portuguese Christians and new Christianized former Jews, the *cristãos novos*. With no unconverted Jewish community existing side by side with that of the *cristãos novos*, the Portuguese New Christians did not experience the tensions that Spanish Jews and New Christians had between 1391 and 1492. They retained a group identity throughout the sixteenth century, and it is not by accident that the Portuguese Inquisition dealt for a longer period and with greater consistency with the problem of Judaizing than did the Spanish Inquisition. This feature also helps to explain the Portuguese urgency in obtaining for itself an inquisitorial tribunal on the Spanish model.

Manoel, the successor of João II, prohibited exclusionary laws against the New Christians, assuming that they would be assimilated into Portuguese Christian society within a few decades, and no inquiry was made into the beliefs and practices of the *cristãos novos* until 1524. Popular feeling in Portugal, however, expressed itself differently. A massacre of New Christians took place in Lisbon in 1506, and from the beginning of the reign of João III in 1521, the king and clergy began actively to seek the establishment of an inquisition in Portugal.

The great earthquake in Lisbon of 1531 brought out further anti-*converso* feeling, and throughout the 1530s João III, with the help of Charles V of Spain, negotiated with the pope for a Portuguese inquisition similar to that in Spain. Although papal reluctance was difficult to overcome and New Christian resistance was often heroic and partially successful in delaying the establishment of the inquisition, the Portuguese Inquisition was established between 1534 and 1540 and its first *auto-de-fé* was held in that year. Between 1540 and 1760 the Portuguese Inquisition, out of 30,000 recorded cases, is estimated to have condemned to execution 1175 Judaizers and burned 633 in effigy. The rate of capital punishment ran considerably higher with the Portuguese Inquisition than it did with the Spanish, and its focus on *conversos* and crypto-Jews remained far more narrow than that of the Spanish Inquisition. Until the reduction of its powers in the 1760s, the Portuguese Inquisition tried a consistently higher number of accused Judaizers than did the Spanish, and even the increase of *converso* trials in Spain in the 1630s seems to have been directed at Portuguese *conversos* who had fled into Spain from the harshness of the Portuguese tribunal.

The flight of Spanish *conversos* to Portugal after 1483, and of Portuguese *conversos* to Spain in the 1630s, were not the only flights from the inquisitions that the sixteenth century saw. Large numbers of Jews and *conversos* fled into the Ottoman Empire, to North Africa, or to those few remaining places in Europe where Jews were permitted to reside. Still others fled to the New World.

One of the greatest powers of the Spanish Inquisition was its legal ability to pursue escapees from its jurisdiction wherever it wished. Thus, even before the establishment of the Portuguese Inquisition, the Spanish Inquisition could pursue escapees into Portugal. With the establishment of Spanish and Portuguese colonies in North and South America and in the Indies, the arm of the Inquisitions also reached across oceans. In 1515 a *converso* was returned from Hispaniola with his family to face trial in Seville, and until the 1530s friars were given inquisitorial authority in the Indies and in Mexico. Their initial activities were directed at *conversos* and at the violation of Christian morals; the first *auto-de-fé* that resulted in executions took place in 1528, when two Marranos were burned, another was reconciled, and two were paraded in penitential clothing. From 1535 to 1543, however, the Franciscan bishop of Mexico, Francisco de Zumarraga, undertook the prosecution of Indian converts to Christianity who were thought to remain crypto-believers in their old religions. In 1569–1570 Philip II of Spain established a formal Inquisition in Mexico, its targets being *conversos* and Protestants. In 1570 an independent tribunal was established at Lima, and another in 1610 at Cartagena. Other inquisitions had already been established in Spain's Mediterranean and Atlantic and Pacific possessions—in Sardinia, Sicily, the Canary Islands, and Manila (see map on p. 100).

In 1561 the Portuguese Inquisition established a tribunal at Goa in India, and besides dealing with *conversos* this tribunal also found itself with crypto-Buddhists and crypto-Hindus to try.

The operation of the inquisitions in the New World offers an important perspective on the self-image of the Spanish Inquisition as a whole. During the first half-century of its operation in Mexico, for example, the Inquisition concentrated more heavily upon the violation of Christian morals, especially in cases of blasphemy, than upon crypto-Judaism. Recent research indicates that a relative toleration existed in the cases of *conversos* until the 1580s. An influx of Portuguese *conversos* during that period, however, spurred the Mexican Inquisition (after 1570 a formal *Tribunal del Santo Officio*) to actively prosecute crypto-Judaism, but the prosecution was brief, ending in 1601. In 1642, however, when relations between Portugal and Spain had deteriorated on the political level and a Portuguese invasion of Mexico was thought to be imminent, anti-Judaizing once again became the focus of inquisitorial activity, culminating in the great *auto-de-fé* of 1649 when most of those condemned were Portuguese *conversos*. Except for these two periods, however, the Mexican Inquisition occupied itself to a far greater extent with offenses against Christian morality than with hunting down and prosecuting crypto-Jews among the *converso* population of Mexico.

The Later History of the Spanish Inquisition

To interpret the Spanish Inquisition and its history in terms of merely one of its functions is to interpret it anachronistically. Although the Inquisition began in an atmosphere of hostility toward *conversos* and revived this concern several times in its history, it is erroneous to see it exclusively as an engine of modern anti-Judaism or anti-Semitism. Although it took up the orthodox Christian attack on Protestantism in the form of prosecutions and censorship, it did not represent the normative Catholic response either to the Protestant Reformation or to the increasingly wide range of sixteenth- and seventeenth-century thought. Although it prosecuted Moriscos as well as Marranos, it cannot be said to have represented all Spanish ideas of Islam. And although it operated in some circumstances according to the doctrine of *limpieza de sangre*, it cannot be said to have inaugurated modern doctrines of racism.

Galicia, 1561

● Santiago

● Logroño, 1489

Barcelona, 1484

● Valladolid, 1488   Zaragoza, 1482

Mallorca, 1488   Sassari

● Madrid, 1638 ● ● Cuenca, 1489   Sardinia, 1492

● Toledo, 1483 ●   Palma

Valencia, 1482 ●

● Llerena, 1485

Murcia, 1488

● Cordoba, 1482

Granada, 1526

Sevilla, 1480 ●

● Palermo
Sicily,
1487

Canary Is., 1507

● Mexico, 1570

● Las Palmas

Cartagena, 1610

A map showing the tribunals of the Spanish Inquisition. Italic names indicate tribunals dependent on the Council's secretariat for Castilla; the rest were dependent on the secretariat for Aragón. Year of founding of each tribunal is shown; Sardinia's was disbanded in 1708, Sicily's in 1782, and the rest in 1820.

● Lima, 1570

The Inquisition was deeply rooted in Spanish culture, and it is as a part of sixteenth- and seventeenth-century Spanish culture—or of Mediterranean Christian culture generally—that it is most accurately studied and understood. Neither a purely economic nor a purely political explanation suffices to explain its history and character. Nor can a narrow selection of cases be cited to explain its entire operation and structure. Jews, Muslims, *conversos*, Moriscos, and Protestants were far from the only victims of the Inquisition, and at times they were far from being the most prominent or most numerous.

For Spanish society excluded others as well from full respect and status, including some fully blooded Old Christians, and the dimension of moral supervision is probably the least studied major aspect of Inquisition activity through the longest part of its history. Blasphemy, sexual deviation, bigamy, solicitation in the confessional, various superstitions, offenses against the Inquisition or its servants, and many other offenses constituted the overall bulk of Inquisition concerns over the longest period. The case of witchcraft offers a very different perspective from other modern points of view.

Although the medieval Inquisitions gradually acquired jurisdiction over the offenses of magic and witchcraft on the ground that they represented a form of heresy, in much of northern Europe (as in the case of other offenses under Spanish Inquisition jurisdiction) these offenses came under secular or diocesan law and remained there. In Mediterranean Europe witchcraft and sorcery came under the authority of the various Mediterranean inquisitions, and in Spain they came under the Spanish Inquisition. Although Spanish inquisitors responded to accusations of witchcraft and sorcery initially with much the same fear and severity as elsewhere in Europe, by the 1530s the *Suprema* insisted upon its right to review all convictions of sorcery or witchcraft. The thoroughgoing method of interrogation, life histories, vast testimonies from numbers of different witnesses (whose quality as witnesses was astutely assessed), and the scope of *Suprema* reviews engendered scepticism concerning such accusations in Spain long before a similar scepticism appeared elsewhere in Europe. A particularly intense outburst of accusations of witchcraft in the Pyrenees in 1610 led to an extensive review of all the evidence by the inquisitor Alonso Salazar y Frias, whose report to the *Suprema* sounded the death knell for prosecutions of this kind in Spain after 1614. Thus the Spanish Inquisition must be considered essentially as an incident in the history of Christianity in fifteenth- and sixteenth-century Spain and understood in those terms. Erected in the late fifteenth century, it lasted for three hundred and fifty years, and its history is the history of an early modern European religious and judicial institution whose purpose was to preserve Spanish Catholicism by visibly and publicly reasserting the religious orthodoxy of Spanish society.

Unlike the medieval inquisitions, the Spanish Inquisition was one of the earliest European institutions which performed such a function with widespread popular support and governmental backing, because it represented a regional response to universal concerns. If the kings of Spain wrested control of the institution from the popes, they did so largely because they were convinced that they knew what was better for Spain than did the papacy; and as the Inquisition entered its last century, the circumstances which transformed and eventually abolished it are the circumstances of eighteenth- and early nineteenth-century Spain.

Much of the support for the Inquisition came from the firmness of Ferdinand and Isabella in the late fifteenth century and from that of Charles V and Philip II in the sixteenth. The rulers' support of their institution, both inside Spain and in their relations with Rome, helped greatly to restrict appeals to Rome, and created the autonomy of the Inquisition within Spain itself. The Inquisition was used very rarely for political purposes by any Spanish ruler, and even its most relentless critics were compelled to admit its popularity within the country.

But Spain itself faced a crisis of great proportions from the early seventeenth century on. Both royal and administrative misjudgment and the structural features of Spanish society and economy precipitated the "decline of Spain," which culminated in the military and economic disasters of the reign of Charles II (1665–1700). With Portugal once again independent, the loss of territorial possessions in Europe, the loosening of ties with the American colonial territories, and the semi-autonomy of Catalonia were increased in the War of the Spanish Succession, which placed the Bourbon prince Philip V (1700–1746) on the throne of Spain and inaugurated a series of governmental reform proposals which constituted an unsettling element in Spain throughout the eighteenth century.

The range of reform proposals, from government to society, education, scientific research, and the economy, characterized successive royal reigns in eighteenth-century Spain, and led to the rise and fall of a succession of reform-minded ministers and royal favorites. In this atmosphere, the status of the Inquisition came frequently under discussion. In the early eighteenth century the royal servant Melchior de Macanaz urged that the royal government take over control and administration of the Inquisition, and in 1703 Philip V virtually took over supervision of the Inquisition's finances and expenditures. Throughout the century proposals for the reform of the Inquisition were frequent and were often made at the highest levels of government. Although the Inquisition resisted reform, it could not resist structural weakness, once its chief victims had disappeared and its newest victims appeared to be political reformers or the heralds of the intellectual enlightenment that had spread from France into Spain by the second half of the century.

The inquisitorial opposition to reform-minded intellectuals like Pablo Olavide in 1778 and, later in the century, to Jovellanos and Campomanes, became entangled with resistance, not only to reform proposals and Enlightenment thought circulating in Spain, but also to the French Revolution of 1789 and the ensuing involvement of Spain in wars with France and England. This relatively mild role as an instrument of political resistance to revolutionary doctrines from France and internal proposals for reform occupied the diminished Inquisition until the Napoleonic wars brought it both temporary abolition and temporary restoration.

In 1808 a revolution against King Charles IV (1788–1808) led to the king's abdication. Ferdinand VII assumed the crown of Spain, but the occupation by French troops in that same year led to the abdication of Ferdinand and the appointment of Joseph Bonaparte, Napoleon's brother, as king. On December 4, 1808, Joseph Bonaparte declared the Inquisition abolished and confiscated its property, although his order was not acted upon. From 1808 to the restoration of Ferdinand VII in 1814 the historian Jaime Vicens Vives has identified four general groupings of Spanish political opinion: moderate traditionalists; traditionalists who sought in Spanish history the solutions to the problems of the late eighteenth and early nineteenth centuries; imitators of French governmental reforms and supporters of Joseph Bonaparte (the *afrancesados*); and reformers who opposed the French but sought a pluralist constitution. The latter convened the *Cortes* at Cádiz and in 1812 issued a constitution for a monarchist Spain free of French domination.

Although the Inquisition was not the chief item of the constitutional agenda, from 1811 on it became a wedge dividing two wings of the liberal anti-French reformers. In 1813, after several years of debate over the question—debate uninformed by any accurate knowledge of the place of the Inquisition in Spanish history, but colored by much picturesque polemic concerning it—the *Cortes* declared the Inquisition inconsistent with the new constitution.

On February 22, 1813, the *Cortes Generales y Extraordinarias* pronounced the abolition of the Inquisition, at the same time reserving to the bishops their right to regulate matters of orthodoxy and heterodoxy and designating the civil authorities as the secular arm of ecclesiastical discipline. The declaration created considerable disturbances when read in Spanish churches, and the papal nuncio to Spain announced that only the pope could dissolve what the pope had created. With the restoration of Ferdinand VII, the Inquisition was reestablished by royal decree on July 21, 1814.

The Institution reestablished by Ferdinand VII in 1814, however, did not long survive its restorer. On July 15, 1834, the regent Maria Christina, acting in the name of the Infanta Isabel II, formally suppressed the Inquisition.

From 1808 to 1834, the Inquisition had virtually ceased to function, its existence chiefly a symbol of Spanish resistance to any reform—whether externally imposed or internally directed—that seemed to stray too far from Spanish ideas. Its victims had long since disappeared, its powers of censorship had been greatly curtailed, and its use as a political device had long since ceased to be needed. It became in itself an *auto-de-fé*— a ritual institution whose existence had come to symbolize the civil Christian life of the Spanish people. Few had any notion of its history or any knowledge of its actual operation.

Chapter Four

The Roman and
Italian Inquisitions

In Spain and Portugal the inquisitors operated according to the universal
language of orthodoxy and heterodoxy common to the Latin Christian
community, but their structure and character reflected regional Spanish
and Portuguese Christianity. To their observers and critics, whether in
Catholic or Protestant Europe, Spanish and Portuguese Christianity appeared indistinguishable from Spanish and Portuguese politics and foreign
policy. Elsewhere in Catholic Europe, especially in the north, the offense
of heresy fell largely under various regional secular or mixed secular-
ecclesiastical jurisdictions. In sixteenth-century Rome, the center of the
older, supra-regional Latin Church, the events of the Reformation did
not elicit another universal, papally-delegated group of inquisitors, but
a local Roman Inquisition, at first loosely linked to territorial inquisitions
elsewhere in Italy, notably in Venice. Except where specified in formal
concordats with territorial rulers, the direct authority of the Roman
Church was confined to those regions it governed directly, that is, to
the Papal States and other territories scattered throughout Italy. There
are few sharper differences between the medieval inquisitorial office and
the inquisitions of early modern Europe than the regional character of
the latter, its reflection of regional culture, and its dependence upon
regional authorities. There is no more dramatic example than that of
Rome itself.

From the sixteenth century on, Christian Europe lived uneasily in
an increasingly regionalized culture, within which a number of different
Christian confessions each professed to have found a universally true
religion. The tension between regional-local culture and the universality
of absolute truth claimed by confessional opponents was heightened

throughout the century by the advancing and rolling back of the Reformation in individual regions, by the reassertion of universal claims by the Roman Church after the Council of Trent (1545–1563), and by the different solutions of the problem of regionalism-universality found throughout Mediterranean and northern Europe. In the case of the Roman Church, its inquisitions operated regionally, but its doctrines and policies had to be exercised throughout Catholic regions that themselves interpreted them and carried them out by local means.

The Early Reformation and the Catholic Response in Italy

The heresies and schisms with which the medieval church had to deal at the universal level shared the structural features of the societies in which they emerged: they tended to be regional, anticlerical, and, with the exception of Catharism, non-doctrinal. The slow development of episcopal inquisitions, legislation by secular authorities, and the papal inquisitors effectively weakened and on occasion suppressed them. In the fourteenth and fifteenth centuries, however, new sources of religious unrest, from the criticism of ecclesiastical abuses, the Avignon Papacy, and the Great Schism of 1378–1415, generated new forms of dissent. Long before the appearance of Martin Luther, movements and demands for reform of the Church had begun in many circles. In the Netherlands and parts of Rhenish Germany, groups or fraternities of devout Christians began in the fifteenth century to meet regularly, and often to live communally, to lead quiet, humble lives, perform charitable works, and discuss Scripture among themselves. Several older religious orders, particularly the Franciscans, also subscribed to considerable reforms, as did individual monasteries and individual dioceses and provinces under reform-minded bishops and archbishops. In Spain and parts of Italy widespread ecclesiastical and clerical reform proceeded from the last decades of the fifteenth century, and the literary and devotional movement known as Christian humanism carried reform ideas into the classes of the learned and their powerful patrons. By the second decade of the sixteenth century, widespread reform movements were active in many parts of Europe.

For the most part, ecclesiastical leaders in Rome were unable or unwilling to coordinate the calls for reform. The pontificate of Julius II (1503–1513) was occupied with political conflict with France and the rebellious anti-Council at Pisa in 1511. Julius responded with a Council of his own, the Fifth Lateran (1512–1517), but the Council failed to achieve lasting reforms, partly at least because the echoes of the fifteenth-century conciliar movement made the popes reluctant to convoke a Council with extensive powers and a strong mandate for reform. Nor did the pontificates of Leo X (1513–1521), Hadrian VI (1522–1523) and Clement VII (1523–1534) display a strong papal interest in ecclesiastical reform.

The protests of Martin Luther that began in 1517 were at first barely noticed by the popes. By the time they were, their influence had spread too quickly and too far for either compromise or control of Luther himself. Protected by a secular prince (as other successful reform movements were protected by independent princes and cities), Luther and his colleagues worked out the principles of the Reformation in the important decade of the 1520s. By the pontificate of Paul III (1534–1549), however, the papacy finally came to grips with what had become a reform movement that had swept much of Europe away from the Roman obedience and threatened to sweep away the rest.

Among the devotional and reform movements that grew up in early sixteenth-century Italy, the Oratory of Divine Love, founded at Vicenza in 1494 and Genoa in 1497, and established in Rome in 1517, played a prominent role in serving the devotional needs of its members and performing charitable works throughout the city. In 1524 a group of Oratorians led by Gian Pietro Carafa, a member of a Neapolitan noble family and bishop of Chieti, founded a new Order, the Congregation of Divine Providence, which became known, from the Latin name of Carafa's diocese, as the Theatines. Driven from the city after the sack of Rome by the soldiers of Charles V in 1527, the Theatine Order moved to Venice for many years, although Carafa returned to Rome in 1536 when he was made a cardinal by Paul III. With the founding of the Oratorians and the Theatines, and the recognition of the Society of Jesus in 1540, the reformed Roman clergy of the Counter-Reformation was established. When Paul III convened an assembly of curialists in 1536 to consider ecclesiastical reform throughout the Church, the information he received in 1537 contained an ambitious reform plan that may be considered in some senses the blueprint for the Counter-Reformation.

In this atmosphere and with a pope who was far more aware of the need of reform than had been his predecessors, the Roman Church undertook both large-scale reforms and the battle against the spread of what it necessarily considered to be the Lutheran heresy. It is clear that a number of reformers in Rome were more than a little sympathetic to Luther's doctrines and, to the extent that Lutheran ecclesiastical ideas resembled their own, they were willing to envision a compromise with

Lutheranism, a view that persisted until the Diet of Regensburg in 1541, when such hopes were dashed, apparently forever.

One of the centers of sympathy with Lutheran reform was the Capuchin Order, which had broken away from the Franciscans in 1520, and whose leader, Bernardino Ochino, was the most popular preacher in Italy. Others besides Ochino and some of his followers were also members of a loose group called "the spirituals," who placed great emphasis upon personal spiritual development and charitable works, rejecting the material aspect of the Church in favor of spiritual reform. Among their number were the Venetian layman Gasparo Contarini, the English cardinal Reginald Pole, and the pious bishop of Verona, Gian Matteo Giberti. Among the spirituals also was the Roman noblewoman Vittoria Colonna, the patron of Ochino and friend of Michelangelo.

In 1536 Paul III announced the summoning of a General Council of the Church, and many of the spirituals, chiefly Contarini, hoped that final reconciliation with Lutheranism would be the result of the Council's work. The failure of the meeting between Catholic and Protestant theologians at Regensburg in 1541, however, and Contarini's own death in 1542, greatly reduced the influence of the spirituals. Carafa, long resistant to the idea of compromise with Protestantism and insistent upon the possibilities of internal reform directed by the papacy, assumed an ascendancy which further increased when, also in 1542, Bernardino Ochino fled Italy and announced his conversion to Protestantism. Ochino's flight greatly discredited not only the spirituals, but also the curial wing which had hoped and worked for a compromise with the Reformation.

Carafa, faced with the failure at Regensburg and the flight of Ochino, urged Paul III to undertake a campaign against heresy in Italy and to do so by the establishment of a new inquisition. Paul III issued the bull *Licet ab initio* on July 4, 1542, establishing the Roman Inquisition. The Roman Inquisition consisted of six cardinals, of whom Carafa was one, called inquisitors-general and empowered to investigate heresy and to appoint deputies when they thought necessary. With the model of the Spanish Inquisition before it, the Roman Inquisition emerged as something quite different from its universal medieval predecessor.

Although the Roman Inquisition began its work moderately and cautiously during the remainder of the pontificate of Paul III, it became stronger and an essential part of the structure of Rome when Carafa was elected pope, in 1555, taking the title Paul IV. The pontificate of Paul IV (1555–1559) launched the Counter-Reformation that Paul III had begun.

The Roman Inquisition

Paul III's decretal not only gave the Cardinal-Inquisitors the power to deputize other inquisitors, but also the power to appoint inquisitors elsewhere in Italy, to supervise their activities, and to proceed against anyone charged with heresy regardless of rank or status except for ecclesiastical and lay authorities. Also in 1542 a list of books prohibited because of doctrinal content or attacks on the Latin Church was issued in Rome, and in 1559 a more ambitious Index appeared, the *Index Auctorum et liborum Prohibitorum*, "The Index of Prohibited Books and Authors." This Index was further expanded in 1564, when as a result of a decision by the Council of Trent, a more comprehensive Index appeared, which remained the basis of further indices until that issued by Benedict XIV in 1758. In 1571, Pope Pius V created a separate Congregation of the Index, although the two institutions shared at least one joint member and the inquisitors were usually called upon to evaluate the content of books. In 1588 Sixtus V erected the Inquisition itself into the *Congregation of the Holy Roman and Universal Inquisition or Holy Office*, one of the fifteen secretariats into which papal government was divided by his administrative reforms.

In general, the procedure followed by the Roman Inquisition was similar to that developed by the medieval inquisitors and considered above. Unlike the Spanish Inquisition, however, the Roman inquisitors conducted their sentencing in private. They conducted their hearings according to a series of *Instructiones* and handbooks of law and procedure which grew considerably more detailed in the late sixteenth and seventeenth centuries. A good example of such a work is the *Directorium Inquisitorum*, written by the Aragonese inquisitor Nicolau Eymeric in 1376 and frequently consulted by later inquisitors in both Spain and Italy. In 1578 Eymeric's *Directorium* was carefully edited, enlarged, and printed by the Spanish canonist and jurist Francisco Peña, working in Rome in conjunction with the Roman Inquisition. Peña was a careful scholar and a well-trained jurist, and he often pointed out areas where Eymeric's text indicated local Aragonese usage which need not be followed by inquisitors elsewhere. Peña also added a collection of historical documents to Eymeric's treatise, commented extensively upon the history of inquisitorial procedure, and cited recent rulings by the Spanish and the Roman Inquisitions. Peña later published a collection of papal letters dealing with heresy and inquisitorial procedure from the thirteenth century to the early seventeenth, and he began but did not finish his own inquisitorial manual, the *Praxis Inquisitorum*, which was not published until 1651. Peña was a thorough collector of materials pertaining to inquisitorial procedure, and his other publications and manuscript materials reflect both a professional scholarly and a confessional interest in the Inquisition. Throughout his edition of Eymeric and his own later writings, Peña emphasizes the authority of the pope and his judge delegates, the inquisitors, and the importance of inquisitorial practice rather than formal theological or legal expositions of inquisitorial authority. In Peña's edition of Eymeric and in his other legal writings, as well as in other similar works of inquisitorial instruction and procedure, it is possible to see the Roman Inquisition in practice as well as theory and to understand the way in which it was conceived by those who created and directed its operations.

Although the Roman Inquisition was nominally superior to the other Italian inquisitions, in practice a number of city-republics insisted that local representatives sit with the inquisitors and that severe sentences be reviewed by secular authorities. The Venetian Inquisition in particular, considered later in this chapter, is a striking example of the partial independence of local Italian inquisitions in the sixteenth and seventeenth centuries. Local bishops also might intervene when their interests were at stake, and the possibility of conflicting jurisdictions was much greater in Italy, for example, than in Spain or Portugal. In addition, it is not thought that the records of the Roman Inquisition were kept as centrally as in Spain or that review of local tribunals was as consistent as it was in the hands of the *Suprema* in the *relaciónes de causas*.

Again unlike Spain, the Roman Inquisition did not primarily—or even significantly—deal with any phenomenon remotely comparable to that of the *conversos*. Although the Roman Inquisition, like earlier inquisitions, had certain authority over Jews and, of course, total authority over Judaizing Christians, the Roman Inquisition never faced the *converso* problem in any significant way. Indeed, many Spanish and Portuguese *conversos*, fleeing Spain and Portugal, often found themselves in Italy, where some were able to live as Jews again.

The chief target of the newly founded Roman Inquisition was the "heresy" of Protestantism. Behind the passion of Carafa lay the prospect of widespread sympathy with and conversions to the doctrines of Luther and other reformers. These concerns appear to have dominated the activities of the Roman Inquisition and its subordinate tribunals until the end of the sixteenth century, particularly during the pontificate of Paul IV (1555–1559) and the period immediately following the closing of the Council of Trent in 1563 and the application of its decrees throughout Catholic Europe.

Like the Spanish Inquisition, the Roman Inquisition and its subordinate tribunals appear to have been generally successful in keeping any substantial Protestant influence from spreading at all widely in the peninsula. Also like the Spanish Inquisition, the Roman Inquisition, once the immediate problem of Protestantism was reduced, turned the bulk of its operations to the question of internal ecclesiastical discipline and to offenses other than Protestantism.

One of the themes common to both Catholic and Protestant reformers in the fifteenth and sixteenth centuries—and one of the major themes of recent research in social history during this period—is the problem of the religion of the laity, or "popular religion." There is little specific agreement about the character of sixteenth-century "popular" religion and little agreement even on the basic terms of the discussion. Who, for example, are "the people"? How is their "religion" measurable? Although inquisitors developed standard measurements for such topics as "superstition" and false beliefs, persecuted the use of legitimate sacramental doctrines for "magical" purposes, and interpreted the variety of religious sensibilities that came before them according to well-known standards, neither their methods nor those of their Protestant counterparts are those of modern social historians and anthropologists.

The inquisitors themselves, whether in Spain or Italy, often displayed a remarkable understanding of the people they interrogated in this category. Although some practices virtually required that a conventional judgment of "witchcraft" or "heresy" be handed down—the work of the brilliant Italian historian Carlo Ginzburg has illustrated this sort of occasion particularly well—in many instances the inquisitors understood very well that the lack of catechesis or consistent pastoral guidance could often result in misunderstandings of doctrine and liturgy, and they showed tolerance of all but the most unavoidably serious circumstances. Thus, although both the Spanish and Roman inquisitions prosecuted the offenses of witchcraft and sorcery very early and vigorously, they also were the first courts to be sceptical of the evidence and mechanics of witchcraft accusations, and they consistently offered the most lenient treatment to marginal cases. In this respect, the Italian inquisitions reflected the aims of the Council of Trent, which, if it would not effect the reconciliation of Catholics and Protestants, was at least strongly determined to elevate the religious behavior of Catholics and to restrict the misuse of orthodox doctrine or practices. In 1576 the Franciscan Fra Girolamo Menghi published *Compèndio dell'arte esorcista,* "The Compendium of the Techniques of Exorcism," a learned work which emphasized the legitimate and illegitimate means that the average Christian had to protect himself or herself against natural or supernatural misfortunes. In order to accomplish these aims, the popes, the Council of Trent, and the Inquisition had to see to the creation of a diligent and competent clergy and to the proper circulation of religious instruction. Thus, the duties of the Roman Inquisition included the regulation of offenses among the clergy as much as among the laity.

From shortly before 1600 throughout the seventeenth century, the cases tried by the Italian inquisitions appear to have shifted markedly from those of Protestantism to offenses generally labelled superstition, particularly magic. Nearly forty percent of all Italian trials seem to have dealt with "superstitious magic" in Italy.

The increasing importance of prosecutions for superstition and magic is reflected in the appearance of specialized *Instructiones* dealing exclusively with this subject for inquisitors, one of the most important of which was the *Instructio pro formandis processibus in causis strigum, sortilegiorum, et maleficorum*, the "Instruction for conducting trial procedure in case of witches, sorcerers, and injurious magicians," circulated by Cardinal Giovanni Garcia Millino, one of the cardinal-inquisitors, sent to a provincial inquisitor in 1624, and printed in 1625. The *Instructio* circulated widely in Italy and Germany in the seventeenth and eighteenth centuries and illustrates the growing caution with which inquisitorial judges treated accusations and convictions for witchcraft and related offenses. The secular courts of Italy had increasingly considered the Inquisition too lax and lenient in its prosecution of those accused of witchcraft, and the treatment of procedure in the *Instructio* supports the impression that inquisitors were far more sceptical of evidence and far more aware of procedural abuses in witchcraft prosecutions than were their secular counterparts in Italy and elsewhere. Although the *Instructio* did not break new judicial ground in its insistence upon uniform procedure, strict rules of evidence, and its prohibition of ad hoc procedures or judicial shortcuts, it insisted that the standards used by the Inquisition at Rome be the same as those applied elsewhere, regardless of popular pressure or the power of secular authorities. On more than one occasion the cardinal-inquisitors in Rome overturned provincial verdicts on the grounds of improper or inadequate procedure.

In addition to insisting upon—and itself following—what for the time were moderate judicial norms, including defense for the accused, often at the Inquisition's own expense, and restriction of the value of the testimony of confessed or convicted witches concerning other witches, the Roman Inquisition appears to have been generally lenient in its punishments. Repentant first offenders were usually let off with penances

or short terms of incarceration (itself a development of inquisitorial jurisprudence, long before it became accepted in secular procedure). Only
after 1623 was witchcraft, for example, made a capital crime, and then
only in cases in which it was established that the witch had actually
injured someone.

The Roman Inquisition was not a static institution, nor were its attitudes
and procedures always identical to those of its founders or most zealous
patrons like Paul IV. The frequency with which the cardinal-inquisitors
in Rome corrected provincial tribunals also reflects the difference in
the power of the Inquisition in Rome and the rest of the Papal States,
on the one hand, and in the rest of Italy, on the other. The historian
John Tedeschi had observed that the Inquisition

> was never admitted into the republic of Lucca and in Naples had to
> operate under the cloak of the episcopal courts. In Genoa, Savoy,
> Venice, and later in Tuscany, lay officials were either members of
> the court, contrary to customary procedure, or interfered freely in
> given cases. In these states any serious action contemplated by any
> ecclesiastical judge, such as arrest, extradition of a suspect to Rome,
> and confiscation of property depended upon the assent of the secular
> authorities.

Like the Spanish Inquisition, its history seems to consist of several
phases: an initial attack on a specific ecclesiastical offense considered
both dangerous and overwhelmingly important (in the case of Spain,
Judaizing; in that of Rome, Protestantism) and a longer and more constant
and routine exercise of authority over offenses against ecclesiastical discipline: magic, witchcraft, blasphemy, bigamy, and the common category
it shared with Spain, "crimes against the Inquisition." As with the Spanish
Inquisition, the latter categories make up the bulk of inquisitorial records.

The Inquisition in Sicily

The power and relatively smooth operation of the inquisitions in Spain,
Portugal, and Rome—and, in a slightly different way, that of Venice—
was not necessarily the norm, for tribunals separated from the centers
of power that created them met with intense local resistance. The histories
of the tribunals of Milan, Naples, and Sicily, for example, read very
differently from those of the larger and better known tribunals in Madrid,
Lisbon, and Rome.

The inquisitorial office in Sicily had appeared in the thirteenth century, as had others, but by the fifteenth century its holders and their operations appear virtually to have ceased. From 1481, however, Sicilian inquisitors were appointed from Aragón, whose king ruled Sicily, and for two decades the Sicilian Inquisition operated fitfully against Jews and *conversos*, enforcing a particularly harsh version of the Jewish expulsion edict of 1492. By 1499, however, the Sicilian tribunal appears to have fallen into disarray through mismanagement and intense local resistance to its procedures. Ferdinand of Aragón reconstituted the tribunal in 1500–1501, and several *autos-de-fé* were held in 1506 and 1511.

In 1511, however, local resistance to the extraordinary extent and detail of inquisitorial privileges grew once more. The next few years appear to have brought a truce, but in 1516 the inquisitor Cervera was forced to depart ignominiously from Sicily, and no Inquisition operated for the next three years. Severe criticism from Spain of the rapacity and illegality of the Inquisition's procedures followed its reestablishment in 1519.

From the 1540s the Sicilian Inquisition, like the other Mediterranean Inquisitions, turned its attention to "Lutheranism," the term apparently only vaguely understood and extended to cover a number of different forms of dissent. Throughout its existence the Sicilian tribunal was a rival of the local royal governor, and this friction, as well as local resistance to the tribunal's methods and the presence of its familiars, was a permanent feature of its existence. Nor was the Inquisition exempt from other troubles. In 1593 the powder magazine of the building in which it operated exploded, killing two prisoners and almost killing the Inquisitor, Luis de Pàramo, its first and most ambitious historian. In 1657 the Inquisitor Cisneros was killed by a prisoner, Diego La Matina, who himself was executed the following year, in an *auto-de-fé* that was one of the most spectacular the island had ever seen.

Not even the shifts in control of Sicily appear to have changed the provincial Spanish character of the Inquisition. When control of the island shifted to Vienna in 1726 the operation of the tribunal appears to have been uninterrupted; when it shifted back to Spain in 1734 it came under the scrutiny of the talented Charles III. In 1784 the Sicilian Inquisition was abolished by royal order, its buildings and finances were confiscated, its records sealed, and its prisoners released.

The Inquisition in Venice

The papal bull *Licet ab initio* of 1542 created the Inquisition in Rome and in the Papal States, but did not specify its authority over tribunals in other parts of Italy, some of which had had an independent existence since the thirteenth century. A number of states outside central Italy jealously guarded the independence of their own tribunals, even when recognizing the general authority of the popes. In Naples, for example, in 1547 there was widespread fear that an external inquisition was about to be established on the basis of the Spanish Inquisition, and even the fact that the model was actually Roman rather than Spanish did not readily calm the population. A similar resentment struck Milan in 1563. Although the history of the spread of the authority of the Roman Inquisition throughout Italy has not yet been written, the case of the Venetian Inquisition offers a particularly striking example of the complexity of the issues involved and the final compromise that was eventually reached.

Like many Italian city-republics and the Kingdom of Sicily in the thirteenth century, Venice had written stiff laws against heresy into its own municipal legal code, and it appears to have enforced them from the early thirteenth century on. The inquisitorial activities in medieval Venice, however, appear to have focused on usury as well as heresy, with the addition of other related offenses later in the thirteenth century; the actual discovery and trial of these cases was done by a lay magistracy. In 1289 Pope Nicholas IV installed a Franciscan inquisitor in Venice, but as in the cases of other city-republics, the office appears to have declined in the late fourteenth and early fifteenth centuries.

The Venetian state and people took considerable—and vocal—pride in their Christianity, and they regarded heretics and other ecclesiastical offenders as much political as civil criminals. For the Venetians, the preservation of the state itself was held to depend upon the orthodoxy of its people's beliefs. Although Venice, because of its location and vigorous trade relationships, permitted the existence of, and limited practice of other faiths by, non-Latin Christians and Jews, the official religion of the state and its protection became early and long remained a fixed idea. Even the interdicts placed upon the city by popes in 1483, 1509, and 1600 did not reflect a Venetian failure of orthodoxy, nor did the long and intense struggles between the Venetian state and the papal state and its various diplomatic and military allies in the fifteenth and sixteenth centuries suggest a breakdown in ecclesiastical affairs or beliefs. Venetians were prominent among the spiritual and ecclesiastical reformers in the early sixteenth century, and a number of Catholic reformers came from the city throughout the sixteenth century. Although the Venetians regarded the papacy on the one hand as a rival political institution whose policies occasionally disagreed with those of Venice and had to be dealt with as such, they also regarded the popes as the spiritual leaders of Latin Christianity. These two quite distinct attitudes came to be severely tested in the history of the Venetian Inquisition.

Throughout the 1540s the papacy urged Venice to seek out and take action against heretics. To Rome the Venetian willingness to permit the residence of Protestants and other "heretical" Christians, as well as Venice's diplomatic negotiations with "heretical" European powers, appeared to be a weakening of Venetian faith; to Venetians, Rome seemed to be confusing state policy with religious orthodoxy. In 1547, however, Venice itself established a magistracy consisting of three prominent and devout Venetian laymen—called the *Tre Savii sopra eresia*, "The Three Wise Men who know about heresy"—who were charged to work with the patriarch of Venice, the papal nuncio, and the Franciscan inquisitor to root out heresy. The prominence of laymen was not at all favored in Rome or elsewhere, and Pope Julius III (1550–1555) strongly criticized such participation throughout Italy. In 1551 the pope and the Venetians reached a compromise according to which the lay participants acted only as observers and witnesses. The compromise also permitted officials in the Venetian dominions to witness examinations and trials, and indicated a certain prominence on the part of the city of Venice itself in relation to its dominions. From 1557 the titles of inquisitor in Venice and inquisitor-general throughout the Venetian dominions came to be held by the same person, thus ensuring the superiority of Venice itself in ecclesiastical affairs throughout its far-flung empire.

One reason for the compromise of 1551 was the fact that since its foundation in 1542 the Roman Inquisition had not undertaken any considerable activity outside the Papal States. During the pontificates of Paul IV (1555–1559) and Pius IV (1559–1565), however, the Roman Inquisition began actively to issue advice and instructions to other inquisitorial tribunals, attempting, as we have already seen, to systematize and make consistent both inquisitorial procedure and sentencing practices. By 1560 the papacy had become the normal authority for nominating Venetian inquisitors, and although a considerable degree of Venetian autonomy survived, by the seventeenth century the inquisition of Venice had come to resemble other inquisitorial districts and that of Rome itself on which it depended, bringing it into line with what might be termed an Italian Inquisition and making it more rigorous.

The unusual combination of lay and clerical members of the Venetian Inquisition is reflected in the different functions of the two groups. The *Tre Savii* appointed by the state were the state's representatives to the Inquisition and the Inquisition's representatives to the state. They were present at trials, might give opinions in particular cases, issued warrants for arrest, and formally delivered sentences. When the sentences were capital, their formal delivery of the sentence to the Council of Ten, the judicial organ of the Venetian state, empowered the council to appoint an official to carry out the death penalty, which in Venice was usually by drowning. The three ecclesiastical members of the Inquisition were led by the inquisitor, who conducted most of the hearings, questioned the accused and the witnesses, and decided upon the sentence. This system of operation placed the theological responsibility and authority firmly in the hands of the inquisitor, who therefore was the most important link with the Roman Inquisition.

The Roman Inquisition kept itself well informed about Venetian affairs, frequently asking for reports on trials in progress and often sending information to Venice. By the mid-sixteenth century, the Venetian Inquisition had begun consulting Rome regularly for advice on procedure and jurisdiction and willingly extraditing suspects to Rome for trial, sentence, or even appeal. The case of Galileo in 1633 illustrates this degree of reciprocity between the Venetian and Roman tribunals, as does that of Giordano Bruno in 1600.

Thus, between 1547 and 1560 the many points of difference in politics and power between Venice and Rome were largely reconciled in the matter of heresy. Although the great early seventeenth-century Venetian historian Fra Paolo Sarpi, in his passionate defense of Venetian autonomy from Rome, made an eloquent case for the historical and juridical autonomy of the Venetian Inquisition as solely an organ of the state, research in the trial records and the communications between Venice and Rome indicate that the reverse was in fact the case, and that, in spite of profound and continuing difference between the two powers, in matters of heresy the Venetian Inquisition cooperated fully with that of Rome, satisfied that its own concessions, the *Tre Savii*, and the participation by territorial governors as observers preserved the honor and status of the Republic. There was thus no need to insist upon independence in the matter of heresy, upon which both Venice and Rome firmly agreed.

The Venetian Inquisition met regularly on Tuesdays, Thursdays, and Saturdays, in winter at the Dominican convent and in summer in the Church of San Teodoro, near the Cathedral of San Marco. Its finances, never substantial, appear to have become more precarious through the seventeenth century, partly because Venetian law dictated that the confiscated goods of heretics reverted to the State. Its procedures fell into line with those of the Roman Inquisition as a substantial literature of inquisitorial jurisprudence and procedure streamed from the printing press. The Venetian Inquisition also appears to have used torture very little and to have issued relatively few death sentences. The execution of capital sentences was held even more secretly than in Rome, and had none of the public dimension of such executions in Spain and Portugal.

Like the inquisitions of Spain and Rome, the Venetian Inquisition appears to have had at least two main stages in terms of the offenses it tried. In the 1500 case records—the *processi*—that survive from the sixteenth century, more than half were directed against Protestantism; the rest dealt with superstitious magic, Judaizing, and offenses against ecclesiastical discipline, prohibited books, usury, bigamy, and blasphemy. In the slightly fewer *processi* that survived from the seventeenth century, the nature of the offenses shifts in importance; nearly half deal with superstitious magic, only around ten percent deal with Protestantism, and about the same proportion with blasphemies and heretical conversation; and they reflect an increased concentration on morals offenses committed by the clergy, including solicitation in the confessional.

The structure of Venetian book censorship reflected the joint character of the Venetian Inquisition. Venice was the printing capital of Europe, and the Venetian presses came under the scrutiny of both state and Inquisition officials. Two state magistracies as well as the Inquisitor dealt with the censorship and approval of books.

Although the Jews of the Venetian *ghetto* (established in the city itself after the mid-sixteenth century) were protected from the Inquisition, the numbers of Spanish and Portuguese Jews who passed through Venice, and the suspicion that they were *Marranos* who were secret Judaizers, brought many Jews to the attention of the Inquisition, and created tensions in the Venetian Jewish Community.

The strongest areas of agreement between ecclesiastical members of the Venetian Inquisition and officials of the state lay in questions of ecclesiastical importance that touched the public security and authority of the Republic as well. In the cases of censorship and of Judaizing, as well as in others, the strongest activities and greatest degree of unanimity in the Venetian Inquisition focused upon aspects of both phenomena that touched state interests. Any book that attacked the religion of Venice, for example, or any case in which it appeared that a secret Judaizer had attempted to deceive the Venetian Inquisition and government, was likely to be treated with extreme severity. In other instances, since Venice possessed a flourishing book trade and necessarily was the home of many Jews, religious and state interests might diverge.

The Inquisition survived in Venice as long as the Republic itself, in spite of conflicts with the papacy in the early seventeenth century and attacks from others later. It disappeared with Napoleon's conquest of Venice in 1797.

The Survival and Transformation of the Roman Inquisition

Although the Congregation of the Holy Office remained one of the major departments of papal government and had wide jurisdictional powers in theory, by the eighteenth century it had virtually no power or influence outside the papal states. The chief occupation of its members during the eighteenth century appears to have been the investigation and censuring of cases of clerical immorality and the censoring of printed books, a task in which it overlapped with the Congregation of the Index.

In terms of censorship, the Indices published during the eighteenth century indicate the randomness with which individual works and authors came to the Inquisition's attention, for there is little consistency in its lists and no evidence of a systematic sweep of all published literature in the search for error. Usually its condemnations were only of Latin, French, or Italian versions of books, chiefly because these were the languages most regularly read in Rome. In 1753 Pope Benedict XIV issued a strict series of procedures for the ecclesiastical censorship of books, and the Index published as a result, that of 1758, was far more thorough than any of its recent predecessors and remained the basic text of the Index until the Index itself was abolished in 1966. Generally, the growth of secular mechanisms of censorship further restricted the influence of the Roman Index in Spain (which had its own Index), France, and the Austrian Netherlands.

As the papacy itself weakened in the late eighteenth century, so did its dependent Congregations, including that of the Inquisition. With the brief revolutionary establishment of the Roman Republic in 1798–1799, Pope Pius VI died in exile in France in 1799 and the Inquisition itself was temporarily abolished by the revolutionary government. In the long conflict between Napoleon and Pius VII (1800–1823) and the Pope's long exile from Italy during 1809–1814, the Papal State was annexed to the French Empire, the archives of many of the Congregations and the papacy itself were confiscated, and the Inquisition was again abolished. From this period dates the scattering of its archives that has so far made the history of the Roman Inquisition so difficult to write. Only recently have scholars traced the lost Inquisitorial archives (including a large number that eventually ended up in Dublin) and begun painstakingly to reconstruct the history of the Roman Inquisition from them.

After 1814, papal rule was restored in Rome and the Papal States, and the Inquisition was reestablished, although its authority was more than ever limited to territories directly governed by the pope.

The emergence of an Italian national state and the restriction upon ecclesiastical authority that followed 1860 further curtailed the activities of the Holy Office, and, its powers reduced to the diminished papal state, it declined further into an advisory committee to the late nineteenth century popes. During the 1907–1908 reaction against Modernism, the papacy appears to have relied as much upon informal response to the Modernists as it did upon institutional restraints. The Jesuit order, the French episcopacy, a newly vocal and popular (and ultramontane) Catholic press, and scholarly journals did much of the papacy's work during the Modernist crisis. The official response was largely conducted by the Congregation of the Index, the administrative manipulation of individual clerical careers by Vatican officials, and official excommunication. Although the Congregation of the Holy Office did participate in the condemnation of certain doctrines and individuals, it appears to have played a far greater advisory than executive role.

In 1908 Pius X changed the name to the *Congregation of the Holy Office*, and its work was merged with that of the Congregation of the Index by the papal secretary of state, Cardinal Merry del Val, in 1917. From 1917 to 1965 the combined congregations constituted a useful instrument for advising the popes, and in several instances, notably in the case of Ernesto Bonaiuti in 1923 and 1926, it generated substantial criticism inside and outside of the Catholic world.

In 1965 Pope Paul VI changed the name once again to that of the Sacred Congregation for the Doctrine of the Faith, and he abolished the Index entirely in 1966. Since that date the Congregation for the Doctrine of the Faith has acted as chief adviser to the popes on theological matters and on matters of ecclesiastical discipline. Although its work is regular and influential, the Congregation can now hardly be thought of as an Inquisition, except by those of its critics who oppose it in particular cases, most recently those of Hans Kung, Edward Schillebeeckx, and Leonardo Boff. On these occasions opponents of the Congregation's decisions often revive the old name of the Inquisition and apply it vigorously. They are sometimes aided by a long tradition of Catholic opposition to the inquisitions, an opposition that became particularly vigorous over the last century.

With the increasing restrictions placed upon the autonomy of Catholic churches by secular governments during the late eighteenth and nineteenth centuries, prelates and clergy turned more and more to Rome—

or toward collaboration with national governmental systems. Those who, fearing the inroads that collaboration with secular governments might entail, and stung by nineteenth-century anticlericalism, turned to Rome, helped to shape the role of the papacy in nineteenth- and twentieth-century world history and gave papal institutions a new lease on life. From 1848 to 1965, the Congregation of the Holy Office acquired more universal authority in Roman Catholicism than it had ever held before, and its continuing existence enabled critics of papal authority to hold up before the world *The Inquisition* as the primary symbol of popish ambitions and ruthlessness. In this respect the last century of the Roman Inquisition served the purposes both of Catholicism and of its enemies.

Chapter Five

The Invention of *The Inquisition*

The Inquisition was an image assembled from a body of legends and myths which, between the sixteenth and the twentieth centuries, established the perceived character of inquisitorial tribunals and influenced all ensuing efforts to recover their historical reality. That body took shape in the context of intensified religious persecution as a consequence of the Reformation of the sixteenth century and of the central role of Spain, the greatest power in Europe, in assuming the role of defender of Roman Catholicism. During the early stages of this process, neither the doctrines and trials of medieval heretics nor the Iberian persecution of Marranos and Moriscos were matters of any concern. Initially, it was the persecution of Protestants, chiefly by the Spanish and Roman Inquisitions, that provoked the first image of *The Inquisition* as the most dangerous and characteristic Catholic weapon against Protestantism, and later, among philosophical critics of religious persecution.

Yet in order to invent *The Inquisition* a number of other equally prominent features of sixteenth-century Europe had to be ignored or transformed. Every European state based its legitimacy on religious grounds, and virtually every European state persecuted religious minorities. What made it possible for Protestant Reformers and Catholic critics alike to distinguish *The Inquisition* from other similar forms of religious persecution was the ecclesiastical character and composition of the Spanish and Roman Inquisitions, the success that their apparently united front experienced in keeping Protestant doctrines out of Spain and Italy, and the fear aroused by the threat of their being instituted elsewhere in Catholic Europe.

As a Protestant vision of Christian history took shape in the sixteenth

122

century, the contemporary inquisitions were identified with the inquisitorial tribunals of the medieval past, and the Protestant Reformers with earlier victims of *The Inquisition.* Catholic defenders of the early modern Inquisitions often made the same argument—that the sixteenth-century Reformers were simply "the heretics of old" and needed to be dealt with in the same way, thereby reinforcing the idea of the continuity of all inquisitorial tribunals.

One great difference, however, between medieval dissenters and sixteenth-century Reformers was that of sheer numbers and state protection. Every Reform movement that succeeded in the sixteenth century did so either because a state protected it or because it came to control a state. Reformers who found no state or state protection suffered as much from Protestant state religions as from Catholicism. In the climate of religious persecution that characterized much of the sixteenth century the theme of martyrdom became first a Protestant, and later a Catholic, form of self-definition and confessional consciousness. In the large and literate Protestant world, the theme of martyrdom was focused upon those Catholic powers that produced martyrs. The most prominent of those powers was that of Spain.

The local experience of England and France during the sixteenth century included several kinds of religious persecution that came very close to resembling Inquisitions themselves, but, as the century ended, neither kingdom had succeeded, and neither kingdom wished to. Both were free to criticize those areas in which Inquisitions had succeeded, and both were willing to do so, particularly when such criticism coincided with foreign policy, particularly in terms of relations with Spain. From the 1530s on, the Spanish Inquisition, originally reconstituted to deal with a particular feature of Spanish religious culture, turned on the new doctrines of the Reformers with the full apparatus and zeal that it had once reserved for *conversos.* At the same time, Spanish political and military power was the greatest in Europe. Resentment against Spain focused equally upon its Inquisition and its diplomatic and military practices. Although both England and France endured conflicts with Spain throughout the century, the flash-point was reached in the Revolt of the Netherlands, when anti-Inquisition propaganda played a large role in uniting both Protestants and Netherlands Catholics against Spanish power and practice.

During these circumstances *The Inquisition* was invented, and, as a myth, it served as a convenient symbol of all religious persecution during the seventeenth and eighteenth centuries, when, first on religious and later on philosophical and political grounds, the idea of religious and civil toleration became the policy of most of the states of Europe. Between the sixteenth and the late eighteenth centuries the invention of *The Inquisition* served a wide variety of purposes, but no matter how different these purposes were, each contributed to the accumulation of detail that shaped the eventual myth.

The Reformation Discovers History and Martyrology

The first concerns of the religious reformers of the sixteenth century were the assertion of a distinct theology that differed from much of that of Latin Christianity, the assurance of a degree of safety in which they might assert it, and the freedom to promulgate the doctrines of "true religion" without hindrance from ecclesiastical or secular powers. During the 1520s, Martin Luther's buoyant confidence in the converting power of the revealed Word and the disorganized character of orthodox response combined to give every sign that the Reformation would succeed. But by the 1540s the pace of the Reformation began to slow; Lutheranism made some gains, but some areas that had turned Lutheran returned to Latin Christianity. Calvinism emerged as a religious "Third force," and the formation of sectarian confessions troubled Protestant and Catholic communities alike. What no one had forseen was the vast religious stalemate that entangled a number of competing creeds, each with universal claims, in the affairs of local communities that came to be the preservers of state religions.

In the course of the development of Protestant theology, no reformer ever argued that his doctrines constituted a "new" religion or that they depended upon anything other than the original divine revelation in scripture and the inspiration of the Spirit working upon the understanding of contemporary sixteenth-century minds. Therefore, the reformed religion of the sixteenth century had to assert a historical tradition nearly as soon as it asserted a theological truth. And it had to explain why, if truth had been revealed in the Old and New Testaments and known to the earliest Christian communities, it had taken until the sixteenth century for it to be fully understood and finally proclaimed. It also had to explain the erratic and often disappointing pace of reform in its own time.

Catholic apologists charged that the Latin Church was the true successor of the evangelical Christian communities of antiquity, and they charged to the Lutherans, as Flaccius Illyricus paraphrased it, that "your church . . . is new, not thirty years since begun and founded by Luther. Therefore, our church and religion, that is, the Roman, and not yours, is true and genuine." Although Protestant apologists like John Foxe could counter-argue that, "if [Catholics] mean the ordinance and institution of doctrine and sacraments now received of us, and differing from the Church of Rome, we affirm and say, that our Church was, when this church of theirs was not yet hatched out of the shell, nor did yet ever see any light: that is, in the time of the apostles, in the primitive age. . . ." The debate required more than assertion and counter-assertion.

The core of the sixteenth-century Protestant argument, except in terms of doctrine, did not go back to the earliest Christian communities during the Roman persecutions, but rather to the period that began with the conversion of Roman emperors and the Empire itself to Christianity in the fourth century; and they pointed to the role of the Latin Church in preserving (from its point of view)—or subverting (from theirs) true Christianity, eventually by outright persecution in the twelfth and thirteenth centuries, and by persecuting or urging others to persecute in its name in the sixteenth-century present. Martin Luther himself posited the existence of a true, hidden, persecuted Church which suffered at the hands of a false, ostensible, persecuting Church which corrupted the Word and usurped otherwise legitimate forms of state power. Thus in the earliest Protestant Church history, the theme of persecuted authentic Christians occupied a prominent place. And their persecutors were the rulers of the Latin Church manipulating secular authority to achieve their corrupt ends.

Although Luther himself never filled out this framework of Church history in detail, later Protestant historians did. At first, Protestant reformers paid little attention to medieval heretics. Neither Luther nor Calvin was prepared to admit all earlier critics of Rome into the "true" Church. The earliest Protestant references to medieval heretics focused upon those of the fifteenth century: Wyclif and the later Lollards in England, the Hussites in Bohemia, and the Waldensians who were persecuted in the late fifteenth and sixteenth centuries in Piedmont and Provence. When Luther replied to Erasmus' inquiry about the history of the true, hidden, persecuted Church, he had simply remarked that the true saints had been hidden; then he sharply asked, "How many saints do you think that the inquisitors have burned over the centuries?," and did not himself give an answer. Even the conversions in the 1550s and 1560s of Alpine Waldensians to Calvinism did not give them—or the medieval Waldensians—a secure place in the Protestant canon.

The full assimilation of medieval heresies—and medieval inquisitors— required two further developments: their identification with the apostolic, and hence the reformed, church, and their role as precursors of the Reformation. On occasion, Catholic opponents of the Reformation assisted in this process. In 1522 Bernard of Luxemburg, a Catholic, published an alphabetical catalogue of heresies, from the earliest Church to the present. Luther, said Bernard, "awoke sleeping heresies." From Bernard of Luxemburg on, one outcome of the debates between Protestants and Catholics about church history was the discovery and publication of much of the surviving source material on medieval heresies, and medieval inquisitorial tribunals. In those sources, the heretics who were identified were usually those who had been discovered, tried, and executed. Luther's question to Erasmus, in the light of Protestant self-definition and the intensification of religious persecution, indicated that martyrdom was the one sign of the hidden church that did not require extensive doctrinal documentation.

The concept of martyrdom had been developed in the early church to describe those who had borne "witness"—*martyrion*—to the truth of Christian belief, both by the perfection of their lives and by their deaths. After the Apostles themselves, the early Christian martyrs became a sanctified group, having imitated Christ's sacrifice in a literal sense. The cult of martyrs had been nurtured by the medieval Latin Church, the ninth-century martyrology of Usuardus becoming a standard work and the cult of the martyrs joining in the broader cult of the saints upon which much of Latin liturgical and devotional life was based. Late medieval books of saints' lives were immensely popular, often graphically illustrated with the sufferings of martyrs, and much attention was paid to the appropriately horrible fates of the persecutors of martyrs.

Although most Reformation doctrines rejected the Latin cult of saints, Protestant identification with the evangelical purity and truth of the early Church did not mean a rejection of martyrdom as well. The persecution of the true Church became a major theme in Protestant self-consciousness, and Protestant writers came to regard the persecution of true Christians in the sixteenth century and earlier as a continuity of the persecution of the earliest Christians. Thus, when the Reformation settled down in an uneasy territorial and polemical map of Europe, the disciplinary activities of the enemies of the reformers came to appear as a continuation of the persecutions of the earliest Roman emperors. Catholic writers counter-attacked by denying both the accuracy of Protestant reports and the quality of devotion that the Protestant martyrs displayed; moreover, Catholics did not hesitate to define Catholics prosecuted and executed by Protestant ecclesiastical or civil authorities as true martyrs. Thus, alongside various kinds of theological and personal polemic, a war of martyrologies commenced.

Martyrologies, whether Catholic or Protestant, reflected the increasing recognition on both sides of the depth of religious conviction in the middle and lower social orders of the population. Because they were graphic and often lurid, often including illustrations, martyrologies on both sides became an immensely popular means of disseminating doctrine and example among a wide range of readers. Often, martyrologies were read and circulated more widely than doctrinal literature and thus constituted part of the broad literature of Reformation polemic, focusing particularly upon the coercive means employed to oppose religious belief.

The earliest Protestant accounts of the new martyrs appeared in Germany and England in the 1520s and 1530s. These were accounts of individual sufferings: Martin Luther's own *The Burning of Brother Henry in Dithmarschen* in 1525, and William Tyndale's *Examination of Thorpe and Oldcastle* in 1535. The appearance of Ludwig Rabus' *Stories of God's Martyrs* of 1552 treated in its first edition only the Christian martyrs of antiquity, but in subsequent editions treated contemporary Protestant martyrs and their persecutors as well. The most substantial tradition of Protestant martyrology stemmed from Jean Crespin's *The History of the Martyrs* of 1554, and the Latin original of John Foxe's *Acts and Monuments* of 1559 and its first English edition of 1563. Crespin's martyrology begins with the martyrs of Christian antiquity and includes a number of executed medieval heretics—notably Jan Hus—as well as a considerable number of sixteenth-century victims of ecclesiastical courts.

Theological tracts, catechisms, and propaganda were the chief media for the communication of complex ideas during the Reformation, but the martyrologies communicated feelings of solidarity and outrage. Read privately or domestically, they and their illustrations sustained individual and small community convictions. Used as material for sermons, they sustained the religious emotions and attitudes of larger communities. In the hands of the great warrior-poet Agrippa d'Aubigné (1522–1630) the theme of martyrology, in the epic poem *Les tragiques* (1577, published in 1616), became the great battle-cry against Rome, and the prophecy of a new age of religious virtue.

Martyrologies became a means of understanding and explaining the sixteenth century to people on each side of the confessional division. From the breakdown of religious and theological negotiations in the 1540s, the first outbreaks of the earliest stage of the wars of religion in the late 1540s, the events of the Council of Trent (1545–1563), and particularly the increasing fury of religious opposition, culminating in the Massacre of St. Bartholomew in 1572, both Catholics and Protestants came to regard themselves as living in an age not at all unlike the age of the earliest Christians under the pagan Roman emperors. In the words of Jean Crespin, the French Protestant martyrologist, modern times displayed "the conformity of the modern history of the martyrs with that of antiquity." As a component of the popular Reformation histories, the martyrologies established, for both Protestants and Catholics, a direct link in time with the earliest Church and its apostolic and evangelical truths.

Repressive legislation on both sides of the Reformation division, dramatic public punishments and executions, exile, and the loss of family and property helped to shape the self-perception of both Catholics and Protestants. The censorship and destruction of books often appeared to be a kind of martyrdom in itself, a martyrdom of the Word, that helped shape the awareness that religious opponents were not merely critics of ideas, but savage and relentless hounders of the true faith. Accusations of conspiracy, assassination plots, treason, and blasphemy came to be as characteristic of much sixteenth-century religious self-definition as theological and ecclesiological differences. Thus, the martyrological tradition contributed substantially to the shift from religious to political opposition that marks the late sixteenth and seventeenth centuries.

In 1563 the great English martyrologist John Foxe published the first English edition of his *Acts and Monuments of These Latter and Perilous Days*, a work that rivaled the English Bible in popularity and familiarity in England over the next two centuries. Foxe's work, popularly known as *The Book of Martyrs*, professed to be a Church history with martyrdom as its central theme. An opponent of religious persecution himself, Foxe worked especially hard to present graphic pictures of the acts of martyrdom, and he linked the persecutions of the sixteenth century not only with those of the pagan persecutions of antiquity, but with those of such more recent English victims as Wyclif and the Lollards and the Oxford martyrs.

Protestant Church history and martyrology were first fully developed in the work of Matthias Flaccius Illyricus (1520–1575), the greatest Protestant historical scholar of the sixteenth century. In 1556 Flaccius published his *Catalogue of Witnesses to the Truth*, in which the "hidden" Church of Luther and the early Calvin took on visibility and specificity, turning the Catholic attack on its head by claiming medieval heretics, not as "heretics of old," but precisely as continuing witnesses to the apostolicity and authenticity of the hidden church from the fourth century to the sixteenth.

Flaccius echoed these sentiments in the volumes of his vast history, the *Magdeburg Centuries* (1559) extending to the twelfth and thirteenth centuries, although the *Centuries* do not treat the inquisitors. The Apostolic origin of the medieval heretics was also asserted by Simon Goulart, the Calvinist continuator and expander of Jean Crespin's martyrology in 1582 and by the *History of the Reformed Churches of the Kingdom of France*, long attributed to Theodore Beza, in 1580. Here as elsewhere, the initial historical spadework of the Lutherans, culminating in the *Centuries*, was taken up and expanded by Calvinists during the second half of the century. The monumental erudition of the *Centuries*, the abundance of medieval texts that it drew upon and printed, and the intelligence and fierce antipapalism of its editors and authors, principally Flaccius, gave to Protestant historiography a solid base that heretofore had been lacking.

By the late sixteenth century the reformed confessions had identified themselves with a number of persecuted medieval heresies, and they identified both with apostolic Christianity. They also defined themselves as martyrs, and their predecessors as martyrs, identifying both also with the martyrs of the apostolic and evangelical ages. It remained for them to identify the agency of that martyrdom and to identify it with the persecuting agencies of the pagan Roman emperors in the first Christian centuries.

For Luther and other early reformers, the great enemy was the pope. Luther's version of history said far less about medieval heretics and their inquisitors than it did about the papal usurpation of imperial and ecclesiastical authority. But sixteenth-century Protestants also knew that they were persecuted in areas where the popes had no direct authority, and in Spain by an institution that appeared to have little connection with the pope and far more with the hated kings of Spain. From this perspective, the agency of persecution, rather than its ultimate authority, offered an effective target of Protestant hostility, and, as their knowledge of their own and the preceding century revealed, that agency was *The Inquisition*, and it was the instrument of the Dominican order.

Dominicans had long been the most vociferous and effective opponents of Luther and of Protestantism generally during the sixteenth century, rivalling the better-known Jesuits in this regard. As the first Protestant reports about the Spanish Inquisition made clear, Dominicans were also those who directed that institution. Although early Protestant thinkers did not particularly condemn St. Dominic and his order, after the mid-sixteenth century anti-Dominican feelings ran high, and the retrieval of medieval source materials indicated how closely the Dominicans had been associated with the inquisitions and particularly with the literature of heresiology, both in theological tracts and handbooks for inquisitors.

During the 1550s the first reports of the Spanish Inquisition's persecution of Protestants were brought to European attention by escaped Spaniards. Hoping to sway the policies of Philip II, a number of these accounts attacked, not the king or the pope, but those who staffed the Spanish Inquisitions, the Dominicans. The Dominicans were a "proud and ambitious sect" who had deceived the noble rulers of Spain into believing that Lutherans were as great a danger to Spanish Christianity as had been the *conversos*. Given power by the king, however, "they erected a new kind of Consistorie of an Inquisition, wherein the poor wretches, instead of better instructions, wherewith there was some hope to win them, should be robbed and spoiled of all their goods and possessions, and either put to the most cruel death, or suffer most intolerable torments by whip or otherwise." As deceivers of the king, the Dominicans could be painted as harshly as polemic required.

So could their founder. In Protestant historiography of the sixteenth century a kind of anti-cult of St. Dominic grew up. Dominic, "a man of fiery and impetuous temper," attacked the Albigenses and other "enemies of the church" with eloquence, the force of arms, the subtlety of his writings, and the "terrors of the inquisition, which owed its form to this violent and sanguinary priest." Just as contemporary Spanish Dominicans deluded Philip II, so the original Dominicans had deluded Pope Gregory IX, perverting his original tribunal into a unique instrument for furthering their own fanticism and greed.

The Roman Church, the Dominican Order, the inquisitions—these filled out the persecuting pattern in Protestant Church history, and they were depicted in history as they were perceived to be in the sixteenth century. The inquisitorial tribunals of different occasions and places slowly became *The Inquisition*, the instrument of the Dominicans and the pope, and now of the King of Spain.

The Spanish Inquisition and the Black Legend

The central role of Spain in sixteenth-century Europe and the identification of Spain with the strongest Catholic opposition to the Reformation frame the place of the Spanish Inquisition in the development of *The Inquisition*. The unification of the crowns of Castile and Aragón during the reigns of Ferdinand and Isabella brought a politically united Spain into the hands of their grandson, Charles V, who had also inherited the Netherlands from his Hapsburg ancestors and was elected Emperor of the Romans in 1519. The personal empire of Charles V made him the greatest ruler in Europe. Although Charles proceeded cautiously during the early stages of the Reformation, not wishing to appear to intrude upon the liberties of his most powerful subjects, his opposition grew stiffer during the 1520s when Protestant doctrines clearly made their way into the Netherlands and into Spain itself. When Charles finally took up arms against his Protestant princely opponents, his victory at Mühlberg in 1547 was the greatest threat the Reformation had had to face, and it offered an opportunity for religious and political opposition to him to coalesce.

The succession of Philip II to his father's territories and the Spanish throne (although not the imperial crown), augmented by the wealth of the Americas, placed an even more dedicated opponent of Protestantism on the most powerful throne in Europe. Spanish influence in Italy, the rivalry with Valois and Bourbon France, the wars of independence in the Netherlands, and the enterprise of the Armada against England generated great political and diplomatic opposition to his rule. His own internal support of the Inquisition and his public role as defender of Catholicism everywhere against Protestantism added a dimension of religious opposition that shaped a distinctive image of Spain throughout sixteenth-century Europe. As Philip wrote to his ambassador in Rome in 1566, "You may assure his holiness that rather than suffer the least damage to religion and the service of God, I would lose all my states and a hundred lives, if I had them; for I do not propose nor desire to be a ruler of heretics." Every step Philip II took vindicated this observation, and his rule placed Spain in such a doubly prominent role that anti-Spanish sentiment was revived. An image of Spain circulated through late sixteenth-century Europe, borne by means of political and religious propaganda that blackened the character of Spaniards and their ruler to such an extent that Spain became the symbol of all forces of repression, brutality, religious and political intolerance, and intellectual and artistic backwardness for the next four centuries.

Spaniards and Hispanophiles have termed this process and the image that resulted from it as "The Black Legend," *la leyenda negra*. Although the term is relatively recent, it has been widely adopted to describe the way in which Spain and the Spanish Inquisition were perceived throughout sixteenth century Europe. Every people, of course, has a Black Legend of its own, that is, a collection of unfavorable images that include ethnic criticism, exaggeration of cultural institutions or traits, and isolated events that are extracted from their original context and elevated to the typical. Such criticism of ethnic and other political collectives developed in medieval Europe, in the multi-ethnic and ethnically organized universities, in large assemblies such as church councils, and in the increasingly national character of warfare and war propaganda. It had been further developed by humanist thinkers, looking back at an idealized vision of Greek and Roman civilizations and freely criticizing the culture and character of contemporary societies, notably Spain and Germany, for their alleged descent from "barbarian" rather than Roman society. Although Spain was not the only target of such criticism, a number of circumstances during the fifteenth and sixteenth centuries greatly sharpened and intensified the character of anti-Spanish criticism.

During the fifteenth century, when Aragonese influence in Italy was especially strong, Italian criticism of Spanish soldiers, political administrators, and merchants in Italy reinforced humanist prejudices. Otherwise routine criticism of Spanish military conduct, unfair advantages seen to be given to Catalan merchants and administrators, and the local outrage at the military sacks of Prato in 1512 and of Rome itself in 1527, intensified anti-Spanish sentiment and increasingly took the form of identifying Spaniards, not with Christianity, but with Judaism and Islam. Since substantial numbers of Jews and *conversos* who fled Spain for Italy were often permitted to settle there, they were identified with Christian Spaniards, even, in the case of the Spanish pope Alexander VI (1496–1503), to the extent of calling the pope a "circumsised Marrano." In Italian anti-Spanish invective, the very Christian self-consciousness that had inspired much of the drive to purify the Spanish kingdoms, including the distinctive institution of the Spanish Inquisition, was regarded outside of Spain as a necessary cleansing, since all Spaniards were accused of having Moorish or Jewish ancestry. After 1492 the term Marrano was virtually identical in Italy with "Spaniard." If the Spanish Inquisition later turned its attention to Lutherans, that was because the Spaniards were naturally prone to Lutheranism as well. In 1547 when a fear arose in Naples that an Inquisition in the Spanish style was about to be established, the Neapolitans were insulted: *they* did not need an Inquisition—the Spaniards, however, did. During the first cycle of the sixteenth-century European wars of religion (1446–1552) that culminated in the victory at Mühlberg, which Protestants called the "Spanish Wars," this invective circulated widely throughout Europe.

First condemned for the impurity of their Christian faith, the Spaniards then came under fire for excess of zeal in defending Catholicism. Influenced by the political and religious policies of Spain, a common kind of ethnic invective became an eloquent and vicious form of description by character assassination. Thus when Bartolomé de las Casas wrote his criticism of certain governmental policies in the New World, his limited, specific purpose was ignored. His *Very Brief Relation of the Destruction of the Indies* of 1552 was circulated by anti-Spanish elements and used to demonstrate that Spanish policies toward the innocent natives in the New World were consistent with the Spanish character and policies that Europeans saw in the Old.

A comparable work to Las Casas' that included the Spanish Inquisition firmly in the context of anti-Spanish invective was A *Discovery and Plaine Declaration of Sundry Subtill Practices of the Holy Inquisition of Spain*, which appeared in Latin in Heidelberg in 1567, attributed to "Reginaldus Gonsalvius Montanus," a purported Protestant victim of the Spanish Inquisition and a native Spaniard. Within a year Montanus' treatise was translated into English, French, Dutch, and German. It was reprinted, excerpted, and retranslated for the next two centuries. *The Discovery and Plaine Declaration* is brief, intelligently designed, and written in a lively and engaging style. Its widespread appeal was based initially on its depiction of the Spanish Inquisition, but its literary merits certainly contributed to making it *the* best known and most influential text on the subject.

The name "Reginaldus Gonsalvius Montanus" has long been known to have been a pseudonym, and the work has periodically been credited to one or another of a known group of Spanish Protestant exiles in the Netherlands. Recent scholarship, however, has identified one such figure, Antonio del Corro, as the real author. Del Corro was a Spaniard from the monastery of San Isidoro in Seville, resident in the Netherlands and writing between 1563 and 1566. Del Corro was a theologian, a close relative of an inquisitor, and a ferocious enemy of the Spanish Inquisition in its campaign to destroy Protestantism.

Montanus has several distinct aims in the treatise. He adopts the device of leading an imaginary victim through all stages of contact with the Inquisition in order to display its horrors effectively, by letting the reader substitute himself for the victim. The horrors once established, Montanus then bases upon them his own argument: that the Inquisition is a form of civil suicide, that it was properly constituted to carry out its initial godly purpose of persecuting false *conversos*, that it has been turned by the Dominicans away from its initial purpose into "a thing . . . burdenous to the world." It is widely unpopular in Spain, Montanus argues, and such unique practices as secrecy deceive the king into thinking that it is doing its proper task.

In his passage through the operations of the Inquisition, much of his information for which is generally accurate, Montanus consistently emphasizes the deviousness and trickery of the interrogation techniques, the variety of horrors in its torture chambers, and the appalling behavior

of its familiars, prison keepers, and torturers. He impugns the derelict
defense counsels permitted the prisoners, and the unsuitability of the
witnesses whose testimony the Inquisition routinely admits. Montanus
concludes the work with twelve case histories, all of Lutherans condemned
by the Inquisition, which he describes as a contribution to martyrology,
a "praise of the pious martyrs of Christ." His martyrology circulated
even more widely than the rest of his work, often simply quoted verbatim
in later collections, as it was in Joachim Beringer's *Hispanicae Inquisitionis
& carnificinae Secretiora* of 1611, and in Michael Geddes' *Spanish Protestant Martyrology* of 1714. From Geddes' text, Montanus' martyrology
was excerpted, again verbatim, in the ecclesiastical History by J. L.
Mosheim of 1726, probably the best known and most widely read Lutheran
church history of the eighteenth and early nineteenth centuries.

Part of Montanus' appeal lay in the base of accuracy upon which he
erected an otherwise extremely misleading description of the Inquisition
to an audience prepared to believe the worst. Taking some of the most
extreme of Inquisition practices as the norm, Montanus portrays every
victim of the Inquisition as innocent, every Inquisition official as venal
and deceitful, every step in its procedure as a violation of natural and
rational law, and its entire operation functioning without the knowledge
of Philip II, who is the creature of the inquisitors. Such a description
paralleled the widely-circulating charges of Las Casas and fitted perfectly
the character of Spain and the Inquisition that had emerged over the
preceding century.

In such a picture other states, Protestant and Catholic alike, found a
standard by which to measure their own experiences and institutions of
religious persecution. Although England, France, and the Netherlands
had very different histories during the sixteenth century, they all faced
the problem of religious dissent and its repression. Although several of
these states had—and the others came very close to having—inquisitions,
the widely circulating image of the Spanish Inquisition and its association
with the evils of Spanish culture and Spanish power permitted them to
distance themselves from it, criticize it as an embodiment of anti-Chris-
tianity, and associate it either with Catholic opposition to true religion
or, in the case of France, with Spanish and papal opposition to the
kingdom of France.

Preparing to Read Montanus: Religious
Persecution in England and France

When Thomas Skinner published his English translation of Montanus
in 1568, England's own recent experience of a Catholic inquisition,

and its deteriorating relations with Spain, made it an ideal and extremely receptive audience to the work and the image of the Spanish Inquisition it contained. With the accession of Elizabeth I to the English throne in 1559, the shifting frontiers of the Reformation in recent English history appeared finally to have stabilized. But the history of the Reformation in England from 1519 to 1559 had raised many examples of religious persecution and had created a distinct dislike on the part of the English for powerful ecclesiastical courts as well as for persecution of religion for its own sake. The rigors of Henry VIII's original reformation, the turn toward Lutheranism under Edward VI, the persecutions of Protestants by Mary Tudor in 1555–1556, and the ongoing problem of a Catholic minority in Elizabethan England all combined to sharpen the attitudes of the English toward heresy, the persecution of religious belief, and the dangers posed by Rome and Spain.

Between 1525 and 1534 Henry VIII, a patron of learning and theology and a bitter enemy of Lutheranism, removed the Church of England from papal obedience and made himself the head of the English Church. Such a state reformation brought ecclesiastical and political notions of crime much closer together, since both were considered ultimately to have been directed at the same person. The Henrician Reformation changed the direction of Henry's earlier attacks on Lutheranism within the kingdom. From 1529 to 1533, as Lutheran doctrines spread vigorously in England, Henry's Chancellor, Sir Thomas More, urged stronger application of those heresy statutes that had been features of English law since the late fourteenth century. Virulently anti-Lutheran himself, More knew a considerable amount of Roman and canon law as well as English common law, and vigorously defended the autonomy of ecclesiastical courts in the pursuit of the new heresy of Lutheranism. Probably no Chancellor of England since Archbishop Arundel had as powerful a sense of the legitimacy of the structures of ecclesiastical and temporal jurisdiction in matters of religious deviance, nor a greater willingness to invoke their power. During his brief Chancellorship, More turned out to be the greatest—and last—defender of the late medieval English system of ecclesiastical discipline. Several scholars have suggested that his plans, if they had been carried out, would have developed that system into an English Inquisition. Protestant critics of More accused him of precisely such a plan. In 1530 Robert Redman of London printed an early Lollard tract which contained a pointed warning about the dangers of ecclesiastical tribunals in matters of dissent:

> The third assault of Antichrist is the Inquisition, as the prophet says, that Antichrist inquires, searches, and harkens where he may find

any man or women who writes, learns, reads, or studies God's law in
their mother tongue. . . .

What defeated More—and, by extension, the fourteenth- and fifteenth-
century judicial system he defended—were the matter of Henry's divorce
and remarriage, and the attacks upon the autonomy of ecclesiastical
jurisdiction made in the name of state (or at least royal) sovereignty
both by legal thinkers and Protestant polemicists. The chief legal opponent
of More's views was Christopher St. German (d. after 1540), who published the enormously influential dialogues between *Doctor and Student*
in 1528 and 1530, reprinted with *New Additions* in 1531. St. German
has been described as the earliest legal theorist of Henrician state sovereignty. One of St. German's most emphatic points was that there was
widespread grievance by the laity against the clergy and that this had
been caused by the clergy's usurpation of rights that belonged to the
common law. More had argued in favor of the correctness of the procedure
in ecclesiastical trials against heretics, reaffirming the right of arrest on
the basis of *fama*, and had even defended the use of secret testimony,
that is, testimony by witnesses whose identity is kept secret from the
accused. It would not be too much to say that between 1529 and 1532,
More's sense of the dangers posed by heresy and his fidelity to the universal
principles of ecclesiastical law might have come very close to establishing
at least a much stronger episcopal inquisition in England, and perhaps
an inquisition of considerably greater presence and power.

With the Act of Supremacy of 1534 and its subsequent reforming
legislation, More's arguments failed and St. German's won out. The
Heresy Act of 1534 swept all previous heresy laws from the books of
England, including now the books of canon law as well. Besides St.
German's juridical indictment of ecclesiastical authority in heresy cases
and of the power of Rome as well, other critics assailed ecclesiastical
jurisdiction on theological grounds. They were led by William Tyndale
(1494–1536), and the criticisms they made ran up to and included the
mighty work of John Foxe.

Tyndale's English translation of the Bible in 1526 was quickly followed
by other treatises on the reformed religion in England, notably *The
Obedience of a Christian Man* (1528). In this and other works, Tyndale
initiated the use of history as a weapon of religious controversy. Violently
anti-clerical, he identified all the clergy of his own day with the "clergy"
who killed Christ and with the later clergy of Rome who turned emperors
and kings into their puppets, "mere names and shadows of power."
Tyndale's asertion that the clergy of any kingdom were servants of a

foreign power and therefore constituted a separate state within a state was echoed in later English constitutional literature.

Tyndale was followed even more vigorously by Robert Barnes (1495–1540), a historical polemicist who insisted on the supremacy of king over clergy. Barnes himself had faced ecclesiastical judges in the matter of heresy in 1526, and he denounced the clergy's assertion that "we proceed after another form of law," to justify their use of secret accusers and witnesses, their refusal to clarify charges of heresy, and their use of judicial trickery.

From the first work of the Reformation Parliament of 1529, the charges against the clergy focus on their independence of the king and their jurisdictional violations: the widespread fear of heresy, the clergy's severity in punishing heresy, the making of laws by the clergy without consulting the laity or the king, and the irregular form of heresy trials. As the Reformation Parliament rolled on, it transformed by statute the legal status of the English clergy: with the *Submission of the Clergy,* incorporated into statute in 1534, the king's appointment of a special commission to investigate ecclesiastical laws, and the repeal of *De haeretico comburendo* and other anti-heresy legislation in 1534, the stage was set for a complete revision of canon law in England, a procedure that culminated in the *Reformatio Legum Ecclesiasticarum* in 1571. Between 1534 and 1571 a series of ordinances and statutes refined the procedures relating to religious uniformity in England. Except for the brief reaction under Mary Tudor (1553–1558), the result of these acts was to strengthen the hand of common law courts in cases of heresy and greatly to reduce the authority of ecclesiastical courts. Thus, from 1534 to 1553, the English Reformation identified itself with the problems of ecclesiastical jurisdiction and identified ecclesiastical jurisdiction in particular as a seditious instrument of hated Rome. In the battle of history and juridical polemic, the case made by Thomas More was not only lost, but arguments like More's became for most English people the very identifying mark of the Catholic Church. The work of Tyndale, Barnes, and St. German succeeded; questions of theology took a remote second in English consciousness: the horrors of ecclesiastical authority were first.

The short reign of Edward VI (1547–1553) marked a substantial turning of England toward continental Protestantism and saw a wide circulation of Protestant literature in England. The judicial reforms of Henry VIII meant that a king who did not wish Protestants persecuted could stay the activities of the common law courts. The Prayerbook of 1552, the Second Act of Uniformity of the same year, and the Forty-Two Articles of 1553 appeared to be heading England into the continental Protestant camp and well away from the dangers that had been posed by More and the ecclesiastical courts a few decades before.

But the accession of Mary Tudor (1553–1558) threatened to return England once more to ecclesiastical heresy tribunals, or worse. Although Mary proceeded cautiously at first, following the advice of Charles V, she married Philip II in 1554, and from that year on, her actions became more determined and raised even greater fears about their consequences. Mary invited Reginald Pole to return to England from his exile in Italy, and Pole returned as a cardinal legate whose mission was to rejoin England to the Church of Rome. In 1554 the Oxford Disputations were deliberately staged to discredit the Edwardian clergy, and in November of the same year Parliament, at the Queen's direction, began systematically to repeal Henry VIII's legislation concerning ecclesiastical jurisdiction and to replace it with the old statutory crime of heresy. During that session, Parliament revived "in full force, strength, and effect, to all intents, constructions, and purposes forever" the old heresy statutes of Richard II (1382), *De haeretico comburendo* (1401), and the heresy statute of Henry V (1414), all such legislation to become law on January 20, 1555. A month after the new legislation became effective, two Edwardian clerics were executed for heresy under the new statutes.

Although Philip II and his Spanish clerical advisers (which included the well-known heresiologist Alfonso de Castro) remained out of prominence in these steps, the substantial criminal Marian legislation against heresy and Mary's willingness to use it far more consistently than her predecessors marked a new wave of persecutions. Prelates like Edmund Bonner and Stephen Gardiner undertook to restore the older forms of ecclesiastical trials, although ecclesiastical courts now had to turn over determined heretics to the secular arm for execution. The trial and execution of Thomas Cranmer in 1556 even involved an investigation of Cranmer's case by the Roman Inquisition. Not by accident did Protestant writers insist that Mary and Pole were creating an English Inquisition, linking it to those of Rome and Spain.

When John Foxe added descriptions of the trials and executions of the Oxford martyrs—Cranmer, Hooper, Latimer, and Ridley—to his *Book of Martyrs*, he was explicit as to the nature of the tribunals that had tried them. Pole was technically a legate charged with the "inquisition of heretical depravity," the technical *inquisitio hereticae pravitatis* of inquisitorial terminology. Foxe's long and vitriolic description of the life and character of Stephen Gardiner, Bishop of Winchester, the "bloody bishop," is a complex and formidable portrait of an inquisitor, as are Foxe's meditations on the career and death of Mary Tudor.

Outside England, the steps taken by Mary and Pole were also recognized as erecting a form of inquisition. In 1554 there was published in London the *Articles to be inquired of the general visitation of . . . the Bishop of London*, a handbook of questions concerning religious belief that were to be used in episcopal visitations, and attributed to Edmund Bonner, Mary's Bishop of London. A year later the work was translated into Latin and German under the changed title, *A New Inquisition of heretical depravity in the kingdom of England . . . so that pious people will know how salutary it is, and how greatly it is to be desired to erect similar Inquisitions in other kingdoms.*

From the accession of Elizabeth I in 1559, under whatever terms a religious settlement was to be reached, the image of ecclesiastical courts endured in England: the contrast between their hated procedures and those of the by now familiar common law courts, their indelible link to Spain and Rome, and their identification with the Inquisitions of those two countries. The 1563 edition of Foxe's *Book of Martyrs* proclaimed it, and the publication of the English translation of Montanus invited English readers to see in the Spanish Inquisition exactly what they had recently seen in that of Mary Tudor and Cardinal Pole.

Montanus' English translator, Thomas Skinner, knew very well the political and religious sensibilities of his likely readers, but he wanted to make sure that none of them missed the point—not the point of Montanus, whose politics are restricted to some advice for the king of Spain, but the point of how English readers should react to Montanus. Skinner's preface, "The Translator to the Reader," pointedly observes:

> Surely, the dangerous practices and most horrible executions of the Spanish Inquisition declared in this boke, which now is brought with fire and sword into the low countries, the sodaine imprisonment of honest men without process of lawe, the pitifull wandring in exile and poverty of personages sometimes rich and welthy, the wives hanging on their husbands shoulders, and the pore banished infants on their mothers brests, the monstrous racking of men without order of lawe, the villanous and shameless tormenting of naked women beyond all humanitie, their miserable deaths without pity or mercy, the most reproachfull triumphing of the popish Sinagoge over Christians . . . the conquering of subiects as though they were enemies, the unsatiable spoyling of mennes goodes to fill the slender quarels picked against Kingdoms and Nations, and all this to hoist up a pield polling priest above all power and authoritie that is on earth. . . . For who is so ignoraunt of the holy Complote and Conspiracie agreed on by the Pope and his Champions for the execution of the counsell of Trent, and the general establishing of the Inquisition? Behold the attempts

in Scotland, the proceding in Fraunce, the executions in Flaunders, and if we Englishmen have one of the last partes, let us be sure as in Tragedies, the last partes and Actes be most dolefull, for we never knew yet what persecution meant in comparison, to that is ment and threatens us now.

The Elizabethan religious settlement at first genuinely did attempt to dampen religious persecution and to remove the worst consequences of Mary Tudor's legislation by repealing it and by discrediting those who had made it. But during the 1570s the Elizabethan courts and government faced a revival of Catholic opinion, triggered by the papal bull of deposition in 1570. To counter this, the Elizabethan government welcomed the linking of Catholicism with rebellion and loyalty to Philip II of Spain. From 1570 on, the Elizabethan government's handling of Catholics suspected to be traitors grew more rigorous. John Felton, who posted a copy of the bull *Regnans in excelsis* in London, was arrested and tortured in order to reveal the names of his accomplices; John Story, a Catholic jurist in the Spanish Netherlands, was kidnapped, returned to England, tortured, and accused of treason and conspiracy and executed. Legislation of 1571 established a number of kinds of religious dissent as treason, and the presence of Catholic missionary priests in England in ever greater numbers strongly influenced both governmental and Anglican measures, threatened as the latter were by a growing Puritan sentiment as well. Although the government of Elizabeth I instituted no formal inquisition and acted against individuals with specific charges, the use of torture to extract additional information and evidence from accused rebels increased, as is seen in the cases of Felton and Story, as well as in the examination and trial of Edmund Campion in 1581. The government continued to insist that it was trying rebels, not religious dissenters, but the increasing pressures from Spain and Rome sustained the search for and trial and execution of Catholics until the reign of James I.

Against Puritanism too, the English church and government proceeded in manners that were often, at least in appearance, extra-legal. The career of John Whitgift as Archbishop of Canterbury (1583–1604) witnessed the establishment of an interrogation system similar to an inquisition in the High Commission's procedures to seek out dissenters. Suspects were put on oath *ex officio*, which committed them to truthful answers before they knew which questions were to be asked, and the entire procedure once again raised questions about the power of the ecclesiastical courts in regard to the common law courts that had troubled England since the early part of the century. Even Burghley, who was not reluctant to torture suspected traitors, complained to Whitgift that the Spanish

Inquisition "use not so many questions to comprehend and trap their preys" as did the High Commission.

Under Richard Topcliffe, an official of the Queen, torture appears to have been used regularly in order to extract information, chiefly from accused Catholics, and always on the charges of treason, rather than religious dissent. Topcliffe and his associates appear to have used the rack regularly, but there was a variety of other instruments and procedures as well, several of them listed in the account of Edward Rishton, himself a victim of Topcliffe's inquiries and methods:

> Of the means or instruments of torture employed in the Tower, there are seven different kinds. The first is the Pit, a subterraneous cave, twenty feet deep, and entirely without light.
> The second is a cell, or dungeon, so small as to be incapable of admitting a person in erect posture: from its effect on its inmates it has received the name of "Little Ease."
> The third is the rack, on which, by means of wooden rollers and other machinery, the limbs of the sufferer are drawn in opposite directions.
> The fourth, I believe from the inventor, is called "The Scavenger's Daughter." It consists of an iron ring, which brings the head, feet, and hands together, until they form a circle.
> The fifth is the iron gauntlet, which encloses the hand with the most excrutiating pain.
> The sixth consists of chains, or manacles, attached to the arms; and
> The seventh, of fetters, by which the feet are confined.

Although religious persecution did not end in England with Mary Tudor's death, it was never to be called Inquisition. To the English, Inquisition was exclusively Spanish or Roman. Nothing that English judges might do to Englishmen of different religious persuasions could imaginably be considered as Inquisition; anyone who doubted this had only to read Montanus.

Like Henry VIII, Francis I of France (1515–1547) began his reign as a patron of letters and the arts, and of some of the learned humanistic reform movements in religion. When the teachings of Luther first appeared in France in 1519 they circulated widely and appealed in many respects to religious reformers and to intellectuals. When the faculty of theology at the University of Paris condemned Luther's teachings in 1521, the *Parlement* of Paris followed suit by prohibiting the printing of religious books in France without the consent of the faculty of theology. Although the king was willing and able to protect individuals when their views seemed to him orthodox, the growing scale of Protestantism

in France and the assault on a number of doctrines that Francis I held
to be absolutely essential to religious orthodoxy—notably the doctrine
of the Eucharist—diminished the king's role over the next several decades
and heightened that of *parlement* and the faculty of theology at Paris.
The king himself appears to have followed the custom in France since
the late thirteenth century of appointing an inquisitor-general from the
Dominican Order. In 1536 he appointed Mathieu Ory to succeed Valen-
tin Lievin to that office, and Lievin himself had been consulted by the
faculty of theology of Paris in a number of cases.

Fear of heresy among the clergy—who were legally immune from
other forms of prosecution—prompted the regent Louise de Savoy to
petition Pope Clement VIII in 1525 for permission to appoint inquisitors
who might proceed against such clergy. Clement's bull not only concurred
with the regent's request, but also directed that the *parlements* might
force bishops to accept their own nominees as inquisitors of heretical
depravity. In the same year the *Parlement* of Paris had appointed a
special commission consisting of two of its own members and two doctors
of theology to prosecute heretics, the commission to be legally empaneled
and deputed by the Bishop of Paris. The alliance between the *parlement*
and the faculty of theology in Paris, and, it must be assumed, the Dominican Order and the Dominican inquisitor-general, constituted the structure
of prosecution of heresy in France before 1530.

In 1527, Francis I attempted to take greater control over the process
of maintaining religious uniformity within the kingdom, first establishing
an episcopal inquisition, which produced a formidable body of legal
and doctrinal legislation, as well as sixteen articles of faith and forty
articles of conduct, which has been termed "probably the first serious
attempt, before the Council of Trent, to define heresy." In 1530 Francis
I ordered all secular judicial officials in the kingdom to participate with
the inquisitors in extirpating heresy; the results of his order are evident
not only in Paris, but in Languedoc as well. Equally stiff procedures
and punishments were directed in 1535 at circulating and possessing
heretical literature, as well as at those who sheltered heretics. In 1540
the *parlement* formally declared heresy to be the secular crime of sedition
and treason as well as an ecclesiastical crime.

The reign of Henri II (1547–1559) witnessed the brief use of the
special court, the *chambre ardente*, for the handling of heresy cases.
But substantial disagreement between the king and the *parlement* over
competent jurisdiction in heresy cases continued well into the reign.
In the edict of Châteaubriant of 1551, Henri II extended to other secular
magistrates outside of members of the *parlement* the right to try heresy

cases without appeal, and to reward informers, to declare heretics ineligible for certain public offices, and to pursue heretical literature and its owners. Several years later a royal edict determined that the houses of convicted heretics were to be destroyed.

In 1555, Henri II proposed a much more comprehensive plan of establishing an Inquisition in France. The measure, which the *parlement* rejected, was designed to be tougher and more comprehensive than the legislation that had recently governed both secular and ecclesiastical courts; the secular judicial apparatus was to have been reduced to the status of a servant and executioner only. With the failure of this proposal, Henri II communicated to the pope in 1557 his request that a papal inquisition be established in France. In the same year the pope appointed the cardinals Bourbon, Lorraine, and Chatillon as inquisitors-general for all of France, with the power to delegate their inquisitorial authority to persons of proven orthodoxy and reliability.

In 1558, however, the new papal inquisition became a dead letter because of the resistance of the *parlement*. Based partly on its own concern for the excessive juridical powers of the papacy within the kingdom of France, *parlement* triumphed over the desires of the king. With the sudden and unexpected death of Henry II in 1559, the first phase of the battle against heresy in France came to an end.

The minority of Francis II (1559–1560), and that of Charles IX (1560–1574), and the vast difficulties facing the queen mother Catherine de Medici, effectively postponed further direct institutional attack on heresy and any further establishment of inquisitorial institutions other than those that already existed in French law. The problem was not fought out in the savage rivalry between Protestant and Catholic factions at the French court and in the kingdom itself. A royal edict of 1560 rescinded many of the provisions made after 1530, restoring judicial competence in heresy cases to the clergy, and emphasizing that it was chiefly the ostensible, public manifestations of religious heterogeneity that now concerned secular judges and the crown.

From 1562, a series of royal edicts began to lay the groundwork for a system of limited religious freedom in the kingdom of France, a process that culminated in the Edict of Nantes in 1598. Between these dates, the events of the wars of religion, the St. Bartholomew massacre of 1572, and the political divisions following confessional lines within France turned the original problem of doctrinal differences into a question of politics, and in the new arena, in spite of Catholic appeals to urgency, the establishment of an inquisition became less and less likely. Although the royal family and a substantial part of the nobility remained Catholic, the civil wars that tore France from 1562 to 1598 clearly demonstrated that varying combinations of religious sentiment and political interest dictated the political and confessional climate. Other strong voices urged that at least outward tranquility in religious matters might be established by a judicious government. Although the political factionalism that directed the wars of religion in France lasted for more than another decade, the slow movement toward separating religious and political differences quickened markedly in the third quarter of the sixteenth century.

Thus, when Montanus was published in French in 1568, the most distinctive movements toward a papal inquisition, a parlementary inquisition, or a royal inquisition had all been very recently tried, and all had failed. France was already on an irregular path to rough forms of religious toleration, but everyone remembered the ferocity of persecutions within their own lifetime, and the old rivalry between France and Spain made the absence of an inquisition in France one of the distinguishing features between the two kingdoms. Although France had arrived at 1568 by a very different route from England, the publication of Montanus encountered a similarly receptive audience, one that made an identical response.

The Netherlands Revolt and the Spanish Inquisition

In spite of the growing concerns in France and England in the 1550s over the question of inquisitorial prosecution of religious dissent, best expressed in Thomas Skinner's operatic and prophetic preface to his translation of Montanus, the greatest step in the invention of *The Inquisition* took place in the Netherlands between 1548 and the outbreak of the Dutch revolt in 1565–1568. In no other part of western Europe, with the possible exception of France, was the printing press and propaganda turned to the service of political reform, with the inquisition as a major focus, on such a wide scale and with comparably devastating effects.

The position of the Netherlands in regard to Spain was the result of a series of complex dynastic and political events that had occurred from the mid-fourteenth to the mid-sixteenth centuries. In 1363 King John II of France conferred the Duchy of Burgundy on his son Philip the Bold, who added Flanders to that legacy in 1384. Between 1384 and 1477, Burgundy and the Netherlands coalesced into "The Great Duchy of the West," an ambitious, wealthy, and powerful state that was dismembered eagerly by a number of powers after the death of Duke Charles the Rash in 1477. Part of Burgundy went to the French crown, but the imperial part of the Duchy, Franche-Comté and the Netherlands, came into the house of Hapsburg and descended by inheritance to Charles V, who also inherited Castile and Aragón and was elected Emperor in 1519. Charles himself added several northern and eastern territories to his vast empire early in the sixteenth century. Technically and legally, each of the provinces of the Netherlands was held personally by Charles, and each had its own customs, governmental structures, laws, and privileges. In 1548 and 1549 Charles V decreased the ties between the Netherlands and the Empire and increased and tightened those between the Netherlands and the dynasty of Hapsburg, thus tying the Netherlands as closely to his dynasty as was Spain. As "The Burgundian Circle" it was a wealthy and crucial part of Charles' personal empire.

When the king himself was not present in the Netherlands, royal interests were the concern of the regent, usually a member of the royal family. The regents of Charles' reign—Margaret of Savoy (1519–1530) and Mary of Hungary (1531–1555)—found that ruling the Netherlands meant balancing the needs and claims of the royal ruler against the local privileges and outlooks of the provinces. They found this to be true in many areas of Netherlands life, but in none as consequentially as in matters of religious uniformity.

From the introduction of Lutheran ideas into the Netherlands, at about the same time as they appeared in France and England, that is between 1519 and 1521, Charles V wished to have no such troubles in his Netherlands as he found on his hands in Germany. In 1520 he began to issue the first in a series of laws, called *ordonnances, plakkaten,* or *placards*—the standard means in the Netherlands for conveying the ruler's will to his subjects—dealing with problems of religious uniformity. In 1521 a *plakkat* banned Luther's books; in 1522 another prohibited the printing or reading of Lutheran literature. According to Netherlands law, only in certain specific instances could the placard of the ruler override local custom and tradition. In the case of the placards, a number of provinces, initially Holland, protested their validity, not out of particular sympathy with Lutheranism nor out of any enhanced idea of freedom of the press, but because they had seemed to violate local provincial privileges. This reaction became consistent from the 1520s on.

Charles V grew adamantly anti-Lutheran during this period, and he issued progressively harsher laws in the Netherlands. In 1522, he instituted an extraordinary tribunal designed as a state inquisition, intended to parallel the already-existing episcopal inquisitions. As had been the case with the validity of the placards, the question of a central royal tribunal that was empowered to summon and judge residents of different provinces also seemed to many of the towns and the nobility a violation of local privilege. In 1529 Charles instituted the death penalty for conviction of heresy, and in 1530 he reorganized the magistracy of the Netherlands. A year later he denounced the leniency of the Netherlands judiciary in heresy cases.

From 1531 on, the ruler's severity grew stronger, and tensions between the central government in Brussels and the provincial estates grew worse. The governmental reorganization of 1531 created a series of royal councils through which the regent governed, including a Secret Council with responsibility over internal affairs and religious dissent. Although these offices were staffed by the local nobility, provincial resistance continued. A letter written in the Netherlands in 1533 mentions the possibility and desirability of erecting an "inquisition in the Spanish Manner" in the Netherlands. Thus, with the problem of placards versus local privileges, royal tribunals versus local tribunals, and the prospect (however frequently denied by Charles V and Philip II) of "an inquisition in the Spanish manner," the three basic features of Netherlands' resistance were in place by 1533.

In spite of the power of Charles' government and its strong support against Protestantism among the different provinces, Mary of Hungary was constantly under pressure to ameliorate the harshest laws and their uniform application in local areas. From 1534 on, the increasing size of the dissenting population became a common matter of discussion and apprehension. There is some evidence that those who had the responsibility of applying the laws of the placards found this task repellent and encountered considerable resistance in carrying it out, particularly the procedure of torture and execution. Provincial councils continued to maintain their right to alter or ameliorate the literal terms of the royal placards. In spite of such mounting pressure, Charles held firm and insisted that the placards be applied to the letter of the law with full severity. Allied with and advised by the theologians of the University of Louvain and the Dominican enemies of Lutheranism, and strengthened by his military victory at Mühlberg in 1547, Charles V was prepared to make no concessions to his Netherlands subjects in the matter of heresy, regardless of Mary of Hungary's difficult position, and of intense local opposition.

It is in the light of Charles' policy in the Netherlands that one should consider the publication in 1548 at Wittenberg of a pamphlet entitled *On the Unchristian, tyrannical Inquisition that Persecutes Belief, Written from the Netherlands.* Charles V, the pamphlet claimed, planned to introduce the Spanish Inquisition into the Netherlands after his victory at Mühlberg. A second pamphlet without place or date of publication made a similar argument. Intermittently from 1548 on, the prospect of the invasion of the Netherlands by the Spanish Inquisition joined other irritants—the local resistance to the placards, the problem of central jurisdiction over heretics, and the prospect of a harsher system of tribunals than the Netherlands had ever seen—as part of the Netherlands' consciousness of Hapsburg policy.

The pamphlets of 1548 were not protesting the existing episcopal and state tribunals, but rather the *Spanish Inquisition*, already known and feared by that name in Charles' Netherlands possessions, probably from descriptions supplied by Spanish students, merchants, and religious exiles, the same community that produced Montanus. That the Spanish Inquisition possessed a character different from those institutions with which many Europeans were familiar had become common knowledge in Europe by 1548. In 1547 a similar rumor that Charles V was planning to introduce the Spanish Inquisition into Naples (he was not, but urged instead a form of the Roman Inquisition) had provoked riots in that city. The memory of the Neapolitan riots also lingered on throughout the sixteenth century and made its way into a number of accounts of the inquisitions from England to the Netherlands.

Yet the rumors persisted. Mary of Hungary had to deny them several times in the face of local complaints, and Charles V explicitly insisted that when the term "inquisition" was used in the Netherlands it referred only to the existing native institution. Only ill-disposed persons, wrote Charles, would use such a threat to disturb the people. Charles' Netherlands adviser Viglius concurred, affirming that although "it is suggested by several books that there is to be a new inquisition founded, which they call the Spanish Inquisition," this rumor is the work of malcontents.

Charles did, however, have in mind yet another reform of the existing Netherlands Inquisitions. In 1550 he instituted the Edict of Blood, which reformed the Netherlands Inquisitions again. In the same year the Lutheran printer Michael Lotter published a description of the operation of the new inquisition entitled *The Form of the Spanish Inquisition Introduced in lower Germany in the Year 1550*, which was prefaced by a "Letter from a certain pious man from a celebrated city in lower Germany, concerning the Spanish Inquisition." In 1558 there appeared the widely read *History of the State of the Low Countries and of the Religion of Spain*, published in French near Strasburg by Francesco de Enzinas, a Spanish Protestant exile. Enzinas' contribution to both the misapprehensions of the Spanish Inquisition and its threat to the Netherlands was substantial.

When Charles V resigned the rule of the Netherlands to his son Philip II in 1555 (he resigned the rule of Spain to Philip a year later), the religious conflicts of Europe underwent yet another major transformation. By 1555 it was clear that Protestants formed substantial parts of the population of most Catholic countries, that reunion among the confessions was unlikely, that Calvinism had begun to displace Lutheranism as the leader of Protestantism internationally, and that Catholic authorities had devised harsh steps in the prosecution of religious dissent. Moreover, the Council of Trent, which sat intermittently from 1545 to 1563, gave a new shape and clarity to Catholic orthodoxy.

One of the first acts undertaken by Philip II as the ruler of the Netherlands was to redesign the structure of ecclesiastical organization. In place of the few bishoprics controlled by metropolitan archbishops in France and Germany, Philip proposed the creation of fourteen new dioceses, all adequately funded by monastic revenues, divided into three native Archbishoprics, to be ruled by the Archbishop of Malines. In each of these new dioceses there would be two canons to serve as episcopal inquisitors. In 1559 Pope Paul IV issued the bull *Super universas* and other enabling legislation that confirmed Philip's changes. During this period Philip apparently had heard a renewal of the rumors about introducing the Spanish Inquisition, since his correspondence and that of his advisers repeatedly denies any such intention. The rumors persisted, nevertheless, partly out of resentment at the vigorous activity of the Inquisitor Peter Titelmans in Flanders during this period. Titelmans, like his predecessors Erard de la Marck and Corneille de Berghe, was an extremely energetic inquisitor, and his and their reputations may have led to Philip II's famous observation that the inquisition of the Netherlands was "much less merciful" than the Spanish Inquisition— *más sin misericordia.*

Although they ruled with far different styles than their predecessors, Philip II's regents in the Netherlands—Margaret of Parma (1559–1568), the Duke of Alva (1568–1573), Luis de Requesens (1573–1576), Don Juan of Austria (1576–1578), and Alexander Farnese (1578–1592)—faced the same problems, which became more pressing after the outbreak of the revolt in 1565–1568. Local customs and privileges were again held up to centralizing royal policies and governors, as were those of Flanders and Brabant in 1562. In addition to Philip's increasingly centralized policies for ruling the Netherlands and the introduction of the new diocesan structure in 1561, he decided to apply the decrees of the Council of Trent to the Netherlands in 1564. The Council had emphasized, among many other things, the responsibilities of bishops for their flocks, and required formidable educational and moral qualifications for episcopal office. Such views alarmed not only many established clergy, but also the families that had hitherto routinely placed their children in high ecclesiastical office. Here too, royal decree encountered local resistance on dangerous ground.

Philip II left the Netherlands for Spain in 1559, never to return. He left the government in the hands of Margaret of Parma whose regency witnessed the transformation of scattered and specific opposition to royal policy into increasingly organized resistance. So strong was the opposition to Philip's choice of Granvelle as Archbishop of Malines and Margaret's chief councillor that Philip recalled Granvelle in 1563. Increasingly, the old attachments that had held much of the nobility to the royal cause weakened. The political structures of the Netherlands became less and less stable as opposition to the government mounted and organized, slowly overcoming old divisions within Netherlands society itself. Economic crises and the spread of Calvinism further eroded old structures, and among people of all social orders a marked willingness appeared in favor of religious toleration. When Philip II sent the Duke of Alva to strengthen the weakening royal government in the Netherlands in 1567, Margaret of Parma resigned her governorship to Alva and retired from political life. The crisis of 1565 was a mark of the failure of her own government and the signal for a turn in the political and religious course of the Netherlands.

Two sets of problems faced the regent of the Netherlands from the 1560s on: widespread concern over the legal procedures of the inquisitions and the emergence of a revolutionary mentality among its hitherto diverse political elements. In terms of legal procedure, one of the very few offenses which permitted the inhabitants of one province to be called out of it for trial elsewhere was the offense of treason. During Charles V's reign heresy had been declared to be treason against both God and the king, and on this principle the inquisitorial courts acted to seize those accused of heresy outside of the province of the accused. There were many debates in local councils over what was often perceived as violation of the *ius de non evocando*—the old right not to be summoned outside one's own province. A second problem arose over the confiscation of property. When a person was convicted of heresy outside his own province, the convicting court, and not the local tribunals, received the confiscated goods. This too, increased local resistance to central tribunals. Finally, the sheer size of the dissenting population meant that religious persecution increased popular resentment on all levels of society and laid the groundwork for ideas of religious toleration.

In 1565 the Count of Egmont was sent to Spain with a plea to Philip II to ameliorate the ferocity of the Netherlands Inquisition. Egmont returned to the Netherlands confident that he had won some concessions from Philip. But in October 1565 Philip wrote to Margaret of Parma his famous letter from the Segovia Woods denying any change of policy and urging her to support the Netherlands inquisitors even more vigorously than she had earlier:

> For as to the inquisition, my intention is that it should be carried out by the inquisitors, as they have done up to now and as it appertains to them by virtue of divine and human rights. This is nothing new, because this was always done in the days of the late emperor my seignior and father, whom God has in His glory, and by me.

The next six months saw a new wave of resentment at the activities of the inquisitors. In 1566 a Confederation of Nobles was formed in the Netherlands modeled after the Huguenot Confederation in contemporary France. In April, 1566, the nobles petitioned Margaret of Parma that,

> We are not in doubt, Madame, that whatever His Majesty formerly ordained and now again ordains regarding the inquisition and the strict observance of the edicts concerning religion, has some foundation and just title and is intended to continue all that the late emperor Charles—blessed be his memory—decreed with the best of intentions. Considering, however, that different times call for different policies, and that for several years past those edicts, even though not very rigorously executed, have caused most serious difficulties, His Majesty's recent refusal to mitigate the edicts in any way, and his strict orders to maintain the inquisition, and to execute the edicts in all their rigor, makes us fear that the present difficulties will undoubtedly increase.

The basis for the Compromise of 1566 that united the nobles of the Netherlands was their argument that Philip II had been deceived by self-serving advisers who persuaded the king to violate his investiture oath,

> and to disappoint the expectations he has always let us cherish, by not only failing to mitigate the edicts already in force, but by reinforcing them and even by introducing the inquisition iniquitous and against all divine and human laws, surpassing the worst barbarism ever practiced by tyrants, it will almost certainly lead to the dishonoring of God's name and to the utter ruin and desolation of these Netherlands.

In the same year Francis Junius urged Philip II to recognize Calvinism, lest libertinism and anarchy spread throughout his Netherlands domains, an argument echoed in a letter from William of Orange to Margaret of Parma.

In 1566 a series of iconoclastic riots rocked part of the Netherlands, sharply polarizing some Catholic and Calvinist attitudes, although Catholics and Calvinists remained allied in the Confederation of Nobles. Other Catholics, however, were drawn to the Duke of Alva, who arrived in the Netherlands in 1567. Those Catholics who remained opposed to the government of Philip II and Alva had to find some grounds for alliance with Calvinists, and they found those grounds in their common opposition to the inquisition.

Until around 1580, the opposition in the Netherlands portrayed Philip II as alternately a prisoner or a dupe of the Inquisition, and therefore the Inquisition bore the brunt of opposition propaganda. In 1556 a pamphlet entitled *Les Subtils Moyens par le Cardinal de Granvelle . . . pour instituer l'abhominable inquisition*, or "The Legend of the Inquisition," accused the Spanish Inquisition of having engineered the resignation of Charles V and of having duped Philip II. In the same year Philip Marnix of Ste. Aldegonde made even stronger accusations against the Inquisition: it was the Spanish inquisitors who had engineered the troubles in the Netherlands, thus compelling Philip II to take even more ruthless action against his loyal subjects.

It was in this atmosphere and this context that Montanus' tract was published at Heidelberg in 1567. Although it circulated more widely than many of its companion tracts, it shared many of their features, particularly in its exaggeration of the practices and ideas of the Spanish Inquisition and its assignment to the Inquisition of precisely the motives most feared in England and France as well as in the Netherlands.

In 1567, when Philip II began the centralization of all his domains on the model of Castile, and Alva instituted the Council of Blood in the Netherlands, the propaganda campaign against the Inquisition grew even more heated. In 1570 Netherlands religious refugees presented a petition to the Imperial Diet at Augsburg, with a long dissertation on the evils and wickedness of the Spanish Inquisition, drawn largely from Montanus, and the petition became extremely influential. An English translation, A *Defence and true declaration of the things lately done in the lowe countrey*, appeared in 1571. Although, like Montanus, the petition did not criticize the extermination of the Marranos and Moriscos by the Spanish Inquisition, it denounced venomously the Inquisition's prosecution of Protestant dissent. And like Marnix of Ste. Aldegonde, the petition also blamed the Spanish Inquisition for instigating the troubles in the Low Countries in order to force Philip II into more repressive acts. This text appears to have been one of the earliest to shift the attack toward the personality of Philip II, although it blames the Inquisition for having arranged the death of Philip's son Don Carlos by deceiving the king. The petition circulated nearly as widely as did the tract by Montanus. Both texts represent the fruits of the revolutionary policy of focusing upon the common enemy—the Inquisition—rather than trouble the fragile alliance of Calvinists and Catholics by focusing upon more immediately divisive issues.

Along with *Les subtils moyens*, Montanus, and the Augsburg Petition, several forged accounts of the Spanish Inquisition's alleged machinations for the destruction of the Netherlands also circulated in the 1570s. Some of them, added to Adam Henricpetri's history of the revolt of the Netherlands, were also translated into English in *A Tragicall Historie of the Troubles and Civile Warres of the Lowe Countries* in 1583. One forgery, composed shortly after 1570, purported to be a decree of the Spanish Inquisition dated 16 February, 1568 and confirmed by Philip II, according to which,

> the entire population of the Netherlands, young and old, men and women, Catholics and Protestants, were, with very few exceptions, declared guilty of lese-majesty and therefore held to have forfeited any right to either life or property.

The determination of this decree as a forgery was not made until the beginning of the twentieth century, and the forgery survived unquestioned in the work of all major historians of the Dutch Revolt and of the history and character of the Inquisition.

From 1572 on, the Revolt developed rapidly, and in a declaration of that year William of Orange indicated that one of his chief reasons for taking up arms was so that "The name of the inquisition shall be erased forever." In 1573 Alva was recalled, his reign of force and atrocity ended, and Luis de Requesens was sent to govern the Netherlands in his place. But in 1574, the States of Holland and Zeeland responded to a communication from Requesens in the same tone as earlier texts had attacked the Spanish government:

> It is clear to all the world that what has been done in these provinces these eight years on behalf of the king, and is still being done, is not the work of the king but of the inquisitors and the pope.

The identification of popery and Catholicism, Catholicism and Spain, Spain and the Inquisition, served the early stages of the Netherlands Revolt effectively. The frequency of the translation of a number of anti-Inquisition works into English in the 1570s and 1580s played upon English apprehensions about Catholicism and Spain and were directed at the one kingdom in which the revolutionaries hoped to find their natural ally. As the Calvinist character of the Revolution asserted itself, moreover, the role of the Inquisition as a focus of propaganda lessened, and the tyrannical character of Philip II replaced it. In 1581 the Act of Abjuration declared Philip II no longer king in the Netherlands, and certainly from that point on, the attack could shift to Philip's own tyrannical character and away from the Inquisition as the evil genius of the Netherlands troubles: the Inquisition became an instrument of Philip, not his evil genius.

But a myth had been created. Besides being the enemy of true religion, the Inquisition was now the subverter of political liberties, the power behind the policies of Philip II of Spain, and the natural enemy of all who loved liberty. It was depicted as such in one of the most influential documents to emerge from the Netherlands Revolt, the *Apologie* of William of Orange, written by the French Huguenot Pierre Loyseleur de Villiers, and published in 1581. It reflects the full Calvinist impact upon Netherlands political thought and discourse. In the *Apologie*, William of Orange describes how he himself warned Margaret of Parma,

> sometime in open counsell, and oftentimes elsewhere: all these their purposes tending to no other ende, but to set up the cruell Inquisition of Spaine, and to establishe the sayde Bishoppes, that they might serve, instede of Inquisitours, burners of mens bodies, and tyrauntes over their consciences.

With the *Apologie*, all of the anti-Inquisition propaganda of the past forty years was enshrined in a political document that validated the entire Dutch Revolt. Much of it had already circulated widely through England and France in translation, and some of its views had spread to Germany. The initial protestations of Philip II, Viglius, and Margaret of Parma were not written for circulation, and would have been believed if they had been. The propaganda added anecdote and accusation to its indictment of the Inquisition as the enemy of political liberty, filling out the portrait in Montanus in even greater detail.

And so the portrait of the Inquisition as the enemy of political liberty entered the mythology of the Inquisition, chiefly through the use of the Inquisition by the propagandists of the early stages of the Dutch Revolt, and it found sympathetic readers in the England of Elizabeth and in Huguenot France. It also entered Inquisition history, since the materials produced between 1548 and 1581 themselves became the sources of later historians, in the Netherlands as elsewhere. There is no better example of the process than *The History of the Reformation*

. . . *in and about the Low-Countries,* written by Gerhard Brandt (1626–1685), the first volume of which appeared in 1671; the work was translated into English by John Chamberlayne beginning in 1719. Brandt's history drew upon earlier histories of the Revolt, but it did not focus on the Revolt, but rather upon "The Reformation" and its activities in the Low Countries.

In Brandt's *History* all of the materials and ideas cited here appear, from the discussion of the proto-Protestantism of the twelfth- and thirteenth-century Albigenses and Waldenses and the origins of "The Inquisition," through the *plakkaten* of Charles V. "A Dreadful Picture of the Inquisition" in Book III describes the political outrage at the Inquisition's rejection of liberties, and the role of the Inquisition in forging the assertion of Netherlands liberties. From Brandt on, and not only in the Netherlands and England, in discussions of the rights of political resistance, the Inquisition was depicted as the universal oppressor of those who sought political liberty as well as true religion. In a series of specific circumstances and the articulation of local experience, the instruments of the Roman Church and the Spanish Empire merged into a single awesome and fearful institution: *The Inquisition.* Serving the diverse purposes of many sixteenth-century thinkers well, *the Inquisition* became a common object of reference in the debates over the problem of religious and civil toleration. Many people who found it difficult to agree with each other on many issues found it easy to agree upon *The Inquisition.* By the beginning of the seventeenth century, they had invented a new and potent idea for the western imagination.

Chapter Five

The Inquisition, the Toleration Debates, and the Enlightenment

The completion of the work of inventing *The Inquisition* fell to the many and varied proponents of religious toleration in the seventeenth century, and to the French *philosophes* in the eighteenth. By the end of the sixteenth century, thanks in part to a widespread and well-planned campaign, *The Inquisition* had become the most commonly recognized symbol of Catholic religious persecution and the dominance of Spain. It was an ideal complementary myth to that used in the self-definition of Protestants as persecuted martyrs, and it conveniently served both anti-Spanish and anti-Roman purposes as well. Although the increased number of Protestant states and the beginnings of limited religious toleration in some Catholic states diminished the direct experience of persecution and martyrdom in Protestant self-consciousness, the image of *The Inquisition* continued to remind even relatively safe Protestants of the past and present dimensions of religious persecution.

At the same time the problem of religious persecution itself took on new dimensions. A number of influential movements grew up that challenged the right of any state or confession to force the consciences of others or to inflict punishment upon others on the grounds of heterodox religious belief alone. In the wide-ranging debates on toleration in the seventeenth and eighteenth centuries, *The Inquisition* served a new purpose. It was held up by thinkers of very different confessional, political, and philosophical positions as the chief symbol of a religious intolerance that became more repugnant to larger numbers of people and states as the seventeenth century went on. As political and religious thinkers attacked religious persecution, *The Inquisition* became their target, grown into the instrument of persecution that caused political and economic disasters in the states that used it. From the debates on toleration, *The Inquisition* was taken up by French *philosophes* and made to stand for the worst of the religious evils of Christian Europe.

By the eighteenth century *The Inquisition* had become not only a sturdy myth, but an unshakeable one as well. None of the considerable changes that had occurred in Spanish or Roman society and government, no aspect of the declining activities and powers of the different inquisitions, no difference in the inquisitions of the eighteenth century as compared to the myth that had been shaped in the sixteenth and seventeenth centuries, had any effect whatsoever on the Enlightenment image. Not only had *The Inquisition* become larger and more terrible to those who were its victims, and more disastrous to the well-being of those who used it, but it became ahistorical as well.

The Inquisition *and the Toleration Debates*

Few modern ideas originated in so many different parts of the culture of sixteenth- and seventeenth-century Europe as that of religious toleration. A widely varied group of thinkers produced a number of initially unrelated arguments against religious persecution. The circumstances in which these arguments were first made were sometimes religious, sometimes philosophical, sometimes political, economic, and cultural. Only in the late seventeenth century did these arguments begin to be drawn together and assembled into a coherent and compelling case for toleration. In all of these, however, *The Inquisition* played a prominent role.

Among the earliest sources for arguments against religious persecution were a number of religious figures on the margins of the Catholic and Protestant worlds. In different ways, such thinkers as Erasmus, Sebastian Franck, Guillaume Postel, Jacobus Crellius, Lelio Sozzino, and Jacobus Acontius all argued that religion was essentially a relation between the individual and God and that its essence was moral rather than dogmatic. In their view, not outward assent, but the individual conscience was the only judge of religious truth, since religious truth was ultimately not naturally demonstrable nor legitimately coercible. Since disputing theologians argued about matters that were incapable of logical demonstration, their conclusions should never be made the basis for interfering with the consciences of others. Although such ideas would remain current, and flourish, for a long time, the intensity of religious conflict until the early seventeenth century prevented their wide acceptance, particularly by those in power. Until Europe had nearly exhausted itself in religious debate and confessional warfare, such doctrines were not generally adopted.

Beneath the level of articulate moral polemic, however, other attitudes also influenced the great movement of Irenicism. First, many Christians, whether Catholics or Protestants, became appalled at the civil disorder to which religious debates had led, and there was a widespread, if not as articulate, distaste for violence in the name of religion on the part of a growing number of people who were neither philosophers nor rulers. A second attitude was that of pointing out the anomalies of the persecuting policies of both Catholic and Protestant states. Martin Luther, for example, had argued that no magistrate had the right to punish anyone for false belief. But Luther also argued that the magistrate did have the obligation to punish blasphemy and that the propagation of false, especially Catholic (but also Anabaptist), doctrine constituted blasphemy. Philip Melancthon extended Luther's condemnation of Anabaptism to the point of arguing that even peaceful Anabaptists ought to be exterminated. Calvin drew the line at anti-Trinitarianism, allowing some leeway for varieties of religious belief but stopping short and permitting persecution at the doctrine of the Trinity, thereby excluding Unitarians from civil protection. Later in the sixteenth century, as England gradually removed heresy from its list of criminal (although not civil) offenses, it nevertheless continued to try religious dissenters, Catholics and Puritans alike, on the formal charges of sedition and treason. Although the anomalies of Catholic practice were widely publicized in the polemical literature, the very invention of *The Inquisition* constituted a perspective from which all forms of religious persecution could be criticized by Irenists, and confessional differences—even on the level of the ordinary Christian— could be held up as potentially destructive of civil peace and the spirit of Christian charity. Even the most extreme forms of the Irenist arguments—that toleration should be extended even to atheists and Jews— served to emphasize toleration among Christians, rather than marking a significant change toward broadmindedness on the part of European thinkers and rulers.

Such views justified condemnation of religious persecution, not on the grounds of sheer numbers of victims, but on the grounds that even a single case might violate the principle of non-persecution for religious reasons. In the case of Michael Servetus, the conduct of Calvin, who had echoed Luther and others in condemning the various inquisitions, created a furor whose consequences echoed for centuries. Servetus (1511–1553) was a Spanish physician, man of letters, and theologian whose views on the Trinity fell afoul of both Catholic and Calvinist authorities. Tried for heresy at Vienne in 1553 by an inquisitorial court, partly, it turns out, on the basis of evidence supplied with Calvin's approval, Servetus fled to Geneva later that year, where he was tried and condemned as a heretic and publicly burned at the stake, the first person ever to be burned as a heretic on the authority of a reformed church (Plate 14).

To many critics of the execution, Protestants and Catholics alike, the fate of Servetus appeared to deny the Protestant assertion that Protestants were the persecuted, not the persecutors. The case aroused great concern throughout Europe, giving Catholic critics a substantial opportunity to attack Protestants for their hypocrisy, but also raising among Protestants profound considerations about the role of religious belief and the state. No one addressed the case as eloquently as Sebastian Castellio, whose treatise *Concerning Heretics: Whether They are to be Persecuted and How they are to be Treated* appeared in 1554 and comprised a vast collection of excerpts from the Church Fathers to the present opposing the prosecution of heretics. Castellio's treatise elicited defenses of the persecution of heretics from both Calvin and Theodore Beza, to which Castellio also responded. The exchanges among Castellio, Calvin, and Beza were taken up by a number of other writers in the decades that followed. Perhaps if the question of the inquisitions had not been addressed so vigorously and pointedly at Spain in the 1540s and 1550s, the tone of these debates might have been more moderate. But the execution of Servetus provided a strong Catholic counter-apology to Protestant criticisms of the inquisitions, and both cases put the question of religious persecution—and its reverse, toleration—squarely into the stream of seventeenth- and eighteenth-century political thought.

The example of Servetus and of the inquisitions, as these had developed in polemic and propaganda since the early sixteenth century, served as a useful tool for Protestants and Catholics alike. Since Spain clearly permitted no religious toleration, and since Spain's reputation had been blackened effectively by 1600, the Spanish Inquisition could freely be cited as an example to all rulers who professed to deny liberties to dissenting subjects. As early as 1524 the Anabaptist Balthasar Hubmaier had charged that,

> The inquisitors are the greatest heretics of all, since, against the doctrine and example of Christ, they condemn heretics to fire, and before the time of harvest root up the wheat with the tares. For Christ did not come to butcher, destroy, and burn, but that those that live might live more abundantly.

From Hubmaier on, the course of arguments for and against religious and political toleration might be traced as the history of commentary on Matthew 13.24–30, the parable of the wheat and the tares, and on Luke 14.21–24, the parable of the guests at the banquet. For the next several centuries these became the scriptural proof texts for arguments on behalf of toleration.

The torture of Balthasar Hubmaier in Zwinglian Zurich in 1525, the execution of John of Oldenbarnevelt in the Calvinist United Provinces in 1619, and other similar cases all were widely publicized and raised the specter of Protestant persecutions, one that was far more troubling to tolerationist Protestants than it was to Catholics. One such writer was Jacobus Acontius. Acontius (1500–1567) was an accomplished engineer, a cosmopolitan convert to Protestantism, and one of the great heralds of religious toleration. Influenced by Erasmus in his dislike of making religious orthodoxy depend exclusively upon a set of doctrines, and by Castellio in his conviction of the arbitrary character of definitions of heresy, Acontius produced his great treatise, *Satanae Stratagemata*, "Satan's Stratagems," at Basel in 1565. Acontius turns on its head the older Catholic and Protestant argument that heresies are the product of the Devil's attempts to confound Christianity. The Devil's chief work among Christians, Acontius argues, is to turn them into persecutors. Thus although Acontius does not single out the Catholic inquisitions (it has been suggested that some of his text reflects the executions of the Oxford Martyrs in Marian England), he isolates the fact—and evil—of religious persecution and attacks it no matter who practices it as a device, a "stratagem" of Satan. Translated into English in 1648, Acontius' work played a substantial role in the larger debates over toleration and religious persecution in the later seventeenth century.

Like Castellio, Acontius raised arguments that at first only a small number of people were pleased to hear. Even Castellio's categorical observation that,

> To kill a man is not to defend a doctrine but to kill a man. When the Genevans killed Servetus they did not defend a doctrine, they killed a man,

did not elicit immediate agreement from either Protestant or Catholic regimes.

In addition to the religious arguments, the philosophical doctrine of scepticism attacked one of the fundamental assumptions of religious persecution, that which asserted that the truth was naturally known and logically certain. On this assumption, any belief or act contrary to the truth could legitimately be persecuted. Scepticism, however, attacked the principle of certainty in religious dogma and its consequent application. The religious thought of Erasmus and his successors could posit a few common principles—essentials—for Christians to believe, and attack any narrowing of these to more specific dogmas. Sceptical thinkers, on the other hand, could argue—whether from a religious or a purely philosophical position—that no truths were self-evident, and that consequently no particular body of dogma could be sufficiently convinced of its own truth to apply it in matters of religious persecution. Scepticism was an old technique of epistemology, but it could coexist with religious faith in the sixteenth and seventeenth centuries.

Scepticism could also operate on a number of different levels. In early seventeenth-century Spain, for example, a sceptical attitude toward the character of the evidence at a number of trials for witchcraft at Logroño in 1610 led to the virtual disappearance of the crime of witchcraft from the work of the Spanish Inquisition itself. Michel de Montaigne attacked the persecution of witches on the grounds that "it is putting a high price on one's conjectures to have a man roasted alive because of them." Once either legal evidence or the application of religious dogma to criminal law could be attacked on the grounds that it was *conjecture*, rather than certainty, states had to find either new grounds for persecution in religious matters or discard it altogether.

On the other hand, those states that practiced persecution on the grounds of conjecture became not only un-Christian (in Acontius' sense), but illogical, because they acted on the basis of conjecture and opinion, not certainty at all. These two originally unrelated strands of thought—that of personal religion and philosophical scepticism—could find in all religious persecutions appropriate targets, but especially in *The Inquisition* could their proponents argue that a single institution, increasingly perceived as marginal to northern Europe, embodied the very principles against which true religion and logic militated.

These arguments, though eloquently stated and philosophically appealing, could not by themselves persuade individual states to undertake policies of religious toleration. Until the problem of religious persecution was squarely faced *within* states instead of *between* contending states with different confessions, it remained an abstraction, and could not be dealt with because of the complacency with which different confessions were content to condemn their enemies' instruments of persecution and to justify their own.

Much more immediate was a pragmatic view of religious toleration, which emerged out of the Netherlands and the French Wars of Religion. By the late seventeenth century the sheer scale of religious dissent and conflict placed any earlier kind of harsh solution outside the realm of possibility. For much of Europe it was no longer remotely a question of sending a few papally commissioned inquisitors to be aided by local authorities in putting down small groups of heretics. Not only Lutheranism and Calvinism, but a number of smaller confessions were virtually international religions, with broad networks of communication and allies and sympathizers throughout much of the rest of Europe. The social discord that religious persecution seemed to produce was increasingly political rather than purely religious. However much the established Catholic or Protestant state confessions might attribute religious deviation to willfulness or satanic inspiration, many individuals had chosen to make religious decisions for themselves. Few early modern political structures had been designed to deal with massive religious conversions, individually made, and they found it difficult to deal with these by repressive means without tearing apart the very fabric of society.

Until the seventeenth century, political theory and practice had assumed that unity and concord were the natural ends of Christian society. Faction, sect, schism, and heresy were thus unnatural. Like political "parties," confessional sects were the very antithesis of the natural order. By the late sixteenth century, however, some French political thinkers, in the wake of the terrible stalemates produced by the wars of religion, began to assert that the state's fundamental and natural purpose was to accommodate the natural sociability of mankind, to preserve itself as a vehicle for this purpose, and to increase the prosperity of subjects and rulers. The state, not the enforcement of a religious dogma, became the focus of their arguments. If civil peace now entailed either repression and persecution on an enormous, repugnant, and ultimately unprofitable scale, the state had to look to its own survival, even if this meant tolerating, within a single community, differences that had always been thought to be irreconcilable.

By the late seventeenth century assumptions about the nature of unity and concord in individual states began to give way to the idea that certain kinds of conflict, diversity of interests, and competition might be more "natural" than the kinds of unity that Europeans had always accepted as fundamental. The doctrine of "asocial sociability" would allow for important areas in which conflict, not unity, better preserved the state. In the late fourteenth century the Florentine historian Leonardo Bruni had observed that "fellow citizens should hate each other in such a way that they do not forget that they are fellow-citizens." In the late

sixteenth and seventeenth centuries many Europeans began to work out
the consequences of Bruni's suggestion. In the political thought of James
Harrington and Algernon Sidney several lines were opened up that,
ran in just over the course of a century to ideas of religious pluralism
within individual societies and to the early thought of James Madison
and *The Federalist* papers.

The first stages of practical religious toleration in northern Europe
occurred where political necessity seemed to demand it, and when alterna-
tives had demonstrably failed. New ideas, employed for political ends,
led to an entirely novel concept of the tolerability of religious as well
as political pluralism in society. Having come about by political necessity,
such policies could in turn be cast aside by later political necessity as
well. But even short-term toleration gave ideas an opportunity to circulate
more widely, with the approval of rulers, so that future reversals of
policy met with greater opposition than they might otherwise have.

The arguments in favor of toleration for purposes of political peace
had focused upon the right of the state to survive and prosper and of
its obligation to do so. Among them was the argument that religious
repression injured a state not only politically, but economically as well.
The expulsion of large numbers of industrious, wealthy, and otherwise
evidently loyal subjects came to be seen as injuring the prosperity of
states. When the economic decline of Spain became obvious after the
middle of the seventeenth century, anti-Spanish propaganda promptly
attributed the decline to Spain's initial expulsion of the Jews and to its
continuing repressive policies against people who were otherwise potentially valuable and productive. To this argument was added the charge
that the confiscations and fines imposed by the Spanish Inquisition were
equally damaging to the Spanish kingdom, since they were alleged to
divert capital from its proper channels and drain it off into such unproduc-
tive areas as clerical support.

A similar argument was made against other persecuting states, especially
in the case of France's expulsion of the Huguenots after the revocation
of the Edict of Nantes in 1685. A number of writers drew parallels
between the decline of Spain and the prospective decline of France for
depriving the kingdom of some of its most productive and enterprising
population. To economic theorists the cost of religious persecution was
too high; to critics of *The Inquisition* the institution's greed, its lust for
land and money, led to the economic catastrophe of seventeenth-century
Spain. The obvious lesson to be drawn by other countries was clear—
do not toy with the idea of renewed persecutions, do not revoke policies
of toleration after political crises have passed.

The new role of *The Inquisition*, as a mortal threat to the state, appeared not only in anti-Inquisition literature, but in political and economic tracts. In 1673 Francis Willoughby concluded his account of *A Relation of a Voyage Made through a Great Part of Spain* with the observation that:

> Spain is in many places, not to say most, very thin of people, and almost desolate. The causes are (1) A bad Religion, (2) The Tyrannical Inquisition, (3) The multitude of Whores, (4) The barrenness of the soil, (5) The wretched laziness of the people, very like the Welsh and Irish, walking slowly and always cumbered with a great Choke and long Sword, (6) The expulsion of the Jews and Moors, the first of which were planted there by the Emperor Adrian, and the latter by the Caliphs after the conquest of Spain, (7) Wars and Plantations.

Willoughby's hierarchy of economic causality, that of an otherwise astute scientific observer, is characteristic of the recognized link between religion and Inquisition on the one hand and economic disaster on the other.

Among the tolerating societies of Europe, those that remained intolerant became the objects not only of contempt, but of social analysis. Their backwardness and economic fragility were assumed, and these in turn were attributed to *The Inquisition*. Portugal, Spain, and Rome were unique in seventeenth-century Europe in terms of their religious unity and their mechanisms of persecution. In European eyes, such unity of religious belief and practice necessarily had to depend upon force or social enervation, for it could no longer be viewed as voluntary

The quest for political order and the identification of the economic consequences of religious persecution did not exhaust the seventeenth century's additions to the image of *The Inquisition*. Increasingly seen as unnatural, *The Inquisition* could only succeed either because the character of a given people is such that it readily succumbs to force or because a people has become enervated and does not have the psychological capacity to resist. That enervation, combined with the coercive force of *The Inquisition* then has further consequences: it stifles imagination, learning, science, literature, and the arts. From the seventeenth century on, these too became a consequence of *The Inquisition*, as its critics began to include "the Spanish character" in their analyses of the unique Spanish institution.

Some of the earliest characterizations of Spain in the invective of the fifteenth and early sixteenth centuries had focused upon an image of alleged Spanish cultural inferiority to Italy. Not all, or even most anti-Spanish or anti-Inquisition invective in the sixteenth century took such a tone. Netherlands criticism, for example, is remarkably free of it, although English criticism reflects it quite strongly. By the seventeenth century, however, criticism of both Spain and the Inquisition implied more than religious, philosophical, political, or economic outrage. For centuries the cultural and intellectual achievements of peoples had been components of ethnography and historical writing, but in the case of Spain and the Inquisition during the seventeenth century they became much more prominent.

Influencing such criticism was the belief that the censorship functions of the Inquisition were an attack, not exclusively upon doctrinal error, but on the expression of ideas itself. The fate of the works of Erasmus and his followers at the hands of Inquisitorial censors, the persecution of such literary figures as Vergara and Luis de León at the hands of the Spanish Inquisition, and the later Spanish censorship of individual works and authors, all contributed to a small but eloquent stream of criticism of Spanish intellectual rigidity and intolerance that grew in volume and familiarity through the early seventeenth century. Since Protestant communities were identified not only with God's Word, but with the powers of human reason to circulate the Word, states that opposed such circulation were necessarily backward and intellectually suppressed.

In spite of the enormous literary and artistic production that flowered in sixteenth- and seventeenth-century Spain, the image of intellectual enervation that accompanied political and economic repression carried over into the repression of the arts, letters, and sciences as well. Since the sixteenth-century Indices issued by the Spanish Inquisition and government focused exclusively upon doctrinal literature, the charge of literary repression does not hold until the seventeenth century. Not until the seventeenth century did the Spanish Inquisition begin to deal with doctrinal representations in the visual arts, and then only intermittently. Nevertheless, adverse judgements on Spanish literature, arts, and science came thick and fast in the seventeenth century, and the despotic governments of Spain or Rome, with the Inquisition as their instrument, were held responsible.

Such judgments did not circulate only in histories of Spain or anti-Inquisition literature. One of the most popular literary genres of the seventeenth century was the traveler's report, and Spain was a popular objective for travelers. Perhaps the most influential of these was the account given by the Countess d'Aulnoy, published in 1691, in which the Spanish character, Spain's artistic and intellectual achievements, and Spanish religion were blackened consistently and articulately. D'Aulnoy's account, with those of Juan Alvarez de Colmenar of 1701, Jean de Vayrac of 1718, and others throughout the eighteenth century provided readers outside Spain with eyewitness descriptive information that confirmed the impression of the disastrous consequences of the Spanish Inquisition. Not without reason has it been pointed out that most of the general knowledge of Spain that Enlightenment writers possessed derived from these late seventeenth-century and early eighteenth-century travelers' reports.

Thus, in the various forms taken by debates over religious toleration and the inquiries into states that practiced religious persecution in the seventeenth century, a large number of originally separate strands of criticism and social analysis combined and focused upon *The Inquisition* as the chief cause of all of the evils that sprang from persecution.

Sectarian Critics and Dissenting Historians

Some of the most effective arguments on behalf of religious toleration—and some of the most eloquent criticism of the inquisitions—came from individuals and groups that could find a place in no state, rather than from those who could dominate in one state and only protest against the persecution of their fellow believers in another. To make their case effectively, those who could find a place in no state had to discover arguments that might justify their finding a place in all.

In the early sixteenth century this was no easy task. Catholics and Lutherans alike professed intense fear of the Anabaptists, and as the century went on other sectarian groups emerged in Catholic, Lutheran, and Calvinist states. Sometimes, as in the case of the seventeenth-century Dutch Remonstrants, these were wings of the state religion itself; sometimes, as in the Unitarian movement in which Sozzino was influential, their doctrines—in this case anti-Trinitarianism—repelled all other Christian states. As the seventeenth century went on yet other groups emerged: Dissenters, Quakers, and Unitarians in England, dissenting wings of both Dutch and French Calvinism in the Netherlands, Mennonites and Unitarians elsewhere. For all of these groups, religion was emphatically an inward rather than an outward matter. Persecuted everywhere, they mounted an attack on persecution itself and in doing so found in *The Inquisition* an image with which to attack not only Spain, Rome, or Portugal, but any state that practiced persecution, stinging even Lutheran and Calvinist states with charges that they, too, possessed inquisitions, regardless of what they called them. Some of the most articulate polemicists and historians of the inquisitions emerged from these societies. Gerhard Brandt, the great historian of the Netherlands Reformation, was a Remonstrant, as was Philip van Limborch, the first great historian of the inquisitions; Gilbert Burnet, the historian of the English Reformation and a great critic of the inquisitions, was a Latitudinarian, as was the English translator of Limborch's history, Samuel Chandler, himself the author of a history of persecutions. Joseph Milner, the eighteenth-century editor of Foxe's Martyrology, was an Evangelical. One could go through all of the anti-inquisition literature of the seventeenth and eighteenth centuries and find a similarly high proportion of those contributing to it defending a sectarian theory of toleration and a parallel hatred of religious persecution.

One target of the sectarian attack was the civil authority of the clergy. Critics of the proposed oath against transsubstantiation forced upon Catholics in England in 1657 claimed that the oath itself was as bad as the Spanish Inquisition. In the eyes of sectarian critics, the excessive power of the clergy in states was the chief cause of persecution, and their campaigns included an extensive criticism of Spain, in particular, for clerical domination of the kingdom and its manifestation in the Spanish Inquisition.

Sectarian and dissenting writers seem particularly to have favored the use of historiography to explain the disasters of religious persecution, and the center of much of their work was in the Netherlands. Although the Netherlands went through a crisis of religious authority at the Synod of Dort in 1618, when the Remonstrant wing of the Calvinist church was exiled and rigid policies against heterodoxy were established, the crisis passed after several years, and not only were the Remonstrants allowed back, but the Netherlands became the publishing center with the fewest restrictions. From the second half of the seventeenth century there flowed a stream of books from the Netherlands—including Locke's own *Letter on Toleration*—and the region became a center of distribution of these works to other countries as well, particularly to England and France. In addition, the Netherlands sheltered a large exile French Huguenot population.

The best example of sectarian and dissenting historiography in the case of the Inquisition is that of Philip van Limborch (1633–1712), professor of theology among the Dutch Remonstrants. Limborch was a great scholar, an influential pioneer in the cause of religious toleration, a powerful force in the attempt to damp the religious passions of the century, a close friend both of the Cambridge Platonists and of John Locke (and for several years the only person who knew that Locke was the author of the *Letter on Toleration*). At some time in the 1680s or early 1690s, a friend had given him a manuscript from the fourteenth century, the *Book of Sentences of the Inquisition of Toulouse*. Limborch, an indefatigable proponent of religious toleration, had no love for popes or inquisitors and decided to edit and print the Toulouse document. But he also decided that the document itself needed an introduction, and to that end he composed his *History of the Inquisition*, publishing the two works together in 1692. His work became widely known, as much for its scholarly quality as for its ideological position, and it was translated into English by Samuel Chandler (minus the *Book of Sentences*) in 1731. Chandler, a kind of English counterpart to Limborch, a proponent of toleration for religious dissenters himself, prefaced his translation of Limborch's history with a long essay on religious persecution, which itself was separately and frequently printed as *The History of Persecution*, and became an influential force in the history of religious toleration in England.

As was the custom of critical historians as well as polemicists, Limborch based his *History* on the writings of Catholic historians and inquisitors. The exceptions are his use of Montanus and Bishop James Usher, although since the latter uses much Catholic material himself, he hardly counts as a Protestant source. Among Limborch's most prominent sources were Peña's edition of Eymeric's *Directorium*, Bernard of Como and other authors of handbooks of inquisitorial procedure, the historians Bzovius and Raynaldi, Charles Dellon's *Relation of the Inquisition of Goa*, and the Inquisition historian Luis de Paramo.

Ignoring the Paramo thesis that the history of the Inquisition begins in the Garden of Eden, Limborch rests his case on the thesis that Christianity was in essence a religion of love, that Charity was Christ's original gift to men, and that God is to be worshipped in the spirit. The mind and will must not be forced, and outside of the basic rules regarding public tranquility, no civil regulations regarding religion have any validity whatsoever. Limborch's history is of the Inquisition, but Limborch's message is wider than a simple denunciation of Catholic persecution. A Remonstrant himself, Limborch was acutely aware of other forms of Christian persecution, and his particular historical description of the Catholic Inquisition is clearly intended to indict all ecclesiastical and secular powers who attempt to legislate on behalf of religious conformity.

Limborch asserts that the early Christians, successors of the apostles, knew no doctrine of persecution; citing the Fathers of the second, third, and fourth centuries to that effect, he concludes:

> This was the most harmless Perswasion of the Primitive Christians, before the World had yet entered into the Church, and by its Pomp

and Pride had perverted the Minds, and corrupted the manners of its Professors.

The turn away from apostolic and evangelical toleration came during the reign of the Christianized Constantine. Faced with the dispute between Alexander, bishop of Alexandria, and the priest Arius, Constantine at first blamed the bishop for being "needlessly inquisitive" concerning Arius' beliefs, and Arius "for his imprudent answers about an unnecessary Question." Later, however, urged on by bishops, Constantine called the Council of Nicaea and he and his successors created civil offenses in matters of religion that entered Roman law. Throughout the early chapters, Limborch keeps up a running dispute with such Catholic apologists as Bellarmine, Jacobus Simancas, and Corrado Bruno, and he pointedly turns to Arian persecution of orthodox Christians, denouncing it as heatedly as he had denounced the initial orthodox persecution of Arians.

From what he regards as the crucial fourth century, Limborch moves quickly to the twelfth and thirteenth and the appearance of the Waldenses and Albigenses. Here Limborch argues that the two faiths were distinct, criticizes Catholic writers for their indiscriminating invective against both, and adds a contemporary touch:

> Particularly the Waldenses seem to have been plain men, of mean capacities, unskillful and unexperienced; and if their opinions and customs were to be examined without prejudice, it would appear, that amongst all the modern sects of Christians, they bare the greatest resemblance to that of the Mennonites.

Having pointed to papal authority as the great cause of religious persecution, Limborch discusses the establishment of the Mendicant Orders by Innocent III as weapons against heresy and asserts that St. Dominic was the first Inquisitor. He then recounts the spread of the medieval inquisition down to the sixteenth century and the reestablishment of inquisitions in Spain and elsewhere.

Earlier historians and polemicists, including Montanus, had noted the early persecution of *conversos* by the Spanish Inquisition, although none of them criticized this, because to them the problem of Jews masquerading as Christians was a heinous offense, and the *conversos* seemed to these writers to have been crypto-Jews. Limborch himself was active in discussions with Jews in Amsterdam, published a friendly debate with one Jewish adversary, participated in the re-conversion of a young Calvinist girl who had been converted to Judaism, and wrote an attack on the criticism of all revealed religions by Uriel Acosta. In his treatment of the *conversos* in the *History of the Inquisition*, Limborch is one of the first Christian writers to express distaste for the persecution of Jews, even if they were pretended Christians. Limborch's opponent in the *Friendly Conference with a learned Jew concerning the Truth of the Christian Religion* (1687) was Isaac Orobio, who himself had escaped Spain and the Spanish Inquisition "by pretending to be a Catholick." The question of toleration in its early stages had always drawn up short at the problem of extending toleration to Jews and atheists. Although Limborch was convinced that both positions were wrong, his treatment of *conversos* in his History suggests that his own idea of toleration extended to Jews, if not to atheists. The full European recognition of the persecution of the Jews by Christians had to wait until the eighteenth century, and it did not become a point of interest for historians of the inquisitions until the nineteenth. But with the work of Limborch, the Jewish *conversos* were at least recognized and remembered, and out of one myth of *The Inquisition* there emerged in Limborch's work the germ of real history.

Limborch's *History* quickly found an echo in very different religious quarters. Much of the seventeenth century in France witnessed Catholic attempts to roll back the limited toleration afforded Huguenots by the Edict of Nantes in 1598. In addition, both Quietism and Jansenism, a variant of Catholic Augustinianism, became the object of attack as well. In an attempt to prove their loyalty to Louis XIV's policy of persecuting the Huguenots—which culminated in the Revocation of the Edict of Nantes in 1685—Jansenist writers adopted Gallican sympathies and undertook to justify the appropriateness of Louis' revocation by comparing it favorably with the horrors of the Spanish and other Inquisitions.

In 1693 the Gallican abbé Jacques Marsollier drew heavily upon Limborch's *History* in his own *History of the Inquisition*. Critical of papal authority, particularly papal disapproval of Jansenism, Marsollier was no less critical of contemporary pleas for general religious toleration, particularly those of John Locke, whose arguments Marsollier's *History* is in part an attempt to refute. Marsollier defends a prince's right to establish a single religion in his own state and to exclude others, but he emphasizes that this is the right of the prince and is not to be imposed upon him by the pope. When the pope commands, Marsollier explains, there is imposed the "terrible yoke" of the Inquisition, "the masterpiece of the court of Rome." Drawing upon the work of Paolo Sarpi, Marsollier compares the policies of Louis XIV and the Venetian State favorably with those of the Inquisitions of Rome and Spain.

Gallican and Jansenist histories of the inquisitions appeared frequently throughout the eighteenth century.

Following the history of Marsollier, Louis-Ellies Dupin (1657–1719), toward the end of a life of vast literary production and historical and theological controversies, produced his own *Mémoires historiques pour servir à l'histoire des inquisitions*, partly derived from Marsollier and substantially increased by his extensive use of Charles Dellon's *Relation sur l'inquisition de Goa* in Vol. II. The extraordinary popularity of Dellon's *Relation* may help to explain why so many historians and polemicists of the eighteenth century deal rather with the Inquisition of Portugal than with that of Spain or Rome. Dupin's and Marsollier's work was added to by the Abbé Goujet and republished in 1759. Goujet, a Gallican and a Jansenist sympathizer, also continued another work by Dupin, the immense *Bibliothèque des auteurs ecclésiastiques*. Thus, French acquaintance with the history of the Inquisition during most of the eighteenth century was with the Gallican histories rather than with Limborch, although Limborch's indirect influence was certainly present.

Pierre Bayle: The Victims Respond

In the work of Pierre Bayle (1647–1706) the scattered strands of the doctrines supporting religious toleration not only found a thinker capable of drawing the strongest of them together, but of doing so in a manner that appealed to eighteenth-century thinkers who had very different presuppositions and very different values. In a lifetime of extensive literary production, Bayle succeeded in secularizing a religious argument to which he himself subscribed on religious grounds. Bayle had grown up in the region of Foix in southwestern France, the son of a Huguenot pastor; he was educated at Puylaurens and (partially by Catholic teachers) in Toulouse. For several years he worked as a tutor, studied intermittently, and became largely self-educated, developing wide literary interests which he tended to express in essays, letters, and in a style that developed a mastery of understatement. After a brief conversion to Catholicism, Bayle focused his studies upon theology and philosophy, taught at the Huguenot academy at Sedan, and fled France to Rotterdam in 1681, when Catholic pressure closed the academy and threatened worse restrictions on French Protestants. As a professor of philosophy at Rotterdam, Bayle espoused the anti-aristotelianism of Descartes and Malebranche, and began the literary career that made him one of the most important French prose stylists and thinkers of his generation.

Bayle had seen enough of persecution to adopt many of the religious and philosophical arguments of his predecessors, and to broadcast them in language that reached a far wider audience. Employing scepticism as a new weapon in polemic, his *General Criticism of M. Maimbourg's History of Calvinism* attacked Maimbourg's use of varied, disorderly, and often conflicting sources. By consistently undercutting the reliability of Maimbourg's sources, Bayle applied to history the same tough criteria of source criticism and methodology that Descartes had applied in other fields. He attacked the argument that the Huguenots were seditionists, and, like many sectarian writers, held up a picture of the apostolic age in which the Huguenots were identified with the persecuted Christians and the Catholics identified with their pagan persecutors. This theme had emerged out of the sixteenth-century martyrologies, but the sectarians had made it their own:

> The communion of Rome has never permitted anyone to contradict her, without exterminating by iron and fire anyone who dared to assume such a liberty. It made great efforts to establish everywhere the Tribunal of the Inquisition, the most infernal, and the most shameful instrument for the maintenance of its authority that was ever displayed by the human spirit, and which was never practiced even by the most abominable religions of paganism, even by those which used to sacrifice human victims to their idols.

In Letter XXI.vii, Bayle takes up Maimbourg's citation of Luke 14. 21–24, the parable of the guests at the banquet, and provides his earliest commentary on what was to become a major work in 1686, an examination of the famous words of the host, "compel them to come in." What would French Catholic writers like Maimbourg do if the English were to conquer France and exercise the injunction of Luke on the French? If any Christian confession accepts the injunction of Luke, then it must admit the right of every other confession to do the same thing. Bayle then cites the example of St. Paul before his conversion, describing him as an inquisitor, examining Jewish consciences and reprimanding heterodoxy by force, while after his conversion Paul used only preaching, instruction, and prayer.

Again and again, Bayle identifies *The Inquisition* with Catholicism, whether that of Philip II of Spain, or of Louis XIV of France. Bayle will not be put off by Maimbourg's ultramontane arguments: Catholicism is the persecutor, and Catholicism establishes the Inquisition wherever it has the power to do so. In Letter XXIII, Bayle unleashes a furious attack on Philip II and his obsession with destroying "heretics;" but he also attacks the execution of Michael Servetus in Geneva.

Bayle's *The True State of Wholly Catholic France in the Reign of*

Louis XIV of 1686 sustained his assault on French persecution of the Huguenots and again cut away Gallican distinctions between the French persecution and those of the Spanish Inquisition. Bayle took up these issues again in 1686–1688 in his *Philosophical Commentary on the words of Our Lord "Compel them to come in,"* a vast extension and development of the argument made in Letter XXI.vii of the *Criticism . . . of Maimbourg*. Here Bayle spells out in vast detail his two principles underlying the argument against religious persecution: the moral superiority of conscience over any set of particular doctrines, particularly over doctrines that propose to use force to persuade the conscience, and the principle of the uncertainty of dogmata that necessarily fails to justify their assertion in ways that will violate the sanctity of the individual conscience. Elevated to a general principle, these doctrines permit Bayle to argue for the toleration of all religions regardless of their doctrinal content.

Behind Bayle's use of the inquisition there lay a vast and complex philosophical doctrine, that of scepticism, and a tough ethical doctrine: that individual conscience in religious matters must never be forced. Bayle, whose own religious faith was probably firm, did not derive his scepticism from the sixteenth-century tradition that had begun with Montaigne. Rather, Bayle based it on his belief that faith and revelation, not reason, were the centers of religious belief and that natural reason's claims were weak and easily refuted in matters of religion. Therefore, reason could not assert religious truth, and final acceptance of its "certainties" must be witheld, particularly when these appear to lead to acts that by other standards appear unethical. For Bayle, conscience, not reason, is what leads to assent. No person or group may force the conscience of another, no matter how certain one may be of the truth of one's own claims. According to Bayle even "erring consciences" must be considered sincere and therefore be respected.

Bayle strengthens his argument about the primacy of conscience by attacking the non-rational means by which people usually accept one religious confession rather than others. Religious truth is ultimately unknowable with natural certainty, and it is unlikely that any one party possesses it; people generally choose the confession of their family and environment, not because they are initially convinced of its truth; if any single group has the right to persecute on the basis of its conviction that it possesses the truth, then it must logically allow the same right to other groups that are equally convinced, even if this means the legitimate persecution of themselves.

By generalizing the claims made by both Catholic and Protestant apologists for religious persecution, Bayle completed the work of sectarian publicists and historians earlier in the century, and he demolished the subtle distinctions drawn by historians like Marsollier between the French persecution of Huguenots and the Spanish and Roman Inquisitions. In the *Philosophical Commentary*, Bayle expressed the hope that some able Spaniard would one day show up the absurdities of the Gallican position and demonstrate that French criticism of the Inquisition by those who otherwise supported the policies of Louis XIV was simply French regret at not having invented the Inquisition themselves.

Bayle also identified *The Inquisition* with all forms of religious persecution, not merely Spanish Catholic or Roman. He elevated it into the instrument, not exclusively of Catholics, but of dogmatic Christianity against the individual conscience. Behind that argument is Bayle's conviction that belief does not determine behavior; that civil authority has no business with conscience, but only with behavior; and that even atheists must be accepted as fully franchised citizens, as must Muslims and Jews. Civil peace is not troubled or endangered by religion except on those occasions when dogmatic Christianity subverts the secular power or when the secular power itself disguises its political ambitions with the precepts of dogmatic Christianity.

These ideas are reflected in Bayle's *Historical and Critical Dictionary* of 1696, which offered a Protestant counter-encyclopedia to those of Catholic writers. Although Bayle's work had no article "Inquisition," his opinion of the inquisitions is made clear in articles on such figures as Carranza and Cornelius Agrippa of Nettesheim. In these articles, much of whose central argument was made in long notes, Bayle's pronounced determination that Christianity was incompatible with religious persecution of any kind is echoed again and again in his denunciation of the inquisitions, not merely on the grounds of freedom of religion, but also on those that inquisitions inhibit the intellectual and scientific development of mankind.

Some of the background to Bayle's treatment of the Spanish Inquisition is to be found in his lack of personal familiarity with Spain and Spaniards and his consequent exclusive reliance on textual evidence. Some of his evidence consisted of the *Relation d'Espagne* of Madame d'Aulnoy, perhaps the most influential description of Spain known to seventeenth- and eighteenth-century French readers, as well as other narratives of this kind. From these Bayle derived his ideas of the Spanish character, its superstitiousness, implacable religious orthodoxy, and its licentiousness. For Bayle, these characteristics led inexorably to Spain's resistance to new ideas and to the institutionalization of that resistance in the Inquisition.

By the time of his death in 1706, Bayle had assembled and woven together the diverse arguments against religious persecution, identified *The Inquisition* with all forms of religious persecution, spelled out the economic and intellectual consequences of persecution, disallowed the state any voice in matters of conscience, and done all this in a literary style that appealed to a broad spectrum of readers. Irony, understatement, virtuoso use of logic and Cartesian rules of evidence, and a taste for the scandalous and outrageous made Bayle's arguments eminently readable, no longer exclusively by sectarians or those with purely religious interests, but by a new reading—and thinking—public, one which Bayle himself termed "The Republic of Letters." It was in the Republic of Letters that Bayle's and his predecessors' influence was most markedly to be felt in the eighteenth century.

Montesquieu and the Political Economy of Inquisitions

The interests of Bayle's Republic of Letters were not exclusively literary. In the work of Montesquieu, constitutional thought and the problems of political economy emphasized the political and economic consequences to states that employed religious persecution. Montesquieu's work is best known for its comparisons between England and France, but he also gave a great deal of thought to Spain, which for him exemplified the worst effects of state mismanagement under the influence of clerical elites. Montesquieu worried that other European states might follow Spain, sapping their vitality and imposing arbitrary force upon the lively and productive civil peace.

In Book XXV of *The Spirit of the Laws*, Montesquieu takes up the vexing problem of religious toleration (XXV.9): "We are writing here as political thinkers, and not as theologians: and, even among theologians, there is a great difference between tolerating a religion and approving it." Montesquieu then observes that when a state tolerates a number of different religions, these tolerated religions must then tolerate each other, "for it is a principle that each persecuted religion becomes a persecuting religion in its turn." It is thus useful for the law to insist not only that different religions do not trouble the state, but that they do not trouble each other.

Montesquieu turns directly toward the inquisitions in a chapter (XXV.13) entitled "A Most humble remonstrance to the inquisitions of Spain and Portugal." This chapter professes to be an appeal from an eighteen-year-old Jewess, burned at Lisbon in the early eighteenth century;

Montesquieu is thus, after Limborch, one of the first thinkers to address the place of the Jews in the Spanish and Portuguese Inquisitions. The text begins by citing, as many eighteenth-century texts on similar subjects did, the practices of religious persecution in Japan. But the inquisitors, states the text, are worse than the emperor of Japan, because they kill those who do not believe as they believe simply *because* they do not believe as they believe:

> We follow a religion that you yourselves acknowledge as having once been dear to God; we believe that God still loves us, and you believe that He does not. And because you judge us thus, you submit to the iron and the fire those who hold so pardonable an error as to believe that God still loves those whom He once loved.

The Inquisition, says the girl, is even more cruel in regard to the children of Jews, burning them simply because they follow what the laws of nature of all peoples have taught in respect to divinity. The inquisitors admit that their religion is younger than Judaism, but they argue that the early pagan persecutions and the blood of the martyrs proves its authenticity; then they themselves take the role of Diocletian and force the Jews to take the role of martyrs. If heaven has loved the inquisitors enough to have permitted them to see the truth, it has given them a great favor; but should the children who have received an inheritance from their father hate those children who have not? The character of truth is its triumph in hearts and spirits and is not conveyed through punishments:

> If your Christ is the son of God, we hope that at least he will reward us for not having wished to profane his mysteries, and we believe that the God whom both you and we serve will not punish us for a religion that He once gave us, because we believe that He has sustained that religion among us.

The Jewess points out that the inquisitors live in a century in which natural reason is more alive than it has ever been, in which philosophy has refined men's minds and spirits, in which the moral message of the Gospels is better known. Therefore, if the inquisitors, in the light of these circumstances, do not give up their ancient prejudices and restrain their passions, it must then be said that they are incorrigible, incapable of all enlightenment and all instruction, and that a nation is truly unhappy "that gives authority to such men as you."

Montesquieu protects himself formally by placing this speech into the mouth of a condemned Jewess and by disavowing her theology in a disingenuous footnote, but the message is clear: the Inquisition can be assaulted upon many fronts as anachronistic, irrational, and irreligious. Moreover, by placing the distribe in the middle of a comparative discussion of the autonomy of religion in the state, Montesquieu clearly regards the chief offense of the Inquisition to be political and social as well.

Among the fragments that Montesquieu did not include in the *Spirit of the Laws* there are several other references to the inquisitions. In a fragment excluded from VI.14, Montesquieu chides the Inquisition:

> It is one of the great abuses of the Inquisition of Spain that, of two persons accused of the same crime, the one who denies it is condemned to death, and the one who confesses it avoids punishment. This difference derives from monastic ideas, according to which anyone who denies the [charge of heresy] is impenitent and damned, while one who confesses appears to repent and is saved.

In a fragment excluded from XXV.12, Montesquieu takes up the theme of the violations of natural reason that have been committed in the name of penal laws made against religion. Citing the case of Charlemagne and the Saxons, he then turns to Justinian and the *Corpus Iuris Civilis*, the public law of Christian Rome:

> In order to amass more wealth, Justinian accused some people of adoring many gods and others of being heretics. He accused still others of pederasty, of having debauched religious women, of having raised rebellion, of belonging to the [Hippodrome] party of the Greens, of being traitors, &c. He established the office of special magistrate whose responsibility it was to seek out crimes against nature, as well as people with unorthodox religious sentiments, and he called this magistrate *inquisitor*. This magistrate confiscated the goods of his victims to the profit of the emperor, and he required no accuser nor any witness against the accused. Here is the very image of the modern Inquisition. It was for similar reasons that the Inquisition was established in Europe. One named no witness, nor any denouncer, and the tribunal confused ideas of Christian charity with a most peculiar barbarism, in its form and foundation, so as to astonish the entire Universe.

This remarkable fragment may have derived from Montesquieu's interest, recorded in his notebook *Le Spicilège*, in a work called a *Study of the History and Methods of the Inquisition*. Elsewhere in the *Spicilège* Montesquieu quotes an anonymous history of the Inquisition describing the ideal social type of the inquisitor:

> It is necessary that there are people separated from society, unhappy by condition, deprived of all sorts of relations, so that they will be hard, pitiless, and inexorable, in order to root out by the most cruel means the births of heresies. Such are the inquisitors.

For Montesquieu, the particulars of the Inquisitions in Spain and Portugal were less significant than the problems raised by certain kinds of religious coercion in eighteenth century Europe. Without profound reform, Montesquieu feared that his own Europe would become the "Europe of the Inquisition," deflected from its promising course by becoming entrapped in the very errors from which his far-reaching and profound political analysis was attempting to preserve it. Nor was Montesquieu content to let political analysis and comparative anthropology alone speak to these issues.

Employing satire in the *Persian Letters*, which purported to be communications from a Persian travelling in eighteenth-century Europe, he undertook to describe the practices of Christian Europe from the point of view of a cultural outsider:

> In Spain and Portugal there are certain dervishes without a sense of humor, and they burn a man as they would burn straw. When one falls into their hands, he is happiest who has always prayed to God with little pieces of wood in his hands, who carries upon his person a little piece of cloth attached to two ribbons, and who has gone once or twice to a province called Galicia. Without these, a poor devil can be mightily embarrassed. When he swears like a pagan that he is orthodox, one certainly cannot refrain from recognizing these qualities, and so one burns him as a heretic. . . .

In political analysis, comparative anthropology, literary eloquence, and satire, Montesquieu draws together for a largely secular readership a number of themes whose origins lie in the sixteenth century and whose convergence in the eighteenth century greatly influenced the image of the inquisitions for the next two centuries. The economic ruin of states, the denial of political liberty, the rejection of tolerance, and the denial of natural law and reason merge in the thought of Montesquieu and of most other writers of the eighteenth and nineteenth centuries. Montesquieu's political criticism of the Inquisitions pointed toward an enlightened and secular analysis of religious movements and institutions that perceived the Inquisition as the implacable and irrational enemy of political liberty and social productivity, not just in Spain and Portugal—but, as Montesquieu emphasized—in "the Inquisition of Europe."

Voltaire and the "Tyrants of the Mind"

No eighteenth-century writer mounted as eloquent and as virulent an attack on religious persecution or as many literary fronts as Voltaire.

Drawing upon the religious and philosophical arguments of Bayle and the political and economic arguments of Montesquieu, Voltaire frequently used *The Inquisition* as the target of literary satire. His enormous readership and intellectual influence completed the invention of *The Inquisition* in a purely secular context. Although, like Montesquieu, he often cited the Spanish or Portuguese Inquisitions specifically, he really intended that *The Inquisition* be regarded as a metonym for all of the most detestable forms of religious persecution. Voltaire, too, would have agreed with Montesquieu's fears of an "Inquisition of Europe," and he employed his pen and his wit relentlessly in pointing out the threat that he considered it to represent both to the intellect and to civil peace.

Voltaire's *Inquisition* did not, however, appear fully developed, but was instead the result of a number of specific occasions in his life and his reading. In the early works, notably the *Philosophical Letters* of 1734, he mentions only in passing that Descartes retired to North Holland to philosophize in solitude at the same time that Galileo languished in the prisons of the Inquisition for having proved that the earth moved. In the rest of the work, however, Voltaire employs his satirical technique on other targets, sharpening it, but showing no particular interest in or familiarity with the inquisitions. This general attitude is also reflected in the *History of Doctor Akakia* of 1752, in which Voltaire mounts an attack on Maupertuis by Doctor Akakia, who enlists the aid of the Roman Inquisition to denounce Maupertuis' ideas as heresy, even including a decree from the Inquisition that indicates some familiarity with its methods and language.

In his early works Voltaire appears to have had the kind of general knowledge of the inquisitions that would have been available from Bayle or Ellies Dupin or Montesquieu, but nothing deeper. The *Story of the Travels of Scarmentado*, printed in 1756, describes an *auto-de-fé*, probably derived from travelers' reports. A superficial knowledge of the inquisitions and Voltaire's willingness to use them for generally satirical purposes is evident in his work until very late in his life, as may be seen in the caricature of an inquisitor in the *Histoire de Jenni* of 1775, which introduces the comic inquisitor Don Jerónimo Bueno Caracúcarador, who almost destroys the hero in an *auto-de-fé* and is only prevented from doing so by the fact that the town, of whose absolute safety he had just given numerous spiritual assurances, is captured by raiders and the victims freed. This use of the inquisitions by Voltaire is simply the casual, routine depiction of the satirized eighteenth-century world, more comic and foolish than deadly.

Even the satire of the Inquisition in *Candide* (1759) reveals no greater knowledge of or concern with the inquisitions than Voltaire's ordinary reading in personal memoirs, travel literature, and history. Candide, having been expelled from his master's house in Germany, is shipwrecked off Lisbon on the eve of the great Lisbon earthquake of 1755. He and his mentor Dr. Pangloss are arrested by the Portuguese Inquisition because a mysterious officer of the Inquisition had overheard Pangloss discussing the cause of the earthquake in terms that imply his doubt of both original sin and human free will. These are positions that Voltaire himself condemned in the thought of Leibniz, and the official of the Inquisition thus serves Voltaire's own purposes.

Voltaire then introduces the infamous *auto-de-fé*:

> After the earthquake had wiped out three quarters of Lisbon, the learned men of the land could find no more effective way of averting total destruction than to give the people a fine auto de fé. The University of Coimbra had established that the spectacle of several persons being roasted over a slow fire with full ceremonial rites is an infallible remedy against earthquakes.

Pangloss and Candide are condemned, along with others guilty of trivial offenses, imprisoned in dungeons, then dressed in paper mitres and sanbenitos:

> Wearing these costumes, they marched in procession, and listened to a very touching sermon, followed by a beautiful concert of plainsong. Candide was flogged in cadence to the music, the Biscayan and the two men who had avoided bacon were burned, and Pangloss was hanged, though hanging is not customary. On the same day there was another earthquake, causing frightful damage.

Candide is let off after his beating, and discovers that his lover, Cunigonde, is now the mistress of two men—a Jewish trader and the Grand Inquisitor. After Candide has killed the Jewish trader, who had discovered him with Cunigonde, the Grand Inquisitor appears for his usual Sunday tryst. Candide kills the inquisitor as well in order to prevent his outcry, and the pair flee Portugal for further adventures.

One of Voltaire's sources for the *auto-de-fé* appears to have been Dellon's *Relation de l'inquisition de Goa*, which was published in 1688 and frequently reprinted during the eighteenth century. However, the entire chapter is a jewel of Voltairean satire. From the mighty conclusions of the University of Coimbra, the deliberate trivializing of the offenses of the accused, the relentless focusing on the evident visual and ritual absurdity of the *auto-de-fé* by depriving it of any meaning other than visual, and the idea of the Grand Inquisitor both having a mistress and sharing her with a Jewish trader, Voltaire introduces the topic of the Inquisition to comic literature (Plate 15).

In Voltaire's moral and historical writings of the same period we see the conventional view of the exterior of the inquisitions as engines of religious persecution, with little knowledge of their interior operation. In the *Examen de Milord Bolingbroke*, revised in the late 1750s, although not printed until 1767, Voltaire simply classes the inquisitions as one more manifestation of the violence with which the adherents of one religion attack those who profess another, condemning both Catholic and Protestant, Calvin's burning of Servetus as well as the inquisitions. In the *Essai sur les moeurs* of 1756, Voltaire treats the medieval and early modern inquisitions historically, deriving his information from earlier histories. Voltaire is cautious about St. Dominic's role in establishing the Inquisition and personally leading the crusading armies in thirteenth-century Languedoc, and he associates the foundation of the medieval inquisition with the suppression of Aristotle's books of natural philosophy at the University of Paris in 1215. Regarding the introduction of the Inquisition in France in 1229 as a blot upon the reign of St. Louis, Voltaire concludes:

> Thus was the Inquisition begun in Europe: and it deserved no better cradle. You understand well enough that it is the ultimate degree of a barbarism that is brutal and absurd to maintain, by means of informants and hangmen, the religion of a God whom the executioners killed. This is nearly as contradictory as to draw to oneself the treasures of peoples and kings in the name of the same God, who was born and lived in poverty. You will see in a later chapter what the Spanish and other Inquisitions were, and to what excesses of barbarism and rapacity some men have gone in order to abuse the simplicity of others.

In Voltaire's early works before 1761, the non-specific Inquisition became the embodiment of an attitude that represented the fanaticism, bigotry, and civil intolerance that had always existed in human societies, pagan and ancient, as well as Christian and modern. Satire, fiction, philosophy, and history were simply different ways of attacking the same abomination.

From 1761 until the end of his life, however, Voltaire's attacks on religious persecution grew sharper and more pointed, his arguments on behalf of religious toleration much more eloquent, and his knowledge of the actual mechanisms of persecution more expert. This change may be understood in terms of several specific cases of religious persecution with which Voltaire became intimately familiar and by his increased awareness of the interior literature of the Inquisition as a result of the work of the Abbé Morellet. A number of these cases are well known, notably those of Calas, Sirven, and the chevalier de la Barre. But the principal case that led Voltaire to the greater knowledge of the procedures of the inquisitions was that of Gabriel Malagrida and the stimulus that the Malagrida case provided to Morellet.

In 1759, as part of his ferocious campaign against the Jesuit Order, the Marquis of Pombal, Prime Minister of Portugal, expelled the Jesuits from Portugal and from Portuguese America, jailed many of them, and turned others over to the Portuguese Inquisition, which he then employed as a political tribunal. Among the Jesuits executed in 1761 was Gabriel Malagrida, a former missionary in Brazil and a man popularly reputed to be a saint. The execution of Malagrida, coupled with Dellon's detailed portrait of the Portuguese Inquisition at Goa, triggered a considerable public outcry throughout most of the rest of Europe. In the same year as Malagrida was burned, for example, Juan Luc Poggi published at Genoa a poem, "The Apotheosis of Father Malagrida, Jesuit . . . strangled and burned at Lisbon at an *auto-de-fé* on September 20, 1761." A three-act tragedy by Pierre de Longchamps, *Malagrida*, was published at Paris in 1763. Voltaire himself wrote the "Sermon of Rabbi Akiba," allegedly delivered at Smyrna on 20 November, 1761, in which he put powerful denunciations of Malagrida's execution into the mouth of a near-eastern Jew. Basing his knowledge of the case on a French translation of the charges against Malagrida, Voltaire includes a sonorous indictment of all forms of religious persecution, concluding with the prayer:

> O Adonai, you who have created all of us and wish no unhappiness for your creatures! Oh God, our common Father, God of mercy make it possible that on our little globe, on this, the least of Thy worlds, there be neither fanatics nor persecutors.

This might have been Voltaire's only concern with the Malagrida case, except for the fact that the case also aroused the wrath of the Abbé Morellet.

Morellet was an immensely learned young man completing his studies at the Sorbonne in the late 1750s when a new outbreak of persecutions struck the Protestants of Languedoc. A representative of the persecuted Huguenots in Paris interested Morellet in their plight, and Morellet decided to produce "a pleasantry, in the manner of the works of Jonathan Swift." Morellet's "pleasantry" was the *Petit écrit sur une matière intéressante*, a satire in which a member of an imaginary French Inquisition protests to the king of France that religious toleration has its dangers and expresses fear that the king will offer toleration to Protestants in North America at the end of the Seven Years War. The short work goes on to suggest some reforms, including the establishment of the Inquisition in North America, the forced ordering of Protestants to believe Catholic dogma, the secret execution by fire of all Protestants in North America, and the argument that France must cease to concentrate on trivial affairs such as material prosperity, and focus instead on important interests such as life in the next world. Morellet's arguments ridiculed only the inquisitorial viewpoint, however, not Catholicism nor the prospect of Catholicism as a state religion in France. Morellet introduced the *Petit écrit* by stating that it was printed on "Inquisition Road, under the Sign of St. Dominic."

A year or two later, in 1758, Morellet was in Rome attending the papal conclave that followed the death of Benedict XIV. The city being overcrowded, he was lodged in the library of the Abbé de Canillac, an auditor of the Roman Rota, and the library was necessarily filled with the works of theologians and canon lawyers:

> In looking over this heap of trash, I fell upon the *Directorium Inquisito-rum* of Nicholas Eymeric, grand inquisitor of the fourteenth century. . . . This text struck me with horror; it was an enormous folio volume which one could ónly sample. I decided to make extracts, under the title *Manuel des Inquisiteurs*, of all that seemed to me the most revolting; and, with a little trouble, I finally managed to give a coherent body and a shape to these scattered atrocities. I arranged them according to the order of [inquisitorial] procedure, beginning with the information [the denunciation of someone to the Inquisition], and finishing with the execution of those condemned. I forbade myself any commentary, because the text alone suggested quite satisfactorily what I would have been able to do.

Morellet's translation, the *Manuel des Inquisiteurs*, appeared in 1762 with a preface that discussed the Malagrida case, as well as the arguments contained in the official Portuguese Inquisition account of the charges and the execution. After pointing out that the Jesuits, who used to approve inquisitions, now oppose them, and that a Jansenist, who used to oppose inquisitions, now approves them in the case of Jesuits, the author of the preface identifies the translator of the *Manuel* as a "friend of the Jesuits," and "if the maxims of the Inquisition here exposed happen to revolt rationality and humanity, it is not the fault of the translator." Morellet added to his excerpts from Eymeric an account of the origins of the Portuguese Inquisition derived from the history of Luis de Pàramo that dealt with the myth of Saavedra, the false inquisitor. Together these works excerpted material that emphasized the least attractive side of the inquisitions, focused exclusively upon the uses of deceit and trickery in order to obtain convictions, and absolutely ignored the vast amount of other material found in Eymeric and Pàramo. The very compactness of Morellet's work, however, increased its appeal and circulation (it is this book that Edgar Allan Poe has Roderick Usher read frequently in "The Fall of the House of Usher"), and provided information about the darker side of the inquisition that few of its harshest critics knew until then (Plate 16).

Morellet's *Manuel* appeared to a chorus of delight from the liberal eighteenth-century world. Frederick II of Prussia wrote him a congratulatory letter, and Voltaire was delighted: "I read with great delight the inquisitors' manual, and I am angry at myself because [I had] Candide kill only one inquisitor: . . . my brothers, I thank you in the name of humanity for having sent me the manual of the inquisition. It is a great pity that the philosophers are not numerous, zealous, or rich enough to destroy by fire and flame these enemies of the human race, and the abominable sect that has produced such horrors; [reading] the pretty jurisprudence of the inquisition . . . has had on me the same effect as the sight of the bloody corpse of Caesar had on the Romans. Men do not deserve to live as long as there is enough wood and fire that they do not use to burn these monsters in their infamous lairs. . . . [I embrace] the worthy brother who has made this excellent work. May it be translated into Portuguese and Castilian as well. The more we are attached to the holy religion of our savior Jesus Christ, the more we must abhor the abominable use of his divine law that men make every day."

Voltaire's reading of Morellet shaped the article "Inquisition" which he included in his *Philosophical Dictionary* in 1769, and it influenced a number of other articles, notably that on "Freedom of Thought," which is a dialogue between an Englishman and a Spanish servant of the Inquisition. The "Inquisition" article is largely a paraphrase of Morellet's extracts from Paramo in the *Manuel des Inquisiteurs*, repeating the story of Saavedra, and denouncing the legal procedure. In 1767 Voltaire again attacked dogmatism and its terrible consequences in the *Questions de Zapata*, a disingenuous list of questions allegedly forwarded to the faculty of theology at the University of Salamanca in 1629 by a young graduate. The sixty-seven questions range across the Old and

New Testaments, raising embarassing problems in terms of official Christian teaching. At the end of the list, Voltaire drily notes that:

> Zapata, having had no response, set himself to preaching the word of God quite simply. He announced to men the father of men, who rewarded and punished and pardoned. He separated out the lies and distinguished religion from fanaticism; he taught and practiced virtue. He was gentle, helpful, modest, and was roasted at Valladolid, in the year of grace 1631. Pray to God for the soul of Brother Zapata.

Voltaire's combination of enlightened humanitarianism, cultural criticism, and satirical discourse gave his portrait of the inquisitions in the context of European cultural history a distinctive character, derived but substantially different from those of the Protestant polemicist historians. It offered cultural grounds for a study and critique of the Inquisition and its development, and, although it gave pride of place to Enlightenment humanitarianism, it placed intellectual oppression and cultural decline a close second. Behind the frivolous and comic misadventures of Pangloss, Cunigonde, and Candide, there lay an enlightened historical vision and a philosophical criticism that directed posterity's glance to the injustice, superstition, and inhumanity of religious persecution, completing the invention of *The Inquisition* in the process.

From Bayle to Voltaire the completed myth of *The Inquisition* was now so adorned as to appeal to all of Enlightened Europe down through the nineteenth century. The cases of Cesare Beccaria, Andreas Zaupser, and Victor Hugo indicate precisely how suitable and appealing it became and remained.

The reign of Joseph II brought the Enlightenment to the Hapsburg Empire and shaped a group of Catholic *philosophes* who opposed many of the practices of the Church of the *Ancien Régime* as vigorously as their counterparts elsewhere. In Milan such a group included the brothers Pietro and Alessandro Verri, eloquent and learned civic reformers, and their protégé Cesare Beccaria. In collaboration with Pietro Verri, Beccaria published in 1764 his treatise on the reform of the criminal law, *On Crimes and Punishments*, which quickly became the most widely read and formally influential work on a subject close to the heart of the Enlightenment. Denouncing what he considered the worst legal abuses of his own day, Beccaria received the enthusiasm of the leading critics of contemporary penal policy, including Helvétius, d'Alembert, d'Holbach, Buffon, Hume, and Voltaire. In 1766 the work was translated into French by none other than the indefatigable Abbé Morellet. *On Crimes and Punishments* criticized many of the assumptions upon which the judicial treatment of religious offenders was based throughout Europe, including the testimony of secret witnesses, the danger of crimes whose proof is difficult, suggestive interrogations, and the use of torture. Beccaria argues that crimes against God are to be punished by God and not by man, and in a highly ironic Chapter XXXVII, he takes up what he calls "A Particular Kind of Crime," the crime of heresy:

> The reader of this work will notice that I have omitted a class of crimes that has covered Europe with human blood and has raised those awful piles where living human bodies used to serve as food for flames . . .

Beccaria's denunciation of inquisitorial tribunals is written with intricate irony, protesting all the while how difficult it is to do justice to the excellent arguments that justify such persecution, and concluding that,

> It would take me too far to prove that, howsoever odious the imposition of force upon human minds may be, gaining for itself only dissimulation followed by debasement, and howsoever contrary it may seem to the spirit of gentleness and fraternity, commanded by reason and by the authority we most venerate, it is, nevertheless, necessary and indispensable.

Even in irony, however, Beccaria points out that crimes against God are to be determined by principles far different from those crude policies of inquisitorial tribunals.

At the other end of the Hapsburg Empire, a Catholic civil servant in Bavaria, Andreas Zaupser, published in 1770 a series of *Letters on the Power of the Church and the Pope*, which criticized the use of punitive authority in religious affairs and urged a broad degree of religious and civil toleration throughout Germany and the Empire. The fourth of Zaupser's *Letters* treated the question "Whether the Church has an independent right to punish breaches of the faith," and it made in passing the argument that "the Inquisition was the most vexing tribunal that the world had ever seen."

The *Letters* made Zaupser some enemies as well as friends, and he continued to publish comments on historical and contemporary Catholicism. Among the enemies he inspired, many were fellow Catholics, notably the Dominican Thomas Aquino Jost, who produced a vitriolic pamphlet attacking the "freethinkers" of his age and urging the creation of an Inquisition in Bavaria to wipe out such freethinking as Zaupser's. Zaupser also became familiar with contemporary inquisitorial cases, particularly that of Pablo Olavide, the Spanish noble who was arrested and imprisoned by the Spanish Inquisition because of his attraction to contemporary French thought. The situation in Bavaria, the case of

Olavide, and the new temper of criticism of Catholic positions sustained Zaupser's and others' polemics against religious persecution.

In 1778 a little tract was published in Munich called *Thoughts on the Inquisition*, anonymous and highly critical. In 1777 Zaupser published his own "Ode to the Inquisition," a long poem, the first half of which attacks the Inquisition, and the second half is a plea to Toleration:

> Debauch and revel by your roaring fires,
> Hag Inquisition,
> Atrocious daughter of Stupidity and Death,
> Plague of Reason and Religion both:
>
> Under your black heels tread down again
> Defrauded slaves into the dust;
> Command again: "No heretic will be spared."
> The monks, your servants, those who confiscate
> The inheritances of orphaned children
> And scream blasphemous prayers at corpses, are
> Like bloody tigers which scatter the peaceful herds
> As they roar out of the forest.
>
> Iberia is already emptied by your dragon-breath.
> Truth, friendship, and the arts all flee;
> The thinker's freedom dies in your smoking pyres.
> Murderess of the Mind, you suffocate it.
>   . . . .
> O Toleration, child of God, springing forth from the wounds of Christ,
> O turn your healing glance to the South,
> Where, with tears, Mankind cries out for aid.
> Hear the screams of the murdered, the death-rattles, moans
> Brought to you by the ash-filled air.
>
> Fly there with angel's strength, strike low that Monster
> So that it flies straight back to Hell,
> And teach that zealous flock, our wayward, wandering brothers,
> That conversion comes with meekness, not the sword.

On Zaupser's large and somewhat operatic scale, *The Inquisition* was the polar opposite of *Toleration*, the hag opposed to the youth. In spite of references in the work of both Voltaire and Zaupser to the specific inquisitions of Iberia, the *philosophe* myth of *The Inquisition* is no longer located in Spain, Rome, or Portugal: it applies wherever there is religious persecution, no matter who does it, no matter the name of the cause in which it is done. The myth has been secularized and universalized well beyond its original Protestant and anti-Spanish beginnings.

As a universal and secularized myth, *The Inquisition* was cited in much the same terms through the nineteenth century, well outside of the circles of Protestant polemic.

When Victor Hugo wrote his "legendary" history of the world, *La légende des siècles* in 1859, he placed his "legend" concerning the Inquisition in Book X, "Les raisons du Momotombo." He had asked a friend in that year to find him materials concerning the reigns of Ferdinand and Isabela and the life of the inquisitor Torquemada. At this period in his life, Hugo was reading Voltaire and accepted much of Voltaire's thought, particularly in matters of religious toleration and persecution. But Hugo was inspired by other sources as well, in this case by the work of an American traveler, E. G. Squire's *Travels in Central America, particularly in Nicaragua*, which mentioned the baptizing of volcanoes in Nicaragua, a custom which seemed to Squire to have dated from the period of the original Spanish conquest. Hugo's epigraph to Book X is taken from Squire:

> The baptism of volcanoes is an ancient custom which goes back to the time of the conquest. All the craters of Nicaragua were thus sanctified, with the exception of Momotombo, from which one never saw return those clergy who had been charged with climbing it and planting the cross.

"The Reasons of Momotombo," then, is Hugo's Voltairean meditation on the Inquisition in the personification of the unbaptized volcano. Momotombo begins his "reasons" by observing that he had never liked the god whom the Spaniards had chased away, since that god had secreted his treasures in the earth, eaten human flesh, and behaved in an utterly repellent way in all other matters. Thus, Momotombo welcomed the Christian Spaniards, since their Gospel was far more to his liking than that of their predecessors. But when Momotombo saw the flames of *autos-de-fé* of the Inquisition in Nicaragua,

> When I saw how Torquemada took those torches and exactly how he used them to dissipate the night of the ignorant savages, how he civilized them, exactly how the Holy Office taught and what it did with light, when I saw at Lima frightful wicker-basket giants, filled with children, roasting on a great fire, which devoured life,

when Momotombo himself was nearly suffocated with the smoke of the *autos-de-fé*, he decided that he had been premature in welcoming the Christians: "I had seen the god of these strangers up close, and I said: 'It isn't worth the trouble to convert.'"

Shielding his criticisms by permitting the volcano to utter them, Hugo gave *The Inquisition* its own place in his history.

That place had been shaped by the *philosophes*, themselves influenced by the varied strands of opposition to religious persecution woven in the sixteenth and seventeenth centuries, integrated by Bayle, and passed down to a group of secular thinkers and writers who universalized them and made their arguments a fundamental part of the Enlightenment legacy.

Chapter Seven

The Inquisition in Literature and Art

The Inquisition had been invented in a literature of religious, political, historical, and philosophical polemic. By the seventeenth century it was sufficiently familiar (and familiarly illustrated in engravings that accompanied polemics) to attract the interest of writers of other kinds of literature and to become part of the literary furnishings of drama and novel. Denounced as an institution that crippled art and literature, it soon became one of their most dramatic components. Literary and artistic depictions of *The Inquisition* varied according to the purposes of the writers and artists who made them, much as did the depiction of *The Inquisition* in the work of religious and philosophical polemicists. And just as one may trace the development of ideas of religious toleration and philosophical enlightenment from the perspective of the way in which *The Inquisition* is used in their causes, one may also trace some of the transformations in early modern European literature and art by the perspective from which writers and artists depicted *The Inquisition*.

The sources of such early literary and artistic depictions were not only the polemical literature of the sixteenth and seventeenth centuries, but also the literature of travel and personal narrative that began to appear in considerable volume in·the seventeenth century. If the sixteenth and seventeenth centuries were fascinated with Inquisition martyrologies, the seventeenth and eighteenth centuries were fascinated with eyewitness accounts of societies in which *The Inquisition* flourished, whether told by returning literary travelers or escaped victims. From these accounts, writers of fiction (often purporting to be "true history") drew a wealth of detail and subjective perception that they then worked into their own narratives. Although travelers' accounts and personal escape narratives had a life and reading public of their own, often for decades after they first appeared, they also provided material for writers and artists that contributed, often in a minor way, to what emerged in the late eighteenth and nineteenth centuries as the literature and art of terror.

From the personal narratives and travelers' reports of the seventeenth century to the work of Edgar Allan Poe and Grace Aguilar in the nineteenth, *The Inquisition* became part of a literary world that varied from picaresque romances to gothic and sentimental novels. From the paintings of Pedro Berruguete to those of Francisco Goya, the verbal myth acquired a visual counterpart, one that developed the myth in greater detail and intensity. In the very centuries in which inquisitions were weakening and even disappearing, writers and artists brought their largest and most horrifying dimensions closer to readers and viewers than even the most articulate polemic or the most detailed of histories. In their work the myth took on an immediacy and imposing presence that greatly strengthened its other roles in religious, political, and philosophical polemic.

Travelers' Reports and Personal Narratives

For all of their tendency to criticize and deplore the culture of Spain and Catholic Europe generally, seventeenth- and eighteenth-century Europeans also were fascinated by it, and many traveled to examine it at first hand. Their reports constituted a source of information and misinformation about *The Inquisition* that had a great impact on northern European opinion and literature in general. Beginning in the early seventeenth century, another genre of narrative—the personal narratives of individuals who had been examined by one of the Mediterranean Inquisitions— became equally widespread and equally popular. The two new kinds of source exerted an influence that went beyond simple polemic; for they influenced the nature of prose narrative itself and contributed to the emergence of the novel. From the original political and economic character of travel accounts the tone shifted in the late seventeenth and eighteenth centuries to the "romantic" character of the Spanish landscape and people; the Spanish and Portuguese Inquisitions also shifted in character from religious tribunals to instruments for suppressing the intellect and persecuting unwary foreigners who fell into their hands. And what was written about an Inquisition in one place soon came to characterize all Inquisitions everywhere.

From the early seventeenth century especially, French travelers brought back accounts of Spanish life and character that greatly influenced French literary and philosophical opinion. French works translated into other languages (or read in French elsewhere) dominated a large literature that included English and German works as well. Few travelers failed to describe and condemn the Inquisition. Its irregular judicial procedures, its use of secret informants and secret testimony, the "turning of what elsewhere in Europe is a criminal execution into a religious ceremony," and the public character of the *auto-de-fé* all excited European readers, including those who had no particular concern for religion at all. The most influential of these accounts, Madame d'Aulnoy's *Relation d'un voyage en Espagne* of 1691, was known to Montesquieu and Voltaire, as we have seen, and her savage and erroneous portrait of the Spanish Inquisition became one of the best-known sources for information and misinformation concerning the institution and its history in northern Europe.

Besides such travel accounts, the reports of former victims of the Inquisitions also became extremely popular in the seventeenth and eighteenth centuries, originally among those who read martyrologies and polemic, but later among a wider readership as well. Among the earliest and most widely circulated of these was the narrative of William Lithgow, a Scottish adventurer who fell first into the hands of the Spanish civil government at Málaga in 1620 and after a few months' confinement was turned over to the Inquisition. Accused of blasphemy, and refusing all attempts to convert him to Catholicism, Lithgow claimed to have suffered in one night eleven different tortures, and later close confinement, starvation, sleeplessness, and the prospect of being burned at an *auto-de-fé* in Granada. Intervention by the English community in Málaga obtained his release just in time, and Lithgow was returned to England and welcomed by the king. Lithgow's account of his experience with the Inquisition at Málaga was originally published in 1632 and reprinted in a longer (and tedious) account of the rest of his travels in 1640. It was subsequently excerpted and paraphrased frequently during the seventeenth and eighteenth centuries.

The personal narrative that had the greatest impact, however was the French physician Charles Dellon's account of his own experiences at the hands of the Portuguese Inquisition in Goa. The *Relation de l'Inquisition de Goa*, was first published at Leyden in 1687; a Paris edition followed in 1688, and the book was widely reprinted, with a distinctive set of illustrations, through the eighteenth century. With the *Relation* of Madame d'Aulnoy, Dellon's account of the Portuguese Inquisition was the most well-known of its kind, and its popularity may account for the fact that, in eighteenth-century literature, the Inquisition of Portugal was as well-known to northern Europeans as was that of Spain. Dellon's *Relation* was the late seventeenth-century equivalent of Montanus, and it circulated nearly as widely.

The octavo volumes that contained the accounts of d'Aulnoy, Lithgow, and Dellon were relatively inexpensive and circulated far more widely than the great folio volumes of Pàramo and Limborch. The smaller, less expensive form of these books made them widely accessible and created a distinctive literary genre that produced a steady stream of accounts for nearly two centuries. Among the most widely circulating tales of personal adventure with various inquisitions several deserve somewhat fuller descriptions. In 1708 there appeared in London *An Account of the Cruelties Exercis'd by the Inquisition in Portugal*. The anonymous author professed to have been a secretary of the Portuguese Inquisition who grew disgusted with his work and fled to Rome in 1672, where he produced an account of his experience and circulated it to some friends, including, presumably, the Englishman who had it printed. The English translator remarks that the author in no way intends to blacken the name of the Roman religion, merely to denounce a particularly ungodly institution. As the *Account* was being set in type, its publisher tells us, he was given another account, this time of the experiences of Louis Ramé in the Mexican Inquisition during the period 1679–1682, and the publisher printed both accounts in the same volume. The Portuguese account focuses much more than most others on the trials of *conversos*, and it gives the account of the trial of three sisters before the Inquisition at Évora in 1660, as well as descriptions of a number of other cases. The interrogation of Ramé, a French-Protestant sea-captain, by the Mexican Inquisition between 1679–1682, is presented in considerable detail with little comment. Ramé had been shipwrecked and washed ashore in Puerto Rico. He was detained and then sent on to Mexico, where he sought work until he could get back to France. In 1678, when the local clergy attempted to convert a dying Dutch citizen to Catholicism, they pressed Ramé into service as a translator for their cause. Upon Ramé's refusal, and his later refusal to pay homage to a procession carrying the eucharist, he was brought to the Inquisition. The trend of Ramé's interrogators was to discover whether he had shown contempt for the Roman Catholic religion. After three years of failing to convert Ramé, the Inquisition remanded to him to the Royal Prison, then transferred him to Vera Cruz, then to Havana, and finally shipped him to Seville, where he remained in various forms of Spanish custody until 1687, when French intervention finally arranged his freedom.

Such works as these, to whatever degree accurate, familiarized new generations of readers with inquisition material, and they were added to periodically throughout the eighteenth and early nineteenth centuries. In 1723 there appeared in London *The Tryal and Sufferings of Mr. Isaac Martin, who was put into the Inquisition in Spain for the sake of the Protestant Religion.* The little book, certified by a number of English prelates and dedicated to George I, tells the story of Martin, an English merchant and tavern-keeper in Málaga, whose rival merchants, Irish papists, denounced him to the Inquisition. He was held for eight months by the Inquisition in Granada, whipped, and banished from Spain forever. His narrative, an attractive, quite unvenomous account of his audiences with the inquisitors and his life in prison, concludes with an appeal for charity, since the Inquisition has ruined him, and denounces the Irish rivals and clergy who denounced him in the first place.

Reports like those of Lithgow, Dellon, the Portuguese Secretary, Ramé, and Martin were reprinted frequently throughout the eighteenth century. Martin's first edition contains a number of illustrations of Inquisition buildings, officials, and victims, all taken from Dellon, and it was quickly translated into other languages—French, probably in Holland, in 1723, and into German in 1724. A second edition appeared in English in 1730, and in 1734 it was included in J[ames?] Baker's *The History of the Inquisition*, along with accounts of the trial of Miguel de Molinos, the experiences of Louis Ramé, excerpts from Gavin's *Master-Key to Popery* (the story of Madame Faulcaut), Dellon's *Relation*, an English translation of a chapter by Dupin's continuator, and other materials. This work was reprinted (without editorial attribution) in 1739, as *An Impartial Account of Many Barbarous Cruelties Exercised by the Inquisition in Spain, Portugal, and Italy.* Baker was obviously a general opponent of religious persecution, and his work rounds out a decade marked by the recent success of Chandler's English translation of Limborch of 1731 and Chandler's own *History of Persecution* of 1736. Baker's sentiments are generally similar to those of Limborch and Chandler. He argues that he is not writing merely Protestant anti-Catholic polemic, for

> Catholicks (as they call themselves) nay, Officers and Judges of the Holy Office, have confessed all this, and more, even with Pride and Exultation of Heart. Far from hiding and denying such things, they imagine them honorable. . . .

In this octavo of 431 pages, illustrated with five of the frequently reprinted engravings illustrating inquisitorial procedures and features, virtually a library of seventeenth- and eighteenth-century personal accounts and excerpts from historical and polemical works is to be found. It is consistent with Baker's own position that this anthology of Inquisition descriptions was probably a contribution to the general Latitudinarian position against religious persecution, although none of its contributors ever intended that their narratives should serve this end, and at least two of them, Dupin and his anonymous commentator, would have been heartily surprised to see their work translated and excerpted into English and published by a Dissenter in the cause of religious toleration.

Lithgow's account of his adventures was separately printed again in 1771, and throughout the later eighteenth century such personal accounts as these appear to have been widely known, cited in later works, including histories, and printed to serve a variety of causes, of which anti-Catholic (or anti-Roman, or anti-Hispanic) propaganda was now but one of several. The cause of religious toleration also produced its substantial number of histories and personal accounts of *The Inquisition*, and from the early eighteenth century on, two other circumstances entered the lists: cases of prosecution for Freemasonry, and personal narratives written by former Catholic priests and inquisitors who turned against Rome and entered the cause of both history and polemic. The best known of the former is the case and narrative of John Coustos; of the latter, those of Anthony Gavin and Archibald Bower.

The first masonic lodge was established in London in 1717. Inspired by the ideas of deism, and as yet not anticlerical, Freemasons recruited their members from the upper classes, invited wide-ranging discussions of religious and philosophical topics in their meetings, and rapidly became a pan-European, and even a pan-Atlantic organization. In 1738 Pope Clement XII, in the bull *In eminenti*, forbade Catholics to become masons, although Catholics did so in significant numbers through the eighteenth and into the nineteenth century. With the political revolutions and curtailments of clerical civil authority from the end of the eighteenth century on, Freemasons became more pronouncedly anticlerical, and in turn they were often blamed by clerics (along with the *philosophes*) for having contributed to the outbreak of revolution and to the discredit of religion.

In 1746 in London there appeared *The Sufferings of John Coustos for Free-Masonry, and for his refusing to Turn Roman Catholic in the Inquisition at Lisbon*, edited for publication by an anonymous Englishman who claimed not to be a mason himself, but whose powerful anti-Roman (and anti-French) sentiments are everywhere evident in the Preface. Coustos had apparently brought not only his own narrative, but materials for a history of the Inquisition, derived from Limborch, Bayle,

and other writers, and the editor arranged these and printed them with
Coustos' story. Thus, the book emerges as a characteristic personal narrative with supporting materials anthologized as a long appendix. Since
the book was printed by subscription, it appeared with three original
engravings of Inquisition torture scenes.

Coustos, a native of Switzerland whose parents lived in and fled France
with other Protestant exiles, worked as a jeweler in France and moved
to Portugal, hoping to be permitted to migrate to Brazil, where he expected
to make his fortune. Prohibited from emigrating by the Portuguese king,
Coustos settled in Lisbon and enjoyed considerable favor and prosperity
in his trade until he was arrested by the Inquisition in its campaign to
crush Freemasonry. Coustos was the master of a lodge, and he implies
that he was a natural target for his enemies for this reason. Coustos
was arrested in 1743, interrogated concerning masonry for several weeks,
urged to convert to Catholicism, and then tortured on the grounds that
he had failed to tell the truth. He claims to have been tortured by the
tightening of ropes around his body, by a kind of horizontal strappado
procedure, and by pressure of a tightened iron chain. Sentenced at an
auto-de-fé, Coustos was sent to the Lisbon prison at hard labor, from
which he was released only by the intervention of the English government.

Coustos' own narrative takes up seventy seven pages; the attached
"Treatise on the Origins of the Inquisition, and its Establishment in
various Countries" occupies 322 pages. That an émigré Swiss jeweler
might have the avocation of collecting materials for the history of the
Inquisition is somewhat improbable. The anonymous editor observes
that the "Treatise" derives from Limborch and other unnamed authors
and that he, the editor, added additional material from Bayle and others.
The version of Inquisition history laid out in the "Treatise" is the common
one: the popes, seeking ever to aggrandize their power, at first threw
down the emperors in the late eleventh century and then set out to
attack those who were "Heretics, or rather enemies to the Pontifical
Authority of Rome." The "Treatise" describes the Albigensian Crusade
and then the establishment of the Inquisition with Dominic as the first
inquisitor, initially subordinate to the bishops, but in the course of the
thirteenth century becoming independent of them. Dominic and the
other inquisitors "came from the Dregs of the People, and had no Kindred,
as it were, or any other Tie which might check the Rigours of this
Tribunal." The social isolation of the Inquisitors, here as elsewhere,
was a point that much exercised the inquisitions' critics. The "Treatise"
then provides brief accounts of the institution of the Inquisition in Italy,
Spain, Portugal, and Lower Germany, and observes that England itself

came very close to an Inquisition several times. The first was during the reign of Mary Tudor, the second shortly before the enlightened eighteenth century itself:

> And hence, that Englishman must read, with the utmost Detestation, the following Words, spoke by a Recorder of London at the Trial of the celebrated Quakers William Penn and William Mead: "Till now, I never understood the Reason of the Policy and Prudence of the Spaniards, in suffering the Inquisition among them. And certainly it will never be well with us, till something like the Spanish Inquisition be in England."

The "Treatise" continues with a description of the Inquisition, largely derived from Limborch and Dellon, a list of examples of the injustice and cruelty of the Inquisition, with a martyrology, a retelling of earlier individual reports including that of William Lithgow, and other stories derived from Montanus. The "Treatise's" favorite spokesman against the claims of the Roman Church and the Inquisition is Pierre Bayle, drawing extensively from Bayle's *Critique générale de l'histoire du Calvinisme de M. Maimbourg* of 1684.

The Inquisitors are worse than cruel, unjust, greedy, and hypocritical; "they are no less ignorant and barbarous than the Goths and Vandals," since they persecute "the most eminent Literati," including, of course, Galileo. From Bayle's *Dictionnaire* came the attack on the Inquisition as an enemy of learning, science, and letters. The author of "the Treatise" then cites the opinions of Erasmus on the Inquisition and the persecution of Lorenzo Valla and that of the Quietist Miguel de Molinos, citing the well-known verse of the Roman satirist Pasquino, à propos the Inquisition and Quietism:

> If we speak, we are sent to the Galleys; if we write we are hanged; if we continue quiet we are clapt up in the Inquisition: what are we to do?

The "Treatise" concludes with an account of the preferable methods by which the primitive Church treated heretics, and a denunciation of the Inquisition. Translated into French and printed in Holland in 1747, and into German in 1756, Coustos' narrative was reprinted in London in 1790 with the addition of some masonic material. The "masonic" version of Coustos' narrative was reprinted in Boston in 1817 and several times later in the nineteenth century, either with the masonic material or with the account of Anthony Gavin in his *Master-Key to Popery Display'd*. The masonic attack on the Inquisition was continued in the remarkable account of his own adventures by Hypolyto José da Costa

Pereira Furtado de Mendonça, and published in England in Portuguese and English editions in 1811, with an extensive translation of the "Bye-Laws of the Inquisition of Lisbon." Like the editor of Coustos, Mendonça denounces the Inquisition particularly as a bastion of ignorance, reprinting the decision against Galileo; also like Coustos and his editor, Mendonça appears to have become an expert in the literature on the Inquisition after his own experience.

In addition to the "masonic" narratives, there also appeared in the mid-eighteenth century the personal accounts of former Catholic priests. Of these, the narratives of Archibald Bower and Anthony Gavin circulated widely; part of Gavin's work, as we have seen, was later reprinted with that of Coustos. Bower, an English Catholic priest in the service of the Inquisition at Macerata in Italy, relates two cases before the Inquisition that inspired him to escape from its service, from Italy, and from Catholicism itself. His short work recounts the case of a man, innocently accused of contempt for the Inquisition, who was arrested, immediately tortured until he was driven mad, and finally released when the real offender was caught. The second story is that of a young husband, arrested for having spoken contemptuously of some penitent monks, who died under the torture. Bower then gives a brief account of his own escape to Switzerland, France, and finally to England. Bower became something of a celebrated controversialist, author of a *History of the Popes*, and his short account was reprinted several times into the early nineteenth century, usually with the English translation of Charles Dellon's account of the Inquisition in Goa.

Like the unnamed Secretary of the Portuguese Inquisition cited above, accounts by former inquisitors and former Catholic priests were popular during the eighteenth century. Anthony Gavin, claiming to have been a secular priest of Zaragoza, fled Spain in the early years of the eighteenth century, became an Anglican priest in 1715, and in 1726 published a French version of his *Master-Key to Popery*, which may have been published earlier in English, but whose earliest English version dates only from 1729 and whose first recorded passages on the Inquisition were frequently excerpted and reprinted until well into the nineteenth century. The *Master-Key* is a three-volume work that attacks the Roman Church from every conceivable eighteenth-century hostile perspective. The first volume deals with abuses of the confessional, the dogmas of the Mass and other sacraments, the adoration of images, and the Inquisition. The second volume contains a scabrous history of the popes and an even more scabrous series of clerical biographies. The third volume deals with the Mass, sanctity, and miracle stories. In all, the *Master-*

Key to Popery is an extensive arsenal of anti-Catholic sentiment, told by an alleged former priest in the Roman Church, and thereby appealingly authenticated for its readers.

Of the whole work, Gavin's account of the Inquisition was especially widely read. He restricts himself to the tribunal of Zaragoza, which he claims to have known at first hand. Gavin describes the personnel of the tribunal, narrates several cases before it, and tells with considerable skill and relish a story from the War of the Spanish Succession that shows the Inquisitors in a discreditable light. In 1706, Gavin says, the French armies entered Spain and began to extract funds from the religious institutions of Zaragoza. When the Dominicans had been forced to make their contribution, they sent the secretary of the Inquisition to announce to de Légal, the French commander, that he was hereby excommunicated. De Légal asked for an opportunity to answer their action the next day, and he did. He sent four batallions under his secretary, who announced that the inquisitors themselves were excommunicated and expelled from their palace; he then quartered his troops there for eight months. The inquisitors could find no redress, although they appealed to the king of Spain. The French liberated four hundred prisoners from the Inquisition, including sixty young women who were the harem of the three inquisitors. Gavin then narrates the story of one of these women, Madame Faulcaut, whom he later met in France. He concludes with the description of a dozen or so other cases that illustrate the horrors and hypocrisies of the Zaragoza Inquisition.

Gavin's tale of Madame Faulcaut is a splendidly created fiction, possibly the earliest instance of the theme of the cruel and erotic inquisitor. Having caught the eye of one of the three inquisitors of Zaragoza, Madame Faulcaut was arrested, threatened with death, and imprisoned until she gave in to the inquisitor's lusts. Treated royally for a time, she soon found herself living in a prison like all of the other young ladies who lived to serve the lusts of the three inquisitors. After several years, she and a companion began to lose favor with their captors and were moved from house to house until the French discovered and delivered them. Both Madame Faulcaut and her companion Leonora married French officers and lived happily ever after. A summary cannot do justice to Gavin's skillful tale, and it is not surprising that the 1739 *Impartial Account* excerpted it. It is one of the best-told stories of the genre of personal narrative of the inquisitions, and one that foreshadows the tales of the later gothic novels nearly a century later.

To anyone setting out to discover something about the inquisitions in the second half of the eighteenth century, the material available was far larger and far more varied than it had been a century earlier. Not only were printed materials on the Inquisition more available, but formidable histories, particularly that of Limborch, offered vast amounts of information, as well as judgment and opinion. In addition to these, the large literature of personal narratives, reportorial or, as in the case of Gavin, fictitious, as well as the periodical issues of polemical pamphlets and books, made the subject far more complex than it had been during the relatively simple confessional and political controversies of the late sixteenth century. Late eighteenth-century satire, and, at the end of the century and the beginning of the next, the emergence of gothic fiction further compounded the complexity of Inquisition source materials.

Picaresque Romance and "True History": Lesage and Saint-Réal

In the seventeenth- and eighteenth-century historiography of Spain the Inquisition vied with Philip II as an object of historians' interest. The earliest sixteenth-century polemical accounts of Spanish history depict Philip II as the dupe of the inquisitors, and the subject that most commonly linked them together was the death of Philip's son Don Carlos in 1568. The Don Carlos theme became immensely popular, not only in polemic and historiography, but in prose fiction and drama from the seventeenth to the nineteenth centuries, culminating in the great play of Schiller and the vast opera by Verdi.

Historically, Don Carlos appears to have been erratic and unstable, and his behavior early gave Philip II considerable concern as to his suitability to inherit the crown. After 1562, Philip II denied his son the customary honors accorded the heir-apparent and finally confined Don Carlos, who died suddenly (and from all the evidence, accidentally) in 1568. Don Carlos' stepmother, Elizabeth de Valois, Philip's wife, died shortly after. By 1570, the *Petition* of the Netherlands Refugees to the Diet of Augsburg already accused the Spanish Inquisition of having caused the death of Don Carlos because the Inquisition feared that Don Carlos would liberate the Netherlands from the bloody regime of the Duke of Alva. In 1581 William of Orange's *Apologie* accused Philip himself of having murdered his own son. Once the Netherlands revolutionaries threw off the image of Philip as the king duped by the Inquisition and directed their wrath at Philip as a bloody tyrant, the case of Don Carlos became that of a potential savior of the Netherlands, murdered by Philip II, the Inquisition, or both.

A number of later historians, Spanish and other, treated the case of Don Carlos, some of them, notably de Thou and Agrippa d'Aubigné, following the version most hostile to Philip II. Dramatists, too, found the subject intriguing, particularly the possibility that Don Carlos was in love with Elizabeth de Valois and that their deaths were connected. From the 1580s these themes were woven into a "myth" of Don Carlos, according to which Don Carlos and Elizabeth had been engaged before Philip II married her as an affair of state. Don Carlos, torn between love and loyalty, turned his attention to the pathetic cause of the Netherlands revolt, and was murdered at the orders of his father and the Inquisition. The themes of frustrated noble love and paternal ferocity remained attached to the Don Carlos myth for several centuries.

The themes of Don Carlos' lost marriage and his love for the Netherlands were emphasized in the *Relaciones* of Antonio Perez, a disgraced favorite of Philip II in exile in England, in 1598. The *Relaciones* and Perez' work in English, A *Treatise Paraenetical*, also of 1598, performed the double role of filling out the appealing literary theme of the tragic Don Carlos and the political theme of Don Carlos as the murdered potential savior of the Netherlands. From 1600 on, writers might emphasize one or the other, usually both, and the literary appeal of the story served as a continuing vehicle for the political ideas that could be woven into it.

The literary and political strands of the Don Carlos legend were woven together, successfully and dramatically, in the novel *Dom Carlos*, published in 1672 by the courtier-diplomat-historian-litterateur César Vichard de Saint-Réal. Although Saint-Réal claimed to have been following the best historical sources (and has been subsequently criticized roundly for doing this so badly), the work is a novel, not a history, and it became very popular.

Saint-Réal, like other seventeenth-century writers of romances, professed "to have drawn this *histoire* from all of the writers, Spaniards, French, Italian, and Flemings, who have written about this period." The profession that the novel is a "history" was not uncommon, but a glance at the mixture of Protestant and Catholic, Spanish and non-Spanish writers, and the serene imperviousness that Saint-Réal displays to their many contradictions suggests that the author looked chiefly for dramatic elements wherever he could find them and paid little attention to any "historical" problems his sources presented. For Saint-Réal, "history" seems to have meant only "in the past, historically intriguing, and dramatically coherent." His novel certainly was all of these.

The novel begins with Charles V's fears for Philip II as he plans to abdicate, notably the threat of war with France. In order to prevent this, Charles agrees to a truce with France, sealed by the betrothal of Don Carlos to Elizabeth de Valois, daughter of Henri II. The truce collapses, however, and in the ensuing diplomatic and domestic events, Philip II becomes widowed and demands for himself the hand of Elizabeth. Don Carlos is horrified, and the remainder of the novel plays out the theme of the older, jealous husband, the love of Elizabeth and Carlos, and Carlos' own political and religious development. One of the earliest of these is Saint-Réal's discussion of Charles V's alleged secret sympathy for Protestantism, followed by the suspicion of Protestantism attached to Charles' advisers Constantin Ponce and Cazalla and the insistence of the Inquisition that they be burned, Don Carlos immediately takes a great dislike to the Inquisition, and, with his friend the Prince of Parma,

> since they were too young to understand that even the most absolute of monarchs possessed none of the rights that are held to be most sacred in the spirit of Peoples, as holy as religion, they spoke publicly of the undertaking of the Inquisition, with all the carelessness that people of their kind are prone to display, and they threatened to terminate the Holy Office and its institution.

Matters are temporarily settled, however, but not without a lingering suspicion of Don Carlos on the part of the inquisitors. The tale goes on. Amidst the love affair and the king's weakness, Don Carlos is converted to the cause of Flemish liberties by Egmont and the visiting Flemish Deputies, becomes the object of the machinations of the wicked Inquisitor-General Spinoza, is tried by the Inquisition after his attempt to go to Flanders and relieve the oppressed population, and condemned to prison. Spinoza, however, is dissatisfied, observing to Philip II that "you have no cage strong enough to hold this bird." Don Carlos is slowly poisoned in prison and finally forced to open his veins in a bath, holding the portrait of the Queen in front of his eyes as he dies. The Queen herself is later poisoned, and the novel ends with a meditation on the brave souls of the two lovers and the horrible ends to which all of their enemies later came.

Dom Carlos, like many works of its kind, enjoyed an enormous popularity and an extremely wide influence. It provided the matter—emotional and political—for other works, some of which developed both themes extensively. It was frequently reprinted, pirated, plagiarized, and translated. An English translation appeared in 1674, and in 1676 Thomas Otway wrote his most successful play, *Don Carlos, Prince of Spain*, based upon the translation, possibly with the help of Saint-Réal himself. Otway also drew upon Shakespeare's *Othello* and Jean Racine's *Mithridate,* both of which contained similar structural elements, thus deepening and refining the literary appeal of the theme.

Although Otway, in the half-Catholic London of Charles II, did not emphasize the Inquisition and the tyranny of Philip II as much as he might have wished to, he did develop a new and important dramatic and political character, the Marquis of Posa, intimate of Don Carlos, and later a favorite spokesman for liberal political principles in other versions of the story, notably Schiller's. Among later versions of the story, that by Vittorio Alfieri, *Filippo II,* of 1783 profoundly blackens the character and tyranny of Philip II and is consequently less focused on the Inquisition. Other writers restored the Inquisition and elaborated upon it considerably. Louis-Sebastian Mercier's *Portrait de Philippe II, Roi d'Espagne* of 1785, a drama based on Saint-Réal, and on Robert Watson's *History of the Reign of Philip the Second, King of Spain,* a violently hostile history which had appeared in English in 1777 and was also widely translated, introduces an actual scene of an *auto-de-fé* onstage and has Carlos turned over to the Inquisition for execution. In most of these versions, eighteenth-century hostility to superstitions, injustice, and cruel, excessive punishment inform the unhappy story of Carlos, Elizabeth, and Philip II.

Besides the "true history"—best exemplified by Saint-Réal's *Dom Carlos*—two other literary genres took up the theme of the inquisitions in the eighteenth century. In the work of Voltaire and Montesquieu we have already encountered one of them: the philosophical satire. The other was the picaresque romance. The picaresque narrative, itself a Spanish invention, generally told the adventures of a roguish hero, whose position, often one of service, permitted the author to satirize and moralize on all social levels and display the folly of the world. Although the Spanish picaresque novels included satires of the clergy and ecclesiastical abuses, they were only lightly censored by the Inquisition in Spain. In terms of depicting the Inquisition, the best example of the genre is the romance *Gil Blas,* by Alain Réné Lesage (1668–1747).

In Book VI, Chapter 1 of *Gil Blas,* three rogues pose as officials of the Inquisition in order to bilk a wealthy *converso* of his fortune. The rogues use accurate Inquisition terminology, and they obtain the same fear and deference toward themselves as real inquisitors would. When a spiteful apprentice of the *converso* denounces him to the "inquisitors," they proceed to his house, terrify him, and secretly steal his money from a closet, which they then close up with an "inquisitor's seal."

Promising to return the next day, they flee the town, mocking the apprentice and the *converso*, pleased with themselves for having invented a new confidence swindle.

In a later expanded version of the novel, the protagonist, who had been with the rogues at the original swindle, has been sent to Toledo (Book XII, Chapter 1) to appraise the talents of a young actress for his master. An innkeeper mistakenly assumes that he has come to see the great *auto-de-fé* scheduled for the next day, and Gil Blas thinks it better to attend the ceremony. Lesage describes the procession of penitents with considerable accuracy. Gil Blas discovers two of his former accomplices among those condemned by the Inquisition, and he leaves after the *auto-de-fé*, quaking with fear and relief, "and I thought I could never be thankful enough to God, for having preserved me from the scapulary and *carochas*."

The picaresque novel, like the Hellenistic romances which it often resembles, depended upon such devices as disguises, impostures, mistaken identities, colorful adventures, and hairbreadth escapes for much of its machinery. To its customary cast of bandits, pirates, grandees, swindlers, and outraged authorities, the Inquisition made an appealing and novel addition. *Gil Blas* permitted the impersonation of inquisitors and thus a satire of the Inquisition itself, while it described the *auto-de-fé* in realistic terms.

Gil Blas was not Lesage's—or picaresque novelists'—only use of the Inquisition. In his later work *Vanillo Gonzalez*, the hero, an apothecary, is arrested by the Inquisition on the charge of sorcery, because rival perfumers and cosmeticians have denounced him as having sold an ointment that restores aged women to youth and beauty. The entire episode is intended as an object lesson to Vanillo about his miserliness, since the Inquisition not only strips him of all his wealth, but retains it after it has freed him. Within that object lesson, however, is a description of the Inquisition that is far more biting than either of the episodes in *Gil Blas*. Vanillo Gonzalez is abruptly visited by a commisary of the Inquisition, thrown into prison, and made to declare the extent and location of his wealth and possessions, which are then confiscated by the inquisitor's officials. Vanillo is reassured by the Commissary:

> You ought not to doubt . . . the integrity of the Holy Office; and if you are not guilty, you may rest assured that all your effects will be scrupulously restored into your hands.

After several sessions with the Grand Inquisitor, each of which is unsuccessful because Vanillo is ordered to state the reason for his arrest—

which he cannot do because he does not know it—Vanillo finally discovers
the nature of the charges against him, and he discovers that the charges
are indeed serious. Two ladies of his acquaintance, however, have used
intermediaries to win the favor of the Count-Duke of Olivares to intervene
in Vanillo's behalf with the Grand Inquisitor, who defers to the royal
minister, except in reserving the right to preserve the Inquisitor's honor
in the matter. The minister agrees, and Vanillo is freed the next day,
but upon the condition that he must formally plead guilty, since only
then can the Inquisition formally extend mercy to him. Since any further
conviction would classify Vanillo as a relapsed heretic, he must leave
the prison a confessed sorcerer, and since the charge of sorcery itself is
sufficient to confiscate all of his goods to the Inquisition permanently,
he also leaves much poorer.

As part of the apparatus of the picaresque novel, as an object of
satire outside the picaresque tradition as well, as the object of polemic
and propaganda, the Inquisition entered the fiction of the seventeenth
century and, for a number of different reasons, retained that popularity
until the late eighteenth century, when other aspects of its myths displayed
a different kind of appeal to novelists and other writers of fiction.

The Gothic Novel and the Pitiless Inquisitor

As the tastes of European writers and readers turned from romances of
adventure to romances of sentiment, both a new aesthetic and new
narrative devices gave *The Inquisition* a new lease on literary life. In
the last decade of the eighteenth century the growing taste for sentimental
romance led writers to medieval settings in which to depict a particular
psychology and atmosphere, inventing the "Gothic" novel. Its chief characteristics were its adventurous treatment of the emotions of characters
and readers, its fondness for depicting innocence in the power of absolute
villainy, its atmosphere of sharply contrasted beauty and pleasure on
the one hand and "agreeable distress"—horror and terror—on the other,
and its distinctive attitude toward the mysterious and the supernatural.
Deriving from a new aesthetic theory, the Gothic genre represented
what the Germans called *Schauerromantik*, the romanticism of terror.

The setting and period of Gothic novels is that of an undetermined
period in the past that combined the most suitable aspects of medieval
Europe, Renaissance Italy, and Spain, or the wilds of the margins of
Europe between 1200 and 1750. The settings are unfamiliar, often terrifying, and usually attractive because of their terrifying character. Gothic

fiction either *deurbanizes* its characters—placing them in old ruins, wild nature, a world of supernatural forces far greater than themselves—or it *urbanizes* them in forbidden, obscure, and mysterious urban settings: convents, religious houses, dungeons, underground passageways and tombs, and prisons of *The Inquisition*.

Its characters are usually youthful protagonists, innocent, "natural," and possessed of a healthy common sense and a benevolent religious creed. They are emotionally unguarded and responsive in their affections. Their elders, usually the ones who put them in danger or leave them particularly vulnerable to it, have been misguided by fanatical religion, bigotry, a dulling of their own affections, unnatural parental cruelty, or dire need. Those youthful characters who enter certain kinds of religious life or a life of pleasure too early and without proper guidance are early perverted into the villains who dupe the elders and exploit the innocent. The characters live through extraordinary emotional extremes, experiencing passion rather than love, hatred rather than honorable hostility.

By the late eighteenth century much of liberal Europe had developed a distinct ambivalence toward medieval and early modern European history, particularly its religious history and the remnants of that history in their own time. On the one hand, aesthetic sensibility grew fonder of the air of mystery, grandeur, emotive power of medieval architecture, often ecclesiastical architecture, and of some, but not all expressions of mystical piety. On the other hand, there was also hatred and fear of contemporary Rome and certain practices of Catholicism, of which religious intolerance was only one. One such controversial practice that attracted much eighteenth-century attention was that of dedicating unwilling young men and women to the cloistered religious life, a subject explored in Diderot's novel *La religieuse*, written in 1760 but not published until 1796. In that work of anticlerical propaganda, Diderot's literary genius had also incorporated the popular theme of forcible religious sequestration, the physical and moral tortures of a young woman "unnaturally" forced into a life of religion, but also the aesthetic of pleasure at depicting her plight. *La religieuse* points to both later Gothic fiction and to such works as the Marquis de Sade's *Justine*. Virtue under coercion, particularly coercion with a sexual dimension, proved extremely attractive to some otherwise highly moral writers and readers at the end of the eighteenth century.

Besides the forcing of youth into unnatural situations, the mechanics of the Gothic novel also displayed a distinct ambivalence toward Roman Catholicism, particularly toward its least known and most feared aspects. Both inside and outside Catholicism, for example, anti-monasticism had long been a constant theme, one that became more acute during the eighteenth century. With anti-Jesuitism—equally appealing because Jesuits were perceived to represent not only the hypocritical, unnatural, equivocating, and devious element in the character of the professed religious, but also the "Machiavellianism" that so distressed enlightened spirits in seventeenth- and eighteenth-century Europe—anti-monasticism colored the appearance of Roman Catholic settings and themes.

In Gothic novels monks, nuns, and Jesuits appear frequently and are depicted consistently in a hostile way. They are subtle and devious, superstitious, false philosophers, sophisticated deceivers, bigoted, mysteriously powerful, and impervious to reason or affection. Their victims possess natural good sense, benevolence, mature judgement, and a degree of religious toleration that infuriates their clerical enemies. Catholic liturgy is mysterious and threatening. Matrimony is usually forced, with the easy compliance of churchmen. Penance is imposed unfairly and grotesquely and may be lifted for the most trivial of reasons or never lifted at all. Churches are designed to depress the spirit. Vows are usually unnatural or perverted. Celibacy is always a sign of sexual repression and unnatural, since "virtue is better tried in the world." The religious life offers no opportunities for the active virtues—benevolence, rational adherence to religion, or helping others.

With such an aesthetic, historical and physical setting, character types, and religious values, Gothic novels did not appeal equally everywhere. They were extremely popular in England and Germany, markedly less so in France. Besides the work of Diderot, and Horace Walpole, one of the earliest examples of the genre which involves *The Inquisition* is Friedrich Schiller's *Der Geisterseher—The Ghost-Seer—*of 1787–1789. In the story, a young and impressionable Protestant prince visiting Venice is cleverly manipulated by a mysterious "Armenian" in the service of the Venetian Inquisition. The Armenian performs marvelous feats of magic and conjuring in order to convert the weak and credulous mind of the young prince to Catholicism and to win back his country from its Protestant sympathies. All of Schiller's disgust at repressive religion emerges bitingly in the story. For Schiller such religion stifles the natural virtues and encourages unnatural vices, opposed to nature in all forms except its perversions.

The sturdy liberal narrator of *The Ghost-Seer* laments his friend the prince's easily exploited and deceived character. Although there is no genuine supernatural activity in the story, the Prince is obsessed with the possibilities and is continually deceived by what Schiller clearly shows to have been the cynical mechanical tricks of a religious charlatan in the service of a monstrous secret organization.

Schiller's choice of the Venetian Inquisition as his target is unusual, since even the most severe critics of the inquisitions tended to exempt that of Venice from their strongest criticisms, on the grounds that Venice was believed to control the excesses of its Inquisition by state supervision, making it a proper court of morals rather than a bastion of religious repression. In Gothic novels, however, all inquisitions are *The Inquisition*, and there are no differences among the literary inquisitions of Spain, Portugal, Rome, Florence, Venice, Naples, or Milan.

The earliest major novel that combines the full range of Gothic features with *The Inquisition* is *The Monk*, written by Matthew Lewis in 1796. The action of the novel is set in Madrid, at an unspecified point in the sixteenth- or seventeenth-century past. The title character, Ambrosio, is an ecclesiastical celebrity, a rigorously austere man whose sermons excite all Madrid. Corrupted by a succubus disguised as a young novice, Ambrosio begins to design the corruption of Antonia, a beautiful young girl who has just arrived in Madrid from Murcia. Intercalated stories tell of the "Legend of the Bleeding Nun" and of the love between Raymond and Agnes, who is put by her parents into a convent, thinking Raymond is dead. Ambrosio commences the seduction of Antonia, who is loved by Lorenzo, a friend of Raymond. Antonia, ill-educated and badly trained in doctrine because her mother has permitted her to read only a heavily-edited, hand-copied Bible, is drugged, kidnapped, raped, and finally murdered by Ambrosio in the cellar of the monastery. Agnes, shut up in the convent under the domination of a tyrannical Prioress, is searched for by Raymond, who invokes officers of the Inquisition in his cause: "at that dreaded word, every arm fell, every sword sunk back into its scabbard." Raymond discovers Agnes nearly dead in a dungeon of her convent, her cell concealed by a clever mechanical moving statue of St. Clare, which the Prioress had given out to be a miraculous image that should not be touched.

With the Prioress punished, a terrible tribunal was called to try Ambrosio. At the end of the novel, Ambrosio is tried by the Grand Inquisitor himself, in a scene that probably informed English readers about *The Inquisition* as much as anything since Montanus. The trial chamber is draped in black; the three stern Inquisitors are also dressed in black. The chamber contains a table on which implements of torture are laid out, and the procedure of the court, considerably shortened for dramatic effect, appears even more terrible:

> In these trials neither the accusation is mentioned, of the name of the accuser. The Prisoners are only asked, if they will confess: If they reply that having no crime they can make no confession, they are put to the torture without delay. This is repeated at intervals either

till the suspected avow themselves culpable, or the perseverance of the examinants is worn out and exhausted. But without a direct acknowledgement of their guilt, the Inquisition never pronounces the final doom of its Prisoners. In general much time is suffered to elapse without their being questioned: But Ambrosio's trial had been hastened, on account of a solemn Auto da Fé which would take place in a few days, and in which the Inquisitors meant to make this distinguished Culprit to perform a part, and give a striking testimony of their vigilance.

Charged with rape, murder, and sorcery, Ambrosio is also interrogated by the Inquisition about crimes he had not committed:

Determined to make him confess not only the crimes which he had committed, but also those of which he was innocent, the Inquisitors began their examination.

Tortured, Ambrosio "suffered the most excruciating pangs, that ever were invented by human cruelty." Horribly tortured again, and faced with the prospect of yet further torture, Ambrosio, unable to face a third session, gives up his soul to the Devil, who tricks him and finally kills him with a horrible, lingering death. As things turn out, the Inquisitors, whose imminent arrival in his cell terrified Ambrosio into selling his soul in return for freedom, were bringing a pardon.

Lewis' use of the Madrid Inquisition is ambiguous. On the one hand the tribunal is necessary to deal with Ambrosio's huge crimes with appropriate gravity and seriousness, and its presence is dramatically necessary: great crimes demand great tribunals. Its officers enable Raymond to discover Agnes, for only they have the authority to overpower the guardians of monasteries and convents. Its officers led to the discovery of the body of Antonia. On the other hand, only a country without true religion would require such a tribunal at all, and only such a country could produce monsters as terrible as Ambrosio. The form and procedure of the Inquisition's court is such as to disgust honest Englishmen, with its sombre decor and costume, its free display of the instruments of torture, its refusal to state a charge or to name accusers, its isolation and repeated questioning and torturing of the accused, its accusation of non-existent crimes, and its unseemly hastening of procedure in order to increase the splendor of a forthcoming *auto-de-fé*. As an instance of terrible justice terribly administered, the sessions of Ambrosio with the Inquisition are outdone only by Ambrosio's final encounter with the Fiend.

Lewis's Inquisition is really a *deus ex machina*, both an object of scorn and a necessary instrument of justice. In Gothic novels, whenever an inquisition functions there seem to be no other tribunals of any kind around. But *The Inquisition* was put to greater and more varied use in Anne Radcliffe's *The Italian*, printed in 1797 and clearly derived from the work of Lewis. In Radcliffe, far more than in Lewis, the Gothic interest in unnatural monasticism, mysterious Catholicism, and the terrors of *The Inquisition* combine to create a much more hostile religious atmosphere than in *The Monk*. In the novel, Schedoni attempts to destroy the lives of another pair of young lovers, Ellena and Vivaldi, by using the conventional forced installment of a young woman in a convent, deceptive manipulation of a parent's conscience, deceiving everyone by the outward form of austere religion. Secrets of the confessional are routinely broken, and the evils of ecclesiastical sanctuary of criminals are early proclaimed.

The Inquisition plays a prominent role in *The Italian*. Schedoni, another monstrous monk, delivers the unwitting protagonist, Vivaldi, to the Roman Inquisition, and black-robed, silent figures lead Vivaldi into its dungeons where,

> Inquisitors in their long black robes, issued, from time to time, from the passages, and crossed the hall to other avenues. They eyed the prisoners with curiosity, but without pity. Their visages, with few exceptions, seemed stamped with the character of demons.

After meditating on the inhuman horrors of such an institution, Vivaldi is led into a room which has a terrible inscription in Hebrew over its door that echoes Dante's inscription over the gate of Hell: "Hope, that comes to all, comes not here." Although Vivaldi had heard (perhaps like Radcliffe's readers) of the customs and laws of the Inquisition, he had only half believed them; now, he saw and experienced them in great detail. Vivaldi's Inquisitors are in a dark room, provided with the instruments of torture and dominated by a huge crucifix. In a long exchange with the chief Inquisitor, Vivaldi, the *philosophe* in the power of the Inquisition, examines and condemns every step of inquisitorial procedure and every principle of inquisitorial law. Many chapters intervene, in order to draw the suspenseful reader back to the Inquisition dungeons, in which it becomes clear that Schedoni had manipulated the Inquisitors with a false accusation, a tactic to which Radcliffe thought the Inquisition was extremely vulnerable. Vivaldi, interrogated again, again failed to convince his interrogators of his innocence:

> The simplicity and energy of truth failed to impress conviction on minds, which, no longer possessing the virtue themselves, were not competent to understand the symptoms of it in others.

The Inquisition is the setting for much of Vivaldi's presence in the novel, and its procedures are gone over again and again in different contexts. Its power, secrecy, tortures, procedures, and officials dominate Vivaldi's world, and only his virtue and courage prevent him from being unjustly destroyed. It is a world, like that of Lewis' Madrid, in which only a false religion, entrusted with extensive, indeed absolute, civil powers, could create as monstrous an institution as the Inquisition, handy though it may sometimes turn out to be, particularly for undoing great villains.

It is hard to imagine anything left unsaid by Radcliffe about *The Inquisition*, but in 1799 William Henry Ireland, a former forger of Shakespeare texts and an aspiring man of more legitimate letters, published *The Abbess*, a work that puts *The Inquisition* to work even harder than Radcliffe. The hero and heroine, Marcello and Maddalena Rosa are falsely charged before the Florentine Inquisition. On the wall of Marcello's cell are painted horrifying demons, as well as a touching written account of the fate of an earlier prisoner, a young girl, who had been tortured and executed. At the end of her account, only scattered words indicate her suffering and despair:

> A new torture then succeeded . . . projecting points of steel . . .
> tortures . . . violence . . . deep . . . wounds . . . excruciating . . .
> lifeless on the ground.

Beneath her text, Marcello discovers the following text from the Inquisition:

> By order of the supreme Inquisitor, the above relation is suffered to remain. The condemned therein confesses her heresy. It is, therefore, to show the rigour of the Holy Office to those who may hereafter inhabit this cell, and teach them not to persist in their contumacy, like Benedetta Cazzala.

The interrogation chamber is familiar from Lewis and Radcliffe: the dark hangings and ominous personnel, the giant crucifix, and the reading of the accusation. Marcello, bound by an oath of secrecy he had given earlier, refuses to answer until the inquisitors produce a large volume and announce to him that:

> And it was further decreed, in a council held at Rome under our most divine apostolic Father, Pope Gregory the Ninth, founder of our Holy Inquisition, at Florence, that the said Inquisitors have power to annul any oath, by which either the informant or prisoner may have bound themselves.

Marcello refuses, denying that the pope had or has such power, although asserting himself to be faithfully "of the Catholic persuasion." Threatened with torture by a characteristically emaciated, hollow-eyed, fanatical Inquisitor, he is instead conducted to a dungeon while Maddalena is interrogated. The Inquisitors attempt to deceive Maddalena by claiming that Marcello had confessed her guilt in the alleged crime. Maddalena resists this "mean duplicity," and her natural innocence and trust in God prevent her compliance.

When Marcello is finally tortured, the scene is luridly painted, the first such prolonged and detailed scene of the inquisitorial torture in a European novel. Ireland discusses at some length the inquisitorial practice of restoring the health of torture victims so that they will be better able to be tortured later, including the presence of a physician. Threatened with the torture of Maddalena, Marcello is about to break his oath when one of the inquisition officials attempts to stab him, prevented only by Maddalena's sudden appearance along with the Grand Inquisitor.

The direction of the hearing is now reversed, and the Inquisitors become the agents of revealing the plot against Marcello and Maddalena. After torture, the villains Vittoria and Ubaldo reveal their crimes and are sentenced to terrible punishments. One of the inquisitors turns out to have been an old enemy of Maddalena's father; through hypocrisy and feigned austerity of character he had been appointed inquisitor and then used his office to torment Maddalena and Marcello. The other villain, Girolamo-Monti, discovered to have been as monstrous a sinner as the abbess, looms at the end of the novel as the ultimate Machiavellian-Satanic protagonist, heroic in his outraged dignity, his thirst for vengeance, and his limitless capacity for evil. Tortured extensively, he finally hears the tolling bell of San Domenico,

> which had so often announced to the innocent victims of that Tribunal their approaching end.

In 1799, the same year as *The Abbess*, William Godwin published *St. Leon*, a large and wandering novel in which the protagonist, after having passed through a very inquisition-like tribunal at Constance, actually is arrested by the Spanish Inquisition during travels in Spain. Perhaps aware that a repetition of *The Abbess* is impossible, Godwin's protagonist observes that, "It is not my intention to treat of those particulars of the Holy Office which are already to be found in innumerable publications." Besides, he had to take an oath of secrecy about the inquisitorial proceedings, and he may just as well keep it. He does not keep it. At one point, an inquisitor delivers a philosophical explanation and defense of the Inquisition which takes up five closely-printed pages, and the protagonist spends twelve years in the prisons of the Spanish Inquisition while the Inquisitors await his confession. On his way to be executed at the grand *auto-de-fé* at Valladolid that had been arranged to celebrate the coronation of Phillip of Spain, the protagonist escapes, simply by dodging from the procession into a maze of alleyways and tiny streets.

By the end of the eighteenth century, *The Inquisition* was virtually a requisite setting for a Gothic novel, although the fertile imaginations of Lewis, Radcliffe, and Ireland would have seemed to have exhausted it. Its mandatory character is shown in its perfunctory appearance in the anonymous *Libertines* of 1800, Anne Ker's *Adeline St. Julian* of 1800, and George Walker's *The Three Spaniards* of the same year. Even Percy Bysshe Shelley's *Zastrozzi* of 1810 included an Inquisition-scene, and Edward du Bois' 1800 parody of Godwin's *St. Leon—St. Godwin: A Tale of the Sixteenth, Seventeenth, and Eighteenth Centuries*—includes a comic parody of the Inquisition-scene, in which the hero, who has been in the cells of the Spanish Inquisition for sixty years, drinks an elixir of youth and escapes, pretending to be a French peasant whom the real St. Godwin had had flown to Spain to take his place in the Inquisition's prisons:

> All this the inquisitor's superstition led him firmly to believe, and taking pity on my apparently deplorable case, he ordered money to be furnished me to defray my expences back to France.

With this kind of parody awaiting the careless Gothic novelist, it required real literary skill to restore the pitilessness of *The Inquisition*. With the publication of *Melmoth the Wanderer* by Charles Robert Maturin in 1820, there appeared the last great Gothic depiction of the cruel *Inquisition*.

Maturin was an Irish Calvinist pastor whom literary ambition and economic necessity spurred to the writing of plays and novels. Vigorously anti-Catholic, Maturin's last work, *Five Sermons on the Roman Catholic Church*, of 1824, is a characteristic confessional polemic. Catholicism is portrayed as inert and stupid, and Sermon Four, a discussion of the Church's misuse of power, culminates in its three most horrible aspects, assassination, massacre, and the Inquisition.

Melmoth is Maturin's masterpiece, a complex structure of stories within stories that tell of a man who sells his soul to the devil in return for immortality and, when he wishes to break the agreement, discovers that he can do so only by finding someone else to fulfill the bargain in his place. The novel uses the device of a young descendant of John Melmoth, also named John Melmoth, slowly discovering the horrible story of his ancestor through encounters with other characters, discoveries of manuscripts, hearing tales told, all in an atmosphere of unrelieved gloom, horror, and largely anti-Catholic emotion. Familiar with Anne Radcliffe's *The Italian*, Lewis' *The Monk*, Godwin's *St. Leon*, and Diderot's *La religieuse*, Maturin also was familiar with seventeenth- and eighteenth-century historiography, particularly in ecclesiastical matters, and of distinct and strong opinions himself. He was also interested in Spain, and most of the stories intercalated in the novel are set in Spain, always with a powerful impression of Spanish Catholicism, and always with the Inquisition involved.

It is in the "Tale of the Spaniard," the first and longest tale in the novel, that the full Spanish atmosphere is displayed: Alonzo Moncada, the illegitimate child of Spanish Grandee parents, is acknowledged by them and sent to a monastery in Madrid as an offering for their sins. The life in the monastery, which displays at great length and detail all of the Enlightenment and Romantic revulsion at the unnaturalness of convent life, is a little masterpiece of horror and human corruption. In an attempt to escape from his monastery, Moncada is captured and imprisoned by the Inquisition. Maturin had clearly read up on the Inquisition, since his technical descriptions are largely accurate. Like Godwin, Maturin cites the oath of secrecy taken to the Inquisition in order to avoid what by 1820 must have seemed repetitious details. "At liberty to mention some general features," Moncada then goes into quite a bit of detail, although his focus is on the mysterious power of Melmoth the Wanderer to insinuate himself at will into even the most closely guarded cells of the Inquisition, and on the ferocity of the Inquisition's condemnation of Moncada himself, this last performed in person by the Grand Inquisitor of Spain, aged and blind. Moncada is spared his fate when a fire destroys the Inquisition's prison and he is set free.

From 1796 to 1824, aside from the artistic requirements of the Gothic novel, the depiction of Inquisitions and inquisitors reflects certain common themes. One of these is a distinctly English and distinctly late–eighteenth-century anti-Catholicism, of which discussions in the novels afford plenty of opportunity. A second common feature is the identical character of all the Inquisitions in the various places in which Gothic innocents end up. Whether in Rome or Florence, Madrid or Toledo, they are all the same, modelled clearly upon popular notions of the Spanish Inquisition. Regional differences are non-existent. A third feature is the implacable secrecy and sternness of the inquisitors. In spite of their irrational theology, unjust procedures, and hardness of heart, Gothic inquisitors often serve the larger purposes of literary justice.

Products of a superstitious and bigoted theology, they nevertheless serve as engines for bringing monsters to justice nearly as often as they indict the innocent—and the innocent are always freed. A number of these features, of course, derive from the necessities of plot and atmosphere.

The cruelty and mysterious remoteness of the Inquisition is sustained in Edgar Allan Poe's "The Pit and the Pendulum" of 1843. The "thousand vague rumors about the horrors of Toledo" echo in the unnamed protagonist's memory as he comes awake in the Inquisition's prisons, having been condemned to death but also having missed a recent *auto-do-fé*. Like Marcello's cell, the protagonist's cell is painted with figures of hideous demons, "repulsive devices to which charnel superstition of the monks had given rise." Subjected to the ingenious slow death-anticipation of the swinging pendulum, the product of "monkish ingenuity in torture," and then the slowly closing, heated walls of his cell, the prisoner is saved by the only force in the world greater than the Inquisition, the French armies liberating Toledo under General Lasalle: "The Inquisition was in the hands of its enemies."

Poe was a learned and ingenious writer, and some of his material certainly came from the recent histories of the Spanish Inquisition that had been translated into English and appeared in Philadelphia earlier in the nineteenth-century. Although most of his story came from other horror tales and his own skillful imagination, the Gothic *Inquisition* served relatively the same purpose for Poe as it had for his predecessors.

During the last decade of the eighteenth century and the first few decades of the nineteenth, the Inquisition-model served in the depiction of other kinds of tribunals as well. Implacable secret tribunals appear to have been much on the minds of late eighteenth-century writers and readers, and where one could not place an Inquisition, one could as easily place a similar institution. In 1794 an English publisher brought out a translation of a German novel of terror, *Hermann of Unna: A Series of Adventures of the Fifteenth Century in which the Proceedings of the Secret Tribunal under the Emperors Wenceslas and Sigismund, are Delineated*. The work of a prolific and many-pseudonymed German woman, Christiane Naubert, the novel tells the story of two lovers, one of whom is tried before an unspecified "Secret Tribunal" that looks very much like the conventional Inquisition of fiction. She is later condemned to punitive imprisonment in a convent. Other German studies and fictions concerning secret tribunals also appeared in English around the same time, usually depicting the *Vehmgericht*, whose legendary reputation matched that of the Inquisition and often appears to have derived from it, and which fascinated even Sir Walter Scott, who depicted it in his *Anne of Geierstein*, which appeared in 1829.

The role of *The Inquisition* as a model for other secret tribunals in nineteenth-century fiction probably reflects a general horrified fascination on the part of early nineteenth-century Europeans both with *The Inquisition* and revolutionary tribunals throughout Europe. The literary motif of the secret, mysterious, all powerful court had a long future ahead of it in the early nineteenth century, and *The Inquisition* had a substantial part in its shaping.

The last nineteenth-century novel to center on *The Inquisition* in this manner is in many ways the most interesting. In 1850 the English woman writer descended from Sephardic Jews, Grace Aguilar, published *The Vale of Cedars, or, The Martyr*, a sentimental novel of Jewish life in the early years of the reigns of Ferdinand and Isabella. Marie Henriquez, a Jewess, has been raised by her parents in an idyllic and secluded vale on the borders of Castile, in which her family has been able to practice its faith without concealment or interruption. Sent to stay with a relative in a Spanish Christian city, Marie meets and falls in love with Arthur Stanley, a noble English exile in the service of Ferdinand of Aragón. But Marie's father presses upon her the need that she marry Ferdinand Morales, a secret Jew prominent in royal military service and a friend of Stanley's. Don Luis Garcia, a mysterious nobleman, engineers Morales' death and Stanley's accusation of the murder. During the court's investigation of the crime, Marie discloses that she is Jewish, is arrested and tortured, but is finally saved through the affection of Queen Isabella and the heroic activities of Marie's uncle, Julien Henriquez, disguised as a Benedictine monk. Julien also provides the evidence to free Stanley and implicate Garcia, but the tortures have mortally wounded Marie, who returns to the vale, says farewell to Stanley, and dies.

All of the action described thus far takes place before the formal establishment of the Inquisition in Spain in 1478, but Aguilar's argument marks the merging of *The Inquisition* theme with the theme of secret societies and secret tribunals, and it suggests the mythical history of Spanish Jewry that came to be widely accepted in the nineteenth century.

Don Luis Garcia is the head of a secret organization known as the

Inquisition, "a secret and terrible tribunal whose power and extent were unknown to the Sovereigns of the land." The "Inquisition" had been introduced several centuries earlier into Aragón by papal authority:

> Confiding in the protection of the papal see, the inquisitors set no bounds to their ferocity: secret informations, imprisonments, tortures, midnight assasinations, marked their proceedings. . . .

But an outraged populace rose up against the Inquisition and destroyed it, or at least its public presence. In fact, the Inquisition survived in secret. "Its subterranean halls were established near almost all the principal cities . . . and its engines were often at work, even in the palaces of kings." The "Inquisition" had profited from the chaos of the fourteenth and fifteenth centuries, but it was threatened by the determined justice and power of Ferdinand and Isabella, whose personalities and court are consistently praised by Aguilar as centers of gallantry, chivalry, and justice. Don Luis Garcia is the Grand Inquisitor of this organization, and it is he who has had Marie Henriquez imprisoned and tortured by his familiars, threatening her with death if she does not accede to his demands and become his mistress!

When the treachery of Garcia is discovered, Ferdinand and Isabella send Francis, the Franciscan Sub-Prior, to Rome in order to obtain a papal bull quashing the secret Inquisition. Pope Alexander VI, however, sneeringly rejects Francis' petition, announcing that he himself is protecting Garcia and plans a high ecclesiastical appointment for him. Francis, who later becomes Cardinal Ximenes, returns to Spain and goes into retirement. Isabella's confessor, Torquemada, then suggests that the royal pair, instead of disbanding the Inquisition, take it under their own control. After heartwrenching indecision on Isabella's part, they agree to do so, setting Torquemada at its head and promising to prevent its zeal from becoming inhumanity.

The novel recounts ten centuries of persecution of the Jews in Spain and justifies the *conversos'* pretended Christianity on these grounds, accepting the argument that all *conversos* were in fact secret, practicing, devout Jews. Liberty-loving Spaniards, thrown into disorder by the chaos of the fourteenth and fifteenth centuries, were being molded into a centralized monarchical state by Ferdinand and Isabella, both being moved by the highest principles of justice and mercy. Although all Spaniards felt considerable revulsion against Jews, Isabella and the court are deeply moved by Marie's personality and plight and they end by permitting her to return to her vale, after attempts at converting her clearly fail. The fault in the novel lies clearly with the surviving secret

"Inquisition" that has profited from political disorder to work its nefarious ways. It and its head, Don Luis Garcia, are the villains of the book, not Torquemada or Isabella. Pope Alexander VI protects his "Inquisition" until his death and it is clearly the original papal charge and continuing papal protection that has directed the secret "Inquisition" from the thirteenth century to the novel's present.

The Vale of Cedars is the first novel to treat the Inquisition from a Jewish perspective, although that point of view is nearly as mythical as the rest of the novel's history. By the time that Aguilar wrote, virtually all of the elements of fictional treatment of the Inquisition were familiar: its secrecy and power; its pliability for the most infamous of purposes, including by then sexual passion; its ruthlessness; its papal authorization; and, finally, its anti-semitism, although this element was distinctly late in arriving. Aguilar's novel went through many editions and translations, and it was nearly as widely read as that of Féréal. The last edition is a Hebrew translation published at Tel Aviv in 1939.

The Vale of Cedars marks the blurring of *The Inquisition* with the favorite nineteenth-century theme of secret societies and tribunals, and it accepts the cruelty and erotic passion of Don Luis Garcia as predictable and routine. It ends the tradition of distinctive inquisitorial pitilessness and cruelty, but it also illustrates a second theme that had grown up around *The Inquisition*, that of the erotic inquisitor.

The Erotic Inquisitor

At its most extensively developed stage in polemic and history, *The Inquisition* was notorious for sparing no one, not the old, the sick, the young, or women, from its implacable search for religious or intellectual deviance. As early as Montanus, *The Inquisition*'s female victims appeared in confessional polemic, and Thomas Skinner's English translation of Montanus did not fail in the preface to mention the "villainous and shameless tormenting of naked women beyond all humanitie." But these and other early references to the treatment of women by *The Inquisition* were largely intended to stir up further moral outrage, not to accuse the inquisitors of prurient interests in their female victims. Historians and polemicists of the seventeenth and eighteenth centuries used inquisitorial cruelty, particularly to those usually exempted in contemporary criminal law, as stock accusations, but in neither case were these accusations intended to engage the reader sentimentally. The inquisitors' cruelty and terrifying secrecy are always the focus, deriving either from "national character," religious fanaticism, or both. Even Voltaire's Cunigonde, mistress of both the Jewish merchant and the Grand Inquisitor, plays no particularly erotic role, except to indicate the hypocrisy of the Grand Inquisitor himself.

But in the eighteenth and nineteenth centuries, another strain of criticism of *The Inquisition* appeared. Both the cruelty and the eroticism of inquisitors became a popular topic in some circles, and in fiction the erotic inquisitor remained popular through the nineteenth century. The figure of the erotic inquisitor is probably related to the general range of charges of sexual irregularity launched against many representatives of the *Ancien Régime* during the eighteenth century and surviving into the nineteenth. Widespread depictions of aristocratic sexual license and degeneration circulated through eighteenth-century English, French, and Italian literature. Such accusations were consistent with the charges of hypocrisy (which applied to inquisitors, the religious in general, and aristocrats) and self-interest that had long since characterized the inquisitors in confessional and political polemic.

The eighteenth century marked the beginning of an extraordinary European interest in the erotic, from Diderot's novels—particularly *La religieuse*—to those of the Marquis de Sade. In most of the fiction considered thus far, however, eroticism was treated as a function of depraved, unnatural religious—whether abbesses, monks, bishops, or heads of religious houses. *The Inquisition* was generally reserved either as an instrument of the wicked or an instrument strong enough to destroy the wicked. None of the inquisitors that Lewis, Radcliffe, Ireland, or Maturin portrayed ever sought out their victims for personal or erotic purposes, even at their most irrational and cruel.

One of the earliest accusations of sexual perversion in connection with *The Inquisition* was Anthony Gavin's *Master-Key to Popery* of 1726. Gavin, professing to have been a priest at Zaragoza, told the skillful and widely circulated story of Madame Faulcaut and her life in the "harem" of the Zaragoza Inquisition. Since much of the rest of Gavin's book focuses upon the psychological instability of Catholic religious sentiment and practice, from the explorations of abnormal psychology in the confessional to the disgraceful lives of the religious, the story of Madame Faulcaut is consistent with the rest of *The Master-Key*, a work that deserves far greater study than it has so far received.

But the figure of the erotic inquisitor was not much further developed or frequently used until the beginning of the nineteenth century, and then not in Gothic novels at all, but in a series of works that seem to be almost *sui generis*, and which we may term *The Inquisition* novel.

Plate 12. *The Sufferings of John Coustos for Free-Masonry . . . in the Inquisition at Lisbon* (London, 1746). A series of engravings were specially commissioned for Coustos' work. This one depicts a kind of torture not mentioned elsewhere in the literature.

Plate 13. J. J. Stockdale, *The History of the Inquisitions* (London, 1811). These three figures in *sanbenitos* were taken by Stockdale from earlier representations individually or collectively in Dellon and Limborch. They belong as much to the official iconography of the Spanish Inquisition as they do to the iconography of injustice, which is their purpose here.

Plate 14. J. L. Mosheim, *Historia Michaelis Serveti* (Helmstedt, 1727). The execution of Michael Servetus became the symbol of the dangers of a "Protestant Inquisition" and was used by many supporters of religious toleration as a counterpoint to the Spanish Inquisition. This frontispiece of Mosheim's biography depicts Servetus—probably inaccurately—as well as his execution in Geneva.

Plate 15. British print on the Lisbon earthquake of 1755. The Lisbon earthquake of 1755 called forth an immensely varied spectrum of explanations, including arguments that the disaster had been caused by the wrath of God. Among the latter (including a sermon by John Wesley) was the further charge that God was outraged by the Portuguese Inquisition. See T. D. Kendrick, *The Lisbon Earthquake* (Philadelphia/New York, 1957).

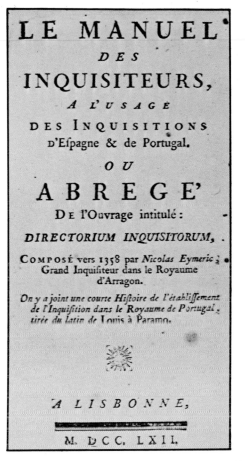

LE MANUEL
DES
INQUISITEURS,
A L'USAGE
DES INQUISITIONS
D'Eſpagne & de Portugal.
OU
ABREGE'
DE l'Ouvrage intitulé :
DIRECTORIUM INQUISITORUM,
COMPOSÉ vers 1358 par *Nicolas Eymeric*,
Grand Inquiſiteur dans le Royaume
d'Arragon.
On y a joint une courte Hiſtoire de l'établiſſement
de l'Inquiſition dans le Royaume de Portugal,
tirée du latin de Louis à Paramo.

A LISBONNE,

M. DCC. LXII.

Plate 16. The Abbé Morellet, *Le Manuel des Inquisiteurs* (Lisbon [false imprint], 1762). The title page of Morellet's widely circulated abridged translation of the *Directorium Inquisitorium* of Eymeric-Peña introduced the most influential text for Enlightenment critics of the inquisitions.

Plate 17. V. de Féréal, *Les Mystères de l'Inquisition* (Paris, n.d.). Illustrators of sentimental fiction took great liberties with traditional Inquisition images as well as with the introduction of new pictorial subjects. The murder of the inquisitor Pedro Arbués in the novel *Les Mystères de l'Inquisition* does not conform to the historical circumstances of his death, but the picture suggests the appropriate vengeance of a wronged woman who has waited for this opportunity for many years.

Plate 18. V. de Féréal, *Les Mystères de l'Inquisition* (Paris, n.d.). Illustrated novels and histories on the Inquisition offered great opportunities for the popular mid-nineteenth-century theme of women in torment. Féréal's (de Suberwick's) novel depicted not only the murder of Arbués, but also the execution of his murderess.

Plate 19. *Storia dell'Inquisizione ossìa Le Crudeltà Gesuitiche*, Vol. I (Florence, 1849). This work is actually an Italian translation of Féréal. Unlike most translations, however, this one dispensed with the conventional pictures (see above, Plates 17 and 18) and included only this one and another (as frontispiece to Vol. II). This half-nude woman awaiting torture, however, echoes the sentiments of the other illustrations of Féréal.

Plate 20. Joaquin Maria Nin, *Secretos de la Inquisición* (Barcelona, 1856). The torture of the character Fanny is characteristic of contemporary depictions and echoes themes of female torment that in the 1850s had become familiar and expected in historical or fictional accounts of the inquisitions.

Plate 21. G. del Valle, *Anales de la Inquisición* (Madrid, 1841). The illustrations of del Valle's *Anales* are a highly stylized and unique pictorial set. This illustration of a woman being tortured on the wheel is consistent with the same kind of scene in contemporary works.

Plate 22. Tomás Bertran Soler, *Vindicación de los Mallorquines Cristianos* (Valencia, 1858). Soler's work contains this depiction of the literary (at the time, asserted to have been historical) burning of Cornelia Bororquia, the heroine of Gutierrez's novel of 1801.

TAJNOSTI ŠPANĚLSKÉ INKVISICI

Plate 23. Josef Hlavac, *Tajnosti Spanelske Inkvisice* (Prague, 1925). This picture is on the cover of a 1925 Czech translation of Féréal's *Mystères de l'Inquisition*. It suggests the continuing pan-European pictorial appeal of tormented naked women in iconography of the late Inquisition.

Plate 24. Tomás Bertran Soler, *Vindicación de los Mallorquines Cristianos* (Valencia, 1858). The picture, in the whimsical and satirical style that characterizes other illustrations in Soler's work, is entitled "Una inquisición de idiotas"—an inquisition of idiots.

Plate 25. "To the greater glory of God!" This plate (from G. Daelli, *A Relic of the Italian Revolution of 1849* [New Orleans, 1850]) is one of a series bitterly criticizing the restoration of papal authority in Rome after the popular revolution of 1849. Here, the statue of a murderous St. Dominic is being raised to a prominent position on a church facade at a location labeled "The Infamous Piazza of the Holy Office." The dogs running down the street are probably the *Domini canes*, the "Hounds of the Lord," the symbol of the Order of Preachers (see Plate 5). The motto, however, is that of the Jesuit Order.

Plate 26. Goya, "For Jewish Descent." This is one of several Goya drawings from the period after the Bonapartist government of 1808–1814 (Gassier-Wilson 1324/Album C 88). The victim, dressed in a *sanbenito* and the *coroza*, emerges with others from a prisonlike tunnel into the area in which sentence is to be pronounced. Goya here reminds the viewer of the powerful anti-Semitic character of the Spanish Inquisition, both in its first years and again in the early decades of Goya's own century.

Plate 27. Goya, "For Having Discovered the Movement of the Earth." Besides his numerous drawings of nameless Inquisition victims, Goya also drew celebrated cases, including some that occurred outside Spain. Here, Galileo is chained to massive, immovable stone blocks, imagined as an ironic punishment for claiming to have discovered the movement of the earth (Gassier-Wilson 1330/Album C 94). Legends of the tortured Galileo circulated widely in the late eighteenth and early nineteenth centuries.

One of the earliest novels to circulate widely on the Continent and deal with the cruelty and erotic interests and characters of inquisitors was *Cornelia Bororquia*, attributed to Luis Gutiérrez and published in Paris in 1801. In a notice to the reader, the author emphasizes the truthfulness of his story, citing "Boulanger's" *La cruauté religieuse*, Langle's *Voyage en Espagne*, and the Inquisition histories of Limborch and Marsollier to prove the truth of the story that

> the young daughter of the Marqués de Bororquia, Governor of Valencia, extremely beautiful, discreet, and virtuous, was publicly burned at the Plaza of Seville, and that her chief crime . . . was that she had refused the advances of the Archbishop of Seville, who was infatuated with her.

The novel is in eighteenth-century epistolary form, the different letters offering different perspectives on her case. The Preface attacks the Inquisition as an unjust and tyrannical tribunal, unfit for a modern, free nation; it is obviously written from the point of view of a liberal Spaniard, drawing arguments for religious toleration from the rich literature of the eighteenth century, and denouncing Spanish backwardness and intolerance.

The novel opens with a letter from Cornelia's father, announcing that the nobleman Bartolomé Vargas has kidnapped Cornelia. The second letter announces that Vargas was not responsible, but its writer cannot say more, quoting the proverb: "With the king and the Inquisition, keep quiet, keep quiet." Other letters indicate Vargas' innocence and inform the Governor that Cornelia has been kidnapped by a servant of the Holy Office acting on behalf of the Archbishop of Seville. Cornelia's letters from the Inquisition's prison [!] tell of the horrors and cruelty of her captors, and one of the Governor's correspondents reminds him, when he raises the fear of family dishonor, that "a wise and reasonable man knows well the cruelty and injustice of the Inquisition, but he must speak about them quietly and in secret," since servants of the "holy, or better, *infernal office*," are everywhere. Vargas, Cornelia's beloved, writes to a friend a letter that reads like a *philosophe* tract on behalf of toleration, citing the case of Socrates and other examples of unjust religious persecution. Vargas' brother writes to Vargas defending the Inquisition, arguing (possibly from the Abbé Morellet's *Petit écrit*) that concerns with such trifling matters as art and letters, economic development and trade, often cost men the gate of Heaven. Further letters describe and denounce the Inquisition's rationale, its personnel, its practices, and its prisons. At the end of the novel there is a final letter from Cornelia to Vargas, a record of her interrogation by the Inquisition, and another letter describing her final moments at the *auto-de-fé*. An escape attempt fails, Cornelia is executed, her father dies of grief, and Vargas embarks for the Netherlands, where he will fight for political justice and religious freedom.

Cornelia Bororquia represents both older and newer literary, emotional, and philosophical interests. In its epistolary form, the arguments for toleration and for curbing ecclesiastical power, and its denunciations of the Inquisition, it shares eighteenth-century *philosophe* sentiments. But in its fascination with Inquisition reasoning and psychological control of its victims, the anguish of parted young lovers, the "monkish gloom" that hangs over it, and the lust of the villain, it is a sentimental novel, one that slowly displaced the earlier literary forms and sentiments.

Other novels sustained the theme of the lustful inquisitors, notably Mikhail Lermontov's 1830 story *Espancy*, in which a Jesuit agent of *The Inquisition* separates two young lovers because of his lust for the young woman. But the most elaborate exploration of inquisitorial eroticism is the enormously popular novel of 1844 by Madame de Suberwick-V. de Féréal, *Les mystères de l'Inquisition et autres sociétés secrets d'Espagne*, elaborately plotted, generously illustrated, and relentless in analyzing the limitless sexual desires of the inquisitor Pedro Arbués.

Dolores Argoso, daughter of the Governor of Seville, is betrothed to Estevan de Vargas, descendant of Moors, but a firm Catholic. The Grand Inquisitor, Pedro Arbués, besotted with lust and given over to all the pleasures of the flesh, has free admission to the Governor's house, where one evening he bursts into Dolores's room and declares his passion. Dolores is kidnapped by a band of thieves who save her from Arbués, and Arbués arrests her father and tortures him to death. The flight of Dolores, aided by the thieves and by Estevan, further aided by clerics and saintly hermits, is punctuated by savage reflections on *The Inquisition*—created by wicked popes and sustained by feeble kings—and by praises of the noble Spanish people, crushed beneath its intolerable burdens.

Ultimately, Arbués is murdered by his favorite, José, a Dominican who turns out to be a woman whom Arbués had ravished and insulted some time before. The execution of José-Paula is described in hideous detail, as are the interrogation rooms, torture chambers, and *autos-de-fé* of an imaginary fifteenth-century Spain, all explained in the editor *Cuendias'* tendentious footnotes. The novel ends with Estevan and Dolores sailing off to combat the Inquisition elsewhere, presumably in the Netherlands.

Clearly written by a liberal French anti-cleric, *Les mystères de l'Inquisition* randomly selects information about fifteenth-century Spain from histories, polemic, and the author's creative imagination. Here, as in other contemporary works, there is a "rehabilitation" of Spain and the Spanish people, the Inquisition now being attributed to the popes and St. Dominic, the "fanatic monk," and sustained by kings eager to hold on to power. Popular resentment against the Inquisition often surfaces in *Les mystères*, although it does not lead anywhere. With *Les mystères*, however, the Gothic austerity and severe asceticism of the Inquisition has disappeared and is replaced by a society of hypocritical voluptuaries, reveling in their greed and lust, utterly devoid of any religious sentiment whatever except hypocrisy. Opposed to them is the pure, philosophical evangelical religion of Dolores, Estevan, and a number of other characters in the novel and the saintliness of Juan de Avila and the "apostle" who shelters the fleeing lovers throughout the novel. This evangelical opposition to Roman Catholic despotism and fanaticism in 1844 probably had a political message as well, coming between the fall of the liberal government in 1843 and the restoration of absolute monarchy in Spain in 1845. But the politics of *Les mystères*, as well as its message of enlightened religion, comes with a strong component of eroticism and sadism, particularly in the scenes of torture and execution.

The twin themes of inquisitorial cruelty and eroticism appeared periodically through the nineteenth century, often in a context that introduced themes of contemporary interest not in the tradition. Perhaps the most important of these works was Josef Schiesl's four-act tragedy of 1875, *Torquemada*, in which the inquisitor, who had been married but had killed his wife when he found her in the arms of a Moor, casts his eye on yet another young woman. She is protected from the inquisitor's lusts, however, by a heroic young German named Fridank. Torquemada thwarted, Fridank returns to Germany, where he later becomes the father of Martin Luther! Torquemada thus ironically becomes the indirect cause of The Reformation of the sixteenth century. *The Inquisition*, a myth invented in the course of the Reformation, thus finally comes around as the assigned cause of the Reformation that invented it.

The Inquisition Displayed

In the escape narratives and histories of the late seventeenth and eighteenth centuries and in the sentimental novels of the nineteenth century *The Inquisition* was presented pictorially as well as verbally. This pictorial tradition was developed from three very different sources: the iconography of the inquisitions themselves; a distinct tradition of the pictorial illustration of criminal punishments, and illustrations of specific scenes described in personal accounts, histories, or fictional narratives. Besides providing readers with graphic pictorial events corresponding to and illuminating the texts, the illustrations of inquisitorial activities also influenced later prose narratives, as well as dramatists and set designers, whether of plays or operas. To a certain extent they also influenced much later cinematographers.

The pictorial history of inquisitions or of *The Inquisition* has never been extensively addressed, and my discussion here is necessarily limited. Its chief purpose is to consider the visual images (in the widest and least specific sense of the term) that printers, illustrators, and readers associated with *The Inquisition*, as well as the particular activities of inquisitors that invited or encouraged illustration. The concentration on the part of illustrators upon certain aspects of inquisitorial activity meant that readers' pictorial images of *The Inquisition* tended to be grouped around certain parts of the inquisitorial process and not around others, much as the focus of much polemic was upon selected points of inquisitorial theory and practice rather than upon the whole structure of inquisitorial procedure.

A number of art historians distinguish between "imagery," which is general and refers to pictorial representation in a broad sense, and "icon," which is a sub-category of imagery, one in which subject matter familiar to the viewer is presented in quickly recognizable settings and readily identifiable methods of composition (Plate 2). One of the important communicative powers of icons is their recognizability when transferred to different subjects; thus, a pictorial representation of a torture chamber, with torturers and victims, becomes transformed when the pure pictorial elements of a seated cleric, scribe, one or two candles, and a crucifix is added, making the scene specifically an icon of *The Inquisition*. By the late eighteenth century, many readers knew accounts of inquisitorial activity and had seen pictures of it. What was of interest was the *way* in which a new set of illustrations appealed within a conventional genre of illustration-types.

The pictorial *Inquisition* has an interesting history, of which this section and the plates in this book offer only a sketch.

The Iconography of The Inquisition

As was the case with many late medieval and early modern institutions, the various Inquisitions encouraged and permitted a certain amount and type of visual identification. Royal coronations and funerals, *joyeuses entrées*, seatings of representative assemblies, memorable executions, and personal portraits all constitute an important dimension of understanding the visual self-definition of early European public and devotional life.

In the case of the Inquisitions such iconography was narrow and intended for specific purposes. Since very little iconographic material is available for most of the Mediterranean inquisitions, this section will focus on that of Spain, but, with little variation, it may serve to describe the others as well.

The Spanish Inquisition possessed its own seal, as did all other legitimate corporate groups, as well as its characteristic emblems, banners, penitential costumes, tribunal decorations, and dramatic sense of liturgy. Some of these elements later made their way into the iconography of injustice—the polemical attacks against *The Inquisition*—but all of these began in an approved context. On occasion, although the Inquisition did not necessarily commission a particular work, the work dealt with inquisition topics and met with the Inquisition's approval. Such an early work was the picture painted around 1490 by the Castilian painter Pedro Berruguete (better known for his studies of Italian renaissance subjects) depicting what might be called "The Triumph of the Inquisition" (Plate 1). In the picture, St. Dominic sits enthroned at the top center, in a line of ecclesiastical and lay dignitaries. Seated and standing just below him are a number of Inquisition functionaries, while at the ground level some military officials lead convicted heretics off to be burned, while others wait for their punishment and, at the lower right, two heretics are actually in the flames.

The picture is an icon displaying the majesty of the tribunal, its saintly director, the cooperation of the secular arm, the punishment of heretics, and, at the far left, the approving witnesses. No such actual event ever took place, of course, and the entire image is artificial. But the icon is consistent with the self-image of the Spanish Inquisition and with such later defenders and historians of the inquisitions as Pàramo. The setting is an *auto-de-fé*, but the quite distinct events and sequence of an actual event are here compressed into a single icon that is intended to convey the legitimacy, grandeur, and power of the Spanish Inquisition.

Since the tenth century, the banner had been used to convey a pictorial message concerning the nature and symbolic character of those who issued it and those who carried it. It had become one of those "signs of lordship and symbols of the state" that later emerged as national flags. A number of legitimate organizations were permitted the use of characteristic banners and seals, and the Spanish Inquisition possessed its own, which may have hung in its tribunals and was certainly carried in the liturgical processions that constituted part of *autos-de-fé* from the beginning. Although it is not known how early the Inquisition possessed its own banner, one is reproduced in Limborch's *History* of 1696 and was reproduced through the eighteenth century and into the nineteenth, in the work of Lavallée and Stockdale (Plate 3). The obverse of the Inquisition banner shows St. Dominic standing beside a coat of arms, the emblem of the Inquisition, on which are represented a cross, a green branch, and a sword, the latter two symbolizing mercy and justice. The inscription is the motto of the Spanish Inquisition, the passage from Psalm 73.22: "Arise, O Lord, and judge thine own cause," with the non-scriptural text below it, "and dissipate the enemies of the faith."

The reverse of the banner shows St. Peter Martyr with the coat of arms of Castile and Aragón. The coats of arms were related to the designs on seals and banners. The seal of the Spanish Inquisition carried the motto from Ps. 73.22 around its outer edge, with a cross in the center flanked by the branch and the sword. Such a device was placed on other banners alone and became the characteristic device of the Spanish Inquisition (Plate 4). The banner of the Inquisition at Goa, which was depicted in Dellon's *Relation* of 1686, showed St. Dominic holding the branch in one hand and a sword in the other, while below him was a dog holding a burning brand in his mouth (the Dominican Order) and an orb surmounted by a cross. A *titulus*, a small banner floating above the figure's head, bore the words *justitia et misericordia*, the "Justice and mercy" that became the motto of the Inquisition (Plate 5).

For the most part, aside from the use of seals on official documents, most of this iconography was focused upon the *auto-de-fé* itself. No Inquisition ever permitted the depiction of its tribunals, torture chambers, prisons, or other functions, since these were kept in secrecy from artists and everyone else. But in the *auto-de-fé* the Inquisition spoke to the entire Christian people (and to enemies of the faith as well), and much of the rest of the iconography of the Inquisition is in fact the iconography of the *auto*.

The Inquisition did permit, indeed, it encouraged both verbal and pictorial representations of its great public ceremony. Sometimes these reached even wider audiences than intended. In 1630 a writer associated with the Spanish Inquisition published in Spanish a long account of the *auto-de-fé* held that year in the presence of Charles II. The account contained a large fold-out line drawing of the event, keyed to numbers and letters identifying individuals in the great assembly, which the text identified accordingly. The line drawing is an impressive and ambitious piece of work, but not nearly as impressive as the painting it inspired, Francisco Rizi's *Auto-de-fé*, painted in 1680, and now in the Prado Museum. Rizi's painting brings the line drawing to rich life and indicates, as does no other painting since Berruguete's, the Spanish Inquisition's success in creating that ceremony as a major public occasion in Spanish culture. Other official and quasi-official illustrations of *autos-de-fé* were done by other illustrators whose task, on a lower scale than Rizi's, was to convey the triumphant ceremony, holiness, and justice of the tribunal's decisions. Allegorical and realistic scenes of triumph and the emblems on seals and banners of course, represented symbolic rather than literal fact. The depictions and their component elements, however, represented literal ceremonies that played an important role in Spanish public life, were often attended by the greatest powers in the kingdom, and were designed as triumphs of the faith over its enemies. The *auto-de-fé* was a liturgical ceremony, and it was attended by all of the detail and pageantry of other counter-reformation liturgy. It was living iconography, reproduced to serve as a reminder and for the sustaining of devotion (Plate 6).

For the inquisitors, heretics must not only be declared to have been heretics, but they must be made to be *seen* as heretics. The costuming of those convicted, whether *in presentia* or *in absentia* (in the latter case by means of effigies appropriately costumed), was the result of careful planning and indicated specific gradations of guilt. There was never a single, simple *sanbenito*, for example, but a different kind of *sanbenito* for different crimes and different degrees of heresy, with corresponding headgear (Plate 13). The garb of the penitents, the procession with inquisitorial banners and crosses, the careful design of the seating and sequence of the ceremony made the *auto-de-fé* itself "a work of art," and the Inquisition permitted and encouraged the pictorial representation of the Church's triumph and the humiliation of its enemies.

Beyond the real and depicted ceremony and its printed accounts, the iconography of the Inquisition did not go. The aim of the *auto-de-fé*, as its name suggests, is the *"act* of faith," that is, the liturgical demonstration of the truth of the faith and the error and evil of its enemies. The iconography of the Inquisition, except in the occasional triumph like that of Berruguete, did not often depict the execution of those condemned to death, because the execution was less important to the Inquisition than the assertion of truth and the penitence of its enemies. Unlike Berruguete's picture, the executions did not take place in the liturgical context of the ceremony, but afterwards, and often at a considerable distance. The mythology of *The Inquisition* omitted the element of *miseri-*

cordia in the Inquisitions' self-definition: what was important was repentance, the concession to legitimate authority, the assertion of truth—not the mechanics of physical punishment or execution, and so the Inquisition did not usually bother depicting these. In its eyes, its own triumphant iconography was more than satisfactory.

Icons of Injustice

Critics and enemies of the inquisitions took up and adapted much of the Inquisition's own iconography, beginning in the late seventeenth century, but they also added a number of characteristic iconic scenes that no Inquisition ever would have permitted, or would have permitted only occasionally and grudgingly. From the late seventeenth century on, readers came to expect a series of readily recognizable icons of injustice in a work on *The Inquisition*, as they did in the later illustrated editions of Casas' *Brief Relation*, and they were amply satisfied over the next century and a half.

An early example of iconic injustice may be seen in the remarkable sequence of plates illustrating Charles Dellon's *Relation*. The title page contains a stylized emblem of the Portuguese Inquisition. The first chapter is illustrated with an accurate picture of two inquisitors interrogating a suspect in a large, windowed chamber dominated by a huge crucifix in the background. This picture is repeated in Chapter 14. In Chapter 30 there is a series of three illustrations of condemned defendants, dressed in different kinds of *sanbenitos* for having been convicted of different kinds of offenses: a self-confessed heretic, a fully convicted, unrepentant (although weeping) heretic condemned to the flames and a heretic who had been condemned to the flames but who has been spared because of his full confession. In Chapter 32 there is an *auto-de-fé*, complete with banners and crucifixes; in Chapter 33 another *auto*, this one inside a great church, and in the 1709 edition a plate was added showing the convicted heretics being led out of the church and burned. Except for the first (showing an actual tribunal at work) and the last, Dellon's illustrations are all consistent with the Inquisition's own iconography. They were also popular: the publishers of Isaac Martin's personal narrative used them (reversing the final plate of the 1709 edition), as did most of the other eighteenth-century illustrated accounts.

The depiction of a tribunal at work (Plate 7) and the post-*auto* removal of the condemned to their execution (Plates 8 and 9) constitute an early instance of extending the Inquisition's own iconography in the direction of an iconography of injustice, in which, tainted by its association with depictions of tortures and executions, the original Inquisition iconography became transformed from the triumphant to the detestable. Philip van Limborch's *History* of 1696 and its English translation by Chandler in 1731 used a number of the Dellon illustrations: the three types of *sanbenito*, the emblems of the Spanish and Goan Inquisitions, the ceremonial procession, the *auto-de-fé* itself inside a church, and the tribunal scene. It added the illustration of an outdoor *auto-de-fé* mounted on a large stage; below it, at ground level, the condemned are mounted on asses and taken off to their punishment.

The *Mémoires historiques* of Louis-Ellies Dupin of 1716 contained the illustrations of the processions and different *sanbenitos* from the Dellon tradition, but it added a scene that was to become perhaps the most widely circulated and reproduced of all elements in the iconography of injustice: Bernard Picart's engraving of an inquisitorial torture-chamber (Plate 10). Picart's illustration, however, derives from other sources than those cited so far. From the fifteenth century on, the illustration of criminal punishments became a common feature of early modern European book illustration. These illustrations in the sixteenth and seventeenth centuries, the best known of which is probably the series of engravings on *The Horrors of War* by Jacques Callot, often depicted in a single scene an entire spectrum of different punishments, most of which would in reality have occurred individually. Recent scholarship has designated these illustrations and the public executions they depicted as a *Theater des Schreckens*—a "theater of horror"—that characterized the public taste for such displays of civil power and justice during the sixteenth and seventeenth centuries. Illustrations of various kinds of torture accompanied the spectacular scenes of various methods of aggravated public execution. Thus, Picart's engraving is, at one level, a representative of a commonplace pictorial genre of the early modern period, the "torture chamber," in which—for the sake of economy and pictorial interest— the various kinds of torture applied are depicted as occurring simultaneously. The addition of a seated inquisitor, another cleric, and a scribe, however, turned the conventional "torture chamber" scene into a depiction of *The Inquisition* at work. The tortures represented are, from left to right, the *strappado*, the water torture, and the application of fire to the soles of the feet, all forms of torture recognized in European civil law and employed in all other courts which used torture, but always applied one at a time to a single individual, never several simultaneously to a number of individuals. No scribe, however competent, could have managed to transcribe the interrogation under torture of several individuals at once, and there is no textual evidence, even in polemic, of such a scene actually occurring.

Besides the "public art" of tortures and aggravated forms of execution, the pictorial sources of *Inquisition* iconography are those graphic depictions of martyrdoms that came to illustrate the martyrologies of the sixteenth and seventeenth centuries and the artistic depiction of traditional religious scenes, particularly the Last Judgement. This diverse body of pictorial sources provided Picart and those who redrew his engraving for the next century with substantial materials for the transformation of the Inquisition's own iconography into the iconography of injustice. As the public taste for pictorial illustrations of tortures and aggravated forms of execution waned in the late seventeenth century, and, as Michel Foucault and others have argued, such forms of torture and execution themselves grew distasteful, they ceased to be produced in their original contexts, but they were preserved in the iconography of injustice associated with *The Inquisition*.

Picart's engraving is the original of all other portrayals of *Inquisition* torture chambers, and it was reproduced virtually once a decade into the early nineteenth century. It is found in the 1739 *An Impartial Account of the Barbarous Cruelties of the Inquisition*; in 1759 in the Abbé Goujet's *Histoire de l'Inquisition* (derived from Marsollier and Dupin); in 1769 in the lavishly illustrated (with scenes of martyrdoms as well) work by Matthew Taylor, *England's Bloody Tribunal: or, Popish Cruelty Displayed*; and in 1783 in an account of the inquisitions in Tuscany, the *Fatti Attenenti all'Inquisizióne . . . di Toscana*, of Modesto Rastrelli. Sometimes reversed, with the inquisitor seated at the right side of the chamber instead of the left, Picart's illustration was also the model for later elaborations on his theme (Plate 11). With the pictures of the tribunal and the execution of heretics, the torture-scene became the single pictorial element that transformed a series of book illustrations originally coming from the Inquisition itself into a pictorial condemnation of Inquisition practices and added a pictorial dimension to *The Inquisition* that substantially contributed to textual polemic.

Most pictorial illustrations of *Inquisition* tortures were derived from Picart. An interesting exception is the personal narrative of John Coustos of 1746, in which, probably because of the subsidy the book received, there are three original engravings of tortures inflicted upon Coustos alone in a torture chamber: the tightening of ropes around the body stretched out on a rack; a kind of horizontal strappado; and a device for tightening a chain around the victim's chest (Plate 12). Although these illustrations did not circulate as widely as that of Picart, they did provide pictorial materials for variations on Picart's picture in the nineteenth century, and they were illustrated in a single scene in Stockdale's *History of the Inquisitions* of 1810, which is a virtual repertoire of the pictorial history of *The Inquisition*, the last such work to appear before the age of sentimental illustration which characterized the tradition in the nineteenth century.

Icons of Sentimentality

The pictorial history of *Inquisition* iconography is summed up in the numerous illustrations of Stockdale's *History* of 1810, but after that date styles of *Inquisition*-illustration took a different turn, one that corresponded to the shift toward sentiment and eroticism that is reflected in fictitious accounts of *The Inquisition*. The earliest and most widely circulated of these were the numerous editions and translations of Madame de Suberwick–Victor de Féréal's *Mysteries of the Inquisition*, nearly all of which were illustrated by the same long series of illustrations. Many of these, of course, continued the familiar iconography of injustice, but many others depicted the most memorable events of the narrative. The illustration of the title page itself surrounds the title with a panorama of images descending to the right and left from the figure of the book's "author," de Féréal, at top center. In descending order around the right is an *auto-de-fé* and the burning of a condemned heretic in a *sanbenito*, ending in a design of winged serpents, crucifixes, swords, implements of torture, weapons, chains, and a skull at the very bottom. Descending down the left side of the page to the skull are scenes of torture, and a somber, mysterious monk. The *Mysteries* is the most extensively illustrated work dealing with *The Inquisition* ever published. Scenes of prison, inquisition tribunals, torture, elaborate forms of aggravated punishment and execution, the burning of heretics, and *autos-de-fé* fill its pages. No scene, however, is more dramatic—or melodramatic—than the murder of the inquisitor Pedro Arbués by the woman he has deceived (Plates 17, 18, and 19). The outraged woman brandishing the knife over the prostrate inquisitor marks the graphic intrusion of sentimentality and melodrama into inquisition illustrations.

De Féréal's *Mysteries* was not the only illustrated *Inquisition*-novel of the nineteenth century. In 1856, Joaquin Maria Nin published at Barcelona his own *Secretos de la Inquisición*, a novel set in the sixteenth century, containing nineteen illustrations, many of them of the characters and scenes of the novel having nothing to do with the Inquisition, but also illustrating an *auto-de-fé*, an inquisitorial tribunal, the Inquisitor-General Diego Sarmiento, scenes of inquisitorial plotting and condemnation, a scene of the torture of the character Fanny (Plate 20), and two

plates in the concluding section of "documents," one depicting Martin
Luther burning a series of papal bulls, and another the execution of
Jan Hus.

Nor were novels the only vehicles for this kind of illustration. The
Anales de la Inquisición of Genaro del Valle, published in Madrid in
1841, contains nearly as many illustrations as de Féréal, done in a
remarkably distinctive style, ranging across the history of heresy and
including virtually every aspect of inquisitorial practice considered so
far. Refraining from neither sadism nor eroticism, the graceful, stylized
illustrations form a small album in themselves, for the first time constitut-
ing an illustration sequence around which a text might be constructed
(Plate 21).

It is in the works of de Féréal, Nin, and del Valle that the illustration
of *The Inquisition*'s treatment of women is most sharply present. Women
before the fire, women on the rack or the wheel, women about to be
tortured, women incarcerated—all in various stages of deshabille—form
the pictorial correspondence to the nineteenth-century interest in the
eroticism of *The Inquisition* and the readers' own interest in the respectable
eroticism of innocent femity in danger and torment. With these novels
and histories, the pictorial history of *The Inquisition* comes to an end
(Plates 22, 23, and 24). Although much of it has been revived in twentieth-
century cinematography, from the work of Carl Dreyer to that of Jean-
Jacques Annaud, cinematographic representations of *The Inquisition*
merely make the old static traditions more powerful, without breaking
new ground, except for the extraordinary kinds of presence that film as
a medium conveys. A number of twentieth-century artists, notably Leon
Golub and José Luis Cuevas, have taken up some of this iconography
in their own works, but their message is a twentieth-century message,
and it speaks to other issues than *The Inquisition*.

The only great artist to illustrate *The Inquisition* was Francisco José
Goya y Lucientes, but Goya's contribution was so distinctive that a
discussion of it belongs to a series of studies on the remarkable use of
The Inquisition by a number of great artists in the course of the nineteenth
century. Utilizing much of the tradition of illustration catalogued in
this discussion, Goya went far beyond both iconography and visual polemic, and he opened one of the most remarkable chapters in the history
of *The Inquisition*.

Chapter Eight

The Power of Art and the Transformation of Myth: Four Nineteenth-Century Studies

Some myths are tougher and more durable than the occasions which first create and employ them. *The Inquisition* was an invention of the religious disputes and political conflicts of the sixteenth century. It was adapted to the causes of religious toleration and philosophical and political enlightenment in the seventeenth and eighteenth centuries. In this process, although it was always anti-Catholic and usually anti-Spanish, it tended to become universalized, until, by the end of the eighteenth century, it had become the representative of all repressive religions that opposed freedom of conscience, political liberty, and philosophical enlightenment. Its origins in the confessional wrangling of the sixteenth century and the Dutch Revolt were long since folded into its wider and more fearsome role as the enemy of modernity on all of the fronts on which modernity clashed with repressive tradition.

The literary and pictorial career of *The Inquisition* was matched by an initially modest but ultimately formidable historiography that developed slowly before the nineteenth century, but emerged as a major branch of historical literature in the last quarter of the nineteenth century. Between these two phases of its mythical and scholarly history, four occasions in the nineteenth century took up the myth once more, continued to universalize it, and completed its erection into the great enemy of the human spirit. Although they are individually well known, it is important to reconsider them in the context of the myth, for they are eloquent testimony to its strength and enduring appeal to the European imagination.

The Dreams of Reason: Moratín and Goya

Throughout the reform-minded eighteenth century, Spain carried on its back the image of seventeenth-century Spain, the Spain depicted so harshly by Madame d'Aulnoy and preserved in the work of Montesquieu, Voltaire, and the various encyclopedists and *philosophes*. As late as 1783 a hostile article on Spain in the *Encyclopédie méthodique* by Masson de Morvilliers prevented the Spanish edition of that work from ever being distributed; five years later, at the urging of Charles III of Spain, a scurrilous little travel book by the Marquis de Langle was publicly burned at Paris for similar reasons. Spain's reaction to the enduring criticism of its seventeenth-century ghost took several different forms. The Inquisition and much of the clergy, having lost considerable power throughout the century, counter-attacked vigorously after the 1770s, with the trial and sentence of Pablo Olavide in 1778 their earliest and most widely known triumph. Reform-minded Spaniards undertook the defense of Spain against outside calumny, often ignoring much of the worst of the Spanish past while asserting the progress that had been made in the eighteenth century, particularly during the reign of Charles III. Finally, a group of satirists and other thinkers attempted to revive the images of Spain's backward past in order that they might expose them to the light of reason which would scornfully blow them away. Until the impact of the French Revolution struck Spain in the early 1790s, these three reactions characterized a broad segment of Spanish society, and both the Inquisition and the "superstitions" of the people played a prominent role in them.

During the second quarter of the century, the great Benedictine scholar Benito Feijóo almost single-handedly began to rehabilitate Spanish thought and brought mercilessly to light the characteristics of Spanish religious culture that could no longer stand up to rational scrutiny and criticism. Feijóo's contemporary, Diego de Torres Villaroel (1693–1770), in 1727–1728 published his remarkable *Visiones y Visitas*, a criticism of popular beliefs cast in the form of dream visions that permitted the writer to depict the values he criticized in an outrageous and monstrous form. After Feijóo's death in 1764, other thinkers took up the task, notably the new periodical press, including the journals *El Pensador*, directed by José Clavijo, and *El Censor*, directed by Luis Cañuelos. The most radical of these critics fully adopted French styles of thought and general Enlightenment attitudes toward the power of the Church and of *The Inquisition* in particular.

The liberal Spanish government and an increasingly reactionary

Church witnessed the French Revolution and attempted in different ways to protect Spain from its consequences. But the Spanish government collapsed before Napoleon in 1808 and from that date until 1814 the *afrancesados* held considerable power. The popular and political reaction to French occupation returned the Spanish monarchy in the person of Ferdinand VII in 1814, and the first liberal period came to an end. With the short-lived revolution led by General Riego from 1820–1823, a second period of dramatic liberalization took place, but with the collapse of the revolutionary government and the second restoration of Ferdinand VII, the hopes of Spanish liberals were dashed once more, and many of them fled to France, never to return.

It is in the context of late eighteenth- and early nineteenth-century divided Spain that the work of Leandro Moratín and Francisco Goya, more effectively and powerfully than any thinkers or artists before them, attacked the most reactionary elements of Spanish culture by dramatizing and portraying them vividly and savagely.

Born in 1746, Francisco José Goya y Lucientes became a popular court painter and was appointed painter to the royal household in 1789. In his life at court, Goya began to meet a number of Spanish reformers, notably the future prime minister Jovellanos, as well as other political figures and writers who professed Enlightenment ideas and bitterly criticized and satirized what they regarded as the worst intellectual abuses of Spanish culture. Goya painted many of these figures, including Jovellanos himself, Cean Bermúdez, and the liberal historian of the Spanish Inquisition, Juan Antonio Llorente. A devastating illness in 1792–1793 cost Goya his hearing and influenced a new direction for his work, one that is marked by an increasingly savage use of satire against anti-Enlightenment practices, represented in his sketchbooks between 1796 and 1799 and by the publication of his drawings called the *Caprichos* in 1799.

The *Caprichos* reflects both the influence of reform ideas on Goya and Goya's transformation of his artistic style in order to represent these ideas pictorially. His first illustration in the volume, which shows the painter asleep, surrounded by creeping and flying monsters, was inscribed by the painter with the title *"El sueño de la razón produce monstruos"*— "when reason dreams, it produces monsters," perhaps an echo of Villaroel. Another inscription informs the viewer that the picture represents,

> The author dreaming. His one intention is to banish harmful beliefs commonly held, and with this work of caprichos to perpetuate the solid testimony of truth.

Goya's use of dreams and fantasies as a device for representing the aspects of Spanish life he most wished to criticize permitted him to depict much of the popular belief in witches and demons, monsters and folly of all kinds, and to attack those institutions that appeared to him to preserve and sustain them. His two prints in the series concerning the Spanish Inquisition (*Caprichos* 23 and 24) depict figures dressed in *sanbenitos*, with ambiguous phrases for titles, some drawn from well-known Spanish proverbs. In the *Caprichos*, however, Goya's target was not chiefly the Inquisition, but a set of superstitious religious beliefs, often less those of the eighteenth century itself than those of the seventeenth century that had recently been popularized. In 1798 Goya painted several scenes of witchcraft in the home of the Duchess of Osuna, and these, too, illustrate beliefs more characteristic of the witchcraft-literature of the seventeenth century.

During the years from 1797 to 1799 Goya became acquainted with the young playwright Leandro Fernández de Moratín, whose portrait Goya also painted in 1799, a devoted *afrancesado* who had developed an interest in Spanish religious beliefs and practices, particularly in witchcraft and the doctrines that permitted its discovery and persecution in the seventeenth century. When he met Goya, Moratín was working on an edition of the *relación* of the famous *auto-de-fé* held at Logroño in 1610, in which eleven people had been burned as witches, another twenty convicted, and several thousand others incriminated by confessions. An official *relación* of the trials and executions had been published contemporaneously with the executions, and circulated widely during the seventeenth century. Moratín undertook to publish a new edition of the *relación* with his own satirical commentary in the form of footnotes to the Spanish text. The work, *Auto-de-Fé celebrado en la Ciudad de Logroño*, appeared in 1811 (and was reprinted in 1812 and 1820) under the liberal Bonapartist government. Goya had known the work—and Moratín's interest in witchcraft beliefs and the Inquisition—since 1797 and much of his pictorial inspiration in the *Caprichos* and later works derived from Moratín.

By the late 1790s both Moratín and Goya had come to believe that by exposing as dramatically as possible the beliefs that opposed and prevented the light of reason from illuminating Spain as it had recently illuminated France, they might help banish the harmful beliefs and practices themselves. In the case of Moratín, this was to be done by meticulously annotating the follies of the inquisitors at Logroño in 1610; in that of Goya, by pictorially depicting things previously existing only in the popular imagination, so that, once these beliefs and practices were *seen*, they would be recognized for the follies and brutalities that they really were, and they would be replaced by the truth. The use of witches, demons, and monsters of various kinds also permitted Goya behind the safe veil of allegory to use these images to attack real social types, particularly clergy, the nobility, and the folk who persisted in superstition.

After the initial fascination with—as well as contempt for—the beliefs for which people had been executed in seventeenth-century Spain, Goya's work between 1799 and 1814 did not focus as extensively on these themes. Occupied with the Bonapartist government and the war, Goya only took them up again with the reaction in 1815. Called before the Inquisition itself in 1815 to explain a number of nude paintings he had done, Goya witnessed the savage popular reaction to the Bonapartist government, and also that of the brief-lived *Cortes* of 1812–1813, led by the king and the Church, with the Inquisition as their chief instrument. During the next liberal period, 1820–1823, Goya turned on the Inquisition with full fury, and in his sketches and paintings after 1814 he elevated his pictorial denunciations into the most remarkable visual art ever produced against that institution.

The years from 1814 to the revolution of 1820 were grim ones for all liberals, particularly those labeled *afrancesados*, and Goya's fury turned more directly upon the clergy and the Inquisition than it had before. In 1819, the same year in which Moratín was denounced by the Inquisition, Goya purchased a country house outside Madrid, the *Quinta del Sordo*, and he decorated its large upper and lower rooms with a series of pictures that have come to be called his "Black" Paintings. Among these is a mysterious and utterly contemptuous rendering of "The Holy Office", which evokes the personnel of the witchcraft trials of 1610 in the wild mountainous country in which the alleged witches had performed their deeds. Some time between 1812 and 1819, Goya had also painted his dramatic condemnation scene, the *Auto-de-Fé*.

After 1820, however, such work could circulate somewhat more freely in Spain. Several salacious comedies about the Inquisition and religious life in convents were performed on the Madrid stage in 1820–1821, and Moratín himself considered mounting a spectacular musical staging of the 1610 witchcraft trials, complete with demons, witches, and dismembered victims. With the fall of the Riego government, Moratín and Goya both fled to France, where they died within a few days of each other in 1828.

Besides the great paintings of *The Holy Office* and the *Auto-de-Fé*, Goya also turned on the Inquisition in a series of sketchbooks, particularly in Album C, which he drew between 1803 and 1824. A number of pictures in Album C, most probably drawn after 1814, savagely excoriate the Inquisition by emotionally depicting its victims, its savage personnel, and its prisons, including a number of world famous figures who had fallen into its hands. The pictures in Album C, especially Nos. 85–115, reflect, more even than the paintings, Goya's fury. In quick strokes and with an ingenious use of figure arrangement and light and shadow, Goya invokes the viewer's sympathy for the victims and utter hostility toward the inquisitors and their servants.

Some of these drawings simply depict forlorn figures in positions of shame or torment with the simple caption—For having done . . . this: For having been born in foreign parts,—indicating the irrational frivolity of Inquisition persecutions. Some of the figures are named, including the Italian sculptor Torrigiano, shrouded in a mantle in a prison cell, and Diego Martín Zapata, chained in a dungeon. One of the most striking is a depiction of Galileo, chained to huge blocks of stone, captioned, "For discovering the movement of the earth" (Plate 27). Nor did Goya ignore what had once been the Inquisition's chief reason for existing. In Album C, Number 88 depicts a procession of figures in *sanbenitos* and *corozas* (penitential miters) emerging from a dark archway into the light, presumably to receive their public shaming or execution. The caption reads "For being of Jewish ancestry" (Plate 26).

Although Goya had begun his new pictorial work in the 1790s, he had originally focused upon customs and superstitions and characters that were uniquely Spanish. By the 1820s, however, he had become much more specific about the Spanish Inquisition, but he also elevated it to the status of a universal enemy of reason and enlightenment. Thus, his depiction of Galileo is pictorially no different from his other drawings depicting victims of the Spanish Inquisition—the Spanish Inquisition has become for Goya *The Inquisition*, the single instrument of reaction that operates the same way everywhere, with the same purpose, and its victims are now no longer the foolish and imprudent, but the innocent, the wise, and the heroic. The early *Capricho* drawings had depicted two people who had committed real offenses, although Goya perhaps doubted whether they should be considered offenses. After 1814, the victims of *The Inquisition* are the least powerful and most heroic representatives of humanity. In these later paintings and drawings Goya speaks, not for *afrancesado* Spain, but for the human spirit, and he universalizes *The Inquisition* into the oppressor of all people everywhere, as a number of his nineteenth-century successors were to do as well.

For Moratín and Goya, the dreams of reason had permitted the artist to release into pictorial existence the horrors that had been real, but not pictorially expressed before. But the horrors themselves were also the products of a place and time that permitted Reason to sleep and to let these things loose upon the Spanish and European mind. At the end, Goya's battle was against the "monsters" of dreaming Reason, many of which he represented in the clutches of *The Inquisition*. Elsewhere in Europe, for political and philosophical purposes, other artists took up the theme as well on a similar scale.

The Further Adventures of Don Carlos: Schiller and Verdi

Goya's universalizing of *The Inquisition* was but one instance of a general eighteenth- and nineteenth-century tendency among thinkers who were concerned less with confessional differences than with the oppression of the intellect or the stifling of political liberty. One of the early commonplace topics of this theme had been the development of the story of Don Carlos, the son of Philip II of Spain, in histories and works of fiction. The story had appealed to polemicists, historians, dramatists, and historical romancers because of its intriguing mixture of romance, passion, and political liberalism. In most versions of the story, regardless of the sentimental variations, the political theme remained prominent, and by the late eighteenth century—the age of liberal revolution itself— the story took on a new lease on life as a popular account of the struggle between freedom and tyranny. In the work of Friedrich Schiller and Giuseppe Verdi, the story found its way into the hands of a poetic genius and playwright and those of a great composer. Their work established the theme as one of the most evocative monuments to human liberty, with *The Inquisition* as its chief enemy.

Friedrich Schiller's *Don Karlos, Infant von Spanien* was written in 1787, based upon the story by Saint-Réal and Robert Watson's *History of Philip II*, an English continuation of William Robertson's *History . . . of Charles V* that was quickly translated into German and depicted the Spanish ruler as a bloody tyrant. Schiller was a great poet and a greater writer than Saint-Réal, however; and he was more genuinely interested in Spain and a far better historian than Watson. Schiller took the political dimensions of the story of Don Carlos as seriously as he took the relationship between Carlos and Elizabeth. These views colored his depiction of Spain and of the figures in the story.

Schiller's *Don Karlos* opens with a discussion between Carlos and the king's confessor, a spy, and flows into Carlos's meeting with a boyhood friend, Roderick, Marquis of Posa, who announces a great new cause to Carlos:

> For I do not stand here as Roderick now,
> Nor as the playmate of the boy-Prince Carlos—
> As deputy of all humanity
> I now embrace you,—and it is the Flemish
> Provinces that weep upon your neck
> And solemnly cry out to you for rescue.
> That land so dear to you is lost if Alba,
> The brutal hangman of Fanaticism,
> Moves into Brussels with his Spanish laws.

Philip, portrayed by Schiller as a heartless monster of a father, does not permit his heart to be moved by pity for his subjects, by the Queen's grace, or by Carlos's own person. Elizabeth, both acknowledging and rejecting Carlos's love for her, urges him to make Spain his great love and to request command in the Netherlands as his new responsibility. Roderick warns Carlos about the dangers of his coming to resemble his father when *he* becomes king, and King Philip refuses Don Carlos command of the Netherlands.

In a discussion between Alva and Domingo, the king's confessor, Carlos's character and utter unsuitability for the throne become a main theme of two of the most repulsive characters in the play. Domingo denounces Carlos as an enemy of both monarchy and Christianity:

> He entertains the monstrous scheme—Toledo—
> The frenzied scheme of being ruler and
> Of making do without our Holy Faith.—
> His heart is all afire for a new virtue
> Which, proud, assured, euffient to itself,
> Does not intend to beg of any Faith.—
> He *thinks!* His head is burning with an odd
> Delusion—he respects mankind.—Duke, is he
> A fit man to become our king?

Domingo proposes to insinuate to the king that Elizabeth and Carlos are lovers, not because he knows this, but because it seems the ideal way to destroy both dangerous characters. Alba and Domingo inform the king of the treachery of Don Carlos and Elizabeth (III. iii). In a stirring scene (III. x) the Marquis of Posa presents ideas of liberal monarchy to the king, almost convincing him of their truth, as Posa prophecies,

> But gentler
> Ages will supplant the times of Philip;
> They will bring milder wisdom; welfare of
> The citizen will walk with Princes' greatness

> In harmony, the thrifty state will cherish
> Its children, and Necessity be human.

Philip claims that he offers peace, and Posa denounces it as "the peace of cemeteries." No force can halt the "transformation of matured Christendom;" moreover,

> . . . the subjects
> That you have lost for the Faith's sake were your
> Most noble ones. With mother's arms wide opened
> Elizabeth [I, of England] receives the fugitives,
> And with the skills of our lands, Britain blooms
> Luxuriantly. . . . Granada lies a waste. . . .

But Philip, although deeply moved by Posa's speech, falls back into the toils of the conspirators, whose devices nearly succeed, until Posa inserts himself as the lover of the queen and is killed in Carlos's presence. Carlos denounces Philip, and the king appears to resign the royal office to his son. The conspirators, however, accuse Carlos once again. In a scene with the Cardinal Grand Inquisitor ("Ninety years of age and blind, leaning on a staff and led by two Dominicans"), Philip begins to confess to the murder of Posa, but is instead harshly rebuked by the Inquisitor for having robbed the Holy Office of a victim it had known of and wanted for years:

> He was murdered wantonly! ingloriously!
> The blood that should have flowed for us in glory
> Was shed by an assassin's hand. The man
> Was ours—Who authorized you to lay hands
> Upon the Order's sacred property?
> To die for us was his excuse for living.
> God granted him unto this epoch's need
> To make of swaggering Reason an example
> By formal degradation of his mind.

The Grand Inquisitor denounces Philip's abruptness; and when the King asks for forgiveness, citing human weakness and his affection for Posa as a human being, the Inquisitor responds,

> Why a human being? Human
> Beings are mere digits, nothing more. . . .

In the final scene, Carlos takes leave of Elizabeth, determined to go to Flanders and lead the rebellion against Philip's tyranny. But Philip and the Inquisitor enter, Elizabeth collapses, and Philip turns Carlos over to the Grand Inquisitor saying,

> Cardinal! I have
> Done what my part required. Do your part now.

The lyric and dramatic powers of Schiller make *Don Karlos* a literary work, but great literary works, as well as inferior ones, may carry political messages, and the message of *Don Karlos* is sharp and eloquent. The unjustly treated wavering prince, strengthened by the friendship and ideas of Posa, gives up his love for the queen and dedicates himself to the salvation of the Netherlands. A brutal and weak king is manipulated by courtiers and confessor into destroying the republican Posa and Elizabeth and Don Carlos as well. The final instrument of Carlos's death is the Inquisition. Thus, in a great drama, the political ideas of the sixteenth, seventeenth, and eighteenth centuries come face to face in a tragedy that is far more human than political, and far more moving than polemic. The king, Carlos, Posa, and the Inquisitor are formidable and memorable literary creations, the Inquisitor particularly playing an awesome presence although he is on stage for the shortest time. Those who knew the polemical history of the Inquisition before reading or seeing *Don Karlos* were certain that they knew far more about it afterwards. For the characters remain in the memory, and they color the reading of even the most objective and analytical historical sources. The domestic tragedy aside, the political and religious tragedy eloquently sums up late eighteenth-century political and religious sentiment.

The lingering influence of Saint-Réal and the dynamic influence of Schiller inspired a large number of *Don Carlos* works throughout the late eighteenth and early nineteenth centuries, including several plays and operas. But the greatest artistic representation of the Don Carlos theme was that of Giuseppe Verdi in 1867. In 1850 Verdi had been approached by two French librettists, Joseph Mery and Camille du Locle, with the proposal that he write for the Paris Opera a work on the theme of Schiller's *Don Karlos.* Although Verdi initially rejected the proposal, by 1866 he had agreed to write the opera, completing it with du Locle after Mery's death in 1866.

As he worked on the original liberetto, Verdi found that its sentiments were not sufficiently republican for his own taste and for his great theme. Continually rejecting his collaborator's drifting away from the original story, Verdi returned again and again to Schiller's text, restoring scenes his librettist had omitted (that between Philip II and the Inquisitor, for example, or the duet on political liberalism between Philip and Posa), and even specifying that it was Schiller's Inquisitor ("whom I should like to be blind and very old") whom he wanted in the opera. During several subsequent recompositions of the opera, these scenes remained in it, although many others were cut, as did the coronation *auto-de-fé* in Act III, Scene ii, which was Verdi's great dramaturgical contribution to the myth.

Verdi had read Alfieri as well as Schiller, and his own republican sentiments and Italian patriotism led him to focus equally on King and Inquisitor as the dark forces of Don Carlos's world. Although Verdi preserved the romantic and individual themes of Schiller, he worked the political themes in early and impressively. In I.ii Carlos is already destined to go to the Netherlands, since his love for Elizabeth is to be sublimated to his love for freedom and justice for the Netherlands. The importance of Posa's ideas is heightened by Verdi by bringing the duet between him and Philip into direct sequence with Carlos' decision in II.ii.

But Verdi's great contribution to the theme is his mounting of the *auto-de-fé* in III.ii, a grandiose spectacle (as far as I know, attempted only by Mercier before him, and that in a stage play) that demonstrated the somber horrors of absolutist Spain, linking the executions to the arrival and pleas of the Deputies of Flanders. Verdi makes a great deal more of the Grand Inquisitor than had Schiller. In Schiller's drama, although the character is distinct and formidable, he is only on stage for two brief scenes. In Verdi's *Don Carlo* he appears in IV.ii, there to harden Philip's heart against Carlo and to remind the king of his stern duties, denouncing Posa and Carlo, isolating the king from all claims of human relationships, and demanding the arrest of Posa who (contrary to Schiller's version) is still alive. Philip's weak query as to whether the throne should once again capitulate before the altar,

> *Dunque il tròno piegar dovrà sempre all'altare!*

is answered by the Inquisitor's silence.

In IV.ii, Roderigo is shot and killed by a companion and servant of the Inquisition. Dying, he reminds Carlo of his glorious duty to Flanders. Just as the revolt breaks out and Philip presents Carlo to the crowd, the Grand Inquisitor emerges once again, dramatically and abruptly, silencing the crowd, quelling the revolt, and assuming dominance over Philip himself.

In Act V, as in Schiller, Elizabeth and Carlo take farewells and are interrupted by the king and the Grand Inquisitor, who commands his guards to arrest Carlo. At the end of Verdi's opera, however, the ghost of Charles V emerges and saves Carlo by drawing him into the cloister of the monastery, San Juste, in which the final scene takes place.

Although Schiller had not mounted an *auto-de-fé*, and although Alfieri had not emphasized the role of the Inquisition in his own drama, Verdi added to Schiller's drama besides what he preserved from it. He added the dimension of the Inquisition to Alfieri's story, probably because it was needed as a support to the more complex and wavering character of Philip II. When the opera was done—and it was revised several times—Verdi insisted upon retaining what he considered the crucial political and ecclesiastical parts, including the *auto-de-fé*, all of it set to some of Verdi's greatest music, thereby not only retaining the political themes of Schiller's republicanism, but increasing and even enhancing the picture of the Inquisition that Verdi had found in Schiller. By the standards of eighteenth- and nineteenth-century republicanism and anticlericalism, the power of *The Inquisition* had less to do with religious belief than with political power, and in the work of Schiller and Verdi particularly, two powerful artists brought that conviction to life—and memory—in a play and an opera. Behind the Inquisitor and the king there lay Flanders and its mythical republican ambitions which had convinced Posa and later convinced Don Carlos. And beyond Flanders lay the world of liberal revolutions. The only obstacle to those political ambitions was the wavering king of Spain and *The Inquisition*—the eternal ally of tyranny and the eternal and universal enemy of political liberty.

Bruno and Galileo, or The Martyrology of Science

In the work of Goya and Verdi, reason and liberty had challenged superstition and tyranny. Although they did not clearly triumph, they battled heroically, and they evoked dramatic and widely admired ideals of heroism and innocent victimization in their great battle. They contended against an increasingly generalized Spain and a universalized *Inquisition*. But they were not the only combatants in the struggle. From the early seventeenth century, a number of natural philosophers had taken up the cause of astronomical and physical theory, postulating a very different physical universe from the Ptolemaic–Aristotelian one that had served the physics and astronomy of medieval and sixteenth-century Latin Europe. Much of the debate centered upon the consequences of the arguments in Nicholas Copernicus' *On the Revolution of the Celestial Orbs* of 1543, but by the early seventeenth century it developed other centers of dispute, perhaps best known being the debate between the followers of René Descartes and the aristotelians that dominated the seventeenth and early eighteenth centuries, and the triumph of Newton. Although not all scientific questions came under ecclesiastical scrutiny, two particular cases in 1600 and 1633 became so well known that they shaped much of the early social and cultural self-perception of modern scientists. The execution in Rome of Giordano Bruno in 1600 and the penance imposed on Galileo Galilei, also in Rome, in 1633 constituted the core of a myth that had its greatest hour in the nineteenth century: the myth of the martyrology of science and the role of the Church, specifically *The Inquisition*, in creating martyrs of science and opposing the progress of scientific discovery.

The thought and writings of Bruno and Galileo were very different: each writer used and understood the work of Copernicus in a very different way. Many historians of science have rightly denied to Bruno a place in the history of science at all. The work of Frances Yates has revealed him to have been a speculative philosopher-magician who misunderstood Copernicus; other scholars have demonstrated that Bruno did not understand "science" outside his Hermetic philosophy, which proposed, among other things, that natural magic, properly deployed, would solve the quarrels of the world and usher in a new age of peace, one to be ruled by wise kings guided by even wiser magicians. As Yates has pointed out, such a world-view could not have been more opposed to that of Galileo:

> Galileo's views were based on genuine mathematics and mechanics: he lived in a very different mental world from Giordano Bruno, a world in which "Pythagorean intentions" and "Hermetic seals" played no part, and the scientist reached his conclusions on genuinely scientific grounds. Bruno's philosophy cannot be separated from his religion.

Yet at the time of their trials and into the nineteenth century, the names of Bruno and Galileo were frequently linked and the cause for which they both suffered was identified as the cause of reason and science, opposed to superstition and obscurantism, represented by theologians and directed by *The Inquisition*.

Bruno (1548–1600) was a former Dominican who had become acquainted with the large body of literature recently translated into Latin that professed to contain the secrets of the "true ancient philosophy"— passed down from Hermes Trismegistus, a contemporary of Moses, corrupted in ensuing centuries, but at last available in its pristine purity to those wise enough to understand and employ it. Among the arguments of Hermetism was that of the divinity of man, the identity of human divinity with that of the stars and planets, and man's ability to employ cosmic forces by means of "natural" magic for the benefit of mankind and the greater restoration of harmony to the universe. Bruno had made a name for himself by producing two works on the art of memory, in which he used his magical-philosophical principles, and he travelled throughout Europe, developing a network of friends and patrons who were fascinated by his combination of religious reform, astrology, cabalism, and magic. When Bruno took up the ideas of Copernicus, he did so not as a mathematician or an astronomer, but as a *magus* who professed to find in Copernicus a set of physical arguments that corroborated his own larger and cosmic vision.

Driven by his vision of a hermetic golden age about to come into existence, Bruno returned to Italy in 1591, possibly with the intention of converting the pope to his views. Arrested by officers of the Venetian Inquisition, Bruno was questioned about his religious beliefs as reflected in his published works, recanted, and requested mercy of the judge. The case, however, was sent on to Rome, probably because of Bruno's notoriety. In Rome, Cardinal Robert Bellarmine presented a list of eight heretical propositions drawn from Bruno's works. Originally promising to recant these beliefs, Bruno later refused. Arguing that he had never been a heretic and that his ideas had been misinterpreted, Bruno was convicted as a relapsed heretic and turned over to the secular arm for execution, possibly (it has recently been suggested) as part of a diplomatic agreement between the pope and Spain.

After the notoriety and the execution of Bruno, anyone wishing to publicly discuss Copernicanism in Italy would have been well advised to avoid any literary form or discourse that remotely resembled Bruno's. But in the early seventeenth century there existed no model for discussions of natural philosophy that were designed to reach a non-specialist audience *without* sounding a little like Bruno. When the case of Galileo came before the Roman Inquisition it appeared to many to resemble that of Bruno much too closely.

Galileo Galilei (1564–1642) spent a long career as teacher of applied mathematics and physics at the universities of Pisa and Padua, and he moved freely in the literary and scientific circles that distinguished the intellectual life of northern Italy. By 1595 he had come to accept most of Copernicus' arguments for a heliocentric universe, and he worked these into his own basic research into astronomy, physics, and mechanics. His work began to take a number of subjects that had hitherto been the preserve of natural philosophers out of their philosophical context and into a physical context of their own, without concerning himself with the way his researches fit into the theological and philosophical world-view of the philosophers. Galileo drew support for his new direction from the appearance of the novas of 1572 and 1604, and his observations on the latter were followed by his experiments with the newly-invented telescope, his discovery of the satellites of Jupiter, and his important astronomical treatise, *The Starry Messenger*, of 1610.

In many respects, particularly to readers unfamiliar with the mathematical and physical technicalities of Galileo's work, *The Starry Messenger* appeared to resemble in an unsettling way some of the style and argument of Bruno. Moreover, Galileo's style antagonized not only philosophers, but rival astronomers and a number of theologians as well. Although Galileo argued that neither philosophers nor theologians should take categorical positions on questions of physical science, in 1616 the Roman Inquisition commanded him neither to hold nor to defend the thesis that the sun is the immovable center of the universe and that the earth is movable and not at the center.

Between 1616 and 1632 Galileo continued his work and his writing, but his name continued to be associated with the misuses of astronomy of Bruno and with a number of other pseudo-scientific philosophies that became widely known and considerably feared during these two decades. In 1632 in Florence, Galileo published his masterpiece, *The Dialogue Concerning the Two Chief Systems of the World—Ptolemaic and Copernican*. Although the work does not absolutely assert the correctness of the Copernican system, Galileo's opinions were sufficiently clear for his enemies to inform Pope Urban VIII, a former friend and patron of the scientist, who called Galileo to Rome and tried him before the Inquisition for having violated the injunction of 1616. Galileo was convicted and sentenced to indefinite imprisonment, quickly commuted to a modified form of house arrest, which continued until Galileo died in 1642.

There is much to be said in favor of the view that Galileo was condemned in the manner that he was because of his association in the minds of theologians and inquisitors with the style and work of Bruno. Yet in neither case were those aspects of their work that most interest modern thinkers the chief issues against them. Although the transcript of Bruno's trial is lost, it appears that he was condemned on relatively familiar grounds—for leaving the Dominican Order without authorization, for positing arguments that were clearly heterodox, and for associating with condemned heretics. In Galileo's case the conviction turned on his disobedience to a command of the Inquisition itself. These cases are interesting precisely because they did not deal directly with the large scientific issues, but rather illustrate the character of how early seventeenth-century inquisitors interpreted the nature of scientific discourse, the atmosphere of academic and professional jealousy and rivalry, and the sensitivity to new and ambitious philosophical physical systems that characterized much of early seventeenth-century Europe.

In the years that followed, although Bruno's name was preserved by a number of sympathetic followers and contributed to what Yates has called "The Rosicrucian Enlightenment," his work was ignored by virtually everyone else until the nineteenth century. But Galileo's was not. Until the 1640s, when Galileo's works began to circulate widely in northern Europe, he was generally known as a natural philosopher who had been condemned in Rome for unknown reasons. To the poet John Milton, who had visited Galileo in 1638, the case was exemplary of the folly of censoring books. As Milton wrote in his *Areopagitica* of 1644,

> I could recount what I have seen and heared in other Countries, where this kind of inquisition tyrannizes; where I have sat among learned men, for that honor I had, and bin counted happy to be born in such a place of *Philosophic* freedom as they supposed England was. . . . There it was that I found and visited the famous Galileo grown old, a prisoner to the Inquisition, for thinking in Astronomy otherwise than the Franciscan and Dominican licensers thought.

Milton did not refrain from holding up the prospect of *The Inquisition* as an analogy to those in England who would license the printing of books: "This practice has crept out of the *Inquisition*, and was catcht up by our Prelates, and hath caught some of our Presbyters." For Milton, Galileo's case illustrates better than any other the dangers of England's own "inquisiturient bishops" who are eager to imitate their popish contemporaries.

A decade later, with the publication of the correspondence of René Descartes, Europeans discovered that in November, 1633, Descartes had written to Marin Mersenne that the condemnation of Galileo had caused Descartes himself to withhold publication of his *Du Monde*, "because I wanted for nothing in the world to issue a discourse in which there might be found the least word which might be disapproved by the Church." Wishing that his other works might find smoother sailing and acceptance, Descartes withheld *Du Monde* during his lifetime (it was published in 1664), perhaps influenced as well by the edict of Cardinal Richelieu of 1624 which prohibited the printing of works which criticized recognized intellectual authorities. Descartes returned to this point more than once in his correspondence, and his biographer, Baillet, emphasized it as well in his *Vie de M. Descartes* of 1691. Mersenne himself had translated into French the inquisitorial decree against Galileo in 1634.

The growth of the reputations of both Galileo and Descartes in the following decades ensured that the fact of Galileo's condemnation and the caution it inspired in Descartes would remain a prominent feature in seventeenth- and eighteenth-century discussions of the freedom of scientific inquiry.

The opposition of *The Inquisition* to science thus joined the opposition of *The Inquisition* to true religion, political liberty, religious toleration, and rational philosophy and the arts in the changing polemic of the eighteenth century. Nor was a particular inquisition—the Spanish or the Roman—solely to blame, but *The Inquisition* in all of its unvarying local manifestations. In 1764 Voltaire observed that,

> If Newton had been born in Portugal [Voltaire had recently become familiar with and fascinated by the Portuguese Inquisition] and if a Dominican had seen a heresy in the inverse ratio of the square of distance, Newton would have been reclothed in a *senbenito* at an *auto-de-fé*.

Almost one hundred years after Marin Mersenne had translated the condemnation of Galileo into French, in Samuel Chandler's 1731 translation of Limborch's *History of the Inquisition* there appeared for the first time in English the condemnation of Galileo and his own abjuration. (Limborch had included the Latin text of the condemnation of Galileo in a chapter on how the inquisitorial process is ended against a person suspected, or suspected and defamed, of heresy.) This part of Chandler's translation was reprinted in *The Gentleman's Magazine* in 1745, probably as part of an anti-Catholic campaign in connection with the rising of Stuart supporters in Scotland. In that article, the cardinals who condemned Galileo are identified as enemies of useful science and true wisdom.

By the mid-eighteenth century, then, the denunciation of Milton, the fear struck into Descartes, the prudence of Mersenne and Gassendi in the face of the ecclesiastical condemnation of Galileo, were added to the traditional invective against Catholicism and the Inquisition, with the substantial assistance of the talented pens of such Enlightenment *philosophes* as Voltaire. It was universally accepted that *The Inquisition* played a role as an instrument of obscurantism and anti-intellectualism, designed to protect superstitions and fanaticism (as well as aristotelianism, the Jesuits, and the religious orders) from the knowledge and discovery of the modern eighteenth-century world. As the Italian savant Algarotti lamented in 1778,

> The imprisonment and condemnation of Galileo have given occasion to many to inveigh against the Roman popes; and the Protestants believed

that they had drawn out an invincible argument against the infallibility of the Church.

The *philosophes* struck through the *Encyclopédie* as well. In the second part of the *Discours préliminaire* of the *Encyclopédie*, published in 1751, d'Alembert, having praised his own and immediately past ages for having revived human thought and launched it on a wondrous new career after centuries of superstition, challenged those who would stifle this intellectual progress:

> A certain tribunal that has grown very powerful in the south of Europe, in the Indies, and in the New World . . . of which France cannot pronounce the name without terror, has condemned a certain celebrated astronomer for having upheld the theory of the earth's motion, and has declared him a heretic. . . . It is thus that spiritual authority, when it is united with temporal authority, forces reason to be silent.

D'Alembert took up the same case and imagery in his article on Copernicus in Vol. IV of 1754; but he added to these the details of Descartes' withholding *Du Monde* from publication for fear of ecclesiastical censure:

> In Italy it is forbidden to uphold the system of Copernicus. . . . The great Galileo was once put to the Inquisition, and his opinion on the motion of the earth was condemned as heretical. . . . [Galileo] was obliged to retract publicly and abjure his pretended error by mouth and by hand, which he did on 22 June, 1633; and having promised on his knees, his hand upon the Gospels, that he would neither do nor say anything contrary to that ordinance, he was put into the prisons of the Inquisition, from which he was later liberated. This event so terrified Descartes, who was very submissive to the Holy See, that it prevented him from publishing his treatise *Du Monde*, which was then ready for publication.

Confessional and philosophical polemic had, by the end of the eighteenth century, found in the persecuted Galileo one of its heroes. But he did not remain alone. In Nelli's *Life and Correspondence of Galileo*, published in 1818, Galileo is linked with Lorenzo Valla, Telesio, and Vesalius as early martyrs in what was about to become "the warfare of science with theology."

Within the double framework of Enlightenment anticlericalism and the Age of Newton, the career of Galileo and his subsequent reputation had been firmly established by the end of the eighteenth century. Since the Inquisition's charge had included the formal mention of torture, and since the biographies of Galileo all noted that he had gone blind in 1637, the additional charges of torture and blinding, as well as prolonged and terrible imprisonment were added to the story.

A number of historians of mathematics and science in the eighteenth century extended Galileo's stay in the prison of the Roman Inquisition from one, to six, to "several" years, when in fact he had lived in the apartment of an official of the Inquisition for twenty-two days. Others assumed that he had been kept in chains and that he had appeared before the Inquisition in a "penitential garment." Although a number of nineteenth-century scholars—and a number of careful biographers of Galileo himself in the eighteenth century—frequently criticized these inventions, they dominated the popular—confessional and scientific— image of Galileo through the nineteenth century and into the twentieth. By the nineteenth century, the case of Galileo served the purposes of historians of science far more than it served confessional hostility to Rome and the Roman Inquisition. But in liberal Protestant histories of the Inquisition written during the late nineteenth century, Galileo's case is added to those of a more directly confessional character. Thus, in Arthur Arnould's *Histoire de l'Inquisition* of 1869, one sees what had by then become a standard short-format for Inquisition histories: reflections on Christianity and persecution, the Christian persecution of dissenters from the fourth century on, the Spanish Inquisition, and the inquisitions down to the author's own day. In Chapter XXI, Arnould arrives at the problem of *The Inquisition* and the freedom of scientific and other intellectual inquiry:

> It is natural enough that the Inquisitors should have accused of magic [!] those men who were elevated so far above all the theologians of the epoch by their knowledge and profound science, and I am not astonished that ignorant monks [!] would have regarded as supernatural beings such men as Pico della Mirandola and Galileo, whose systems were condemned at Rome.

Giordano Bruno had no such consistent career as an admired natural philosopher as Galileo, although he came to enjoy a similar degree of respect during the nineteenth century. Partly because of his own interest in philosophical magic, Bruno and those who followed him, notably the Englishman Robert Fludd, were roundly condemned during that period when "natural philosophy" was separating out the natural sciences from the philosophical and poetic sciences of the sixteenth and early seventeenth centuries. Mersenne, to whom Descartes confided his reluctance to publish *Du Monde,* was a bitter enemy of Fludd and condemned Bruno, thus banishing both of them from the elaborate network of scientific correspondents Mersenne had established throughout Europe, and therefore from the early pantheon of Science itself.

The first full-scale account of seventeenth-century scientists as martyrs was the collection of articles by David Brewster, published in London in 1846 as *The Martyrs of Science: Lives of Galileo, Tycho Brahe, and Kepler*, and reprinted through the nineteenth century and even into the twentieth. Much of Brewster's work on Galileo derived from the earlier *Life of Galileo* by Lord Brougham that had appeared in 1829. Brougham's *Life* was particularly interesting because it claimed that Galileo received much of his knowledge from Giordano Bruno, and throughout the nineteenth century the names of Bruno and Galileo, both "victims" of the Inquisition, became early entries in the martyrology of science.

Brewster's Galileo, martyr though he is, is an ambivalent martyr. Brewster took the view that Galileo was an inveterate and devious enemy of the Church who deliberately circumvented explicit instructions in 1616 and caved in ingloriously out of fear in 1633. Yet Brewster condemns the Inquisition of Rome as well:

> Abhorring, as we must do, the principles and practice of this odious tribunal, and reprobating its interference with the cautious deductions of science, we must yet admit that, on this occasion, its deliberations were not dictated by passion, nor its power directed by vengeance. By yielding to their power, [Galileo] riveted for another century the almost broken chains of spiritual despotism.

It was not until the nineteenth century that the reputation of Bruno as a martyred philosopher and scientist began successfully to overcome the criticism of Mersenne and others. Besides the work of Brougham, it was powerfully aided by an increasingly strong current of Italian national (and largely anti-papal) sentiment, especially after 1849 (Plate 25). Although Bruno's reputation since the seventeenth century seems to have been preserved chiefly among literary historians, the publication of his work in Italian by Adolph Wagner in 1830 provided nineteenth-century readers with the materials of a new appreciation of Bruno (whom Wagner compared somewhat freely with Luther, Melanchthon, Erasmus, Pomponazzi, and Pico as one who helped "to drive away the clouds of ignorance" from Europe). The anticlerical nineteenth century also appreciated Bruno's martyrdom at the hands of the Inquisition. In 1868 the Italian patriot and scholar Doménico Berti published his *Life of Giordano Bruno*, and from that date until the end of the century a steady stream of Bruno studies flowed into European readerships. Berti, who also published the first complete set of Galileo trial documents in 1876, also published other documents concerning Bruno in 1880. As Owen Chadwick has pointed out,

Not only was Giordano Bruno burnt as a heretic in 1600, but the antipapal forces of the eighteenth-eighties used his death as a stick with which to beat the Papacy and to show how, as in the trial of Galileo, priests stopped scientists by force.

Among the most pointed expressions of liberal Italian opposition to the papacy was the dedication, on July 9, 1889—the Feast of Pentecost—of a statue of Giordano Bruno in the Campo dei Fiori, the very place where Bruno had been executed in 1600. Moreover, a secret society also called "Giordano Bruno" was formed in the late nineteenth century in Rome as a circle of freethinkers. During the second half of the nineteenth century, the history of ecclesiastical discipline was invoked again and again against papal authority, and the pontificate of Pius X (1903–1914) was scorned in liberal newspapers as reviving the ancient Roman Inquisition.

With the martyrology of Science now having come to include—indeed, virtually to have been founded by—Bruno and Galileo, it was possible for nineteenth-century critics of ecclesiastical interference in scientific investigation to depict the struggle of science in their own day as a potential martyrology.

The Darwin controversy created at least the fear of still more martyrs. From the late eighteenth century to the mid-nineteenth, most of the larger Christian confessions, as well as many of the smaller ones, had come to terms with much of the scientific thought of the eighteenth century and the materialism of the nineteenth. By 1835 the Roman Church had dropped its opposition to theories of a geocentric universe, and material evidence was accepted by most Christians as proof of both divine creation and divine providence. God as the creator of a harmonious Nature could as readily be deduced from scientific observation as from revelation. Even the considerable moments of turbulence in a number of mid–nineteenth-century confessions, notably the Church of England, or the controversies over the historical criticism of Scripture, did not at first signal the self-conscious break between religion and science that became a commonplace of discussion at the end of the century.

The publication of Charles Darwin's *On the Origin of Species by Means of Natural Selection: or, The Preservation of Favoured Races in the Struggle for Life* in 1859 did not change the relationship between religion and science overnight. Darwin's work fit into an older debate about materialism and revelation, and its full implications did not circulate very widely until the end of the century. For several decades, Darwin's theories of randomness and mechanical evolution were often accomodated with Christian doctrines of a divine purpose and teleological development in nature. Even the most extreme positivisitic interpreters of Darwin could fit readily into some of the main religious professions of the period.

Although theologians and scientists were able for much of the century to accomodate each others' world views, a number of historians were not. Out of the scientific mode of explanation for the mathematical and physical sciences in the late eighteenth century there also emerged the theory of a "scientific" history, that is, an idea that civilizations also develop according to measurable laws. Although Auguste Comte is generally credited with popularizing positivistic history, in England the work of Henry Thomas Buckle was extremely influential, particularly since Buckle advocated the comparative study of civilizations, with considerable attention paid to cultural and intellectual achievement as a standard measure. Buckle's famous observations of 1861 on "the Spanish Intellect," for example, represented one of the most extensive manifestations of the Black Legend, condemning the Spaniards' lack of intellectual and artistic achievement as a function of the nation's fanatic subordination to clerical interests:

> [Spain] is proud of everything of which she should be ashamed. She is proud of the antiquity of her opinions; proud of her orthodoxy; proud of the strength of her faith; proud of her immeasurable and childish credulity; proud of her unwillingness to amend either her creed or her customs; proud of her hatred of heretics, and proud of the undying vigilance with which she has baffled their efforts to obtain a full and legal establishment on her soil.

The appeal of Buckle's method and the persuasiveness of his judgments assured that intellectual, scientific, and artistic characteristics now could be routinely included either as causes or results of a nation's character. Spain, for Buckle, was the antithesis of modernity, and therefore Spain's perversity needed to be explained by the new historical method. Cultural comparativism was a dangerous new tool in the historian's hands.

Buckle's notion of scientific history and Buckle's assessment of Spain in that history laid the groundwork for much development of historical theory in the nineteenth century, particularly when a number of writers, often moved by the case of Darwin, began to emphasize the autonomy of science as an element in comparative cultural analysis. In 1874 John William Draper, an American scientist, published his *History of the Conflict between Religion and Science,* one of the earliest and best known examples of a genre of polemic that became immensely popular during the second half of the nineteenth century and the first half of the twentieth. In his work, which deals less with "Religion" than with Roman Catholicism, Draper announced yet another achievement of the Reformation of the sixteenth century: its enabling a scientific view of the universe to develop against the resistance of Catholic Europe. For Draper, science was the sister of the Reformation, and *The Inquisition* was the chief Catholic instrument for thwarting both. Draper assembled the Galileo myth full blown and applied it to his own age and to all times past. In his work, all of the anti-Inquisition elements coalesce without a seam.

In 1869 Andrew Dickson White, President of Cornell University, gave a famous address at the Cooper Union in New York City, entitled "The Battlefields of Science." Far less sanguine than Draper, White's remarks at Cooper Union and his subsequent development of them in his book *A History of the Warfare of Science with Theology in Christendom* of 1896 charged all dogmatic religions, including Protestantism, with impeding the development of scientific thought, and hence progress, and of using either inquisitions or the equivalents of inquisitions to achieve their obscurantist ends.

Although it was in no way similar, the case of Darwin, in the view of the Buckle-Draper-White theory of historical development, began to look very like the cases of Galileo and Bruno; that is, as a martyrology. A number of modern historians of science, notably James Moore and Ronald Numbers, have emphasized the frequency of military and battle-metaphors in the discussions of science in the late nineteenth and twenti-eth centuries; White's "Warfare" being merely the best known of many, and the tone of the discourse not confined to English-language publics or publications. It may be useful to suggest that the metaphors of martyrology are not inconsistent with those of warfare in the language of the period.

Long before Draper and White, "Darwin's bulldog," Thomas H. Huxley, had sounded the alarm of martyrology and warfare against the Catholic Church of the late nineteenth century. As James Moore has pointed out, as late as 1889 Huxley professed a fear of the revival of the Inquisition, this time with scientists, rather than heretics, as its victims:

> The wolf would play the same havoc now, if it could only get its blood-stained jaws free from the muzzle imposed by the secular arm.

In his attacks on any sort of intellectual constraint in matters of scientific investigation, Huxley took the extreme positivists as well, and like Bayle, who in 1691 had warned against a "Protestant Inquisition," Huxley now warned against a Positivist Inquisition:

> The logical, practical result of [Comtean Positivism] would be the establishment of something corresponding with the eminently Catholic, but admittedly anti-scientific institution—The Holy Office.

With the conceptual vocabulary in place that identified the Inquisition as the enemy of true religion and political liberty, and as the culmination of obscurantism and superstition, secular nationalist historians—as in Italy—as well as the new historians of comparative cultures and science found that vocabulary ready at hand when they assessed either the impact of religious culture on scientific, intellectual, and artistic development across Europe, or the history of scientific discovery and its impeded circulation. The work of Huxley, Draper, and White added the last chapters to the myths of the Inquisition, building on earlier myths and modernizing them to take contemporary concerns into account.

The Grand Inquisitor

The most powerful and influential literary depiction of an inquisitor (and, by extension, *The Inquisition*) in European literature occurs in Book V, Chapter 5 of Fyodor Dostoievsky's novel, *The Brothers Karamazov*, planned by Dostoievsky since 1868 and first published serially in the January, 1879 issue of the journal *Ruskij Vestnik, The Russian Messenger.* The novel's serialization was completed in November, 1880, and the work appeared separately in 1881. Set in Dostoievsky's contemporary Russia, one of its themes is the glorification of the author's particular vision of Russian Orthodox piety; another is the criticism of westernization. That this novel should select as one of its central episodes a highly literary and explicitly stated "fiction" set in sixteenth-century Spain, involving a monologue directed by the Grand Inquisitor at Jesus Christ, troubled critics in Dostoievsky's own day and has troubled readers ever since.

In the nineteenth century both Spain and Russia developed ambivalent attitudes toward their own pasts and toward the western European culture that they both admired and feared. Like Moratín and Goya, Spanish liberal critics bitterly resented a number of religious aspects of Spain's past and urged a closer affiliation with the culture of France and England. A similar attitude in Russia is found in the work of Turgenev, the critic Vissarion Belinskij, and among the members of the Petrashevsky circle, with which Dostoievsky was affiliated in Moscow in the 1840s. Conservative critics in Spain were reluctant to criticize Spain's religious past and were far more apprehensive of Spain's place in the modernization of the European world. The conservative Spanish tradition in the nineteenth century produced one literary masterpiece, Marcellino Menendez y Pelayo's *Historia de los heterodoxos españoles*, whose publication overlaps with that of *The Brothers Karamazov.* Conservative critics in Russia also vaunted the Russian religious tradition and grew increasingly apprehensive about westernization, as did Dostoievsky himself during his imprisonment and penal exile for political offenses between 1849 and 1859. *The Brothers Karamazov* is the literary masterpiece of this movement. At first glance, then, Spanish and Russian conservative cultural critics would appear to have had much in common, and historical contacts between the two cultures would appear to support such a thesis.

Both Spain and Russia had long been the settings of the conflict between Christianity and other religions, indeed the two main areas on the margins of western Europe where such coexistence and conflict was both prolonged and profound. In both countries the position of the Jews was crucial, and the case of the Muslims in Spain paralleled that of the Mongols in Russia between the thirteenth and the sixteenth centuries. Both countries had developed a xenophobic awareness of Christianity, partly as a result of the contrast of Christianity to other religions. In the late fifteenth century Russian prelates expressed admiration for the steps taken by Ferdinand of Aragón and his "cleansing" of Christian Spain. There is some evidence that Russia in the sixteenth and seventeenth centuries modelled its own methods of ecclesiastical discipline upon what it knew of the Spanish inquisitorial techniques, although ecclesiastical inquisitorial procedures were foreign to Orthodox Christianity in the Byzantine and older Russian traditions.

Russian interest in Spain continued through the eighteenth and nineteenth centuries, and this interest may have been one of the sources for Dostoievsky's selection of Spain as the setting for the episode of *The Grand Inquisitor.* But there were others as well, for Dostoievsky shows no sense of the parallel situations of Spain and Russia, and his treatment of the Spanish Inquisition is, of course, distinctly hostile, as hostile as Dostoievsky ever showed himself toward Spain, Catholicism, or to the West in general.

Dostoievsky's conversion to his unique vision of Russophilism drew both upon traditional Russian anti-western views and his own experiences in western Europe during his travels from 1862 to 1871. During these years, which began with the publication of *The House of the Dead* in 1862 and included the great decade of literary production that ranged from *Crime and Punishment* in 1866 to the writing of *The Brothers Karamazov,* Dostoievsky estranged himself from his former liberal associates and admirers and worked out his great vision of Russian religion and his indictment of western Europe.

Both aspects of Dostoievsky's thought during these years—his vision of Orthodoxy and his antiwesternism—must be considered if the episode of *The Grand Inquisitor* is to be fully understood. For Dostoievsky, Orthodoxy was the true Christianity, unique to the Russian people, preserved in prayers and hymns rather than in sermons and theological doctrines, and thus embodied in the hearts of the people, in their love and piety, and above all in their history of suffering. The suffering of the Russian folk provided the opportunity for their redemption, and their redemption has given them an apocalyptic role in providential history. Besides the simple devotion of the people, Dostoievsky increasingly regarded the Orthodox monasteries as repositories of the purest Orthodoxy. Monasteries provided the heroes of the future, and monasteries would guide the redemption of Russia.

Although a number of contemporaries and later critics and historians criticized Dostoievsky's portrait of idealized Russian religion, it is this portrait that anchors the episode of *The Grand Inquisitor*. Dostoievsky, after all, called *The Grand Inquisitor* episode one of the *two* "culminating points" of the novel. The other, Dostoievsky's counterpoint and refutation of the arguments of the Grand Inquisitor, occurs in Chapters 2 and 3 of Book VI, *The Russian Monk*, Dostoievsky's account of the life and teachings of Father Zosima, the teacher of Alyosha Karamazov and Dostoievsky's embodiment of the soul of Russian religion. The episode of *The Grand Inquisitor* is unthinkable without the counterweight episode of *The Russian Monk*.

Against his vision of Russian religious piety Dostoievsky set his indictment of Europe, its soulless materialism, and especially its godless religion. For Dostoievsky, the Roman Catholic Church was a continuation, not of the Christianity of the Gospels, but of the Latin domination of all life that had first taken form in the Roman Empire and later absorbed the Latin Church into it. Roman Christianity had become a state, no longer a Church. Although Dostoievsky argued that an entire culture in all of its forms of organization ought ultimately to be a spiritual community, hence a church, he decried the Latin Church's arrogation to itself of state power without roots in popular piety. If all states should ultimately become churches, the failure of the Latin Church was its having willingly become a materialistic state, preserving only the guise of a Church.

Not even Protestantism impressed Dostoievsky. Given the Lutheran reluctance to assume civil authority, Germanic "Protestantism" would remain forever incomplete, a failure like the Latin Church. But the least developed or least flawed by human error in history, and hence the form of Christianity with the greatest potential for the eventual realization of true Christianity, was the Christianity of the Slavs. It is precisely in this comparative view that Chapters 2 and 3 of Book VI of *The Brothers Karamazov* play their role. The story of *The Russian Monk* is presented by Dostoievsky in the language of the *zhitie*, that of the saint's life popular in Russian Orthodox literature, and the language of Father Zosima echoes the simplest, most intimate, and oldest popular expressions of Russian piety. Against his view of incomplete Protestant Christianity and of perverted Latin Christianity, Dostoievsky denounced those Russians who had been seduced by the perversions of the Latin Antichrist, the mystic Peter Chaadeev (1794–1856) and the Russian aristocrat turned Catholic and Jesuit in 1843, Ivan Gagarin. Such figures are echoed in *The Brothers Karamazov* in the figure of Pyotr Alexandrovich Miusov. Dostoievsky took particular pleasure in western campaigns against the Jesuits and the popes, and he praised Bismarck's *Kulturkampf* against Roman Catholicism.

It is against the twin themes of Russian redemptive Christianity and the politicization of Latin Christianity (and the irrelevance of Protestantism) that the episodes of *The Grand Inquisitor* and *The Russian Monk* must be understood. Dostoievsky places his indictment of Latin Christianity (and western Europe in general) in the form of a "poem" composed by the westernized, abstractly intellectual, soulless Ivan Karamazov as told by Ivan to Alyosha, the disciple of Father Zosima. The narration of the "poem" follows a discussion between Ivan and Alyosha on the subject of theodicy—the problem of divine justice, which Ivan refuses to accept, since no concept of divine justice for him is adequate to account for or justify the suffering of the innocent, particularly children.

Ivan begins with a preface, in which he explains that in sixteenth-century literature it was common for literary works to depict the powers of heaven returned to earth, not only in texts, but on stage in popular drama and pageant. Such would have been Ivan's poem if he had written it in the sixteenth century. But the sixteenth century also saw the challenge of Protestantism to such a faith, and the despair of the faithful had grown so great that people actually prayed for a Second Coming, and Jesus returned. He came back to earth in Seville, "in the most terrible time of the Inquisition, when fires were lighted everyday to the glory of God, and

> In the splendid *auto-de-fé*
> The Wicked heretics were burnt."

Jesus' return was only a visit, "to the hot pavement of the southern town in which on the day before almost a hundred heretics had, *ad majorem Dei gloriam* ["to the greater glory of God"—the motto of the Jesuits] been burned by the cardinal, the Grand Inquisitor, in a magnificent *auto-de-fé*, in the presence of the king, the court, the knights, the cardinals, the most charming ladies of the court, and the whole population of Seville."

Instantly recognized by the crowd, Jesus is arrested by the Grand Inquisitor, "an old man, almost ninety, tall and erect, with a withered face and sunken eyes, in which there is still a gleam of light, like a firey spark. He was not dressed in his gorgeous cardinal's robes, as he was the day before, when he was burning the enemies of the Roman Church; at that moment he was wearing his coarse, old, monk's cassock." The familiars lead Jesus to the prison of the Inquisition, where the Grand Inquisitor denounces him for his return, claiming that Jesus has no right to add anything further to the revelations he once made, and threatens to burn Jesus the next day. For if Jesus were to reveal anything further, he would take from men their faith and their freedom, by compelling them to believe. And the Grand Inquisitor is furious precisely at the terrible burden of freedom that Jesus has placed on humanity, having had far too high expectations of mankind. Because mankind cannot bear such freedom, the Grand Inquisitor and his colleagues have taken it upon themselves to relieve men of their freedom, and men have happily given it up to them. Citing the episode of the three temptations of Jesus as told in Matthew 4.1–3 and Luke 4.5–13, as indicating Jesus' heartless failure to recognize the weak nature of human beings, the Grand Inquisitor indicts Jesus' failure to recognize in the temptations the great question of "miracle, mystery, and authority" which is the only key to making human life endurable on earth. Jesus resisted the temptation to turn stones into bread, to cast himself down from the heights, and to become king of the earth, because he wished belief to be given freely. But humans have no wish for such freedom and no capacity to follow its dictates: Jesus has given mankind an impossible injunction, and the Inquisitor and his fellows have compensated for Jesus' inhuman legacy by assuming the burden of freedom themselves and deceiving the weak and freedom-hating human race into thinking that it was following Jesus' injunctions.

Alyosha interrupts Ivan's terrifying poem to protest: "That's not the idea of it in the Orthodox Church. . . . That's Rome, and not even the whole of Rome, it's false—those are the worst of Catholics, the Inquisitors, the Jesuits. . . ." But Ivan denies that he is engaging in the usual anti-Catholicism. His Grand Inquisitor is an ascetic, one who has spent many years in the desert fasting and praying, a monk, and a Jesuit. The Grand Inquisitor loves humanity and is willing to accept its burden of freedom in order to make life bearable for the weak mass of mankind. Ivan suggests that the Masons, like the Catholics who hate them so much, share this sense of mystery, "to guard it from the weak and the unhappy, so as to make them happy." Having finished his denunciation of Christ for having overestimated the human capacity for freedom, the Inquisitor awaits Christ's reply:

> The old man longed for Him to say something, however bitter and terrible. But He suddenly approached the old man in silence and softly kissed him on his bloodless aged lips. That was all His answer. The old man shuddered. His lips moved. He went to the door, opened it, and said to Him: 'Go, and come no more . . . come not at all, never, never.' And he let Him out into the dark squares of the town. The Prisoner went away.
> And the old man? [asks Alyosha.]
> The kiss glows in his heart, but the old man adheres to his idea.

Implicit in Ivan's poem is Dostoievsky's religious vision of western European history: the Roman Catholic Church had absorbed the Roman Empire and turned itself into a dominating force in Europe; just as Roman Catholicism had created Europe, Roman Catholic Europe created Socialism; Socialism is the source of atheism, and the entire course of European history proclaimed its coming collapse and revealed in materialistic atheism the full and inevitable flowering of the seeds planted by the Roman Empire in the Latin Church. Roman Catholicism, having failed to live up to Jesus' demands by rejecting suffering and freedom, created an illusion of freedom and insisted upon material sufficiency for all men. Mankind, lacking the knowledge and the will to resist, accepted the Latin formula, with Socialism and atheism being the inevitable result.

Dostoievsky had raised many of these issues in his earlier work. *The Possessed* also treated the three temptations; *The Idiot* took up the theme of Rome as Antichrist; Father Zosima himself speaks of the Latin Church as having become of its own will a state instead of a Church. Nor is Dostoievsky willing simply to leave Roman Catholicism as a cynical manipulation of human weakness and gullibility by "Machiavellian" Jesuits. Ivan insists that his Grand Inquisitor has acted from a more profound understanding of and sympathy with the human condition than Jesus himself. For the Grand Inquisitor has also been a monk and an ascetic; he is wearing his coarse monastic habit when he encounters Jesus, indicating that it is closest to his heart and that his cardinal's robes are for public display only. The Grand Inquisitor's monastic/ascetic credentials are ostensibly as good as those of Father Zosima. He has taken power but does not revel in it, and he has done so out of a love of humanity that has sought only to relieve its impossible burdens. Like Ivan, he too has seen the tortures of the innocent, and he speaks with a passion and fury never equalled in European literature. As Dostoievsky himself remarked of the episode, "In all Europe there have been no expressions of atheism, past or present, as powerful as mine." The author's contemporaries fully agreed, and many wondered about the relation among the Grand Inquisitor, Ivan Karamazov, and Fyodor Dostoievsky himself.

Dostoievsky also remarked that he had "carried the thought of the Grand Inquisitor in his soul during his entire life." And yet there is a recognizable background for his choice in the tradition of inquisitorial historiography and literary representation that suggests, if the general idea had long been in Dostoievsky's imagination, the specifics of the episode are traceable to several distinct sources. As scholarship has long suggested, Schiller was an influence on Dostoievsky, not only in terms of the inquisitorial role in *Don Karlos*, but in the manipulations of unstable temperament in *Der Geisterseher*. Dostoievsky's old patron Belinskij had also denounced *The Inquisition*, as did most nineteenth-century liberals.

At some points, however, Dostoievsky's Grand Inquisitor greatly departs from the Schillerian prototype. The *Grand Inquisitor* is sighted, possesses far less reserve than Schiller's, and strikes to the heart of his vision of Christ's failure, a scene that would have been extremely unlikely for Schiller to have written. Moreover, the Grand Inquisitor is not merely a bigoted manipulator of kings. Dostoievsky will not accept such an argument; his Grand Inquisitor does what he does furiously, and he is willing to justify himself even to the face of Jesus. For the most and greatest part, of course, the Grand Inquisitor is Dostoievsky's own invention. But there is another source besides Schiller that may cast a bit more light on the external features of Dostoievsky's creation.

Schiller and Belinskij were not Dostoievsky's only sources of information on the inquisitions and their history. There was not only Protestant polemical history and the works of the Enlightenment, but nineteenth-century histories available to Dostoievsky, and some of these treated the inquisitions in the light of nineteenth-century progressive ethical values, often not without considerable literary skill.

One of the most popular of these was the long study of Philip II of Spain by the American historian William Hickling Prescott. In the first volume of his history, Prescott portrayed the Inquisition in its attacks on Protestants as luridly and dramatically as any writer from Montanus on. In 1858 Prescott's *Philip II* was translated into Russian as *Istoria tsarstrovaniia Filippa utorogo, korolia ispanskoga*. Dostoievsky acquired a copy of it, for one has been ascertained to have been in his library. In Prescott's treatment, the historical inquisitor Fernando Valdes occupies the center of much of Prescott's description of the Inquisition, and Prescott's technique of following a prisoner of the Inquisition from arrest through the *auto-de-fé*—originally designed by Montanus in 1567—offered a grim and influential portrait of the techniques of the Inquisition. Far severer than the portrait of the Inquisition in Prescott's earlier *Ferdinand and Isabella*, the portrait of the Inquisition in *Philip II*, centering on Valdes and the machinery of the Inquisition—and its impact on victims and readers alike—offered Dostoievsky, and Ivan, whom Dostoievsky tacitly implies had also read the Russian translation of Prescott, the ideal character and form of the "prose-poem" with which Ivan chooses to perplex and outrage the sensitive and pious Alyosha.

But we must not press Dostoievsky's interest in and knowledge of the historical inquisitions too far. Our point is the success of his artistic use of historical and quasi-historical traditions to create a character and scene, and to raise a devastating critique of the western version of the Christian message that would be offset by his own Russian counterpoint—the piety and religious sentiment of Father Zosima that must survive in Alyosha in spite of Ivan's formidable challenges. Dostoievsky uses the myth of *The Inquisition* and one superb literary creation—the figure of the old Inquisitor himself—and a few spare details about the darkness of the Inquisition's prisons and the terrible threats about its powers that the Inquisitor utters to Jesus. There is little else about the Inquisition that concerns or interests Dostoievsky. Its very name invokes the myth that enveloped it; the figure of Jesus facing the Inquisitor rivets the attention, and the Inquisitor's long diatribe is the focus of the Chapter. What there is of the Inquisition, and the gist of the Inquisitor's speech, is a message from the West, and it was a message that Dostoievsky enhanced as fully and as dangerously as he could in order to refute it at its strongest and most sympathetic manifestations—its relentless insistence on the wretchedness of human suffering, and upon the weakness of mankind. For this, the Grand Inquisitor suited Dostoievsky far better than his conventional targets in other works and in his correspondence and diaries—Pope Pius IX, the Jesuits, or even the Russian converts to Catholicism and westernism.

In his creation of the Grand Inquisitor Dostoievsky indeed drew upon recent traditions and historical materials, but he far transcended Schiller and Prescott, for his purpose was far greater and more ambitious than theirs. In achieving it he created the most memorable of all literary inquisitors, whom he left to other later writers who would treat it in very different ways from his own. And he created his Grand Inquisitor at a time when the older myths of *The Inquisition* were giving way to history. His own great passion and talent, however, did as much to preserve the myth in the face of history as had that of any other nineteenth-century figure.

Chapter Nine

From Myth to History

Myth stubbornly haunts the assertions of history, and history continually challenges the veracity of myth. From the sixteenth century to the present the western tradition has consisted of the joint existence of both, with myth continuing to shape conceptualization and belief and an autonomous discipline of history asserting standards according to which myth should lose its legitimacy. Except for a number of slowly widening circles of thinkers, however, no inverse Gresham's Law operates in this process: good history does not always immediately and permanently drive out bad myth. The emergence of history itself has a history, and the emergence of the history of inquisitions out of myth and polemic is a complex and illustrative story.

Sometimes myth asserts itself to be history, as it did in the debates about Church history in the sixteenth and seventeenth centuries. So does some fiction. Grace Aguilar, for example, asserted that her novel *The Vale of Cedars* was based on actual history, and she cited two sources: the *Travels in Spain* by de Langle and John Stockdale's *History of the Inquisitions*. De Langle's work, published in 1796 but actually written in 1784 by Jean-Marie Jérôme Fleuriot and burned by order of the Parlement of Paris at the request of Charles III of Spain in 1788, is an extremely tendentious, wrong-headed, and largely fictitious work; Stockdale's *History* of 1810, an elaborate and lavishly illustrated account, was originally intended explicitly to prevent the acquisition of political rights by Catholics in Britain. Through the wide popularity of Aguilar's novel, Fleuriot's fictions and Stockdale's fancies became *the* "history" of *The Inquisition* for many English readers during the second half of the nineteenth century. As long as historical method was sufficiently uncertain and undeveloped, history survived as a component of myth. But as historical research became more complex, acquired access to new sources, and developed standards of source-criticism, it began to free itself from the larger and increasingly different scope of myth. In the case of *The Inquisition* this process was distinctive and difficult, for it involved not only the revaluation of a part of myth that continued to evoke powerful emotions through the nineteenth century, but the revaluation of religious history itself, a process that touched many minds and emotions powerfully and distinctively during that period.

The emergence of inquisition history out of the mythology of *The Inquisition* took no predictable, clear path. Its own history consists of unlikely events and improbable assertions.

The Inquisitors and Other Catholics Write History

Tyndale and Foxe put their fingers on a profound Reformation truth when they asserted that Church history must not be left to those who opposed them on religious grounds. It did not take long into the sixteenth century for both Protestants and Catholics to realize that salvation history was an essential component of theological debate. As early as 1522 Gregorio Cortesi had urged Pope Adrian VI to oppose Luther by the use of Church history to identify and discredit heretics and to preserve the faith. By the mid-sixteenth century in Rome itself a lively historical interest developed among learned and non-learned people, encouraged by St. Philip Neri, who led pilgrimages to the ancient churches of the city and urged scholars and antiquarians to provide historical and archaeological information on a broad series of topics connected with the early Church of Rome, which would emphasize the antiquity and holiness of Rome itself. Such enterprises as these played a substantial role in strengthening the Latin conviction that history was a powerful weapon in the theological controversies of the century. Printed editions of early documents of ecclesiastical history, the writings of the Church Fathers (often edited by Dominicans), and the growing ecclesiastical use of print for many purposes by the mid-century all pointed toward a new Church history, one to be written with the problems of the sixteenth century firmly in mind, but also one to be written from the best texts of the best sources.

In 1558 Neri asked Caesar Baronius, a young and talented scholar, to provide a series of lectures on Church history for the Roman Oratory, a religious foundation visited by devout laypeople with an interest in ecclesiastical scholarship and antiquarianism. Baronius' lectures were popular, and when the question of a quasi-official Catholic Church history came up, Baronius was urged to take up the task. Initially, there was no thought of shaping Baronius' history to refute the Protestant *Magdeburg Centuries* (1559–1574), since Baronius did not even possess a copy until 1577. But in 1571 Pope Pius V appointed a commission to study the *Centuries*, and although Baronius had started work on his own history in 1564, by the time his first volume of the *Annales Ecclesiastici* appeared in 1579, the Roman Church adopted his work as a kind of answer to the great Protestant history. By the time of his death in 1607, Baronius had published twelve volumes of the *Annales*, reaching the year 1100, and had begun work on the thirteenth.

The theme of the *Annales*, which was continued by several successors after Baronius' death, was that the Roman Church had never deviated from Christ's charge, and that the early Church history of Eusebius had set the standard for all later Church history. Over the centuries, twenty-one complete editions of the *Annales Ecclesiastici* were printed, and this work became the standard by which all subsequent Roman Church histories were measured. Thus, Inquisition-Histories constituted a subsection of a larger Catholic conception of Church history.

The broad framework of Church history erected by Baronius and continued down to 1572 by his Oratorian successors Odovicus Raynaldi and Jacobus Laderchii gave full range to the Church's treatment of heresy and heretics as well. Besides printing, often for the first time, thousands of documentary sources, these *Ecclesiastical Annals* constituted a meticulous year-by-year account of the continuity of Church history. When Raynaldi reached the Reformation of the sixteenth century, he was more than able to consider it in terms of the long history of heresy and the early inquisitors that had been established by Baronius in his early volumes.

In addition to the continuation of Baronius by Raynaldi and Laderchii, however, there also appeared simultaneously another continuation, by the Polish Dominican Abraham Bzovius. The work reached the year 1535 (a posthumous continuation of Bzovius reached 1572). Bzovius was far more interested in heresy than were Raynaldi and Laderchii, and his history, which circulated widely, constituted a rigorous investigation of the nature of heresy and the origins of the Inquisition.

These works were, of course, confessional. Their authors did not for a moment doubt either the truth or the accuracy of their sources, and they wrote from a conviction that was as powerful as it was necessary. Their authors' access to original documents, the cooperation of other

scholars in Rome and elsewhere, and their turning of massive histories
into a tool of confessional debate, mark the great outpouring of documentary sources for the historiography of the seventeenth and eighteenth
centuries. Any response to their arguments required the publication of
folio volumes as large and as detailed as theirs. The seventeenth century
was the century of very large books of history which contained as much
documentation as narrative or polemic, and they changed the way by
which history was used by everyone.

The first historical work devoted exclusively to the inquisitions, however, was that of Luis de Pàramo, Canon of Leon and Inquisitor of
Sicily from 1584 to 1605. Paramo published his *On the Origin and
Development of the Office of the Holy Inquisition, and on its Dignity
and Fruitfullness* in two books (with a third on *The Power of the Roman
Pontiff*) in Madrid in 1598. The work was prefaced with the permission
of Philip II and contained an *Approbatio* by the theologian Pedro Lopez
de Montoya asserting that the work contained "nothing adverse to the
Catholic faith or to good morals." Pàramo's is a triumphant history,
and to later centuries and readers with different points of view it seemed
bizarre. Cited by most later historians of the inquisitions, whether pro
or con, parts of Pàramo's work dealing with the Portuguese Inquisition
were summarized—and other parts translated—by the Abbé Morellet
in the same volume as his Eymeric translations in 1762, thus revealing
Pàramo to the world of the Enlightenment, and inspiring Voltaire to
the scathing satire of his article "Inquisition" in the *Dictionnaire philosophique*.

Unlike the work of Baronius, Raynaldi, and Bzovius, Pàramo's history
did not discuss the Inquisition in terms of a larger Church history.
Pàramo rather wrote Church history, from the Creation to his own
age, in terms of the Inquisition. The first title of his Book I, for example,
considers the sin of Adam, and the second title considers the inquisitorial
procedure by which God proceeded against Adam and how it constituted
the prototype of the procedure of the Holy Office: "God therefore quickly
became the first and greatest teacher of the Inquisitors of heretical depravity, himself providing them with [the example] of a just and legal punishment."

Pàramo's history goes on to consider heresy and idolatry in the Old
Testament according to the theological scheme of the six ages of the
world. Book I ends with the establishment of the sixth and final age
with the coming of Christ, "the first Inquisitor under the Evangelical
Law," and of John the Baptist, who also exercised inquisitorial functions.
Peter, Paul, and the other apostles were also inquisitors, and the Christian

bishops, successors to the apostles, inherited their inquisitorial powers and responsibilities.

The three titles of Book II, the most important section of the work, treat the development of a special office of inquisitor, the spread of the Inquisition throughout the world, and an analysis of the Inquisition's operations under the title "On the dignity, usefulness, and fruits of the Holy Inquisition." One of Pàramo's key assertions is that the bishops, through negligence or the press of other obligations, failed to prevent the growth of heresy—that is, they failed to fulfill their "inquisitorial" function. "The highest pontiffs, therefore, upon mature deliberation, chose several learned and Catholic men to exercise the holy office to the extent that papal authority permitted them to." To Pàramo, then, the papal power to delegate office created in the thirteenth-century inquisitors an order virtually parallel to that of bishops. Saint Dominic was the first Inquisitor-General. Pàramo then traces the offices of officials of the Inquisition, recounts the particular indulgences given to inquisitors, and comments on the large number of Dominicans who were chosen to be inquisitors, including, of course, Nicolau Eymeric.

The second title of Book II sweeps quickly into the sixteenth century and traces the history of the Roman Inquisition from the thirteenth century to his own day. Pàramo then spends considerable time on the Inquisition of Spain, which he knows in considerable detail, concluding with a survey of the establishment of inquisitions throughout the world. Pàramo prints a number of important documents from the history of his own inquisition of Sicily, particularly important because, as Pàramo says, an explosion in the castle of the Inquisition in Palermo in 1593 destroyed much of the archive of the Inquisition, and Pàramo himself seems barely to have escaped with his life.

In his discussion of the history of the Portuguese Inquisition, Pàramo comments on the well-known story of the impostor Saavedra, who appeared in Lisbon in 1539 armed with papal bulls comissioning him as the Inquisitor-General of Portugal. Saavedra, an accomplished forger of official documents, had even devised exact copies of official seals and convinced King João III of the authenticity of his charge. Having borrowed huge sums in Spain on the strength of his imposture, Saavedra also collected a fortune in confiscations in Portugal. Discovered by one of his Spanish creditors, Saavedra was tried and sentenced to a term in the galleys, but Pope Paul IV eventually approved the activities of the Portuguese Inquisition under Saavedra's control.

Although the inquisitions were not particularly interested in making themselves public, Pàramo's history may well be considered the inquisitors' own view of their place in Christian history. Never since has the story of the inquisitions been told in such a triumphant and institution-centered manner.

Pàramo's was not the only work, however, that included extensive documentation. The histories of Baronius, Raynaldi, and Bzovius, Peña's editions of Eymeric's *Directorium*, Eliseo Masini's *Sacro Arsenale* of 1625, and other works that circulated widely made considerable documentation available to both Catholic and Protestant historians and polemicists. Printed editions of inquisitors' handbooks of procedure, such as those of Alphonso de Castro of 1534 and Bernard of Como of 1556, as well as local collections of documents such as those of Venice, used by Paolo Sarpi in his own critical history of the Venetian Inquisition in 1638, opened up the source material for discussions of the inquisitions from medieval to early modern times. Materials in Catholic territories that had become Protestant also became available to scholars, as did medieval manuscript materials that appeared in print in greater and greater numbers during the seventeenth century.

Another feature of Pàramo's and Raynaldi's historiography should also be noted. A common feature of the polemic on both sides of the Reformation divide was the argument that each church—both the Latin Christian and the "true, hidden" church of Martin Luther and others—was the only direct successor of the evangelical church of the early Christians, the single church founded by Jesus Christ. From the Catholic point of view, this position led to the unavoidable conclusion that sixteenth-century reformers and seventeenth-century Protestants were simply the latest in a long line of "heretics of old." From the Protestant point of view, the continuity of the "hidden" church led to the unavoidable conclusion that the Latin Church was simply the latest in a long line of persecutors of true religion. In each church, a line of martyrs to the truth paralleled the long line of heretics and persecutors. The views expressed by a number of critics of the inquisitions that the origins of the inquisitions lay in the fourth century and that the history of the inquisitions was really a history of *The Inquisition* from the fourth century on was virtually identical with that of Pàramo, who placed the origin of the inquisitions even further back in time, into the Garden of Eden itself. Thus, the commonplace idea in much Protestant polemic and history that the inquisitions were one and reached far back in time was not exclusively a Protestant invention. From an entirely different point of view, Pàramo would have accepted it completely, and the meticulous annalistic works of Baronius and Raynaldi would have confirmed Pàramo, even though they otherwise represented a very different kind of church history.

In the work of Pàramo, church history becomes inquisition history, and salvation history becomes the history of the battle between truth and error. The inquisitorial function becomes the essence of the Roman Church. From a Protestant point of view, Pàramo's argument is far from unacceptable, although it was interpreted far differently from its author's intentions. *The Inquisition* was indeed the essence of the Roman church, but tyrannous, hostile to the truth, and Satanic. It had begun by the intrusion of the "World" into religious affairs, surely no later than fourth century. It was indeed coeval with Roman Catholicism. Pàramo and the Protestant historians and polemicists agreed; it was merely that their interpretation of the agreed-upon facts were polar opposites.

Pàramo's was a spectacular case, not of the Church driving the Inquisition, but of the Inquisition identifying and driving the Church. Pàramo's Sicilian Inquisition, however, was part of the larger organization of the Spanish Inquisition, and not all Catholics agreed with him, either about Church history or about the place of the inquisitors in it. Many French and Bavarian Catholics, for example, would have accorded the Inquisition no such role, either in Church history or in French or Bavarian society. A very different Catholic account may be seen in the work of Paolo Sarpi of Venice, one of the most able historians of the seventeenth century, and one with a very distinctive view of inquisitions and the place of the Venetian Inquisition in their history.

During the seventeenth century Venice was the one Catholic power generally admired in Protestant Europe. Its republican form of government, its control of ecclesiastical authority, and its often acerbic relations with Rome singled it out to many northern Europeans as a progressive society, and in the usual denunciations of inquisitions, the Venetian Inquisition was often made the exception. Part of the "myth of Venice" was the result of the historical and apologetic work of Paolo Sarpi, Venice's literary spokesman to the rest of the world, and Sarpi had some very distinctive notions about the Venetian Inquisition and its place in history, notions very different from those of Pàramo.

Sarpi (1552–1623), a Servite friar and theological consultant to the Republic of Venice after 1606, was a dispassionate examiner of the issues dividing Catholics and Protestants, a scientific investigator, and, most important for our purposes, a remarkable historian of ecclesiastical institutions. In 1606 a dispute between the Venetians and Pope Paul V led to the placing of a papal interdict on Venetian territory. As theological consultant and canon lawyer to the Republic, Sarpi undertook the responsibility of responding to papal charges, and one of the ways by which he did this was to write a number of historical studies of some of the claims of the counter-reformation clergy and the papacy. His first work was a long memorandum, intended for private circulation, on the events in Venice in 1605–1607. His second work was the great *History of Benefices* of 1609, for which he drew on the incomparable secret Venetian archives and argued for the time-bound and contingent character of ecclesiastical doctrines on the subject. In his massive *History of the Council of Trent*, published in Italian in London in 1619, Sarpi used extensive documentary evidence, allowed for purely temporal causality in ecclesiastical history, and wrote Church history in a vein similar to those in which historians of purely temporal institutions worked. Sarpi's treatise *On the Office of the Inquisition* of 1615 emphasized the requirements of due process in its procedures and the right of the Venetian Senate to control its operations rigorously. Sarpi's own attitude towards religious persecution was extremely harsh. He categorically criticized the attacks on harmless dissenters and pointed out with relish that religious persecution had not worked in the Netherlands and had provoked serious resentment in England and France. But Sarpi was also evenhanded: he condemned Calvin's burning of Michael Servetus, and at the same time questioned the motives of inquisitors and other persecutors, denouncing the Index itself for having been a later invention with no apostolic authority for its foundation.

The popularity of Sarpi's criticisms of the Council of Trent and such institutions as the Inquisition was considerable. The London first printing of the *History* suggests the breadth of Sarpi's appeal and its similarity to other early seventeenth-century currents of thought. Sarpi was also popular in non-Catholic Europe for his criticism of Spain and Spanish power, as well as for his attacks on ecclesiastical institutions. Here in the early seventeenth century was a Catholic attack on several important aspects of Roman Catholic institutions, one made in the name of historical truth, but for the purpose of serving a Republican state and asserting its autonomy even in matters generally considered spiritual elsewhere in Europe.

Sarpi's *Historia della Sacra Inquisizióne*, first published in 1638, begins emphatically with the assertion that "Heresy, by divine permission, was sown throughout the world at the same time as was founded the Holy Church, that is, after the ascension of Our Lord into Heaven. . . . nevertheless, the particular Office of the Inquisition against the heretics did not begin until after the year 1200." Observing the apostolic strictures that were limited to reprimand and expulsion, Sarpi notes that the Christian Roman emperors asserted their right to make heresy a secular offense. There are three parts to every criminal judgment, Sarpi pointed out: the definition of the legal offense, the determination of fact, and the sentence. In the case of heresy, the first of these is to be determined by ecclesiastics, but the second and third are purely secular; therefore, bishops may be called in by the secular authority to determine whether heresy is involved, but the secular authorities then assume their normal responsibility for the remainder of the process.

With the failure of secular authority and the growth of heresy after the year 1000, the popes established the Franciscans and Dominicans as Inquisitors; but, Sarpi emphasizes, "they had no tribunal, but at all times exercised the authority to banish or otherwise punish those heretics whom they found." The laws of Frederick II were the first to impose the death penalty for heresy, and these laws were used by Popes after Innocent IV to erect the inquisitors' function into a distinctive tribunal. This attempt, however, led to great confusion, by separating the right of ecclesiastical discipline from the office of bishop and by diminishing the authority of the secular magistrates. Although the sixteenth-century Inquisitions continued to do this, notably in Spain, the Venetians created a more proper form of Inquisition, leaving appropriate authority in the hands of secular magistrates and giving ecclesiastics a consultative authority only.

Sarpi's history, with its focus on Venice, offered a very different Catholic picture from that of Pàramo, one far more acceptable, not only to Venetians, but to Europeans generally, who tended to regard the Venetian Inquisition as a court of morals rather than as a tool of militant Catholicism. The reputation of the Spanish, Portuguese, and Roman Inquisitions elsewhere in Europe also generated different Catholic versions of inquisition history. As we have seen, such Gallican defenders of French royal policy later in the seventeenth and eighteenth century as Marsollier, Dupin, and Goujet, freely wrote inquisition history that criticized the Spanish and Portuguese Inquisitions while praising the "moderation" of the religious persecutions of Louis XIV and Louis XV, much to the displeasure of Pierre Bayle.

Pàramo's history, then, represented less a "Catholic" point of view than it did a single Catholic point of view that existed at one extreme end of a relatively wide spectrum of Catholic historical opinion through the late eighteenth century. If Pàramo may be said to have created a Catholic "White Legend" of *The Inquisition* intended to offset the Protestant and anti-Spanish "Black Legends," then certainly not all Catholic historians of the inquisitions participated in the White Legend. In the eighteenth and nineteenth centuries, other Catholic historians tended to align themselves with the methods of historians of other confessions, or of no confessions at all, although the Pàramo strand remained obvious in the most conservative and ideological of Catholic historians through the nineteenth and into the twentieth century. In Catholicism itself, myth survived along with the beginnings of history.

Like Sarpi's, a number of later Catholic Church histories were produced with a view toward establishing Catholic rights in countries where such rights were withheld. The late eighteenth-century English Catholic historian Joseph Berington argued for a rational Catholicism in which the most extreme papal claims were regarded as non-essential for religious belief. By denying claims that the most extreme forms of papal authority were integral parts of Catholic belief, Berington argued that Catholicism, no less than other confessions, could obtain a legitimate place in modern civil societies. Twelfth- and thirteenth-century heresies were products of times and places, not of an enduring body of Catholic orthodoxy, and inquisitions too were historical constructs, having none but a historical basis and not germane to current problems at the turn of the nineteenth century.

From fifteenth-century Spain, Venice, and the sixteenth-century Netherlands there had always been Catholics who either opposed the inquisitions outright or wished their competence and activities to be drastically curtailed. From the sixteenth and seventeenth centuries there were also Protestants who opposed religious coercion and persecution on the part of Protestant societies, and there were both Catholics and Protestants from the seventeenth century on who urged civil governments to adapt even wider policies of civil toleration, policies that might include atheists and Jews as well as Catholics and Protestants. The Jansenist Gallicans in seventeenth- and eighteenth-century France supported the restrictions placed upon Protestants by Louis XIV and Louis XV while criticizing the inquisitions of Rome and Spain. By the time of the great revolutions of the late eighteenth century, the list of Catholic opponents of the inquisitions had grown longer, and revolutionary circumstances in Spain, Portugal, and Italy between 1808 and 1848 lengthened it even further. By the late nineteenth century such Catholic writers as Ignaz von Döllinger and his protégé Lord Acton could denounce the history of religious persecution as vigorously and categorically as any Protestant or philosophically liberal writer, and they felt no need to spare Rome.

Acton was an unsettling combination of a great and critical historian and rigorous moral judge. Throughout much of his adult life he barely escaped censure from Rome and Westminster and on several occasions thought himself about to be excommunicated. Although he publicly accepted the principle of ecclesiastical authority, he also bitterly condemned those occasions in the past and present when he believed that authority was used illegitimately. In 1897 he wrote to Mandell Creighton criticizing the Protestant Creighton's lenient treatment of the late fifteenth and early sixteenth-century papacy in his *History of the Popes,* particularly singling out papal moral responsibility for the inquisitions. Historical truth, Acton argued, was not so relativist as to be obliged to spare those who exercised otherwise legitimate authority in demonstrably unjust ways:

> We all agree that Calvin was one of the greatest writers, many think him the best religious teacher, in the world. But that one affair of Servetus outweighs the nine folios, and settles, by itself, the reputation he deserves. So with the medieval Inquisition and the Popes that founded it and worked it. That is the breaking point, the article of their system by which they stand or fall.

Acton was as harsh about the early modern inquisitions as he was about the medieval, and he argued that great leaders are not exempt from moral judgment; indeed, they are more subject to it than are others. He then went on to make a subsequently famous observation, one that is often taken out of context;

> If there is any presumption, it is the other way about holders of power, increasing as the power increases. Historical responsibility has to make up for the want of legal responsibility. Power tends to corrupt and absolute power corrupts absolutely. Great men are almost always bad men, even when they exercise influence and not authority. . . .

Acton's denunciation of the moral responsibility of the papacy in the historical instances of the inquisitions is far more explicit and harsh than some of his earlier cautious concessions to the legitimacy of ecclesiastical authority, but the principles are the same: legitimate authority in spiritual matters may exercise a certain discipline, but not one that transgresses a fundamental moral code. The problem of the limits of legitimate authority became, in the papacy and elsewhere, one of the central problems of the twentieth century.

Side by side with Acton's commitment to historical accuracy was his reservation of the historian's right and even obligation to judge morally. In the case of the inquisitions, Acton's moral judgment overcame his historian's caution and set the tone that was later echoed in the wake of the Second Vatican Council, when much of the history of the Roman Catholic Church came under heavy internal criticism and was subjected to substantial reform.

From Acton's day to our own, however, most Catholic and non-Catholic historians have tended to use identical historical methodology and to have ceased to approach the history of inquisitions from the perspective of Black or White legends. Although there have been several exceptions to this generalization on both sides of the confessional line, the historical achievements of the late nineteenth and twentieth centuries have made a return to the myths, among professional historians of any creed at least, virtually impossible.

The Protestant Histories

The great sixteenth-century interest in Church history was a direct result of the conflicts caused by the Reformation, and Reformation differences long dominated both Protestant and Catholic salvation histories. The authority of the popes, the sacramental powers of the clergy, the role of religion in civil society, and the nature of heresy all constitute the key points around which Church history was written during the seventeenth and eighteenth centuries, and the history of inquisitions is part of this larger history.

One of the central disputes of the sixteenth-century competing views of history was the problem of the relation of the sixteenth-century reformers to earlier reformers—in the Protestant view—or to earlier heretics—the Catholic view. Both Protestants and Catholics, of course, asserted their origin in the apostolic community of the first few centuries of the common era. Catholic historians, formidably and in enormous detail in the case of Baronius and his successors, then asserted the continuity of the Catholic Church with the apostolic community and identified the heretics of the early church and of the Middle Ages with the "heretics" of the sixteenth and seventeenth centuries. At the end of the seventeenth century, one of the most influential Catholic historians, Jacques-Bénigne Bossuet (1627–1704), in his *History of the Variations of the Protestant Churches* of 1688 strengthened the traditional Catholic viewpoint by identifying the proliferation of sects as an essential characteristic of heresy and by characterizing the Reformation as the most recent cause of sectarian division. From Bossuet to the nineteenth century, this view underlay the Catholic view of Church history and legitimized earlier forms of inquisitorial persecution. Although Bossuet himself was an avid proponent of ecclesiastical reunion and no particular admirer of contemporary inquisitions, his historical views remained internally influential within Catholicism.

Opposing the Catholic view of Church history was the Protestant view of the identification of the apostolic community with those true Christians who had not been won over to worldliness and superstition by the conversion of the Roman Empire to Christianity, but survived as a hidden Church until their revelation in the sixteenth century. Although the Protestant "adoption" of medieval heretics was not uniform or universal, it was greatly strengthened by the martyrologies and by the Protestant response to the Catholic attack. Official Protestant churches themselves were noticeably anxious over the growth of sectarianism, however, and, like the early use of inquisition history in the toleration debates, the full acceptance of medieval heretics in the Protestant pantheon was more the work of sectarian historians than those of established Protestant churches. The most influential of these works was Gottfried Arnold's *Nonpartisan History of Churches and Heresies* of 1699, a work that troubled both Protestant and Catholic authorities, because it celebrated all forms of dissent as signs of the manifestation of true, personal, living religion opposed to dogmatic theology and state-bound churches.

Debates about the place of medieval heretics—and the steps used to discipline them—continued in a lively way into the twentieth century, and only in this century has the problem begun to be seen in a historical light, stripped of the emotional and dogmatic commitments of four centuries of polemical debate.

As long as two such conflicting views of Church history contended, not only in scholarship but in popular and learned culture as well, it was virtually impossible to obtain a more reliable and less partisan Protestant Church history than a Catholic. What changed in Church histories concerning the inquisitions during the seventeenth century was not the governing framework itself, but the increasing amount of documentation made available to historians, the increasingly sophisticated methods of source-criticism used by historians of all confessions, and the new perspectives opened up and pioneered by scholars who were as apprehensive of established Protestant authority in religious matters as they were of Catholic authorities. One of these, in many ways the most remarkable and original of all early histories of the Inquisitions, as we have already seen, was Philip van Limborch's *History of the Inquisition* of 1697. Limborch, a dissenting Dutch Calvinist, employed scrupulous methodology, immense learning, and a powerful ethical opposition to all forms of religious persecution, but his editorializing about the evils of persecution did not prevent him from the accurate use of source materials, the publication of carefully edited texts, and his refusal to permit his history to be merely a "Protestant" attack on "Catholicism." In the work of Limborch, as in that of others, the sectarian historians were the first to point the way to an Inquisition history out of Inquisition polemic and ideology.

Although Limborch's *History* was widely used during the eighteenth century, its lessons were rarely taken to heart by either Protestants or Catholics. To be fully effective, sectarian historical values—and skills— needed the influence of rationalist critics and a transformation of both Catholic and Protestant historical ideologies, and these did not become fully available until the nineteenth century. Until then, although strengthened by new documentation and improved by the wider use of historical methodology, Protestant histories of the Inquisitions differed chiefly in perspective from those written by Catholics.

Perhaps the best-known, most frequently translated, and most widely read Protestant history in this vein is the *Ecclesiastical Institutes* (1726), by Johann Lorenz Mosheim (1694–1755). Mosheim's treatment of the inquisitions is virtually a Protestant reversal of Pàramo. For Mosheim, the deviance of the early Latin Church was caused by the intrusion of pagan philosophy and worldly authority into the structure of the Church, leading inevitably to a lowering of Christian standards, the proliferation of unnecessary ceremonies, superstition, and clerical ambition. The culmination of this process was the establishment of a papal monarchy by Gregory VII in the eleventh century, when true Christian doctrine was utterly corrupted and ambitious clerical authority persecuted those who charged the clergy with corruption. Such an atmosphere produced Dominic, "a man of fiery and impetuous temper," who set out to defend papal authority against its honest critics:

> This enterprise he executed with the greatest vigor, and we may add fury, attacking the Albigenses and the other enemies of the church with the power of eloquence, the force of arms, the subtlety of controversial writings, and the terrors of the *inquisition*, which owed its form to this violent and sanguinary priest.

Mosheim's portrait of the Latin Church is bleak and vicious. Dominic's *inquisition* created "that strange system of inquisitorial law, which, in many respects, is contrary to the common feelings of humanity and the plainest dictates of equity and justice."

The popes then turned their inquisitors against the Lutherans, scourging all Europe, driving some into exile and others into a purely hypocritical acceptance of Rome. Stout European resistance prevented the voracious Inquisition from gaining a sure foothold anywhere except in Spain, Portugal, and Rome. In emphasizing the political successes of the Reformation in freeing much of Europe from popish ambition, however, Mosheim tended to identify the Reformation itself with a political triumph, to narrow his depiction of its religious achievements, and to emphasize heavily the instruments by which Rome resisted this process, chiefly the inquisitions. Thus, Mosheim's is a very different history from that of Limborch, and his influence touched even later sectarian historians who otherwise might have been more influenced by the line of thought opened by the proponents of religious toleration.

Such a historian was the English Evangelical Joseph Milner (1744–1799). An able historian with considerable interest in the religious history of the devotional lives of ordinary people, aware of the attacks on conventional history by sceptical historians and Enlightenment thinkers, Milner nevertheless undertook to establish the old and increasingly outmoded thesis of identifying the medieval Waldenses with the apostolic community and with his own Calvinism, thereby entailing a stout attack on papal authority and papal means of repression of dissent. A close and avid reader of Foxe's *Book of Martyrs,* Milner is usually best known for his *The History of the Church of Christ,* of 1794–1797, but he was also the author of a history of persecution similar to that of Samuel Chandler, which began with the persecutions of pagan emperors and concluded with *The Inquisition.* Milner's little work on persecutions was frequently reprinted into the nineteenth century, and, with the history of Mosheim, represented both established and sectarian preservation of the myth of *The Inquisition* in popular histories. In some respects, before the mid-nineteenth century, Protestant histories had too heavy an investment in *The Inquisition* to give up the myth that easily.

Nor was the confessional character of Catholic or Protestant histories of inquisitions much altered by the transformation of historical theory and methodology that affected other kinds of history in the eighteenth century. Such enlightened historians as Edward Gibbon and David Hume, for example, represented too strongly the Enlightenment reaction to "superstition" and religious coercion to have been sufficiently interested or able to offer a history different from those of Catholic or Protestant writers. Not for nearly a century did historical standards enable a number of writers to damp confessional or philosophical passions enough to begin the process of writing a nonpartisan history of the inquisitions.

The characteristic features of encyclopedias did not change considerably over the eighteenth century. The characteristics of seventeenth-century encyclopedias and their eighteenth-century reissues—confessional partisanship, editorial neutralization when the subsequent editor was of a different faith from the original writer, and polemical judgments based upon the literature of myth—characterized most eighteenth-century encyclopedias. The article "Inquisition" in Ephraim Chambers' *Cyclopedia: or, an universal dictionary of arts and sciences* of 1727 turned much of the literature of myth into widely circulating reference works. Catholic encyclopedias, for example Gianfrancesco Pivati's *Nuovo dizionario scientifico e curióso, sacro-profano* (1750–1761) contained a short article entitled "Inquizione," but ecclesiastical censorship prevented the article from expressing anything concerning inquisitions in any detail, and Pivati restricted himself to commenting briefly only on the harshness of the inquisition in the New World.

Rather than transforming the historical treatment of inquisitions, critical history driven by Enlightenment principles and encyclopedias and other reference works usually did no better than polemic and myth. With the exception of Limborch's work, a history of the inquisitions had not emerged in any significant sense before 1800.

The Archives Begin to Speak: Juan Antonio Llorente

Virtually all of the histories of inquisitions written before the first quarter of the nineteenth century were based upon printed material produced by the inquisitions themselves (e.g., Pàramo, Masini's *Sacro Arsenale*, or Eymeric-Peña), personal narratives, martyrologies, other histories, and occasional inquisitorial documents (e.g., Limborch's use of the *Book of Sentences . . . of Toulouse*). Inquisition archives themselves were sealed, even to Catholic historians. Although they may have been periodically destroyed by accident, they were not dispersed or made available to non-inquisitors until after the age of revolution in the late eighteenth and early nineteenth centuries. When they were, they opened a new chapter in the writing of inquisition history.

In 1808 and 1809 two events dramatically signalled a change in the history of the archives. In 1809 the French General Miolis, then in command of Rome, was ordered by Napoleon Bonaparte to send to Paris the archives of the Vatican, part of Napoleon's grand design of an international archive in France. Miolis was instructed particularly to send the archives of the Holy Office, a task which he completed in 1811. In 1808, as a result of the Napoleonic invasion and conquest of Spain, Joseph Bonaparte summarily abolished the Spanish Inquisition and turned its archives over to Juan Antonio Llorente, an *afrancesado*, former secretary of the Madrid Inquisition, and a friend of Moratín and Goya, who once painted his portrait. With these two events, the archives of the Roman and Spanish Inquisitions began to speak.

Neither event, however, permanently abolished either inquisition. After a second abolition by the revolutionary *Cortes* at Cadiz in 1813, the Spanish Inquisition was reestablished by Ferdinand VII in 1814, reabolished by the revolutionary government in 1820, and lingered on in the ensuing age of reaction until its permanent abolition in 1834. Although it regained custody of its archives in 1814, many were scattered or destroyed in 1820, and after 1834 the archives of the Spanish Inquisition became part of the national archives of Spain. The fate of the archives of the Roman Inquisition was worse. Although the Holy Office was reestablished after the fall of Napoleon, many of its archives, and much other Vatican material, did not return from France. Much was lost, stolen, or sold off. The dispersal of the archives of the Roman Inquisition has made its history extremely difficult to write with the thoroughness that the archives of the Spanish Inquisition have permitted. A large number of documents, for example, passed through English hands, ending up in the library of Trinity College, Dublin, in 1854, where they have remained ever since. Some individual cases that were particularly famous, notably that of Galileo, took a much longer time to be discovered and returned to Rome. The trial records of Giordano Bruno were never found.

Those archives that became available, even for a brief period after 1808 and 1809, vastly expanded the available source materials for inquisition histories. Historians now possessed a very different set of sources for inquisition history from those they had acquired by the end of the eighteenth century. Against archival research could be tested, not only the earlier polemical and confessional histories, but the personal narratives, pamphlets, and formal accounts of statutes and *autos-de-fé* that had comprised their source material for two centuries. In terms of source materials for inquisition history, the armies of Napoleon in Spain and Italy accomplished nearly as much as Limborch more than a century earlier.

Nor did the age of reaction that followed the fall of Napoleon in 1814–1815 even begin to completely restore the status quo that existed before the French Revolution. In a number of states, inquisitions never recovered their lost wealth, power or records. In Naples, for example, the prosecution of heresy, which was still an offense, was now undertaken by secular courts. Even though the restoration of the Spanish Inquisition was part of Ferdinand VII's rejection of the revolutionary past, it never achieved its former standing or power. Moreover, inquisitions in the Spanish Americas disappeared as the early nineteenth-century revolutions cut the ties of the former colonies with Spain. In Italy the restored Roman Inquisition saw its authority confined to the Papal States. Except for Spain, where the restoration of the Inquisition was part of a nationalist and political reaction to the French occupation, inquisitions were not high on the list of things to be restored after the fall of Napoleon. Few were, and those that had been did not long survive. Except for some of the archives of the Holy Office in Rome, which were returned after the fall of Napoleon, and remained closed, all of the archives of all of the inquisitions were slowly opened to historical inquiry during the nineteenth century. A new age of inquisition research had been born.

When Joseph Bonaparte turned the custody of the archives of the Spanish Inquisition over to Juan Antonio Llorente in 1808, he inadvertently patronized the first historian of any inquisition to write directly from the archival sources. Born in northern Castile in 1756, Llorente had received a good ecclesiastical education, was ordained a priest in 1779, and quickly received a number of promotions because of his intellectual abilities. In 1782 he was named Vicar-General of Calahorra, in 1785 he became associated with the Inquisition at Logroño, and in 1789 was made Secretary-General of the Madrid Inquisition. From 1785 he also became exposed to Enlightenment criticism of religious authority. In 1789 the Inquisition itself was controlled by reform-minded ecclesiastics, and one of Llorente's accomplishments was to draw up a plan for Inquisition reform. During these years, Llorente, a member of the Inquisition, came to know the Inquisition's archives extremely well.

He was invited by the inquisitor-general himself, Abad y la Sierra, to revise inquisitorial censorship procedures and to establish appropriate legal procedures as well. With the fall of Abad y la Sierra in 1794, Llorente also lost royal favor and his position on the Inquisition. From 1805 on, however, Llorente regained royal favor. He was made a canon of Toledo in 1806, a member of the Royal Order of Spain in 1807, and by 1808 he had emerged as a conservative sympathizer of governmental and ecclesiastical reform and a prominent figure in the highest councils of Spain on the eve of the Napoleonic invasion.

On May 5, 1808, Charles IV and Ferdinand VII resigned the crown of Spain to Napoleon Bonaparte at Bayonne. Napoleon established his brother Joseph Bonaparte on the Spanish throne and surrounded him with a council of Spanish advisers, among whom was Llorente, from that time on identified prominently as an *afrancesado*, a sympathizer of reform to be directed by the French government. When Bonaparte abolished the Inquisition, confiscated its archives, and turned them over to Llorente, the latter decided to reveal to his countrymen for the first time the nature and extent of the Inquisition's role in Spanish history by using the Inquisition's archives as an unrivalled source.

Even part of the Spanish resistance to the Bonapartist government agreed that the Inquisition had been a disaster for Spanish development, and in the *Cortes* held at Cadiz from 1810 to 1813, a number of savage debates concerning the Inquisition took place until the *Cortes* itself declared the Inquisition abolished in 1813. For five years, from 1808 to 1813, Llorente had absolute access to the Inquisition's records, and he worked with great speed, if not always with great judgment. But the Spanish resistance to Bonapartism made the reformist ideas of Llorente and the *Cortes* of 1813 obsolete. When Ferdinand VII ascended the throne in 1814, he reestablished the Inquisition. Llorente, deeply implicated, even though he had not been wholeheartedly in favor of the French government, fell with it and fled to France, where his great work and his great troubles began. He brought with him his notes, but not the archives, and for nearly a decade he remained in France, where he published his great *Historia crítica de la inquisición de España* in a French translation between 1817 and 1818.

As short as was his control of the archives of the Inquisition, Llorente did not waste time. Moreover, having been a member of the tribunal himself, he knew the archives already and was much better prepared to go through them than anyone else would have been. In one sense, he echoes Páramo, as he himself remarked:

> In order to write an exact history, it was necessary to be an Inquisitor, or Secretary of the Inquisition. In this way alone could be seen the bulls of the popes, the orders of the kings, the decisions of the Council of the Inquisition, the original trials and other papers of its archives. Perhaps I am the only one, who at the present time can possess all of these documents. I was Secretary of the Inquisition at the court of Madrid in the years 1789, 1790, and 1791. I knew its establishment sufficiently to consider it vicious in its origin, constitution, and laws in spite of apologetic writings in its favor.

Llorente worked quickly. In 1811 there appeared two editions of his *Memoria historica sobre cual ha sido la opinión nacional de España acerca del Tribunal de la inquisición.* A year later he published two volumes of his *Annales de la inquisición* and reprinted the *Memoria historica*, which was reprinted again in 1813.

These early works were written from archival sources, but they were certainly not free of a particular kind of polemic. Llorente argued that the Inquisition had been imposed upon a resisting Spanish society, and it had forced critics into silence until now. Llorente's historical works of this period appear to have influenced the deliberations of the *Cortes* at Cadiz, in spite of its political differences with the *afrancesados*. In

1817–1818, Llorente completed his greatest work, whose title deserves to be cited in full:

> The critical history of the Inquisition of Spain, since the epoch of its establishment by Ferdinand V to the reign of Ferdinand VII, drawn from the original materials of the archives of the Council of the Suprema and of those of several subalternate tribunals of the Holy Office. By Don Juan Antonio Llorente . . . Translated from the Spanish, from the original manuscript and under the eyes of the author by Alexis Pellier.

Llorente's vast history, although it was written from a distinctly reformist point of view, nevertheless set a new standard for inquisition scholarship. The materials from the archives not only presented vast amounts of new evidence, but informed many Spaniards who had had no idea of the historical role of the Inquisition in Spain. Bitterly critical of its "vicious" character, Llorente's work showed signs not only of haste but of ideology, and it generated considerable hostility to him. As early as 1814, 1815, and 1816 savage criticism came from opponents of both the French government in Spain and of the reform movement itself, notably in José Clemente Carnicero's two-volume attack on Llorente and defense of the reestablishment of the Inquisition in 1816. Llorente replied with his *Defensa canónica* of the same year, and he continued to justify himself in his autobiography, the *Noticia biográfica*, of 1818. With the revolution against Ferdinand VII in 1820 (and the second abolition of the Inquisition), Llorente was able to return to Spain, where the first Spanish edition of the *Historia critica* appeared in 1822–1823, again to mixed praise and blame. Llorente died in Madrid in 1823, but the furor raised by his historical work and his editorial perspective raged through the nineteenth century and in other places besides Spain.

Llorente's *Historia critica* was translated into Italian in 1820, into Dutch in 1821, German in 1823 (the year of its first Spanish publication), and English in 1826—in both Britain and the United States. At the same time, it was abridged, and the abridgments were translated at a similar rate. Within a decade of its publication in Paris, Llorente's history had become familiar to the European and Atlantic world. At first, not surprisingly, Llorente's work merely added fuel to the conventional flames of myth and polemic, and his scholarly impact took considerably longer to reach a suitable audience. Although the early and mid-nineteenth century witnessed a new and more rigorous conception of scholarly history, the subject of the Inquisition resisted such discipline, since confessional, philosophical, and political feelings ran as high after the fall of

Napoleon as they had before. Moreover, Llorente's was not the only work on the Spanish Inquisition to emerge from the years 1808–1813. In 1811, for example, Antonio Puigblanch published, under the pseudonym of Natanael Jomtob, *La inquisición sin máscara*—*The Inquisition Unmasked*—a scurrilous attack on the Inquisition, its history, its destruction of both the spirit of Christianity and the development of Spain. Puigblanch's work, although far inferior to that of Llorente, also influenced the deliberations of the *Cortes* of Cadiz and is said to have been instrumental in its abolition of the Inquisition in 1813. An English translation appeared in 1816. Inside Spain both works ran afoul of the reactionary temper of the years 1814–1820; outside Spain they appealed to the same public that had always discredited the Inquisition on religious, philosophical, or political grounds.

Nor did Llorente's work initially dominate inquisition literature during the first half of the nineteenth century. In 1809, for example, Joseph Lavallée, Marquis de Boisrobert, published his two-volume *Histoire des inquisitions religieuses d'Italie, d'Espagne et de Portugal*. The account of Lavallée was based upon a slight reading of the then well-known sources: Sarpi, Limborch, Marsollier, and others, with some original inquisitorial documents appended without explanation of their source. An English translation of Lavallée's book appeared in 1810, and the work was used as the basis of John Joseph Stockdale's own 1810 *The History of the Inquisitions; Including the Secret Transactions of those Horrific Tribunals*, a work of no historical value whatsoever but of considerable polemical value in England, where the debate over granting civil liberties to Roman Catholics was considerable during the first decades of the nineteenth century. Stockdale admitted that the purpose of his work was to discredit the supporters of Catholic civil liberties, and he included twelve grisly plates to emphasize his point.

Works like those of Lavallée and Stockdale remained far more appealing than the heavily documented volumes of Llorente, and they were supplemented by a continuing though slightly diminished flow of personal narratives. One of the best known of these was *The Memoirs of Don Juan Van Halen; comprising the Narrative of His Imprisonment in the Dungeons of the Inquisition at Madrid*, which was published in London in 1830 and frequently reprinted. In spite of the promise of its title, it turns out that very little happened to Van Halen, a Spanish officer of Dutch ancestry, except for what even he admitted to be an accidentally broken thumb.

In addition to the continuing appeal of polemical treatments of the Inquisition, the opposition to Llorente moved from within Spain to the general European world of reaction and restoration. In 1822 there appeared in French the posthumous *Lettres sur l'Inquisition* by Joseph de Maistre, one of the most influential spokesmen for the repression of revolution and liberalism of the early nineteenth century. Not only did de Maistre's *Lettres* take the side of the supporters of the Inquisition in Spain after 1814, but it too was translated into other languages, and the story of its first English translation is an interesting chapter in American history.

In 1820 the short-lived revolution against Ferdinand VII resulted in the sacking of a number of palaces of the Inquisition in Spain and the scattering of the local archives. Among the records of the tribunal of Barcelona that were not destroyed or lost on the spot were several that made their way to Boston, Massachusetts, where they were translated and printed by Samuel Goodrich in 1828 as the *Records of the Spanish Inquisition*. The United States had inherited the traditional Protestant views of the Spanish (and generally Roman) Inquisition, and the 1821 volume of the *Port-Folio* carried an interesting notice of the work of Puigblanch; in 1825 the *American Quarterly Review* published a long and sophisticated anonymous review of the Madrid Spanish edition of Llorente's *Historia crítica*. Probably stung to retort by these publications, a Boston priest, T. J. O'Flaherty, published the first English translation of de Maistre's *Letters on the Spanish Inquisition* in 1830 as an unofficial response to the *Records* of 1828.

In Spain the greatest nineteenth-century critic of Llorente was Marcellino Menendez y Pelayo, who was born in 1856, educated at the University of Barcelona, and published in 1876 *La Ciencia Española*, a blistering historical attack on the residual Enlightenment criticism of Spanish intellectual backwardness and lethargy. Menendez y Pelayo also attacked the companion thesis that religious intolerance was the cause of Spain's backwardness, in what is perhaps the most eloquent attack on the generalized criticism of Spain and the Inquisition and the Black Legend in general:

> Why was there no industry in Spain? On account of the Inquisition.
> . . . Why are Spaniards lazy? On account of the Inquisition. Why
> are there bull-fights in Spain? On account of the Inquisition. Why
> do Spaniards take a siesta? On account of the Inquisition. . . .

Although *La Ciencia Española* was not a major work, it earned Menendez y Pelayo a national reputation, and in 1878 he took up the chair of the History of Spanish Literature at the University of Madrid. Between 1880 and 1883 he published the three large volumes of his *Historia de los heterodoxos españoles,* a vast and immensely learned study of Spanish religious dissent, highly critical of Llorente, but fundamentally flawed in itself. Menendez y Pelayo chose to emphasize the purity of the Spanish "race" and to emphasize well beyond the limits of his sources that heterodoxy had always been an import into Spain, and had never originated locally. He identified Spanish patriotism with Spanish Catholicism, and he was particularly suspicious of those eighteenth-century reformers who imported French free thought into the Iberian Peninsula. He defended the history of the Inquisition on these grounds, and out of religious obligation. Within Spain, if not always outside it, Menendez y Pelayo's work damped the ardor of liberal nineteenth-century historians, and no major work on the archival materials of the Inquisition appeared in Spain by a Spanish author during the nineteenth and early twentieth centuries.

Among scholars who were less driven to defend or criticize Spain's history one of the first to use Llorente's work with profit and effectiveness was the Scottish historian Thomas M'Crie. In 1827 M'Crie had published a *History of the Progress and suppression of the Reformation in Italy in the Sixteenth Century,* and in 1829 he published at Edinburgh his *History of the Progress and Suppression of the Reformation in Spain in the Sixteenth Century,* a work in which he relied heavily on Llorente, although not without criticism, and that strongly influenced the young American historian of Spain William Hickling Prescott.

Inspired by his Harvard teacher George Ticknor, and unable to undertake any other career because of an eye injury, Prescott began the study of Spanish history in 1826. From the publication of *Ferdinand and Isabella* in 1837 until his death in 1859 following the publication of the third volume of *Philip II,* Prescott was the greatest and most influential student of Spanish history in North America. Initially, Prescott's introduction to history was that of the eighteenth-century man of letters. He read and properly praised Voltaire, Thierry, Sismondi, Mably, Montesquieu, and Gibbon as both moralists and historians. Unlike many of his Enlightenment predecessors, however, Prescott was understanding of and sympathetic toward religion. Although he believed that the Reformation had marked religious progress, he does not seem to have set out to write as a Protestant historian, nor does he seem to have regarded the religion of Ferdinand and Isabella in a hostile sense. For him, their Catholicism was the belief of energetic, heroic, and simply pious people in an archaic period of history. His work even includes sympathetic observations made of individual Catholics and Catholic beliefs, and throughout his life Prescott prided himself on his evenhandedness in matters of Catholicism. On his visit to New York in 1844 he twice noted that Bishop John Hughes had praised his fairness in *Ferdinand and Isabella* and *The Conquest of Mexico;* and he greatly resented accusations of anti-Catholic bigotry that were launched in reviews in Baltimore and Dublin.

Although Prescott did not intend at the outset of his work to deal at any length with the Spanish Inquisition, he read the work of M'Crie closely, and from M'Crie was led to Llorente's *Historia critica.* But Prescott also relied on Mosheim, Limborch, and Pàramo, and his treatment of Torquemada in *Ferdinand and Isabella* places the blame on the inquisitor, not on Isabella, for the establishment of the Inquisition. In his treatment of Philip II, however, Prescott found himself unable to avoid a detailed discussion of the Inquisition, particularly when his sources increased in number and focused upon Philip's persecution of Protestants instead of Marranos and Moriscos. Focusing his discussion on the character of the Inquisitor Fernando Valdes, Prescott borrowed from the most polemical invective used by his sources. Valdes becomes a monster, not only of religious persecution, but of the destruction of the Spanish intellect:

> Folded under the dark wing of the Inquisition, Spain was shut out from the light which in the sixteenth century broke over the rest of Europe, stimulating the nations to greater enterprise in every department of knowledge. The genius of the people was rebuked, and their spirit quenched, under the malignant influence of an eye that never slumbered, of an unseen arm ever raised to strike.

Prescott's portrait of Valdes, read by Dostoievsky in the Russian translation of 1858, contributed perhaps as much as Schiller to the portrait of Dostoievsky's Grand Inquisitor.

The liberal Catholic reformism of Llorente, the philosophical liberalism of Lavallée, the liberal Protestantism of Prescott, and the scholarly Presbyterian sympathies of M'Crie thus colored the earliest uses of the archival materials of the inquisitions. In Portugal too, the great liberal historian Alexandre Herculano began to issue his monumental *On the Origin and Establishment of the Inquisition in Portugal* in 1854 (the two remaining volumes appeared in 1855 and 1859). Since the Inquisition in Portugal had been dissolved in the revolution of 1820, the subsequent political chaos in that country did not permit its reestablishment. Its records were joined to the royal archives, and thus Herculano's task was not difficult, at least in one sense. In another, it was prodigious. There had been, in spite of the voluminous eighteenth-century literature on the Portuguese Inquisition based largely on Dellon's *Relation de Goa*, no serious historical work on the Portuguese Inquisition, and the flimsy chapters of Lavallée's 1809 *Histoire des Inquisitions* devoted to Portugal (and largely taken from Dellon) were Herculano's only model. Moreover, Portuguese inquisitorial history was also tangled in legend, including the legend of Saavedra the impostor. In addition, Herculano was inclined to see in the history of the Portuguese Inquisition an unsettling combination of fanaticism and hypocrisy, as well as a power struggle, an object lesson to his own contemporaries. Thus, although it is still a major work of history, even Herculano's history resembled to a large extent the work of his political and philosophical contemporaries.

Between the publication of Llorente's *Historia critica* in 1817–1818 and the work of Prescott and Herculano at mid-century, the archives had only begun to speak. The power of confessional polemic and rationalist criticism remained too great to permit an objective historical investigation of inquisition history. But, also by mid-century, much archival material of the inquisitions of Spain and Portugal had moved to national archives and remained accessible to historians. In Inquisition history, as in other types, archival research slowly transformed the nature of source materials upon which historians relied. In Germany, the enormous influence of Leopold von Ranke and his predecessors established archival research and close documentary criticism as the historian's most useful tools. After mid-century, the archives, even those of the Inquisitions, began to speak more clearly.

The Inquisitions' Historian: Henry Charles Lea

The English and Continental writers who took up the theme of inquisition history between the sixteenth and the late nineteenth centuries generally wrote with other, often larger agendas in mind than that of inquisition history alone. Even Llorente, as his own history shows, wrote on behalf of a reformed Spain, its new path illuminated, as it had been for Moratín and Goya, by its ancient errors. Even the revolution in historical theory and method, adapted by Leopold von Ranke from the transformation of classical scholarship and applied to medieval and early modern historical documents, did not take up the problem of inquisition history until the end of the nineteenth century. Church history generally lagged behind other kinds of historical research, and confessional feelings still ran sufficiently high as to make the history of inquisitions a difficult and disputed topic. It remained for a citizen of the United States, far removed from both confessional and professional history as practiced on the Continent, to begin a new approach to the history of inquisitions—one not restricted by contemporary passions and institutional mainstreams, focusing specifically on the inquisitions, but insisting at the same time that they must be understood in their historical setting. The publication of Henry Charles Lea's A *History of the Inquisition of the Middle Ages* in 1887 opened what has been called "the golden age" of inquisition history.

Lea was born in Philadelphia in 1825. His family operated the publishing house founded by his grandfather Mathew Carey in 1785. After a promising start as a scientist and man of letters, Lea entered the family firm, in which he worked until his retirement in 1880. Tutored at home, and later self-educated, Lea never attended a school or college, never held a teaching position, and never intended to be a historian at all. A breakdown in 1847 caused by overwork prohibited the continuation of his literary and scientific work, and a few years of desultory reading of seventeenth- and eighteenth-century French court memoirs led him back to the French Middle Ages, in which he developed a considerable interest. His first historical work, a forty-page still unpublished essay on the rise of the house of Capet before 987, indicates the earliest direction of his historical interests.

In order to undertake such work in the United States of the 1850s, Lea had literally to purchase his own private library; even the excellent holdings of local Philadelphia libraries could not provide him with the materials he needed. As he began to read widely in medieval history, free of academic constraints, and hence of academic models, Lea became convinced that much of medieval European history had been written from the wrong perspective, that, to be understood, it had to be read in terms of its own culture, not from the point of view of nineteenth-century standards superimposed upon the past. What struck Lea particularly was the inadequacy of political history and the excessively confessional character of Church history for such a task. Lea turned instead to the history of law, because, as he said,

> At the commencement of my historical studies I speedily became convinced that the surest basis of investigation for a given period lay in an examination of its jurisprudence, which presents without disguise its aspirations and the means regarded as best adapted for their realization.

In 1866 Lea published his first book, a collection of essays on the judicial ordeal, legal compurgation, the judicial duel, and torture, which he titled *Superstition and Force*. His *Sketch of the History of Sacerdotal*

Celibacy of 1867 reflected a topic that was a matter of considerable debate in his own day. In 1869 he published a miscellany of essays, *Studies in Church History*, which includes studies of the temporal power of the Church, the church and slavery, benefit of clergy, and excommunication. All of this work was produced during a period when Lea was fully involved in operating, then directing as owner, his family's prosperous publishing house. In 1866 and 1867 Lea turned his attention to events in Rome, and in 1870 he published a review of Janus, *Pope and Council*, in which he was able to correct even the great Ignaz von Döllinger on points of Church history. In 1866 Lea also discovered his last major formative influence, the work of W. E. H. Lecky, *History of the Rise and Influence of the Spirit of Rationalism in Europe*, of 1865. Lecky's central concern with what would now be called cultural rather than political history enabled him to focus on religious issues as cultural problems without placing confessional concerns as central in his study. As Lea wrote to Lecky in 1866,

> We have had enough of annalists to chronicle political intrigues and military achievements; but that which constitutes the inner life of a people and from which are to be drawn the lessons of the past that will guide us in the future, has hitherto been too much neglected.

By 1868 Lea could write to one of his correspondents that "I hope it leisure serves to write a history of the Inquisition."

In 1865 Lea acquired M'Crie's *History of the Progress and Suppression of the Reformation in Spain*. In 1868 he acquired Páramo and Montanus. From these years on, Lea's library, which had focused on medieval materials more and more after 1850, now began to burgeon with inquisition materials, not only all printed sources (Lea possessed every work cited in this book that appeared before his death in 1909), but manuscripts as well, and finally, when manuscripts were not available for purchase or loan, on transcripts from the original archives themselves. Between 1864 and 1871 Lea acquired nearly all of Llorente's works on the subject. In 1869 Lea began a correspondence with G. B. de Lagrèze, whose study *Histoire du Droit dans les Pyrénées* Lea had favorably reviewed in 1868. He indicated his new interest to de Lagrèze, who responded that his relative, the King of Sweden, had told him of an Inquisition manuscript in Copenhagen that might be of interest to Lea. In the same year Lea managed to borrow the Moldenhower Codex from the Royal Library in Copenhagen and hand-copy it for his own use. The acquisition was extremely important at that stage of Lea's development. In the 1780s the Danish theologian D. G. Moldenhower acquired in

Madrid, by means still unknown, a large working dictionary of the laws and procedures of the Spanish Inquisition, obviously issued by the *Suprema* itself, which covered three centuries of legislation and practice and was the most extensive work of its kind. Nothing in print in the 1860s, and no known manuscripts, offered as rich a source for inquisition history. Not even Llorente had such a tool for his own work.

Lea's wide reading in all kinds of medieval source material and his reading of the Moldenhower Codex may have been the triggers that marked the first important phase of his inquisition work: he decided that the medieval period of inquisition must be treated separately from the early modern Spanish Inquisition. Thus breaking the myth of a single institution extending from late antiquity to the present, Lea was probably also daunted by the enormous amount of source material that had never before been used, and simply could not conceive a single historical work that could encompass both the medieval and early modern phases. As it turned out, A *History of the Inquisition of the Middle Ages* consisted of three large volumes of six hundred pages each; A *History of the Inquisition of Spain* (1906–1907) consisted of four large volumes of the same length, with the addition of three more volumes containing studies of related topics. Lea had undertaken research on inquisition history on a scale never before attempted. Not only heresy, but social, political, and legal structures, philosophy, and theology, framed the work, and for the first time the medieval phase of inquisition history was put into a coherent framework that drew from historical sources alone. By 1870 Lea began to expand the remarkable network of correspondents which included diplomats, booksellers, scholars, travellers, fellow Philadelphians, lawyers, and amanuenses through which he sent out his requests, received responses, selected his materials, bought books and manuscripts, and hired and paid copyists, all from his growing library at 2000 Walnut Street, Philadelphia. He worked only after business hours until he retired in 1880, and he was prevented from intensifying his historical research by another breakdown in 1880–1884. After 1884, however, he worked continuously, first, on his *History of the Inquisition of the Middle Ages* and then, after its publication in 1887–1888, on his massive *History of the Inquisition of Spain*, which appeared in 1906–1907, as well as on a number of related research projects.

Lea's *History of the Inquisition of the Middle Ages*, although a distinct and separate work, nevertheless implies that it deals with the medieval phase of *The Inquisition*. Despite its lack of full local data and its misleadingly centralized presentation of the papal office of inquisitor, Lea's work is arguably still the most exhaustive study of the inquisitorial office and function in medieval Europe. With Lea's inexhaustible capacity for finding and wisely using source material, his *History* overcomes both its defects and its residual editorial characterizations of Catholic temporal power. Not only was Lea's work the first study to focus only on the medieval period, but it virtually opened up medieval history in the United States in a way in which no book written before or long after it did. It remains the basis for much work done today in medieval ecclesiastical and legal history.

Having completed the "medieval" Inquisition, Lea turned to the Inquisition of Spain. Although he had no particular interest in Spain or in Spanish history, the Spanish Inquisition rather than the Portuguese or the Roman attracted his interest, since, as he once wrote to Lecky, "the Spanish Inquisition is the controlling factor in the career of modern persecution." Here too, Lea was probably driven by Enlightenment principles and his own great personal distaste for the possession of civil authority by ecclesiastical institutions. His choice, however, was wise. Neither Portugal nor Rome could have offered the research opportunities in the 1880s and 1890s that Spain did; moreover, the resources at Simancas were available and well-catalogued, and if Lea had undertaken a project similar to, say, that of Lavallée, to write on all of the early modern inquisitions, he would not have produced a work as substantial as his masterpiece.

The years between 1873 and 1914 were indeed the golden age of Spanish Inquisition historiography. The archives at Simancas drew José Toribio Medina (1852–1930), the historian of the inquisitions in Latin America, as well as the great Ernst Schäfer (1872–1946), whose *Beiträge zur Geschichte des spanischen Protestantismus und der Inquisition im sechzehnten Jahrhunderts* appeared at Gutersloh in three large volumes between 1902 and 1903. Between 1889 and 1906 the Belgian historian Paul Fréd ericq's *Corpus documentorum inquisitionis hereticae pravitatis neerlandicae* was a multivolume collection of edited documents relating to the history of the medieval and early modern inquisitions in the Netherlands. In 1880 and 1887 Charles Molinier produced important studies of heresy in the south of France. Celestin Douais produced superb editions of medieval inquisitorial registers and a French translation of the handbook for inquisitors written by Bernard Gui. The quality of the work of Toribio Medina and Schäfer rivaled that of Lea, and in Schäfer's case his extraordinary ability to print meticulously edited texts without characterizing the Inquisition in any way made him, even more than Lea, a model of dispassionate and objective scholarship.

But Lea's vast *History of the Inquisition of Spain*, in its scholarship, range, extensive use of sources, and critical method, remains the greatest and most extensive history of the Spanish Inquisition ever written. Although Lea was virtually unknown in Europe when he began his research on the Inquisition in the late 1860s, by the time of his death in 1909 he was world famous, and with him North American scholars joined the European historians of the inquisition and have remained prominent in it ever since.

The standards set by Lea, Herculano, Toribio Medina, Schäfer, and other scholars of the "golden age" finally succeeded in erecting inquisition history into an historical subject in its own right. The extensive use of archives, the use of critical editorial standards, the insistence that source materials should shape historical discourse, and that historical research should reveal the life of the past without editorializing about its quality—the same standards, in short, that were being invoked for history generally—were now routinely applied to the problem of the inquisition. Although confessional broadsides still appeared into the twentieth century—and occasionally still do—the "myth" of the Inquisition was by World War I among historians, at least, merely a myth. A century of superb and detailed scholarship had brought the inquisitions, not only out of their own secrecy, but out of the jumble of myth and polemic that had characterized their place in European literature since the sixteenth century. The battles in whose service myth and polemic had been used had, by the early twentieth century, all been fought and ended, if not won. With their causes removed or muted, myth and polemic could move on to serve other purposes and other kinds of historical discourse. The Inquisitions now belonged primarily to historians.

The Historians' Inquisition

Lea and his contemporaries had demonstrated that inquisition history, like any other history, must be studied and described in the context of its own times and places and is distorted when presented as the illustration of a confessional or philosophical idea of the proper uses of history. As vast as their works were, however, both medieval and early modern history had left more sources than even they had used. After the great works of the "golden age" had been absorbed by historians of the early twentieth century—and corrected in occasional detail—inquisition history did not attract a great deal of scholarly attention until after 1930. Even then, two world wars, the removal of the Spanish archives from Simancas to Madrid and their subsequent recataloguing, and a general shift in the directions of historical research in Europe and the Americas all militated against extensive research in inquisition materials for both the medieval and early modern period.

Some of the directions of historical interest and research that became prominent after 1930 brought historians back to inquisitorial subjects by extremely circuitous routes. The ecclesiastical history of medieval and early modern Europe came to be dealt with in less confessional ways and to be regarded as part of the social and intellectual history of Europe. Detailed studies of the history of the papacy, for example, were able to tone down the papal component of medieval inquisitorial history as historians came to understand more precisely the nature of papal authority and, more important, the extent of papal resources during the twelfth and thirteenth centuries. When Herbert Grundmann published his masterly account of *Religious Movements in the Middle Ages* in 1935, he opened up a new framework for the history of religious dissent and the place of ideas of heresy within it. The work of several generations of historians of medieval canon law has made far clearer the legal character of the office of inquisitor.

With the new interest in social and economic history that characterized the years after 1945, researchers slowly came to discover in the records of the various inquisitions a treasury of detailed information on classes of people about whom few other records spoke, and in the inquisition records historians sometimes heard them speaking in their own words. Although the French historian Pierre Chaunu had called attention to the value of these materials as early as 1956, it has taken several decades for individual historians and groups of historians to work up a methodology that makes this usable. The work of the Italian historian Carlo Ginzburg has demonstrated the eloquence with which the inquisition records of Italy permit "the people without history" to speak. Once the main focus of inquisition history, larger doctrinal offenses have given way to study of the full range of inquisition offenses, including relatively minor ones, as the proportion of major and minor cases within particular archives and historical fields of investigation has come to be better understood. Finally, regional studies for both medieval and early modern Europe have at last become possible, and in most cases, precisely in those areas where such historians as Lea and Herculano were limited, modern research is casting light on regional tribunals and the communities with which they worked.

Just as "religious history" has greatly expanded to include dissent as well as orthodoxy, social history has found in the materials of the inquisitions a virtually inexhaustible source of information on precisely the least documented strata of European society, as well as access to regional history usually unrivaled elsewhere. Thus, from 1965 the journal *Cahiers de Fanjeaux* has published research on the culture of southern France, principally in terms of heresy and the inquisition of Toulouse and nearby regions. Virtually all of this research is "ecumenical"—that is, the confessional affiliations of scholars do not impede professional contact and mutual influence. And conferences have been held more often during the past decade and a half than ever before, the conference publications representing the current state of what is now a prominent and productive area of historical research.

Further, no historian now senses an obligation to work narrowly upon the Inquisition alone, nor to trace its development from the fourth or the twelfth centuries to the nineteenth. Like most historical subjects, inquisition history is now worked on in detail by specialists, and only through their work is a book like this one possible.

For better or worse, the inquisitions and inquisitors now belong to historians. And historians ask different questions in the twentieth century. In approaching a particular source, usually one stemming from the inquisitors themselves, they now ask about the individual inquisitors, their training and experience, and their awareness of the size of the phenomenon they encounter in their investigations; the place of the source at a particular stage of the Church's response to dissent and heresy; the nature of the heresy discussed, its local or transregional character, and the nature of the place and time in which the source was produced. A source must be analyzed in terms of its language, the concepts of orthodoxy and heterodoxy it reflects, and the complex process by which vernacular interrogations and statements made their way into the Latin language of the sources.

There is now, too, a sociology of the inquisitions and inquisitors, and of heretics as well. Inquisition history is sometimes also a study of means of social control, and among its components are the beliefs and behavior of the faithful as well as those of the heretics. If we can no longer designate medieval and early modern heretics as witnesses to a hidden, true church, neither is it possible to designate them with the blanket term "heretics" derived from an unchanging category of theology and canon law. The history of the use of the terms "heresy" and "heretic" themselves has revealed shifting definitions and ideas. Above all, we now possess a far more detailed and complex picture of the culture of Europe during the Middle Ages, one that permits simple answers neither for questions of heresy and inquisitions nor for other kinds of questions.

The same must be said for the history of early modern Europe. Once the work of the Spanish Inquisition, for example, was understood in terms of the full universe of cases and offenses it dealt with, it became easier to understand the great categories of offenses—Judaizing and Lutheranism—that had once been the exclusive concern of historians. The Roman and Venetian Inquisitions have also found historians whose interests are different from those of their predecessors, who simply grouped all inquisitorial tribunals together as *The Inquisition*. In fact, *The Inquisition* has disappeared from scholarly literature. It is revived only in journalism, confessional propaganda, films, and occasional comedy routines such as those of Mel Brooks and Monty Python, themselves echoes of the satire of Lesage and Voltaire, Morellet, Goya, and Gilbert and Sullivan.

From the perspective of the late twentieth century, inquisition history has become far more than the stuff of polemic or fiction—and more interesting and useful. It has become one of the keys to understanding past societies in their entirety, especially important because it is one of the few areas in which different strata of society become linked and where it is possible to see popular as well as learned beliefs and practices being put to the test by representatives of a dominant culture, informed by a wide literature and a professional training. It has availed itself of the computer and the anthropologist, the statistician and the folklorist, the legal historian and the theologian. It now constitutes, with other kinds of history, a distinctive point of access to the past, one that must be linked with other points of access, not isolated and erected into a separate and distinct field of research.

Chapter Ten

Materials for a Meditation

Although the work of late nineteenth- and twentieth-century historians largely replaced the confessional and ideological mythology of *The Inquisition* with a genuine history, it did not lessen the appeal of the idea. Lea, Schäfer, Molinier, and Fréderícq produced their histories in an age that believed it had overcome those irrational forces in history that had produced the inquisitions in the first place. The civil authority of ecclesiastical institutions was disappearing, and most of its worst features had gone the way of the rest of the *Ancien Régime*. The *Ancien Régime* itself had disappeared, and a seemingly republican, democratic, modernized, humane Europe stood in its place. Torture had been abolished, and a professionally liberal although socially conservative judiciary was determined that it would never reappear. Even the wars between nation states seemed to be diminishing in frequency and intensity.

But between 1914 and 1932 all of this changed. The First World War; social and political upheavals, the ominous presence of the authoritarian state, and repressive ideologies not only destroyed the confidence of an earlier generation but also turned attention back to the distant and so recently discarded past to seek out models of comparable repression of individual liberty that might arouse the twentieth century to the dangers of the new—or revived—threats on the horizon.

Once more *The Inquisition* became a potent force. It was needed no longer to invoke resentment against Catholicism, popery, Spain, or the *Ancien Régime*; its depiction in confessional or tolerationist form was unnecessary. Its wealth of familiar images and associations were reinterpreted and applied to a puzzling new complex of ideologies and politics, first generally throughout a disenchanted Europe, then specifically in a number of particular cases: Soviet Russia, Fascist Italy, Nazi Germany, Communist Poland, and the United States. In a series of imaginative literary works, studies in the social sciences, and in the common usage of journalists and politicians alike, the myth of *The Inquisition* returned, stripped of its original functions and redesigned to provide a framework for explaining some of the most problematic features of public life in the twentieth century. It functions that way still.

It is not surprising that the earliest signs of the revival of *The Inquisition* should be found in the hands of writers of imaginative fiction. During the early twentieth century the accepted standards of literature, too, came under attack, and some novelists opened up the new career of the myth dramatically, in fiction and in literary criticism, before it was taken up by social scientists, journalists, and playwrights later in the century.

D. H. Lawrence and Others Reread Dostoievsky

There is no better example of the revived appeal of *The Inquisition* than in the two very different readings of Dostoievsky's "Grand Inquisitor" episode from *The Brothers Karamazov* made by the British novelist D. H. Lawrence, the first in 1913 and the second in 1930. After first reading the episode in 1913, Lawrence was entirely indifferent to it, "fascinated but unconvinced." When the critic John Middleton Murry suggested that the episode was the key to all of Dostoievsky, Lawrence asked, "Why? It seems to me just rubbish," dismissing the Grand Inquisitor as a pretentious, cynical pose, one in which Dostoievsky was "just showing off in blasphemy." By 1930, however, when Lawrence was asked to write the introduction to a separately printed edition of the "Grand Inquisitor" episode, he treated it very differently. The criticism of Christ now seemed "a deadly, devastating summing up. . . . It is reality versus illusion, and the illusion was Jesus, while time itself retorts with the reality." Human demands for miracle, mystery, and authority now indeed seemed dominant and rendered humans unfit to accept the unadorned message of Jesus, requiring instead its own Grand Inquisitors,

> For the Grand Inquisitor finds that to be able to live at all mankind must be loved more tolerantly and more contemptuously than Jesus loved it.

Lawrence saw in the wake of the First World War and the social dislocations that followed it a twentieth-century version of the Grand Inquisitor's indictment:

> Today man gets his sense of the miraculous from science and machinery.
> . . . The same with mystery: medicine, biological experiment, strange
> feats of the psychic people, spiritualists, Christian Scientists—it is all
> mystery. And as for authority, Russia destroyed the Tsar to have Lenin
> and the present mechanical despotism, Italy has the rationalized despo-
> tism of Mussolini, and England is longing for a despot.

Lawrence saw the Grand Inquisitor, with his insistence on the relentless-
ness of human longing for miracle, mystery, and authority, as a model
of the twentieth-century political totalitarianism that had overtaken Soviet
Russia and Fascist Italy. Two years later Lawrence saw Germany go
that way as well, and he fully expected (not without reason) England
to follow along.

For Lawrence in 1930, as for many others, the Grand Inquisitor
and the dilemma he proposed challenged all earlier images of good
and reasonable state authority. He embodied instead a new and lethal
form of coercion which exercised itself in the name of humanity in
the only form that humanity itself was capable of accepting, maintaining
itself by fulfilling humanity's demands for miracle, mystery, and authority
in its terrible flight from the freedom offered by Jesus or by states that
proposed to live according to other standards. In his grasp of absolute
power and his ruthlessness in using it, the Grand Inquisitor now antici-
pated and personified the impersonal, pervasive, and total control exercised by a growing number of twentieth-century states. Lawrence thereby
appropriated and infused a new political meaning into Dostoievsky's
Grand Inquisitor, one that served other twentieth-century thinkers as
well.

Lawrence's was one of the most dramatic, but it was not the first or
the only literary transformation of Dostoievsky's creation and its application to political purposes in the wake of the First World War.

About the same time that Lawrence was shaping his new political
reading of Dostoievsky, the Russian dramatist and novelist Evgeny Zamyatin also applied the metaphor of inquisition/heresy to his analysis of
the place of freedom and oppression in early Bolshevik Russia. Zamyatin
(1884–1937), trained as a naval architect, became a political revolutionary
in the early years of the twentieth century. Although he welcomed the
revolution of 1917, he soon began to criticize the revolutionary government of the Soviet Union for freezing the October Revolution, its myths,
and its doctrines, into an unalterable program of state. Profoundly critical
of the restrictions on personal freedom engendered by the civil wars of
1918–1921, Zamyatin argued that the Soviet government itself was becoming an old European-style state religion, and in 1919 he described

it as having achieved a parallel course and structure to earlier state religions:

> The *prophetic stage*, of course, contained most of the peaks, the grandeur, and the romanticism. The Christians in the catacombs. In the *apostolic stage* they preach openly, but they still struggle ideologically, they have not conquered. And finally, in the *ecclesiastical stage*, they have conquered on the *earthly* plane. And as all conquerors, the Christians begin forcible salvation: by force, by sword, by fire, by prisons. Christ becomes the Grand Inquisitor.

Zamyatin developed the figure of "the heretic" as embodying the unending human struggle for freedom, expressing in dissent the true direction in which the human spirit should move. Anything that impeded such movement was, by definition, orthodoxy, whether defined by church or state, threatening all individual liberty and the creative spirit by labeling them as heresies and persecuting them:

> Only the heretics discover new horizons in science, in art, in social life; only the heretics, rejecting today in the name of tomorrow, end the eternal ferment of life and ensure life's unending movement forward.

These ideas pointed Zamyatin to his first significant expression of the modified Dostoievskian approach, the play *Ogni svjatogo Dominika (The Fires of Saint Dominic)*.

In 1919 Maxim Gorki proposed to the Major Art Council of the Department of Theaters and Spectacles in Petrograd that it commission a cycle of dramas depicting the history of the world in terms of human intellectual development, with superstition and religion contrasting with science and reason. Zamyatin undertook to write the portion of the cycle dealing with the Inquisition, and he appears to have finished *The Fires of St. Dominic* by 1920, although it was not published until 1922.

The play is set in Seville in the second half of the sixteenth century. Rodrigo de Santa Cruz, who has just returned to Spain from the Netherlands, is denounced to the Inquisition by his brother Balthasar, a Dominican monk, because he possesses a version of the New Testament in Castilian. Rodrigo is condemned and burnt by the Inquisition, denouncing at the end of the play the slavish populace which permits the perversion of humanity that the Inquisition represents. Zamyatin received heavy criticism from Soviet critics, who rightly saw the play as a thinly veiled attack on the Soviet system couched in Zamyatin's favorite terms of heresy, religious persecution, and the Inquisition as a symbol of all repression of the human spirit.

In his anti-utopian novel *We*, written around 1920, but only published for the first time, and then in English, in 1924, Zamyatin transposed his themes of heresy and inquisition from the historic myth that he had borrowed from nineteenth-century tradition to the secular plane of utopian and philosophical fiction. We depicted a totally collectivized society that dealt brutally with its dissidents. At one point in the novel the protagonist meditates on the superiority of his own United State to the irrationality and anxiety of earlier religions: rational totalitarianism is far superior to that generated by irrational superstitions and fears. At another point, the protagonist complains that his own United State and its methods of interrogation and execution are sometimes thoughtlessly compared "with the ancient Inquisition," although his own state is more rational, since it seeks only its own preservation and not some unattainable transcendental good.

Like Lawrence, Zamyatin transformed Dostoievsky's image of the Grand Inquisitor and his institution into a flexible metaphor for a number of aspects of twentieth-century life, flexible enough so it could be applied to any regime that was perceived to be oppressive. In 1936 the exiled German Jewish novelist Hermann Kesten published his *Ferdinand and Isabella*, which attacked the German persecution of the Jews through the thinly veiled story of Ferdinand and Isabella's shaping of state authority in fifteenth-century Spain, through manipulation of the inchoate fears of the lower classes with the cooperation of the fanatic and self-interested clergy. At a crucial point in the novel, when the Jew Isaac Abravanel offers Ferdinand and Isabella vast sums of money to stay the Inquisition, Torquemada himself challenges the rulers to even try to avoid the will of God and the people for money; they are now prisoners of their own invention, and the Inquisition is implacable. Miracle, mystery, and authority will rule the state, and Abravanel in despair predicts the consequences:

> The Inquisition harries us, it does not smite us. It smites Spain. And Spain shall wither. Its inhabitants shall be enslaved, trembling, dazzled, fearing the secret, crying for the miracle, its rulers ever needy—is that no punishment? Is that not Hell?

Kesten echoes Dostoievsky indeed, denouncing Nazi Germany in the guise of the Spain of Ferdinand and Isabella, and, like Lawrence and Zamyatin, finds in the episode of the Grand Inquisitor a parable of the racist and political monstrosities of the twentieth-century totalitarian state. In his 1938 continuation of *Ferdinand and Isabella*, *König Philip der Zweite*, Kesten takes up again the totalitarian mentality, its dependence upon unreflecting popular fanaticism, and its instrumental use of the clergy and their power:

> King Philip loved mankind in the aggregate and in its masses. Individu-
> als, however, seemed to him to be threatening. . . . The individual
> is dangerous. One must eliminate the individual. The people as a
> whole will never resist our royal might. Only individuals resist us.
> The individual is the limit of our power. Write it down! It is good to
> write down the wisdom of the old. I have grown old contentedly. I
> have a fine understanding. And God loves me. I have ruled men
> according to their worth. I, the king.

The worth of human beings and the estimate made of it by twentieth-
century totalitarian governments was as much a theme of Kesten's as it
had been of Lawrence and Zamyatin. The use of historical myth drew
more on popular memory than on historical knowledge, but nothing
in Europe's past appeared to be as effective a metaphor as *The Inquisition*
to explain the horrors of totalitarian states. Kesten, moved by the destruction of the German Jews, reached back into the European past for a
comparable and well-known episode, and he found it in the reigns of
Ferdinand and Isabella, where he also found and tapped *The Inquisition*.

In their different ways, Zamyatin and Kesten were not particularly
subtle about their application of the metaphor of *The Inquisition* to
contemporary political regimes. Other novelists, however, had begun
to perceive that the direct application of inquisitorial metaphors did
not adequately convey the complexities of twentieth-century state activity.
One of the earliest, and arguably the best example of these, was the
work of Stefan Andres.

In the same year as Kesten's *Ferdinand and Isabella* there appeared
the far more subtle work of Stefan Andres, the novella *El Greco malt
den Grossinquisitor (El Greco Paints the Grand Inquisitor)*. Like Kesten,
Andres was an opponent of the Nazi regime and its policies, but Andres
was an internal resister, remaining in Germany throughout the Nazi
period. The novella begins with a summons issued without any reason
to El Greco to appear before the Grand Inquisitor. The painter immediately begins to fear for his life, wonders who could have denounced
him to the Inquisition, and is told to bring along his painting equipment.
After a threatening exchange with the Inquisitor's messenger, who asks
whether El Greco's parents might have been schismatics, since they
were Greeks, El Greco thinks of his friend Cazalla, whose brother was
executed at the Inquisition's command. But he is informed that he is
merely to paint the Grand Inquisitor's portrait. The novella consists of
a series of conversations between El Greco and the Grand Inquisitor
during the sittings, between El Greco and Cazalla, who has come to
Seville to treat the Grand Inquisitor, and between the Grand Inquisitor
and Cazalla. As the portrait develops into that of a "holy hangman,"

the fanaticism of the Inquisitor becomes clearer and clearer, and against this fanaticism and the fear it inspires, only the physician Cazalla and the artist El Greco represent the voices of reason and mercy. Although Andres was no historian, his portrayal of El Greco's Inquisitor Nino de Guevara is probably the most subtle portrait of an inquisitor in all literature, and *El Greco Paints the Grand Inquisitor* fully explores the puzzling contrasts of humanitarianism and the use of terror in religious and political sensibilities that produce both the painter and his subject.

In Andres' novella, the particular tenets of anti-Semitism are subordinated to a general humanism of which *The Inquisition* appeared to have been the enemy. Andres' great strength was his willingness to dispense with the traditional trappings of Inquisition allegory. The Grand Inquisitor Guevara is never seen except alone or with a few people. In one striking episode, as Cazalla is treating him, Guevara makes the point of telling an assistant that if he dies during the treatment, it is purely a pathological phenomenon and not to be attributed to human agency. The only procession of penitents in the novella is observed by El Greco alone at a window. All of the material in the Inquisition myth that so fascinated other novelists, dramatists, and composers is absent from Andres' work. There are only individuals speaking to each other, thinking alone, and painting or curing. And yet Andres' treatment of the subject is by far the more artistically satisfying.

Andres displayed considerable ambivalence, a love–hate relationship, with Catholicism. A Catholic humanist, Andres attempted to separate the institutionalized and persecuting Church from a more authentic religion of love and mercy. Andres indicts his own Catholicism as much as he does the mentality of the Grand Inquisitor as an allegory of twentieth-century state power:

> Witnesses of the Cross have appeared seldom, and we have seen instead: the executioners of God's judgments, organizers of salvation, moral policemen, traders in souls, temple capitalists, clerical dwarfs, fetishists of sacramentals, and pensioners of eternity.

Just as twentieth-century peoples failed to pierce the humanitarian rhetoric of those whom they permitted politically to enslave them, so Andres' Catholic church was so self-satisfied that it was unable to prevent a political inquisition from reviving the older inquisitions.

As arresting and dramatic as was the conversion of Lawrence and the metaphors of Zamyatin, Kesten, and Andres, even they realized that the mechanical revival of *The Inquisition* had limited applicability to twentieth-century totalitarian regimes. The twentieth century was not the fifteenth or sixteenth, and the historical studies of inquisitions that had begun in the late nineteenth century weakened the old power of the myth. For the most part, later novelists who took up the theme tended to use *The Inquisition* and inquisitor-figures rather as primitive evolutionary stages of twentieth-century political culture in its most fearsome aspects rather than as direct metaphors. This is the treatment of the theme in the novels of Arthur Koestler and George Orwell.

Five years after Kesten's and Andres' Inquisition allegories, in 1941, Arthur Koestler's *Darkness at Noon* invoked the Inquisition myth in the name of political and ideological oppression in a nameless modern state. Koestler did not name the Soviet Union, but it is clear that his work was a reflection on the Purge Trials in Russia during the 1930s and it introduced into mid-twentieth century culture the person and perspective of the political prisoner. Jail and torture became the natural setting of humanity, and the absolute dogmas of a ruling ideology dictated the treatment and state of human beings.

To introduce the protagonist Rubashov's meditation on his own earlier party activities and the work of the earlier inquisitors, Koestler uses as an epigraph a text from the fifteenth-century conciliarist Dietrich von Niem's treatise *On Schism* of 1411, indicating the freedom of the Church from the normal moral obligations when its survival is threatened:

> We resembled the great Inquisitors in that we persecuted the seeds of evil not only in men's deeds, but in their thoughts.

Similar religious imagery is used by Rubashov's interrogator Ivanov. Ivanov explains the theology of instrumental reason that dictates the circumstances of his and Rubashov's world in religious terms:

> *Apage Satanas.* . . . In the old days, temptation was of carnal nature. Now it takes the form of pure reason. Satan . . . is thin, ascetic and a fanatical devotee of logic. He reads Machiavelli, Ignatius of Loyola, Marx and Hegel; he is cold and unmerciful to mankind, out of a kind of mathematical mercifulness. He is damned always to do that which is most repugnant to him: to become a slaughterer, in order to abolish slaughtering, to sacrifice lambs so that no more lambs may be slaughtered, to whip people with knouts so that they may learn not to let themselves be whipped, to strip himself of every scruple in the name of a higher scrupulousness, and to challenge the hatred of mankind because of his love for it—an abstract and geometric love.

The passage echoes Dostoievsky, Lawrence, and Zamyatin. Linking the new instrumental rationality with a reversal of the temptations of Christ by Satan has by now become a conventional *topos* in the uses of the

Inquisition myth. From anti-Catholic polemic to the Enlightenment invention of Inquisition allegory and its invocation by nineteenth-century romantic political writers, the work of Andres and Koestler has developed the figure of the inquisitor into that of the geometric and scrupulous agent of an absolutist ideology, and the earlier religious persecutions are now regarded as premature and amateurish attempts to control life as now it finally can be controlled.

Koestler's Rubashov and Ivanov are old revolutionaries; they remember the world before the Revolution, and they dimly remember the historical past, and so Ivanov, Rubashov, and Koestler himself can invoke images of the inquisitions and expect to have them recognized by their interlocutors or readers. Gletkin, the new man of the Revolution, has no need of history or of inquisition myths, since he lives in a world that does not require historical imagery in order to define itself in its own eyes or in the eyes of others.

George Orwell, a reader and friend of Koestler who empathized with much of Koestler's pessimism, used faint echoes of the inquisition in his work. Orwell's own life and thought had made him sympathetic to socialist revolutionary movements and hostile to the capitalist, class-bound society of England and France. But Orwell's growing disillusion with Communism in the Spanish Civil War and later in the Soviet Union itself, and his unique ability to see the similarities as well as the differences among ideologically opposed kinds of modern state, led him to take a broader and more cynical view of twentieth-century options. He grew impatient with conventional means of condemning the misuse of state power and sought new forms and images to advance his polemic.

A theme that emerges fully in the 1946 novel *Coming Up for Air* is sounded early in a 1939 review of N. de Basily's book *Russia Under Soviet Rule:*

> The terrifying thing about modern dictatorships is that they are something entirely unprecedented. Their end cannot be foreseen. In the past every tyranny was sooner or later overthrown, or at least resisted, because of "human nature" which as a matter of course desired liberty. But we cannot be at all certain that "human nature" is constant. It may be just as possible to produce a breed of men who do not wish for liberty as to produce a breed of hornless cows. The Inquisition failed, but then the Inquisition had not the resources of the modern State. The radio, press-censorship, standardized education and the secret police have altered everything. Mass-suggestion is a science of the last twenty years, and we do not know yet how successful it will be.

Although Orwell's knowledge of the inquisition seems to have come chiefly from general information, he is known to have read and commented briefly on Elphège Vacandard's history of the Inquisition, which had been published in French in 1906 and reprinted several times since. It was translated into English in 1908. Orwell was suspicious of Vacandard's Catholic account ("It is a Catholic history, so you can be sure that you're getting, so to speak, the minimum of everything"), but his view of the Inquisition indicates that he knew some of the limitations of the myth for twentieth-century purposes. In 1944 Orwell wrote that modern collectivism is not inherently democratic, "but, on the contrary, gives to a tyrannical majority such powers as the Spanish Inquisitors never dreamed of." As it was for Koestler, the Inquisition, even the myth of the Inquisition, was becoming less relevant for twentieth-century polemic.

In spite of his somewhat conventional anti-Catholicism and his occasional use of some of the old myths about the inquisitions, Orwell was not a romantic political idealist who might invoke a mythical past institution in order to stimulate the liberty-loving present. Rather, in his masterpiece, *1984*, he discards the past as a standard by which to measure the atrocities of the present: "Even the Catholic Church of the Middle Ages was tolerant by modern standards." When Orwell's protagonist O'Brien does mention the inquisitions, he is contemptuous of them:

> You have read of the religious persecutions of the past. In the Middle Ages there was the Inquisition. It was a failure. It set out to eradicate heresy and ended by perpetuating it. For every heretic it burned at the stake, thousands of others rose up. Why was that? Because the Inquisition killed its enemies in the open, and killed them while they were still unrepentant; in fact, it killed them because they were repentant. Men were dying because they would not abandon their true beliefs. Naturally, all glory belonged to the victim and all the shame to the Inquisitor who burned him.

The new horror state has a sharper purpose and better means, and consequently the Inquisition is relegated to the dustbin of history, a history that itself will soon be utterly eliminated. For Orwell, Lawrence's and Zamyatin's metaphor is no longer adequate to contain the horrors of the present and the even greater horrors of the possible future. In the wake of Fascism and the Holocaust the anti-Semitism of the early Spanish Inquisition appeared paltry and inefficient; in the wake of examples of total state control, other Inquisitions appeared arbitrary and worked on far too small a scale to be interesting. Perhaps the work of the historians was beginning to place earlier inquisitions in a comprehensible scale of purpose and effectiveness. Orwell's brief notes on his reading of Vacandard certainly give that impression. As an institutional model for the totalitarian state, *The Inquisition* and the Grand Inquisitor had disappeared from the political novel by the 1950s.

In the work of Andres, however, another legacy of Dostoievsky had been caught: that of *The Inquisition* as a metaphor for mind. Without displaying any of the inquisition's apparatus, Andres, like Dostoievsky, had displayed its greatest consequences, not in the *autos-de-fé*, the tortures, or the vast social power it possessed, but in its power to shape a particular kind of mentality in those whom it touched. This metaphor, more durable because less mechanical, came to life brilliantly in Jerzy Andrzejewski's 1957 novel *Ciemnosci Kryja Ziemie* (A *Darkness Covers the Earth*). The 1960 English translation is entitled *The Inquisitors*.

The novel is set in Spain between 1485 and 1498. Its central character is Diego Manente, a young Dominican who is taken up by Torquemada and slowly turned from his original liberal piety and kindness into a formidable inquisitor, one so dedicated that he outdoes his own teacher. Early in the novel, which is narrated by a voice purporting to retell extracts from "an old Spanish chronicle," Torquemada provides a rationalization of *The Inquisition*:

> What can man achieve when he is left to his own devices? The kingdom of God, my son, has not yet penetrated the consciousness of men. Does this mean that humanity will not win salvation? No. It's necessary to bring salvation to people against their will. For a long time to come it will be necessary to nurse human consciousness: to destroy in it everything that's evil or that's delaying the advent of the kingdom of God. Don't you understand, my son, that men have to be guided and ruled? That's our task. This great burden rests on our shoulders in the Holy Office.

Diego's consciousness, too, is nursed. Surprised by the humanitarian tolerance and tireless devotion of Torquemada, Diego begins his own conversion, lacking the will and the ability to resist such a force. He makes his own hesitant first denunciation, then he denounces a former friend in his old convent. At the end of the novel, Torquemada falls gravely ill, experiences a hallucinatory conversation with the Devil, and at the end repents, begging Diego to begin the destruction of the Inquisition. Diego, however, turns on his master, disgustedly striking the face of Torquemada's corpse, and prepares to assume his former teacher's role.

Although Andrzejewski's novel contains a number of scenes of the inquisitors at work, overcoming popular resistance, and conducting trials, its action is primarily upon the mind of Diego. In the work of Lawrence,

Zamyatin, Kesten and other novelists, the apparatus of *The Inquisition* as a metaphor of cynical social control had been the chief purpose of reviving the myth. But in the work of Andres and Andrzejewski, the apparatus and the external role of *The Inquisition* are subordinated to the problem of *the inquisitorial mind.* In this respect Andres and Andrzejewski have universalized a problem, drawing on one of the many strands of thought in Dostoievsky's complex creation, "rereading" *The Grand Inquisitor* to strike a deeper significance than had their predecessors: not the impact of the twentieth century and its ideologies on the body politic or the body human, but on personality itself is their study.

The external use of *The Inquisition* in fiction has generally ceased, and it is unlikely that it will return, since the late twentieth century now understands both its own and more remote history more clearly and painfully than it did half a century ago. Utopian fiction now draws upon its own imagination, stimulated by events that make even the old *Inquisition* pale by comparison. Some of the myth survives in historical fiction, but not very successfully, not even in the deft and mercurial games of a novel like *The Name of the Rose*, whose inquisitor, identified as the historical figure Bernard Gui, is actually a composite of a myth created several centuries after the early fourteenth century period in which the action of the novel is set. The character of Bernard Gui is simply Umberto Eco's tour de force at recreating another Torquemada or Pedro Arbués out of nineteenth-century fiction, and he is neither a cautionary figure for the twentieth century nor a historically accurate reconstruction of any fourteenth-century inquisitor.

In this sense, Dostoievsky's creation has run its course. But in a deeper sense, that which focuses upon the creation of a certain kind of mind, the legacy of the great Russian novelist has not been exhausted, nor is it likely to be. Great fiction works far less well as a social program than it does in its own natural element, the human mind and personality. Dostoievsky, Andres, Andrzejewski and even Orwell on occasion, have found in *The Inquisition*, not a metaphor for politics, but one for personality. And that too is part of Dostoievsky's universalizing of a western European myth in order to lay bare, not the perversions of western power, but the dangerous transformation of the western soul.

Political "Inquisitions" and "Witch-Hunts" in the Twentieth Century

Other writers besides novelists, however, focused public attention on the behavior of governments by drawing analogies with the myth of

The Inquisition, particularly in the United States after the Second World War. With *The Inquisition* they also used a distinctly North American reference, one that pointed to the late seventeenth-century witch persecutions in colonial New England, mythologized as *Witch-Hunts* and applied, with *The Inquisition*, to the activities of a number of governmental agencies and Congressional investigatory bodies. Although some of the inspiration for such metaphors surely came from the tradition of twentieth-century political fiction, much of it came from a distinctly American intellectual experience, one that differed from that of European novelists and historians.

Aside from the historical work of Lea, most Americans derived their knowledge of inquisition history from lively confessional polemic and the ideological histories of such writers as Prescott and John Lothrop Motley, as well as from occasional works of fiction, notably those of Poe. To most people in the United States, even those who did not read Poe, hear Verdi, or see the paintings of Goya, *The Inquisition* was a stock item of faith and fear. Besides confessional appeal it possessed political appeal as well, standing for the unnatural alliance of throne and altar that was anathema to a democratic society. For those who did read Poe and Dostoievsky—and Hawthorne—inquisitions and witch-hunts both were lively metaphors for religion and civil authority employed with fanatic zeal and carelessness.

In the United States, far more than in Europe, *The Inquisition* remained an evil abstraction, sustained by anti-Catholicism and supported by political opposition. The witch-hunts of colonial North America fared little better; they, too, found no defenders, and, like the inquisitions, they represented a past from which the United States had escaped. By the end of the First World War, little change in the images of both inquisitions and witch-hunts had taken place in the United States. Extensive research into the phenomenon of witch beliefs and persecutions, in spite of the pioneering work of Lea himself and the German archivist Joseph Hansen, did not begin until the 1960s.

The European political writers who took up the theme of the Grand Inquisitor and inquisitions in general and applied them to political phenomena in Europe from the First World War on—Lawrence, Zamyatin, Kesten, Andres, Koestler, and Orwell—came from a historical tradition that routinely encompassed more of Europe's past than did that of American writers at the same period. The United States had its Inquisition history second hand and at a great temporal and geographic distance. Even its own witch trials of the late seventeenth century seemed remote and archaic to Americans caught up in the traumatic modernization of society from 1914 to 1932. During the Red Scare of 1919–1920, for example, neither the polemic of the leftists nor that of the liberal defenders of the victims of local and federal governmental prosecution appear to have invoked images either of inquisitions or of witch-hunts. In spite of the substantial and dangerous steps that American society and government had taken in curtailing civil liberties from World War I on— extensive treason, espionage, and sedition legislation and litigation, a new and omnipresent insistence on loyalty to the state in all occupations, and widespread claims of the existence of "hidden" political enemies in the teaching profession and in union organizations—the language in which these actions and their consequences was criticized was that of constitutional reference. For example, in 1920, when the National Popular Government League issued its report on *Illegal Practices of the Department of Justice*, the report attacked extremist government practices during the Red Scare of 1919–1920, but its language hewed closely to that of the Constitution, citing particularly violations of the Fourth, Fifth, and Eighth Amendments. Other critics accused government officials of trying to "Prussianize" government and society, or of launching a "White Terror."

At the same time, the government itself built a large and irregular investigative apparatus on a national and local level, first in its well-publicized campaign against violent criminals during 1933–1935, and later in the process of Nazi-hunting. Until well into the 1940s the expression "police state" was reserved in American usage for Germany, Italy, and the Soviet Union. The Wickersham Report of 1931 criticizing American police methods spoke only of "the third degree." As yet, *Inquisition* and *Witch-Hunt* were terms not commonly in use in the United States.

During the three decades following 1920, however, both terms appeared frequently in American criticism of some governmental activities, and by 1950 they had become commonplace. This was in part the result of a process of popularizing the images of *Inquisition* and *Witch-Hunt* and in part the influence of the work of European writers and their timely rereading of Dostoievsky.

This new popularization may be traced in drama and film, in popular histories and novels, and in the adaptation by journalists and social scientists of images first developed by gifted and perceptive writers of fiction. In 1920, the same year in which the National Popular Government League report appeared, Joan of Arc was canonized. Over the next several decades several works dealing with Joan's career appeared, beginning the modern fascination with her life and its lessons for the twentieth century. In 1923 George Bernard Shaw's *Saint Joan* was first performed, creating an image of the heroic saint and depicting an inquisitorial hearing, although Shaw represented the inquisitorial trial of Joan as a rational and fair proceeding. At the same time, inquisitorial tribunals began to appear in film. One of the earliest representations of *The Inquisition* on film was that in Carl Dreyer's 1919 film, *Blade af Satans Bog* (*Leaves from Satan's Book*), Dreyer's own imitation of D. W. Griffith's earlier film *Intolerance*, with the addition of an inquisition. The depiction of an inquisition in Dreyer's 1919 film was considerably expanded and detailed in his 1928 film, *The Passion of Joan of Arc*. Dreyer's inquisitors, unlike Shaw's, were human monsters. The film opens with a close-up of the trial manuscript itself and then cuts to Joan, played by the actress Falconetti in the most powerful portrayal of a tortured saint in all of cinema. The power of the medium and Dreyer's relentless examination of an inquisitorial trial brought *The Inquisition* to life in a way that no polemic or novel ever had, with the possible exception of Verdi's and Dostoievsky's work.

From the 1920s on, drama and film were joined by a large number of popular histories and literature containing accounts both of inquisitions and of witch trials.

Besides the 1908 English translation of Vacandard, there appeared in 1920 A. S. Turberville's critical history, and in 1928 the English translation of Jean Guiraud's work, *The Medieval Inquisition*. In 1929 the pugnacious G. G. Coulton published his own *The Inquisition*. A number of these works integrated the history of heresy and inquisition into the broader history of medieval and early modern Europe, began to study its social and economic roots, and described it in the new discourse of social science history, which created a considerable opportunity for comparisons—often naively reductionist—across time and space. At the same time, the still youthful discipline of anthropology began to come to the attention of intellectuals, sometimes in peculiar dress. In 1921 Margaret Murray published *The Witch Cult in Western Europe*, a widely read and discussed thesis that European witchcraft was the survival of pre-Christian cults of Diana. Almost two decades later, in 1939, there appeared the American edition of the eloquent nineteenth-century French historian Jules Michelet's *Satanism and Witchcraft*, which depicted those accused of witchcraft as popular rebels against a corrupt and archaic regime.

In 1929 George Lyman Kittredge's *Witchcraft in Old and New England* linked what had hitherto been the specifically local European and North American phenomena with the practices of peoples in different parts of the world. The work of Murray and Kittredge brought the image—and the problem—of witchcraft well to the fore of public familiarity. Montague Summers published seven books on witchcraft, vampirism, and were-wolves between 1926 and 1946, and added translations into English of key works from the period of the witchcraft persecutions, notably the *Hammer of Witches* in 1948; his enormous productivity brought these subjects too before a wide literate audience, whom they fascinated.

In 1938 a Works Progress Administration project in Essex County, Massachusetts, produced a large typescript transcription of the witchcraft trials at Salem Village in 1692, opening the difficult old records to new readers. In 1949 Marion L. Starky's very readable and popular *The Devil in Massachusetts* relied on these documents to produce a popular and widely read history of the trials.

Galileo also joined Joan of Arc and the Salem witches. As early as 1933, the six-hundredth anniversary of his trial, the German playwright Bertolt Brecht conceived of writing a play based upon the trial and submission of Galileo. Brecht wrote his first version of the play in exile in Denmark in 1938–1939, and it was performed in Zurich in 1943. In 1941 Brecht arrived in the United States, and a few years later began to revise and translate the play for an American production, in collaboration with the actor Charles Laughton and other friends. Brecht's *Galileo* is a puzzling play, not least in its treatment of Galileo and the Inquisition. In the first version, Galileo appears as the hero of science fighting obscurantism and religious authority in the name of the human spirit. Such a vision was not uncommon in the Galileo tradition. Between 1939 and 1945 Brecht transformed his central figure into a different Galileo, a self-indulgent gourmand whose uncontrollable appetites led him to defy authority, capitulate, and destroy his daughter. The new Galileo is an enemy of the people, for he uses his discoveries for his own ends and glory, not in the service of humanity. In the Laughton version of the play, the Inquisition, although present, is far closer to that of Shaw: it condemns Galileo in proper form, on legitimate grounds. Like the Inquisition of the early Gothic novels, its power is necessary.

Brecht was not the only German writer in exile in the United States to concern himself with the inquisitions. During the late 1940s the German novelist and playwright Lion Feuchtwanger began work on his drama *Wahn oder der Teufel in Boston* (*The Devil in Boston*), first produced in 1952. Feuchtwanger had read the works of Cotton Mather and was particularly struck by what seemed to him the contrast between Mather's learning and his passion for persecution. Feuchtwanger turned his account of the Salem Village trials into a parable of Cold War repression, but he also took up the topic of inquisition history from another angle in his novel *Goya*, begun in 1943 but not published until 1951 (English title, *This Is the Hour*).

Feuchtwanger not only expounds upon the Spanish Inquisition extensively in Part II of *Goya*, but he also mythologizes Goya himself, making the painter the great artist who captures the spirit of revolution and opposition to a decadent ruler and to the Spanish Inquisition and emerges unscathed. Feuchtwanger's *Goya* in English translation was an enormous popular success in the United States. Although an American film project did not materialize, it was made into a film in East Germany in 1971, and the book was subsequently translated into twenty-four languages. Through Feuchtwanger's influence alone, both the Spanish Inquisition and Goya became extremely familiar to Americans and others from 1951 on.

American concern for civil liberties and intellectual freedom was reviving, and now the terms "Inquisition" and "witch-hunt," used by Feuchtwanger and others, were much more widely used.

In 1950 Carey McWilliams published his *Witch-Hunt: The Revival of Heresy*, a study of the activities of the House Un-American Activities Committee and the early career of Sen. Joseph McCarthy, in which McWilliams invoked the metaphors of "heresy," "the Inquisition," and "witchcraft" as a master-key to understanding the current American hysteria centered on anti-Communism. McWilliams used recent social science research for his socio-psychological analysis, and he cited an abundance of recent historical studies to justify the metaphor. In 1973 McWilliams' metaphorical political sociology was updated to the year 1960 and even more elaborately developed in Cedric Belfrage's *The American Inquisition, 1945–1960* and echoed as late as 1982 in Stanley Kutler's *The American Inquisition: Justice and Injustice in the Cold War*. McWilliams' influential metaphor became widely popular, is still used in common speech, and proved sturdy and appealing enough to invite Belfrage, Kutler, and others to re-use it in later works.

In spite of its novel title, the first two parts of McWilliams' *Witch-Hunt* of 1950 are generally straightforward liberal criticisms of the policies of Congress, the courts, and government agencies in a series of specific cases. Book Three, however, "The Strategy of Satan," is an extensive essay in psychosociology that lays out a typology of social fear and a typology of the mechanisms that societies use to deal with it. McWilliams himself terms his essay "the sociology of heresy," drawing heavily on much of the literature since 1920 discussed above, also drawing precise and provocative analogies—even identities—between early European persecutions of heretics and witches and contemporary American social and political procedures. The victims on the left are identified with the heretics, as both heroes and victims, while the institutions and social temper that prosecuted them are identified with the Inquisition and the society that supported its activities. Although McWilliams' knowledge of the history and character of the inquisitions was superficial, and his sociology overgeneralized, he created in popular usage the very terms "inquisition" and "witch-hunt" as bywords—at least in a large and vociferous part of the American political community—for the anticommunist movement of the late 1940s and 1950s.

Like some early twentieth-century novelists, McWilliams was chiefly concerned with the external and ideological similarities of inquisitions, witch-hunts, and contemporary governmental investigative procedures. But the playwright Arthur Miller, in the same intellectual climate and with similar political views, chose to focus, as had Andres, Feuchtwanger, and others, on the effects of such a climate on human personality.

Miller's *The Crucible*, a play dramatizing the Salem Village witch trials of 1692, was produced in New York in 1953. Miller later observed that he had long known about the New England witchcraft phenomenon, and had been interested in it well before he wrote the play. Americans of Miller's generation had recently come to know rather a lot about the witch trials of New England, particularly with the increased availability of easily readable records after 1938 and the enormous popularity of Marion Starky's *The Devil in Massachusetts* in 1949. But by 1952 that general interest was easily alignable with political and ethical concerns, as it had been for McWilliams. Miller himself pointed out that:

> It was not only the rise of "McCarthyism" that moved me, but something which seemed much more weird and mysterious. It was the fact that a political, objective, knowledgeable campaign from the far Right was capable of creating not only a terror, but a new subjective reality, a veritable mystique which was gradually assuming even a holy resonance. . . . I had known of the Salem witch hunt for many years before "McCarthyism" had arrived, and it had always remained an inexplicable darkness to me. When I looked into it now, however, it was the contemporary situation at my back, particularly the mystery of the handing over of conscience, which seemed to me the central and informing fact of the time. . . . I saw accepted the notion that conscience was no longer a private matter but one of state administration.

Miller decided that some element of personal guilt must have inspired both the persecutions and the capitulations, and in his dramatization of the Salem trials he focused upon the manipulation, by ruthless judges and terrified and envious neighbors, of the guilt felt by an otherwise heroic victim.

Miller's remarks of 1958 bear a striking resemblance to those of D. H. Lawrence of 1930. A topic or episode, long known but little understood or sympathized with, suddenly becomes an explanatory device for a profound dilemma and affords meaning and appropriate symbols that until then had been lacking. McWilliams found this in 1950, Miller in 1952. McWilliams used comparative sociology and popular history to draw the analogy; Miller saw it in the dramatic conflicts between individuals, between individuals and communities, and in the power of officials to make purely personal guilt serve public ends. With these two works, two years apart, the United States had acquired an image for understanding its own recent experience of Cold War hysteria, that of the Inquisition and its historic accretions. Neither McWilliams nor Miller was without his critics, nor had Brecht been. But outrage at McWilliams' bad history and sociology or at Miller's "distortions" of history and misreading the location of moral virtue in both Salem and Washington did not prevent the wider use of "inquisitions" and "witch-hunts" in the common language and common mentality of Americans.

Both imaginative literature and mass media have shaped the late twentieth-century usage of such terms as *Inquisition* and *Witch-Hunt*. They have inspired diverse products: L. Cepair and S. Englund have written of *The Inquisition in Hollywood* (referring to the blacklisting of a number of film professionals, not the films of Mel Brooks). Cedric Belfrage's *American Inquisition, 1945–1960* takes the popularization process a step further. For Belfrage, *Inquisition* is no longer a metaphor, as it had been for McWilliams and Stanley Kutler, but something identical to American governmental activities during the period he writes about. For Belfrage, the metaphor no longer mediates: the House Committee on Un-American Activities and Senator McCarthy *are The Inquisition*. Belfrage's justification for his assertion may be seen in an examination of two repositories of common knowledge and linguistic usage, two dictionaries.

The Random House American College Dictionary of 1959, its definitions little changed from the edition of 1947, defines *inquisition* as follows:

> 1. An act of inquiring; inquiry; research.   2. an investigation, or process of inquiry.   3. an inquiry conducted by judicial officers or such non-judicial officers as coroners.   4. the finding of such an inquiry.   5. the document embodying the result of such inquiry.   6. (*cap.*) *Rom. Cath. Ch.* a special tribunal (officially the *Holy Office*) for the defense of Catholic teaching in faith and morals,

the judgement of heresy, the application of canonical punishment, and the judgement of mixed marriages and the Pauline privileges.

This definition is consistent with other early and mid-twentieth century English dictionaries, indicating primacy of meaning to neutral or technically legal senses, and considering the special Roman Catholic usage with neutrality and politeness. In *The Random House Dictionary of the English Language* of 1966, however, the dictionary cited by Belfrage, the definition is very different:

> 1. an official investigation, esp. one of a political or religious nature, characterized by lack of regard for individual rights, prejudice on the part of the examiners, and recklessly cruel punishments. 2. any harsh or prolonged questioning. 3. act of inquiring; inquiry; research. 4. an investigation, or process of inquiry 5. a judicial or official inquiry. 6. the finding of such an inquiry. 7. the document embodying the result of such inquiry. 8. (*cap.*) *Rom. Cath. Ch.* the special tribunal established in the thirteenth century and active until early modern times, engaged chiefly in combatting and punishing heresy.

The Inquisition of twentieth-century mythology has become the definition of *inquisition* in a respected and widely used dictionary, and its special Roman Catholic sense no longer includes the defense of faith and morals, mixed marriages, or the Pauline privileges. The difference between the two definitions is not that of the seven years between the two editions of *The Random House Dictionary*, but of the difference in American usage of the term *inquisition* between the end of the Second World War and the present. In the current state of its history, both inquisitions and *The Inquisition* have managed to find a place in the same dictionary entry. History and myth, even now, refuse to be separated.

Literary Inquisition: A Bibliographical Essay

No single bibliography can contain adequate references to all of the matters touched on in this book. I have tried to indicate the best recent historical accounts and the best bibliographies dealing with the subjects treated above, chapter by chapter. I have tried to omit nothing concerning inquisitions or *The Inquisition*, although I have not been able to list literature on the larger questions touched upon in this book.

Where bibliographical references tend not to be readily available, I have extended my own bibliographical coverage here in some areas far more than in others. This unevenness is the result of omissions in some modern scholarly literature. Even to select from the immense literature on the later Middle Ages, the Spanish Inquisition, the Reformation, the rise of religious toleration, the Enlightenment, Gothic and sentimental fiction, nineteenth-century uses of *The Inquisition*, and twentieth-century political consciousness has been a trying task. What is not included here will generally be found in one of the works referred to in the pages that follow.

Introduction (pp. 1–10)

The most convenient introduction to modern ideas of political mythology is that of Leonard Thompson, *The Political Mythology of Apartheid* (New Haven, 1985). See also Henry Tudor, *Political Mythology* (London, 1972).

Ernst Cassirer, *The Myth of the State* (New Haven, 1946) is also the subject of a collection of related papers, Haralds Biezais, ed., *The Myth of the State* (Stockholm, 1971). See František Graus, *Lebendige Vergangenheit* (Cologne and Vienna, 1975), and Leon Poliakov, *The Aryan Myth: A History of Racist and Nationalist Ideas in Europe* (New York, 1977).

Alan Ryan's remarks are from his review of Thompson in the *Times Literary Supplement*, December 13, 1985.

There are several accounts of related phenomena in Eric Hobsbawm and Terence Ranger, eds., *The Invention of Tradition* (Cambridge, 1983).

The only recent general account of inquisition history is the short work by Edward Burman, *The Inquisition: Hammer of Heresy* (Wellingborough, 1984). Ch. 14 deals very briefly with some of the themes treated in the second half of this book.

Chapter 1. The Law of Rome and the Latin Christian Church (pp. 11–39)

The best general account of Roman law is that of W. W. Buckland, *A Text-Book of Roman Law from Augustus to Justinian*, 3rd. ed., rev. by Peter Stein (Cambridge, 1975). There are shorter accounts of the appearance of inquisitorial procedure in John Crook, *The Law and Life of Rome* (Ithaca, 1967) and A. H. M. Jones, *The Criminal Courts of the Roman Republic and Principate* (New Jersey, 1972).

The *Digest* of Justinian has recently been newly translated under the editorship of Alan Watson, *The Digest of Justinian*, 4 vols. (Philadelphia, 1985).

An up-to-date bibliography of the emergence of the concept of heresy in the early Christian communities is contained in Edward Peters, *Heresy and Authority in Medieval Europe* (Philadelphia, 1980). The most ambitious general history of the period is Hubert Jedin and John Dolan, eds., *Handbook of Church History*, Vols. 1 and 2 (Freiburg and London, New York, 1965, 1980). On doctrine, see Jaroslav Pelikan, *The Christian Tradition*, Vol. 1, *The Emergence of the Catholic Tradition (100–600)* (Chicago, 1971).

For matters of ecclesiastical discipline, I have relied heavily upon the early chapters of Henri Maisonneuve, *Études sur les origines de l'inquisition* (Paris, 1960), a work that has also guided me in Ch. 2.

On early medieval inquests and inquisitorial procedure, see Julius Goebel, *Felony and Misdemeanor* (rpt. Philadelphia, 1976) and François Louis Ganshof, *Frankish Institutions under Charlemagne* (New York, 1970).

Chapter 2. Dissent, Heterodoxy, and the Medieval Inquisitorial Office (pp. 40–74)

The most thorough general history is Henry C. Lea, *A History of the Inquisition of the Middle Ages*, 3 vols. (New York, 1887), reprinted many times since its publication, abridged one-volume edition edited by M. Nicholson (New York, 1961), extracts concerning legal procedure published separately and edited by Walter Ullmann (London, 1963; New York, 1969). Lea's perspective led him to posit a considerably more centralized and organized "Inquisition" than recent scholarship has allowed. Bernard Hamilton, *The Medieval Inquisition* (New York, 1981) tends to follow Lea's argument. The present book does not, nor does Richard Kieckhefer, *Repression of Heresy in Medieval Germany* (Philadelphia, 1979).

There is an extensive bibliography of both heresy and inquisition in Carl T. Berkhout and Jeffrey B. Russell, *Medieval Heresies: A Bibliography, 1960–1979*, Pontifical Institute of Medieval Studies, Subsidia Mediaevalia 11 (Toronto, 1981), esp. pp. 142–152. Edward Peters, *Heresy and Authority*, has several chapters on the period and its problems. Walter L. Wakefield and Austin P. Evans, *Heresies of the High Middle Ages* (New York, 1969) is the most extensive collection of documents in translation.

Two collections of essays contain indispensable material: Jacques Le Goff, ed., *Hérésies et sociétés dans l'Europe pré-industrielle, lle–18e siècles* (Paris and The Hague, 1968), and W. Lourdaux and D. Verhelst, eds., *The Concept of Heresy in the Middle Ages (11th–13th C.)*, Mediaevalia Lovaniensia, Series I, Studia IV (Leuven and The Hague, 1976). R. I. Moore, *The Formation of a Persecuting Society* (Oxford and New York, 1987), contains an important assertion that between the tenth and the thirteenth centuries Christian Europe became a persecuting society that shaped later forms of state and ecclesiastical persecution down to the twentieth century. Moore regards the activities of medieval inquisitors less as introducing forms of law in place of mob violence than as a manifestation of the power of central authority. Moore's work and the present book differ in emphasis, but *The Formation of a Persecuting Society* is essential for the period.

The short work by Albert Clement Shannon, O.S.A., *The Medieval Inquisition* (Washington, D.C., 1983) offers a recent scholarly Catholic interpretation. Some of the new range of studies on medieval heresy and inquisitorial practices are brilliantly illustrated by R. I. Moore, *The Origins of European Dissent* (rpt. Oxford, 1985), and Brian Stock, *The Implications of Literacy: Written Language and Models of Interpretation in the Eleventh and Twelfth Centuries* (Princeton, 1983), Part 2 of Stock's work deals with the emergence of heresies as "textual communities," alternative forms of spiritual association centered upon a particular written text and its teacher.

Henri Maisonneuve, *Études sur les origines de l'inquisition* is indispensable for the legal procedure, as is the collection of essays, *Le crédo, la morale, et l'inquisition*, Cahiers de Fanjeaux 6 (Toulouse, 1971), particularly the essay by Raoul Manselli, "De la *persuasio* à la *coercitio*," pp. 175–197. In the collection *The Concept of Heresy in the Middle Ages*, the study by Othmar Hageneder, "Der Häresie–Begriff bei den Juristen des 12. und 13. Jahrhunderts," pp. 42–103, is an important supplement to Maisonneuve, as is the study by Helmut G. Walter, "Häresie und päpstliche Politik: Ketzerbegriff und Ketzergesetzgebung in der übergangsphase von der Dekretistik zur Dekretalistik," pp. 104–143.

The manual for inquisitors at Carcassonne has been translated and studied in Walter L. Wakefield, *Heresy, Crusade and Inquisition in Southern France,*

1100–1250 (Berkeley and Los Angeles, 1974). There are a number of important studies of inquisitors in *Bernard Gui et son monde*, Cahiers de Fanjeaux 16 (Toulouse, 1981).

The long and complex story of the relation between the Cathars and the inquisition in Languedoc is best told by Élie Griffe, *Le Languedoc cathare et l'Inquisition (1229–1329)* (Paris, 1980).

On the history of torture, see Edward Peters, *Torture* (Oxford and New York, 1985). On the regionalization of methods of repression in early modern Europe, see William Monter, *Ritual, Myth and Magic in Early Modern Europe* (Athens, Ohio, 1983).

There is an extensive bibliographical survey of recent European research by Giovanni Gonnet, "Bibliographical Appendix: Recent European Historiography on the Medieval Inquisition," in Henningsen and Tedeschi, *The Inquisition in Early Modern Europe*, 199–223. Several important Latin texts are printed in Kurt Victor Selge, *Texte zur Inquisition* (Gutersloh, 1967).

On the semantic history of some key terms, see Theodor Bühler–Reimann, "Enquête—Inquesta—Inquisitio," *Zeitschrift der Savigny–Stiftung für Rechtsgeschichte, Kanonistische Abteilung* 92 (1975), pp. 53–62.

MAINTAINING RELIGIOUS UNIFORMITY IN ENGLAND, FRANCE, AND GERMANY

A large literature exists on late medieval religious life in England. The career and later historiographical reputation of John Wyclif has recently been summarized by Vaclav Mudroch, *The Wyclif Tradition*, ed. Albert Compton Reeves (Athens, Ohio, 1979). Of particular importance are the studies of Norman Tanner, *Heresy Trials in the Diocese of Norwich, 1428–31* (London, 1977), and *The Church in Late Medieval Norwich, 1370–1532* (Leiden, 1984). On the former work, see the important review article by Margaret Aston, "William White's Lollard Followers," *Catholic Historical Review* 68 (1982), pp. 469–497, John A. F. Thomson, *The Later Lollards, 1414–1520* (London, 1965).

Important studies by Margaret Aston bring the English scene into useful perspective: *Thomas Arundel: A Study of Church Life in the Reign of Richard II* (Oxford, 1967); *Lollards and Reformers: Images and Literacy in Late Medieval Religion* (London, 1984), esp. Chs. 7 and 8, the latter of which complements the study of Mudroch on the Reformation reputation of John Wyclif. In addition, see now Anne Hudson, *English Wycliffite Writings* (Cambridge, 1978), Peter McNiven, *Heresy and Politics in the Reign of Henry IV* (Suffolk and New Hampshire, 1987). Anthony Kenny, ed., *Wyclif in His Time* (Oxford, 1986) is a good introduction to the English theologian.

On the problem of Lollardy and its continuity, see A. G. Dickens, "Heresy and the Origins of English Protestantism," in A. G. Dickens, *Reformation Studies* (London, 1982), pp. 363–382.

For France, see Joseph R. Strayer, *The Reign of Philip the Fair* (Princeton, 1980), and for the Templars, the brilliant study of Peter Partner, *The Murdered Magicians: The Templars and Their Myth* (New York, 1982), a book that has served in many ways as a model for this one. On the Parlement, see J. H. Shennan, *The Parlement of Paris* (Ithaca, 1968).

The peasant Cathars in the Ariège have been studied in the well-known, but not entirely convincing work of Emmanuel LeRoy Ladurie, *Montaillou: The Promised Land of Error*, trans. Brabara Bray (New York, 1979). There is additional material in Peters, *Heresy and Authority*, Ch. 9. On early sixteenth-century Languedoc, see Raymond A. Mentzer, Jr., *Heresy Proceedings in Languedoc, 1500–1560* (Philadelphia, 1984).

On the role of universities, particularly that of Paris, see Guy Fitch Lytle, "Universities as Religious Authorities in the Later Middle Ages and Reformation," in Guy Fitch Lytle, ed., *Reform and Authority in the Medieval and Reformation Church* (Washington, 1981), pp. 69–98, and James K. Farge, *Orthodoxy and Reform in Early Reformation France: The Faculty of Theology of Paris, 1500–1543* (Leiden, 1985).

For Germany, see Richard Kieckhefer, *Repression of Heresy in Medieval Germany* (Philadelphia, 1979).

The most recent study of heresy and inquisition in Italy is the ongoing work of Mariano d'Alatri, of which one volume has so far appeared: *Erètici e Inquisitóri in Italia: Studi e documenti*, Vol. 1, *Il Duecènto* (Brindisi, 1986). Although d'Alatri's work covers only the thirteenth century, it is a mine of information on many of the subjects for the inquisitorial office generally in medieval Europe. The best general study in English is Brian Pullan, *A History of Early Renaissance Italy from the Mid-Thirteenth to the Mid-Fifteenth Century* (New York, 1973). A fourteenth century inquisitor's manual from Italy has been edited by Lorenzo Paolini, *Il "de officio inquisitoris." La procedura inquisitoriale a Bologna e a Ferrara nel Trecento* (Bologna, 1976).

On late medieval Bohemia, see the indispensable work of Alexander Patschovsky, *Die Anfänge einer ständigen Inquisition in Böhmen* (Berlin New York, 1975), and Patschovsky, *Quellen zur böhmischen Inquisition im 14. Jahrhundert* (Weimar, 1979).

Chapter 3. The Inquisitions in Iberia and the New World (pp. 75–104)

The greatest history of the Spanish Inquisition is still that of Henry C. Lea, *A History of the Inquisition in Spain*, 4 vols. (New York, 1906–1907), used by all subsequent historians. Most recently in English, see Henry Kamen, *Inquisition and Society in Spain in the Sixteenth and Seventeenth Centuries* (Bloomington, 1985).

From the late fifteenth century to the present, the most valuable bibliographical research tool for the history of the inquisitions is Emil van der Vekene, *Bibliotheca Bibliographica Historiae Sanctae Inquisitionis*, 2 vols. (Vaduz, 1982–1983). Van der Vekene's work lists 4,808 items concerning the inquisitions over a period of nearly five hundred years in all western languages. Its descriptive categories make its use far easier than most ambitious bibliographies. It should be consulted for all material in this book from 1500 on.

Several studies on the Spanish Middle Ages have greatly illuminated our knowledge of the troubled fifteenth century. See J. N. Hillgarth, *The Spanish Kingdoms [1250–1516]*, 2 vols. (Oxford, 1976, 1978), and Peter Linehan, *The Spanish Church and the Papacy in the Thirteenth Century* (Cambridge, 1971); Linehan, "The Spanish Church Revisited: the episcopal *gravamina* of 1279," in Brian Tierney and Peter Linehan, eds., *Authority and Power: Studies on Medieval Law and Government Presented to Walter Ullmann* (Cambridge, 1980), 127–148, and Linehan, "Religion and National Identity in Medieval Spain and Portugal," *Studies in Church History* 18 (1982), 161–199. These studies and others are collected in Peter Linehan, *Spanish Church and Society, 1150–1300* (London, 1983). A number of studies by Angus MacKay should also be consulted, notably his "Ritual and Propaganda in Fifteenth-Century Castile," *Past & Present* No. 107 (1985), and the other studies collected in MacKay, *Society, Economy and Religion in Late Medieval Castile* (London, 1987).

The reign of Henry IV in Castile has recently been intelligently reassessed by William D. Phillips, Jr., *Enrique IV and the Crisis of Fifteenth-Century Castile*, Speculum Anniversary Monographs Three (Cambridge, Mass., 1978). See also Téofilo Ruiz, "La Inquisición medieval y la moderna: paralelos y contrastes," in Angel Alcalá y otros, eds., *Inquisición española y mentalidad inquisitorial* (Barcelona, 1984)

Two classic works are Albert Sicroff, *Les controverses de statuts de 'pureté de sang' en Espagne du XVe au XVIIe siècle* (Paris, 1960), and Stephen Gilman, *The Spain of Francisco de Rojas: The Intellectual and Social Landscape of La Celestina* (Princeton, 1972).

The best study of "popular religion" is that of William A. Christian, Jr., *Local Religion in Sixteenth-Century Spain* (Princeton, 1981).

In the past decade, a number of individual and especially collaborative works have taken up the history of the Spanish Inquisition from the point at which Lea left it in 1909. In 1980 some of the initial results of the new research were published in a volume edited by Joaquín Pérez Villanueva, *La Inquisición Española. Nueva visión, nuevos horizontes* (Madrid, 1980). Drawing on the work of more than fifty specialists, Villanueva's collection reflected the entry of inquisitorial scholarship into modern historiographical method, as had the slightly earlier anthology of essays edited by Bartolomé Bennassar, *Inquisición española: Poder political y control social* (orig. French, Paris, 1978; Spanish, Barcelona, 1981). An international symposium on the Spanish Inquisition was held at Brooklyn College, New York, in 1983, and its proceedings have appeared as Angel Alcalá y otros, eds., *Inquisición española y mentalidad inquisitorial* (Barcelona, 1984).

The results of these different directions of research are summed up in the new multi-authored history of the inquisitions under the general editorship of

Joaquín Pérez Villanueva and Bartolomé Escandell Bonet, *Historia de la inquisición en España y América*, of which Volume 1 has so far appeared (Madrid, 1984).

At last, the modern historical study of the Spanish and other Mediterranean Inquisitions is being brought into comparative study. In October, 1985, under the direction of Professors Stephen Haliczer and John Tedeschi, Northern Illinois University and The Newberry Library in Chicago sponsored an important conference on the topic of *The Inquisition as Court and Bureaucracy*, which drew together Spanish, Italian, English, and American scholars, heralding the comparative study of the Mediterranean inquisitions as the next major step in the history of inquisitions.

Some of the papers from this conference are now available in Stephen Haliczer, ed., *Inquisition and Society in Early Modern Europe* (New Jersey, 1987). Of particular importance are the essays by Haliczer, Nicholas Davidson, and Jaime Contreras on Jews, heretics, and Protestants in Spain, Portugal, and Italy. The essays by Sara Nalle, Mary O'Neil, John Martin, Jean-Pierre Dedieu, and Mary Elizabeth Perry deal with the increasingly important subject of the inquisitions and popular culture. The concluding essay by Virgilio Pinto deals with censorship and thought control.

Another conference volume indicates the variety and quality of current research: Gustav Henningsen and John Tedeschi, with Charles Amiel, *The Inquisition in Early Modern Europe: Studies on Sources and Methods* (Dekalb, Illinois, 1986).

The most recent study of Spain in early modern history is that of R. A. Stradling, *Europe and the Decline of Spain: A Study of the Spanish System, 1580–1720* (London, 1981). The important works of J. H. Elliott, *Imperial Spain* (London, 1963), and John Lynch, *Spain under the Habsburgs*, 2 vols. (Oxford, 1969) are essential background.

Several review articles are useful: Antonio Marquez, "Estado actual de los estudios sobre la Inquisición," *Arbor* 396 (1978), 86–96; Gustav Henningsen and Marisa Rey-Henningsen, "Inquisition and Interdisciplinary History," *Dansk Folkemindesamling, Studier* Nr. 14 (Copenhagen, 1981), 119–125; Antonio Marquez, "La Inquisición: Estudio de las investigaciones inquisitoriales," *Revista de Occidente* 6 (1981), 147–156.

There is an extensive bibliographical commentary on recent work on the Spanish Inquisition in Angel Alcalá's *Prologo* to the Spanish translation of Henry C. Lea, *Historia de la Inquisición española*, Vol. 1 (Madrid, 1983), pp. xxv–lxxxi.

Another recent review article is that of Geoffrey Parker, "Some Recent Work on the Inquisition in Spain," *Journal of Modern History* 54 (1982), 519–532, admirable for its comparative approach to the inquisitions in Spain and Italy.

The literature on medieval anti-Judaism is large and growing. Vols. 3–8 of Salo W. Baron's *A Social and Religious History of the Jews* (New York, 1957) offer a detailed survey, and Jacob Marcus, *The Jew in the Medieval World*

(New York, 1965), offers an extensive collection of translated and annotated documents. A classic work is that of Joshua Trachtenberg, *The Devil and the Jews: The Medieval Conception of the Jew and its Relation to Modern Antisemitism* (New Haven, 1943).

Viator 2 (1971) contains five important essays by major scholars on the general theme "Reflections on Medieval Anti-Judaism," pp. 355–396. Particularly useful are the papers of Amos Funkenstein and Gavin Langmuir. On the whole setting of the Talmud trials of 1240, see Joel E. Rembaum, "The Talmud and the Popes: Reflections on the Talmud Trials of the 1240s," *Viator* 13 (1982), 203–223, and the more extreme position taken by Jeremy Cohen, *The Friars and the Jews: The Evolution of Medieval Anti-Judaism* (Ithaca, 1982).

On Jewish polemic, see David Berger, ed. and trans., *The Jewish-Christian Debate in the High Middle Ages: A Critical Edition of the 'Nizzahon Vetus'*, *with an Introduction, Translation, and Commentary* (Judaica, Texts and Translations, no. 4) (Philadelphia, 1979), and Berger's article, "Christian Heresy and Jewish Polemic in the Twelfth and Thirteenth Centuries," *Harvard Theological Review* 68 (1975), 287–304.

The most important study of the inquisitors and the Jews is that of Yosef Hayim Yerushalmi, "The Inquisition and the Jews of France in the Time of Bernard Gui," *Harvard Theological Review* 63 (1970), 317–376, with extensive discussion of theories of forced baptism, and, more recently, Joseph Schatzmiller, "Converts and Judaizers in the Early Fourteenth Century," *Harvard Theological Review* 74 (1981), 63–77.

Two recent studies of the blood libel are Gavin Langmuir, "Thomas of Monmouth: Detector of Ritual Murder," *Speculum* 59 (1984), 820–846, and Langmuir, "Historiographic Crucifixion," in *Les juifs au regard de l'histoire. Mélanges en l'honneur de Bernhard Blumenkranz* (Paris, 1985), 109–127.

Of other studies that illuminate various aspects of the subjects discussed in this section, among the most important are the following by Solomon Grayzel: "Changes in Papal Policy toward the Jews in the Middle Ages," *Fifth World Congress of Jewish Studies*, Vol. 2 (Jerusalem, 1972), 44–54; "Bishop to Bishop I," *Gratz College Anniversary Volume* (Philadelphia, 1971), 131–145; "Popes, Jews, and Inquisition, from *Sicut* to *Turbato*," *Essays on the Occasion of the Seventieth Anniversary of The Dropsie University* (Philadelphia, 1979), 151–188, and several studies of Gavin Langmuir: "Medieval Anti-Semitism," Henry Friedlander and Sybil Milton, eds., *The Holocaust: Ideology, Bureaucracy, and Genocide* (Millwood, N.Y., 1980), 27–35; "From Ambrose of Milan to Emicho of Leiningen: The Transformation of the Hostility Against Jews in Northern Christendom," in *Gli Ebrei nell'Alto Medioevo*, Settimane di Stùdio del Centro Italiano di Studi sull'Alto Medioevo XXVI (Spoleto, 1980), 313–368; "*Tanquam servi*: The Change in Jewish Status in French Law about 1200," in Miriam Yardeni, ed., *Les Juifs dans l'histoire de France* (Leiden, 1980), 24–54.

On the panic of 1321, see Malcolm Barber, "The Plot to Overthrow Christendom in 1321," *History* 66 (1981), 1–17, and Carlo Ginzburg, "The Witches'

Sabbath: Popular Cult or Inquisitorial Stereotype," in Steven L. Kaplan, ed., *Understanding Popular Culture* (New York), 1984), 39–51.

On Jewish political status generally, see Robert Chazan, *Church, State, and Jew in the Middle Ages* (New York, 1980).

The fundamental work on the Jews in medieval Spain is that of Yitzhak Baer, *Toledot haYehudim biSefarad haNotzrit* (2 vols. Tel Aviv, 1945; 2nd. ed. 1 vol. Tel Aviv, 1959), translated into English as A *History of the Jews in Christian Spain*, 2 vols. (Philadelphia, 1966). This work is based upon Baer's earlier collection of expertly annotated documents, *Die Juden im christlichen Spanien. Erster Teil, Urkunden und Regesten* (Berlin, 1929), which should be used in the reprint edition (London, 1970), containing a new Introduction by Baer and a note on "Select Additional Bibliography" by Haim Beinart.

Baer's greatest student, Haim Beinart, has produced a splendid edition of the activities of the Inquisition at Ciudad Real: Haim Beinart, *Records of the Trials of the Spanish Inquisition in Ciudad Real*, 4 vols. (Jerusalem, 1974), with a useful introduction.

Compare Eliyahu Ashtor, *The Jews of Moslem Spain*, trans. Aaron Klein and Jenny Machlowitz Klein, 3 vols. (Philadelphia, 1973, 1979, 1984).

Two studies raise the question of persecution compared over time: Caesar C. Aronsfeld, *The Ghosts of 1492: Jewish Aspects of the Struggle for Religious Freedom in Spain, 1848–1976* (New York, 1979), and Yosef Hayim Yerushalmi, *Assimilation and Racial Anti-Semitism: The Iberian and German Models*, Leo Black Memorial Lecture 26 (New York, 1982).

Aside from occasional expressions of interest on the part of Christian historians of the Spanish and Portuguese Inquisitions from the late seventeenth century on, the role of anti-Judaism in their early and occasionally later stages was not systematically considered until the very end of the nineteenth century by either Christian or Jewish scholars. Virtually the first scholarly study in English from a Jewish perspective was the work of Cecil Roth, *The Spanish Inquisition* (London, 1937; rpt. New York, 1964).

The *Repertorium Inquisitorum* has recently been translated into French by Louis Sala-Molins, *Le dictionnaire des inquisiteurs, Valence 1494* (Paris, 1981), although Sala-Molins' introductory material should not be accepted uncritically. As is the case with his translation of Eymeric, and a number of volumes in the series he edits (notably, for our purposes, Hélène Vedrine, *Censure et pouvoir. Trois procès: Savonarole, Bruno, Galilée* [Paris and The Hague, 1976]), Sala-Molins has a violently anti-papal agenda which does not make his scholarly judgments above reproach.

There is a detailed study of the great *autos-de-fé* of 1559 and the shift of interest on the part of the Spanish Inquisition to Protestantism in Jesús Alonso Burgos, *El Luteranismo en Castilla durante el siglo XVI: Autos-de-fé de Vallado- lid de 21 de Mayo y de 8 de Octubre de 1559* (Madrid, 1983). See also Jaime Contreras, "The Impact of Protestantism in Spain, 1520–1600," in Haliczer, *Inquisition and Society*, pp. 47–66.

The classic study of Spanish inquisitorial censorship of works of the Enlightenment is that of Marcellin Defourneaux, *L'Inquisition espagnole et les livres francais au XVIIIe siècle* (Paris, 1963); Spanish translation by J. Ignacio Tellechea Idigoras, *Inquisición y Censura de Libros en la Espāna del siglo XVIII* (1973), incorporating additions and corrections by Defourneaux. See now Virgilio Pinto, "Thought Control in Spain," in Haliczer, *Inquisition and Society*, pp. 171–188. From another perspective, see Augustín Redondo, ed., *Les problèmes de l'exclusion en Espagne (XVIe–XVIIe siècles)* (Paris, 1983).

There is a useful bibliography in the important study by Miguel Avilés, *Erasmo y la inquisición* (Madrid, 1980).

Among the most important recent works dealing with the finances of the Spanish Inquisition is that of José Martinez Millan, *La Hacienda de la Inquisición (1478–1700)* (Madrid, 1984).

On the inquisition in Portugal, see Alexandre Herculano, *History of the Origin and Establishment of the Inquisition in Portugal*, trans. John C. Branner (Stanford, 1926). This work should be used in the reprint edition (New York, 1972), because the Prolegomenon by Yosef Hayim Yerushalmi contributes important views and new bibliography. See also Yerushalmi, *From Spanish Court to Italian Ghetto* (New York, 1971). The archival materials are discussed by Charles Amiel, "Les archives de l'Inquisition Portugaise," in *Arquivos de Centro Cultural Português de Paris* (Paris, 1979), 7–29.

On the massacre in Lisbon in 1506, see Yerushalmi, *The Lisbon Massacre of 1506* (Cincinnati, 1976) and Yerushalmi's great book, *Zakhor: Jewish History and Jewish Memory* (Seattle, 1982).

The case of the impostor Saavedra is briefly discussed and dismissed by Yerushalmi in his Prolegomenon to the reprint edition of the English translation of Herculano's *History . . . of the Inquisition in Portugal*, p. 22 and note. The topic evidently appealed to Spanish playwrights, since several comedies treat it. See Edward Glaser, *Estudios españo-portugueses: relaciones literarias del Siglo de Oro* (Valencia, 1957), 221–265.

On the Spanish Inquisition in the New World the classic work is that of Richard Greenleaf, *The Mexican Inquisition of the Sixteenth Century* (Albuquerque, 1969).

A recent example in English scholarship of the internal affairs of the Spanish Inquisition is John Edwards, "Trial of an Inquisitor: the dismissal of Diego Rodriguez Lucero, inquisitor of Córdoba, in 1508," *Journal of Ecclesiastical History* 37 (1986), 240–257.

The most recent study of the process by which the Spanish Inquisition was abolished is that of Francisco Maria Gilabert, *La Abolición de la Inquisición en España* (Pamplona, 1975).

The best study of the relations between Spanish church and government during the late eighteenth and early nineteenth centuries is that of William J. Callahan, *Church, Politics, and Society in Spain, 1750–1874* (Cambridge, Mass., 1984).

Chapter 4. The Roman and Italian Inquisitions (pp. 105–121)

The best general study of early modern Christianity is that of John Bossy, *Christianity in the West, 1400–1700* (Oxford and New York, 1985), and, for the Roman and other Italian Inquisitions, Nicholas Davidson, *The Counter-Reformation* (Oxford and New York, 1987).

On the Roman Inquisition see the studies of John Tedeschi, "Preliminary Observations on Writing a History of the Roman Inquisition," in F. F. Church and T. George, eds., *Continuity and Discontinuity in Church History* (Leiden, 1974), 232–249; "Organización y Procedimientos Penales de la Inquisición Romana: Un Bosquejo," in Alcalá, *Inquisición espânola*, pp. 185–206; "The Roman Inquisition and Witchcraft: An Early Seventeenth-Century 'Instruction' on Correct Trial Procedure," *Revue de l'histoire des religions* (1983), 163–188, and, with E. William Monter, "Toward a Statistical Profile of the Italian Inquisitions, Sixteenth to Eighteenth Centuries," in Henningsen and Tedeschi, eds., *The Inquisition in Early Modern Europe*, 130–157.

On Eymeric-Peña, see Edward Peters, "Editing Inquisitors' Manuals in the Sixteenth Century: Francisco Peña and the *Directorium Inquisitorum* of Nicholas Eymeric," *The Library Chronicle* 40 (1974), 95–107; Patricia Jobe, "Inquisitorial Manuscripts in the Bibliotèca/Apostòlica Vaticana: A Preliminary Handlist," in Henningsen and Tedeschi, *The Inquisition in Early Modern Europe*, 13–32; Agostino Borromeo, "A Propòsito del *Directorium Inquisitorum* di Nicolas Eymerich e delle sue edizioni cinquecentésque," *Critica Stòrica* 20 (1983), 499–547. There is an abridged French translation of parts of the work by Louis Sala-Molins, Nicolau Eymerich, Francisco Peña, *Le manuel des inquisiteurs* (Paris and The Hague, 1973). See also bibliography for Ch. 6.

THE INQUISITION IN SICILY

The fullest account in English is that of Henry C. Lea, *The Inquisition in the Spanish Dependencies* (New York, 1908), whose first chapter deals with Sicily (other chapters treat the inquisitions of Malta, Naples, Sardinia, Milan, the Canaries, Mexico, the Philippines, Peru, and New Granada). Lea's research depended, as usual, on what original and printed documents he could obtain and on the pioneering scholarship of Vito La Mantia. La Mantia's work, long out of print, has recently been assembled and reprinted as Vito La Mantia, *Origine e vicende dell'Inquisizióne in Sicilia* (Palermo, 1977). La Mantia's greatest successor, Carlo Alberto Garufi, published an important series of studies between 1914 and 1921, and these have been reprinted as Carlo Alberto Garufi, *Fatti e personaggi dell'Inquisizióne in Sicilia* (Palermo, 1978). In 1964 the Sicilian novelist Leonardo Sciascia published a long essay entitled *Morte dell'Inquisitóre*, which was republished in 1967 and translated into English by Judith Green with another work: Leonardo Sciascia, *Salt in the Wound, followed by The Death of the Inquisitor* (New York, 1969). Sciascia's essay is the most recent study in English, although its scholarship is not definitive. Sciascia's notes naturally do not indicate the subsequent reprinting of the work of La Mantia and Garufi.

THE INQUISITION IN VENICE

The most detailed accounts of the Venetian Inquisition are contained in the recent and excellent studies by Paul F. Grendler, *The Roman Inquisition and the Venetian Press, 1540–1605* (Princeton, 1977), which is also the best recent account of pre-modern censorship of the press, and Brian Pullan, *The Jews of Europe and the Inquisition of Venice, 1550–1670* (Oxford, 1983), which suggests the extraordinary kind of social history that some inquisition records permit in the hands of first-rate scholars.

See now the work of Nicholas Davidson, *The Counter-Reformation* (Oxford, 1987), and "The Inquisition and the Italian Jews," in Haliczer, *Inquisition and Society.*

There are several studies of the dispersal of the Roman archives in 1808–1811. The best is John Tedeschi, "The Dispersed Archives of the Roman Inquisition," in Henningsen, Tedeschi, and Amiel, eds., *The Inquisition in Early Modern Europe* (DeKalb, 1986), 13–32. See also Owen Chadwick, *Catholicism and History: The Opening of the Vatican Archives* (Cambridge, 1978), Ch. 1. The story is anecdotally told in Maria Luisa Ambrosini, with Mary Willis, *The Secret Archives of the Vatican* (Boston, 1969).

Very little literature exists on the institutional transformation of the Holy Office–Inquisition/Congregation for the Doctrine of the Faith in the twentieth century, a surprising fact, considering the increasingly wide and various use made of the term in so many different areas.

There is a large bibliography on Lord Acton, but the volume most readily useful for matters discussed here is Gertrude Himmelfarb, ed., *Lord Acton, Essays on Freedom and Power* (Cleveland, 1955).

Lester Kurtz, *The Politics of Heresy: The Modernist Crisis in Roman Catholicism* (California, 1986) is extremely ambitious and original in its treatment and extensively documented, although it, too, oddly neglects the transformations of the Roman Inquisition that occurred during the period it covers and were closely connected to its events. Other English accounts of the modern papacy are equally reticent; e.g., Karl Otmar von Aretin, *The Papacy and the Modern World*, trans. Roland Hill (New York, 1970). John O'Brien, *The Inquisition* (New York, 1973) represents the post-Vatican II apologetics at their least appealing, and least scholarly.

There is an excellent depiction of an important aspect of the Modernist crisis in Claude Nelson and Norman Pittenger, eds., *Pilgrim of Rome: An Introduction to the Life and Work of Ernesto Bonaiuti* (Welwyn, 1969). A strongly pro-papal account of the nineteenth and twentieth centuries is that of

Anthony Rhodes, *The Power of Rome in the Twentieth Century: The Vatican in the Age of Liberal Democracies, 1870–1922* (New York, 1983).

On the Schillebeeckx case, see Leonard Swidler and Piet F. Fransen, *Authority in the Church and the Schillebeeckx Case* (New York, 1982).

There is an interesting general Catholic discussion of the broadest aspects of the problem in Maurice Bévenot, S. J., "The Inquisition and Its Antecedents," *The Heythrop Journal*, VII, 3 (1966), pp. 257–268; VII, 4 (1966), pp. 381–393; VIII, 1 (1967), pp. 52–69; VIII, 2 (1967), pp. 152–168.

Chapter 5. The Invention of The Inquisition (pp. 122–154)

REFORMATION POLEMIC: PROPAGANDA, MARTYROLOGIES, AND MONTANUS

There is a large literature on Reformation polemic and propaganda, most of it conveniently summarized in Steven Ozment, ed., *Reformation Europe: A Guide to Research* (St. Louis, 1982).

On martyrologies in the formation of Reformation historiography, see A. G. Dickens and John M. Tonkin, with Kenneth Powell, *The Reformation in Historical Thought* (Cambridge, Mass., 1985), pp. 39–57. Several important studies by Donald Kelley have dealt with the place of martyrologies in larger intellectual contexts: "Martyrs, Myths, and the Massacre: The Background of St. Bartholomew," *American Historical Review* 77 (1982), pp. 1323–1342, and *The Beginnings of Ideology: Consciousness and Society in the French Reformation* (Cambridge, 1981), esp. Ch. 3. For England, see Helen C. White, *Tudor Books of Saints and Martyrs* (Madison, 1963). For Crespin, van Haemstede, and Rabus, see *The Reformation in Historical Thought*, pp. 41–42, 49–51, with further references in the notes.

On the martyrologies as contributors to the idea of "precursors" of the Reformers, see Pontien Polman, *L'Élement historique dans la Controverse religieuse du XVIe Siècle* (Gembloux, 1932), pp. 178–200.

On John Foxe, see the references in the section dealing with him in Dickens and Tonkin, *The Reformation in Historical Thought*, pp. 44–49, and John Hazel Smith, ed., *Two Latin Comedies by John Foxe the Martyrologist* (Ithaca, 1973). Although I have checked the first edition (1563) of the *Acts and Monuments*, I have cited texts from *The Acts and Monuments of John Foxe*, 4th ed., ed. Josiah Pratt, with an introduction by John Stoughton, 8 vols. (London, 1877). Foxe's observations on the popularity of such a work in English are found in Vol. 1, p. 8; on San Romanus and the image-maker, as well as Foxe's account of the Spanish Inquisition, see Vol. 7, pp. 447–458; for the cases of Nicholas Burton and John Frampton, see Vol. 8, pp. 513–516; for the case of Richard Atkins, burned at Rome, see Vol. 8, pp. 742–743.

On Foxe and historical thought and writing, see William Haller, *Foxe's 'Book of Martyrs' and the Elect Nation* (London, 1963), Ch. 4, and V. Norskov Olsen, *John Foxe and the Elizabethan Church* (Berkeley and Los Angeles,

1973). There is a brief but useful discussion of Foxe's role in informing England about the Spanish Inquisition in William Maltby, *The Black Legend in England*, Ch. 3.

The most important, thorough, and best documented study of Montanus is now that of B. A. Vermaseren, "Who Was Reginaldus Gonsalvius Montanus?" *Bibliothèque d'Humanisme et Renaissance* 47 (1985), pp. 47–77. Vermaseren's footnotes indicate the comprehensive scholarship on the text, its author, and its impact. The political circumstances surrounding its circulation and use will be considered in Ch. 6. Further information on the life of Antonio del Corro is provided in Paul Hauben, *Three Spanish Heretics and the Reformation* (Geneva, 1967), although Hauben does not identify del Corro with Montanus.

On the subsequent use of Montanus' martyrology, see A. Gordon Kinder, *Spanish Protestants and Reformers in the Sixteenth Century: A Bibliography* (London, 1983), nos. 74, 208, 216–219, 144–159 (for del Corro). For Michael Geddes, I have used the second edition of the work: *Miscellaneous Tracts: In Three Volumes*, by Michael Geddes, Vol. 1 (London, 1714), Tract 7, pp. 553–576.

On the *autos-de-fé* at Valladolid and Seville between 1559 and 1562 and the practice of the Spanish Inquisition of labelling various kinds of dissent as "Luteranismo," see Paul Hauben, "Reform and Counter-Reform: The Case of the Spanish Heretics," in Theodore K. Rabb and Jerrold E. Siegel, eds., *Action and Conviction in Early Modern Europe: Essays in Memory of E. Harris Harbison* (Princeton, 1969), pp. 154–168.

REFORMATION POLEMIC: CHURCH HISTORY

The best general study of Luther's ideas about history is that of John M. Headley, *Luther's View of Church History* (New Haven and London, Yale, 1963), especially Chs. 3, 5, and 6. On the polemical character of sixteenth century church history, see Pontien Polman, *L'élément historique dans la controverse religieuse de XVIe siècle* (Gembloux, 1932), which contains detailed accounts of many of the works cited in this chapter.

The best general guide is Dickens and Tomkin, *The Reformation in Historical Thought*. A. G. Dickens has published several preliminary studies on individual historians in several essays: "Contemporary Historians of the German Reformation," and "Johannes Sleidan and Reformation History," both in A. G. Dickens, *Reformation Studies* (London, 1982), pp. 509–536, 537–564. For Mosheim, see Dickens and Tonkin, pp. 131–135.

Polman, *L'Élement Historique*, pp. 178–200, deals in part with the idea of "precursors of the Reform," but his work should be supplemented in the case of medieval heresies by Vol. 14 of the Cahiers de Fanjeaux, *Historiographie du catharisme* (Toulouse, 1979), especially the articles by M.-H. Vicaire, "Les Albigeois ancêtres des Protestants. Assimilations catholiques," pp. 23–46, and Guy Bedouelle, "Les Albigeois, témoins du véritable évangile: l'Historiographie protestante du XVIe et du début du XVIIe siècle," pp. 47–70, which broaden the discussion of Polman, with particular attention to Bernard of Luxemburg, Flaccius Illyricus, and others.

The history of the Alpine Waldensians is taken up in the fine study of Euan Cameron, *The Reformation of the Heretics: The Waldenses of the Alps, 1480–1580* (Oxford, 1984). For the historiographical problems, see Ch. 16.

THE BLACK LEGEND

The term was invented by the Spanish journalist Julian Juderias, *La leyenda negra: Estudios acerca del concepto del España en el extranjero* (Madrid, 1914; many subsequent editions). The best recent discussions of a problem now with an immense literature are those of Charles Gibson, ed., *The Black Legend: Anti-Spanish Attitudes in the Old World and the New* (New York, 1971); Philip Wayne Powell, *Tree of Hate* (New York, 1971); Henry Kamen and Joseph Pérez, *La imagen internacional de la España de Felipe II: 'Leyenda negra' o conflicto de intereses* (Valladolid, 1980). The modern classic on the subject is Sverker Arnoldsson, *La leyenda negra: Estudios sobre sus orígines* (Goteborg, 1960).

ENGLAND PREPARES TO READ MONTANUS

There is a vast literature on the English Reformation that need not be cited here, since our purpose is to identify the particularly political and anti-clerical character of the English scene. For Henry VIII and Thomas More, see Jasper Ridley, *Henry VIII* (London, 1984), and idem, *Statesman and Saint: Cardinal Wolsey, Sir Thomas More, and the Politics of Henry VIII* (New York, 1982), esp. Ch. 15, both with extensive references.

There are many perspectives to Thomas More. Besides Ridley's study, which focuses particularly on More as an opponent of Reform, see also Richard Marius, *Thomas More* (New York, 1984), and Alistair Fox, *Thomas More: History and Providence* (New Haven, 1982), esp. Chs. 4–7. F. M. Powicke, *The Reformation in England* (Oxford, 1941) is particularly astute in topics considered in this section, as is A. G. Dickens, *The English Reformation* (London, 1964).

Thomas More's ecclesiology is extensively considered by Brian Gogan, *The Common Corps of Christendom: Ecclesiological Themes in the Writings of Sir Thomas More* (Leiden, 1982), although for More's views and activities on heresy this must be supplemented by R. J. Schoeck, "Common Law and Canon Law in Their Relation to Thomas More," in Richard S. Sylvester, ed., *St. Thomas More: Action and Contemplation* (New Haven, 1972), pp. 15–56, and, especially for the issues between St. German and More, John Guy's essay "Thomas More and Christopher St. German: The Battle of the Books," in Alistair Fox and John Guy, *Reassessing the Henrician Age: Humanism, Politics and Reform, 1500–1550* (Oxford, 1986), pp. 95–120. The same exchanges are considered from another important point of view in Rainer Pineas, *Thomas More and Tudor Polemics* (Bloomington, 1968), Ch. 6.

The best recent account of the actual behavior of the English ecclesiastical courts is that of Ralph Houlbrooke, *Church Courts and the People during the English Reformation, 1520–1570* (Oxford, 1979), and, for the governmental side, G. R. Elton, *Policy and Police* (Cambridge, 1972).

Two recent and intelligent studies of English religion and English national identity and history are those of John W. McKenna, "How God became an Englishman," in Delloyd J. Guth and John W. McKenna, eds., *Tudor Rule and Revolution: Essays for G. R. Elton from his American Friends* (Cambridge, 1982), pp. 25–44, and A. J. Fletcher, "The Origins of English Protestantism and the Growth of National Identity," in *Religion and National Identity*, Studies in Church History 18, Stuart Mews, ed. (Oxford, 1982), pp. 309–318.

On Tyndale's "New History," see Pineas, *Thomas More and Tudor Polemics*, Ch. 2; for Barnes, Ch. 3, and for Tyndale's influence on John Bale, see Pineas, "William Tyndale's Influence on John Bale's polemical Use of History," *Archiv fur Reformationsgeschichte* 53 (1962), pp. 79–98, and Pineas, "John Bale's Non-Dramatic Works of Religious Controversy," *Studies in the Renaissance* 9 (1962), pp. 218–233.

The relevant constitutional documents may be found in G. R. Elton, *The Tudor Constitution* (Cambridge, 1962), Chs. 7 & 9, and in C. H. Williams, ed., *English Historical Documents*, Vol. 5, 1485–1558.

On the interruption and continuity of polemic, see Edward Baskerville, *A Chronological Bibliography of Propaganda and Polemic Published in English between 1553 and 1558 from the Death of Edward VI to the Death of Mary I* (Philadelphia, 1979).

Useful introductions to the reign of Mary Tudor and the scholarly literature dealing with it are D. M. Loades, *The Reign of Mary Tudor: Politics, government, and religion in England, 1553–1558* (New York, 1979), and the brief but useful work of Robert Tittler, *The Reign of Mary I* (London, 1983). For the Marian trials and executions, see D. M. Loades, *The Oxford Martyrs* (London, 1970), and Jennifer Loach and Robert Tittler, eds., *The Mid-Tudor Polity* (London, 1980).

For the important links between England and Rome following the death of Mary and the accession of Elizabeth, see C. G. Bayne, *Anglo-Roman Relations, 1558–1565* (Oxford, 1913; rpt. 1968). Bayne points out that the Roman Inquisition attacked England's efforts to secure outward conformity. The Inquisition's opinion is printed on pp. 296–297.

SIXTEENTH-CENTURY FRANCE PREPARES TO READ MONTANUS

The best work in English on the topic of the inquisitions in sixteenth-century France is that of N. M. Sutherland, *The Huguenot Struggle for Recognition* (New Haven, 1980), and Sutherland, "Was there an Inquisition in Reformation France?" in Sutherland, *Princes, Politics and Religion, 1547–1589* (London, 1984), pp. 13–30. For the faculty of theology at Paris, Sutherland's work may be supplemented by Farge, *Orthodoxy and Reform in Early Reformation France*.

Some of the climate change in regard to religious persecution is conveniently discussed in Henry Kamen, *The Rise of Toleration* (New York, 1967). The best comprehensive account of the period from 1559 on is that of Richard S. Dunn, *The Age of Religious Wars, 1559–1715*, 2nd ed. (New York, 1979); and J. H. M. Salmon, *Society in Crisis: France in the Sixteenth Century* (London, 1975).

For the south of France in the sixteenth century, see also Raymond A. Mentzer, *Heresy Proceedings in Languedoc, 1500–1560.*

The most important comparative study is that of Perez Zagorin, *Rebels and Rulers, 1500–1660* (Cambridge, 1982), Vol. 2, Ch. 10.

On the means of repressing heresy outside the ecclesiastical inquisitions proper in France, see Nathaniel Weiss, *La Chambre Ardente* (Paris, 1889; rpt. 1970), and for propaganda, see Vittorio de Caprariis, *Propaganda e pensièro politico in Francia durante le guèrre di Religióne* (Naples, 1959).

THE NETHERLANDS REVOLT AND THE INQUISITION

The best general account in English is that of Geoffrey Parker, *The Dutch Revolt* (Ithaca, 1977). Many of the relevant texts are translated in the important work by E. H. Kossman and A. F. Mellink, *Texts Concerning the Revolt of the Netherlands* (Cambridge, 1974). For the Spanish background, see A. W. Lovett, *Early Habsburg Spain*, Ch. 10, and Perez Zagorin, *Rebels and Rulers, 1500–1660*, Vol. 2 (Cambridge, 1982), Ch. 11.

The best study in English of the early problems of the inquisition in a particular province (Holland) is James D. Tracy, "Heresy Law and Centralization under Mary of Hungary: Conflict between the Council of Holland and the Central Government over the Enforcement of Charles V's Placards," *Archiv für Reformationsgeschichte* 73 (1982), pp. 284–307. Alastair Duke, "Salvation by Coercion: The Controversy Surrounding the 'Inquisition' in the Low Countries on the Eve of the Revolt," in Peter Newman Brooks, ed., *Reformation Principle and Practice: Essays in Honor of Arthur Geoffrey Dickens* (London, 1980), pp. 137–156, offers a wider scope than Tracy's study and complements it nicely, particularly in matters of jurisdictional conflict. The extremely important essay by K. W. Swart, "The Black Legend during the Eighty Years War," *Britain and the Netherlands*, Vol. 5 (The Hague, 1975), pp. 36–57, devotes a very important section to the problem of the inquisitions and should be read with the essay of Vermaseren, "Who Was Reginaldus Gonsalvius Montanus?"

An important textual source has been edited by H. Wansink, *The Apologie of Prince William of Orange against the Proclamation of the King of Spain* (Leiden, 1969) in a fuller version than those printed in Kossman and Mellink and elsewhere.

Further material on the climate of religious surveillance and persecution in the Netherlands is provided and discussed in R. W. Truman and A. Gordon Kinder, "The Pursuit of Spanish Heretics in the Low Countries: the activities of Alonso del Canto, 1561–1564," *Journal of Ecclesiastical History* 30 (1979), 65–93.

There is an excellent short study of the Revolution by J. W. Smit, "The Netherlands Revolution," in Robert Forster and Jack P. Greene, eds., *Preconditions of Revolution in Early Modern Europe* (Baltimore, 1970), pp. 19–54.

Smit has also provided a useful introduction to the great seventeenth-century Netherlands history by Gerhard Brandt, *The History of the Reformation . . . In and About the Low-Countries* (London, 1720; rpt. New York, 1979). On the importance of Brandt's *History* in the development of Reformation Historiography, see the studies in A. C. Duke and C. A. Tamse, eds., *Clio's Mirror: Historiography in Britain and the Netherlands* (Eighth Anglo-Dutch Historical Conference: Britain and the Netherlands, no. 8) (Zutphen, 1985).

On the international character of Calvinism, see now Menna Prestwich, ed., *International Calvinism, 1541–1715* (Oxford, 1985), particularly Chs. 3 and 4, by Menna Prestwich and Alastair Duke, respectively.

Chapter 6 The Inquisition, the Toleration Debates, and the Enlightenment (pp. 155–188)

The best introduction to early modern political theory is Quentin Skinner, *The Foundations of Modern Political Thought*, 2 vols. (Cambridge, 1978), particularly Vol. 2, *The Age of Reformation*. As Skinner points out, the focus of sixteenth-century political thought was upon the character and extent of civil authority and the problem of rights of resistance. Within this framework, the inquisitions played a minor role. More recently, for Luther, see W. D. J. Cargill Thompson, *The Political Thought of Martin Luther*, ed. Dr. Philip Broadhead (Sussex, 1984), and Prestwich, *International Calvinism*, esp. Ch. 11, "French Calvinist Political Thought, 1534–1715" by Myriam Yardeni, pp. 315–338.

On Sarpi, see William Bouwsma, *Venice and the Defense of Republican Liberty* (Berkeley and Los Angeles, 1968). Sarpi's treatise *Sopra l'Officio dell'Inquisizióne* of 1613 is edited in Fra Paolo Sarpi, *Scritti Giurisdizionalistici*, ed. Giovanni Gambarin (Bari, 1958), pp. 121–220.

The fullest general account of the rise of toleration is still that of Joseph Lecler, S. J., *Toleration and the Reformation*, 2 vols. (New York and London, 1960); the short work of Henry Kamen, *The Rise of Toleration* (New York, 1967), is also very accessible and useful. On Servetus, see Roland Bainton, *Hunted Heretic: The Life and Death of Michael Servetus, 1511–1553* (Boston, 1953), and on Castellio's treatise, Bainton, ed., *Concerning Heretics* (New York, 1935).

For Limborch and other dissenting historians, see bibliography for Ch. 9. On the manuscript of the Toulouse Inquisition that Limborch edited, see M. A. E. Nickson, "Locke and the Inquisition of Toulouse," *British Museum Quarterly* 26 (1971–1972), 83–92.

On the sources for Bayle's knowledge of and attitude toward Spain, see Kenneth R. Scholberg, *Pierre Bayle and Spain*, University of North Carolina

Studies in the Romance Languages and Literatures, No. 30 (Chapel Hill, 1958). The best general discussion in English is that by Elisabeth Labrousse, *Bayle*, trans. Denys Potts (Oxford, 1983). There is an extensive discussion of Bayle's influence on later French thought in H. T. Mason, *Pierre Bayle and Voltaire* (Oxford, 1963), and on Bayle's *Dictionnaire* in the context of other contemporary and later encyclopedias in Frank A. Kafker, ed., *Notable Encyclopedias of the Seventeenth and Eighteenth Centuries: Nine Predecessors of the Encyclopédie* (Oxford, 1981).

On some of Bayle's difficulties, see Walter Rex, *Essays on Pierre Bayle and Religious Controversy* (The Hague, 1965), esp. Ch. 5.

There is much useful scholarship in Myriam Yardeni, ed., *Modernité et Non-conformisme en France à travers les âges* (Leiden, 1983).

On the arguments from political economy that favored the toleration of religious minorities and further depicted the Inquisition in Spain as a disasterous economic policy, see Myriam Yardeni, "Naissance et vie d'un mythe: La Révocation de l'Édit de Nantes et le déclin économique de France," in A. Grabois, ed., *Les mythes en France*, Troisième Colloque de Haifa (forthcoming). For the consequences in Spanish historiography concerning both the economic decline of Spain and the alleged centrality of the Spanish Inquisition in this process, see Jean-Pierre Dedieu, "Responsabilité de l'Inquisition dans le retard économique de l'Espagne? Éléments de Réponse," in Bartolomé Bennassar, ed., *Aux origines du retard économique de l'Espagne* (Paris, 1983), pp. 143–153.

There is a good discussion of Montesquieu on this theme in Mark Hulliung, *Montesquieu and the Old Regime* (Berkeley and Los Angeles, 1976). For the texts I have used the *Oeuvres Complétes de Montesquieu*, ed. André Masson, 3 vols. (Paris, 1950).

On the perplexities of *philosophe* support of toleration, see Geoffrey Adams, "A Temperate Crusade: The Philosophe Campaign for Religious Toleration," *Ideas in History: Essays Presented to Louis Gottschalk*, ed. Richard Herr and Harold T. Parker (Durham, 1965), 65–84.

The *Histoire du Docteur Akakia* is in Voltaire, *Mélanges*, pp. 289–300; separately printed, with introduction and notes, by Jacques Tuffet (Paris, 1967).

Morellet discusses both the *Petit écrit* and his translation of Eymeric in his *Mémoires*, 2 vols. (Paris, 1821), Vol. 1, pp. 32–39, 58–63. There is a brief discussion in Alan C. Kors, *D'Holbach's Coterie: An Enlightenment in Paris* (Princeton, 1976), pp. 122–124. On Morellet's activities as a translator and their impact, see Dorothy Medlin, "André Morellet, translator of liberal thought," *Studies on Voltaire and the Eighteenth Century*, ed. Haydn Mason, Vol. 174 (Oxford, 1978).

On Voltaire on Calvin and Servetus, see the discussion in Graham Gargett, *Voltaire and Protestantism*, Studies on Voltaire and the Eighteenth Century, Vol. 188 (Oxford, 1980), esp. pp. 57–66.

I have used René Pomeau, ed., Voltaire, *Essai sur les moeurs*, 2 vols. (Paris,

1963), and Voltaire, *Mélanges*, ed. Jacques van den Heuvel and Emmanuel Berl (Paris, 1961). For *Candide* I have used the critical edition by René Pomeau, in *The Complete Works of Voltaire*, Vol. 48 (Oxford, 1980), and Voltaire, *Candide*, ed. and trans. Robert M. Adams (New York, 1966), and for other works, Voltaire, *Romans et Contes*, ed. Henri Bénac (Paris, 1960).

On Beccaria, see the most convenient edition, Césare Beccaria, *On Crimes and Punishments*, trans. with an introduction by Henry Paolucci (Indianapolis–New York, 1963). There is an exchange of correspondence between Beccaria and Morellet, with other contemporary comments on *On Crimes and Punishments* in the French edition by J. -A. -S. Collin de Plancy, *Des Délits et des peines par Beccaria* (Paris, 1823).

I have not been able to obtain a full text of Zaupser's *Ode*. I have loosely translated the selection printed in Jürgen Schreiber, *Jerzy Andrzewskis Roman 'Ciemnosci kryja ziemie' und die Darstellung der spanischen Inquisition in Werken der fiktionalen Literatur*, Slavistische Beitrage, Bd. 146 (Munich, 1981), 39–40 (cf. van der Vekene, Vol. 1, 1:22). The only detailed study is that of Karl von Reinhardstöttner, "Andreas Zaupser," in *Forschungen zur Kultur- und Litteraturgeschichte Bayerns* I (Munich and Leipzig, 1893), 121–226. For the *Gedanken*, van der Vekene No. 4548, 1721.

For Victor Hugo, I have used Victor Hugo, *Légende des siècles*, ed. Paul Berret, Vol. 2 (Paris, 1922), 653–662. The event that Momotombo has in mind was probably the great *auto–de–fé* held at Lima in 1639. The only contemporary account is that of Jose Cisneros, *Discurso Que En El Insigne Auto De La Fé, Celebrato En esta Real ciudad de Lima* . . . (Lima, 1639). A copy is in the Lea Library of the University of Pennsylvania.

The most recent exploration of questions of toleration generally is the collection of essays edited by John Horton and Susan Mendus, *Aspects of Toleration* (London and New York, 1985).

Chapter 7. The Inquisition *in Literature and Art* (pp. 189–230)

TRAVELERS' ACCOUNTS AND PERSONAL NARRATIVES

The best general study of Spanish travelers' accounts is that of Elena Fernandez Herr, *Les origines de l'Espagne romantique. Les récits de voyage 1755–1823* (Paris, 1973), with extensive bibliography. There is a collection of sample extracts from seventeenth-century accounts in José María Diez Borque, *La sociedad española y los viajeros del siglo XVII* (Madrid, 1975), with the Inquisition illustrated on pp. 176–190. For Enlightenment travel reports, see Gaspar Gomez de la Serna, *Los viajeros de la Ilustración* (Madrid, 1974).

Madame d'Aulnoy's account is particularly criticized in detail in El Duque de Maura and Agustín González-Amezúa, *Fantasias y realidades del viaje a Madrid de la Condesa d'Aulnoy* (Madrid, n.d.).

Other dimensions of these accounts are discussed in Bartolomé Bennassar,

The Spanish Character, trans. Benjamin Keen (Berkeley and Los Angeles, 1979).

There is an exhaustive inventory of personal narratives and travelers' reports, with extensive printing histories in van der Vekene, nos. 1687–1868. Aside from those narratives discussed here, the most widely circulated accounts were those of Katharine Evans and Sarah Cheevers (London, 1662); Giuseppe Pignata (chiefly an elaborate escape-narrative by a Molinist arrested by the Roman Inquisition), published by the imaginary Pierre Marteau at "Cologne" in 1725, well-known in English because of the translation published by Arthur Symons (New York, n.d. [1930]); Simon Berington's Memoirs of Sgr. Gaudentio di Lucca (London, 1737); Christian Friedrich Rudolph, *Der reisende Buchbindergeselle* (Stockholm [Copenhagen], 1753). Most of these were frequently reprinted into the nineteenth century, and many were translated into different languages. I have used the original editions of all works cited. Some of the texts discussed in this chapter may be regarded as forerunners of the widely read memoirs of Joseph Blanco White, *Letters from Spain* (London, 1822), and of George Borrow's *The Bible in Spain* (London, 1842).

The best modern study of "the Spanish character" is the subtle and graceful work of Bartolomé Bennassar, *The Spanish Character*. For some of the material with which this book deals, see Ch. IV, "Catholic Faith and Dissidence." The relation of writers to the Inquisition in Spain has been extensively mapped by Antonio Marquez, *Literatura e Inquisición en España (1478–1834)* (Madrid, 1980).

The liveliest of *Gil Blas* translations is that of Tobias Smollett. I have used for Vol. 1 the edition of London, 1864, and for Vol. 2 that of London, 1853. On Lesage's use of the Church in *Gil Blas*, see Katharine Whitman Carson, *Aspects of Contemporary Society in Gil Blas*, Studies on Voltaire and the Eighteenth Century, ed. Theodore Besterman, Vol. 60 (Oxford, 1973). I have used the French text of *Gil Blas*, edited by Roger Laufer (Paris, 1977). There is an English translation of *Vanillo González* (New York, 1890). On *Gil Blas* and the picaresque genre, see Jennifer Longhurst, "Lesage and the Spanish Tradition: *Gil Blas* as a Picaresque Novel," in J. H. Fox, et al., eds., *Studies in Eighteenth-Century French Literature presented to Robert Niklaus* (Exeter, 1975), 123–137.

During the eighteenth century the nature of historical thought and writing was a matter of considerable debate. Although highly accomplished critical work was still being produced in history's auxiliary disciplines, learned history was still looked upon as non-literary, while history that seemed too literary was written off as romance. Historical Pyrronism vied with didactic ideas of history, and only toward the end of the century did a line of critical historical thought and form of literary expression emerge in the work of Gibbon and others. On the general problem, see Arnaldo Momigliano, "Ancient History and the Antiquarian," in Momigliano, *Studies in Historiography* (New York, 1966), 1–39; J. H. Brumfitt, "Historical Pyrthonism and Enlightenment Historiography in France," in Charles G. S. Williams, ed., *Literature and History in the Age of Ideas: Essays on the French Enlightenment presented to George R. Havens* (Ohio, 1975), 15–30.

THE CRUEL AND EROTIC INQUISITOR

There is a large literature of and about Gothic novels, which I do not feel obliged to cite here. Elements of the movement that touch directly upon the matters of this chapter were early identified and illuminatingly discussed by Mario Praz, *The Romantic Agony* (1933; rpt. New York, 1956). The best recent studies are those of Maurice Levy, *Le roman "gothique" anglais: 1764–1824*, Association des Publications de la Faculté des Lettres (Toulouse, 1968), and R. I. Letellier, *An Intensifying Vision of Evil: The Gothic Novel (1764–1820) as a Self-Contained Literary Cycle* (Salzburg, 1980), esp. pp. 211–221 and the extensive bibliography. There is a précis of some of Levy's work in Jean Ducrocq, Suzy Halimi, and Maurice Levy, *Roman et société en Angleterre au XVIIIe siècle* (Paris, 1978), Chs. 14–15.

To these more recent works must be added, of course, that monstrous farrago of inexhaustible—and indispensible (when it is true)—knowledge about Gothic fiction, Montague Summers, *The Gothic Quest: A History of the Gothic Novel* (1938; rpt. London, 1968). There is a brief survey of subsequent criticism of the Gothic genre in William Emmet Coleman, *On the Discrimination of Gothicisms* (New York, 1980).

There is an astute study of the treatment of Roman Catholicism in Gothic fiction, written as a doctoral dissertation at Catholic University in 1946, by Sister Mary Muriel Tarr, *Catholicism in Gothic Fiction* (rpt. New York, 1979). Tarr considers the themes of "Monkish Superstition," "Monastic Gloom," "Morbid Devotion," and "Melancholy Pleasure" as the main foci of her study and as the organizing principles of Gothic treatment of the subject. On pp. 104–105 Tarr includes a convenient census of English Gothic novels in which the Inquisition is used as a setting. There is considerable data on the misunderstanding of Catholic office and ritual in this vein in Summers, *The Gothic Quest.*

For *Cornelia Bororquia*, I have used the edition of Paris, 1819, in Spanish. For the circulation of the work, see van der Vekene, Vol. 2, *Register*, s.n. Gutiérrez, Luis. Van der Vekene lists twenty-nine reprintings, translations, and editions of the work in the nineteenth century, the last edition being that of Madrid, 1881. The original publication date is disputed, 1800 or 1801.

Schiller wrote *The Ghost-Seer* between 1787 and 1789. I have used the partial English translation published in New York, 1796.

For *The Monk*, I have used Matthew Lewis, *The Monk: A Romance*, ed. with an introduction by Howard Anderson (London, 1973). I have used Ann Radcliffe, *The Italian, or the Confessional of the Black Penitents: A Romance*, ed. with an Introduction by Frederick Garber (London, 1968).

I have used William Henry Ireland, *The Abbess: A Romance*, 4 vols., (rpt. New York, 1974), and for Godwin's *St. Leon*, the New York, 1975, reprint of the 1835 London edition. For the parody, see Edward Du Bois, *St. Godwin:*

A *Tale of the Sixteenth, Seventeenth, and Eighteenth Centuries* (rpt. New York, 1974).

For Maturin, I have used Charles Robert Maturin, *Melmoth the Wanderer: A Tale*, ed. with an introduction by Douglas Grant (London, 1968). The most comprehensive study is that of Claude Fierobe, *Charles Robert Maturin (1780–1824). L'Homme et L'Oeuvre* (Paris, 1974), with a thorough bibliography. There is a useful study of cross-national and literary influences by Syndy M. Conger, *Matthew G. Lewis, Charles Robert Maturin and the Germans: An Interpretative Study of the Influence of German Literature on the Two Gothic Novels* (Salzburg, 1977).

For *Herman of Unna* and the nineteenth-century literature of Secret Tribunals, see Summers, *The Gothic Quest*, pp. 124–136. Walter Scott's *Anne of Geierstein* appears to have introduced the theme of the non-Inquisition secret tribunal into English literature. The similarity between the two was perceived long before Summers, however. In her 1850 novel *The Vale of Cedars*, the first novel of the "Inquisition" written from a Jewish perspective, Grace Aguilar observed:

> I may be accused in this scene of too closely imitating a somewhat similar occurrence in Anne of Geierstein. Such seeming plagiarism was scarcely possible to be avoided, when the superstitious proceedings of the *vehmic* tribunal and the *secret* Inquisition of Spain are represented by history as so very similar.

The reason for the similarity, of course, is the very process of historical and literary *representation*. For Aguilar's *Vale of Cedars* I have used the edition of New York and Philadelphia, 1850.

For Mme. de Suberwick-Victor de Féréal, *Les mystères de l'Inquisition et autres sociétés secrètes d'Espagne*, I have used an undated mid–nineteenth-century Paris edition (1846) as well as the German translation (Brünn, 1862), an Italian translation of Milan, 1862, a Spanish translation of Mexico City, 1850, and another 1845 Italian translation with the misleading title *Stòria dell'Inquisizióne*.

I have not seen Schiesl's *Torquemada*. There is a brief discussion in Schreiber, pp. 50–51.

One of the most striking aspects of the novels of Suberwick and Aguilar is the extremely favorable light in which Spanish people and values are portrayed. Although the inquisitors and Inquisitions are as wicked as ever—with the added dimension of sexual evil—the romantic interest in Spain and Spanish history is clearly evident in the novels written after 1824. On the romanticizing of Spain and Spanish history, see Elena Fernández Herr, *Les origines de l'Espagne romantique. Les récits de voyage, 1755–1823* (Paris, 1973), with full bibliography. In the United States the process seems to have begun with Washington Irving and George Ticknor.

IMAGES OF THE INQUISITION

The best introduction to the place of judicial punishment in art history is that of Samuel Y. Edgerton, Jr., *Pictures and Punishment: Art and Criminal Prosecu-*

tion during the Florentine Renaissance (Ithaca, 1985). Edgerton's work provides far more information than the title suggests. Much of the visual background to contemporary forms of punishment elsewhere in Europe and in the next several centuries as well is provided in Hans Fehr, *Das Recht im Bilde* (Munich and Leipzig, 1923) and *Das Recht in der Dichtung* (Bern, n.d.). An extensively illustrated work, dealing with other topics as well, is that of Miroslav Hroch and Anna Skýbová, *Die Inquisition im Zeitalter der Gegenreformation*, German translation from the Czech by Wolf B. Oerter (Stuttgart, 1985). A particular virtue of the Hroch–Skýbová book is its wealth of pictures from Czech sources as well as its reproduction of rarely seen images like the auto-de-fé held at the Church of Santa Maria sopra Minerva in Rome in 1657, rendered by Arnold van Westerhout (fig. 38); a large full-color reproduction of Feo Rizi's painting of the *auto-de-fé* of Madrid of 1680 (fig. 61); an unusual engraving of a *strappado* process by Theodor Goetz (fig. 68); and a full color reproduction of Eugenio Lucas's early nineteenth-century painting of a Spanish inquisitorial trial (fig. 71).

An excellent example of the detailed discussions of public punishment in early modern Europe is Jacob Döpler, *Theatrum Poenarum, Suppliciorum et Executionum Criminalium* (Sondershausen, 1693), and the modern scholarly discussion by Peter Spierenburg, *The Spectacle of Suffering* (Cambridge, 1984). There is an interesting example of the identification of inquisitions and torture in the exhibition catalogue *Inquisition/Inquisición*, ed. Robert Held (Florence, 1985).

Chapter 8. The Power of Art and the Transformation of Myth (pp. 231–262)

THE DREAMS OF REASON

The most complete catalogue of Goya's work is that of Pierre Gassier and Juliet Wilson, *Goya, His Life and Work, With a Catalogue Raisonné of the Paintings, Drawings and Engravings* (London, 1971), which includes a superb biographical study as well. There is a lively if highly opinionated introduction to a number of the topics treated here in Gwyn A. Williams, *Goya and the Impossible Revolution* (New York, 1976), which relies heavily, as have I, on the brilliant scholarship of Edith Helman, chiefly her article "The Younger Moratín and Goya: On *Duendes* and *Brujas*," *Hispanic Review* 27 (1959), 103–122, reprinted in her *Jovellanos y Goya* (Madrid, 1970). Helman's *Trasmundo de Goya* (Madrid, 1963), is equally important.

On Moratín's interests in witchcraft beliefs and illustration, see Luis Felipe Vivanco, *Moratín y la Ilustración Mágica* (Madrid, 1972). For Moratín's edition of the 1610 *relación*, I have used the edition of the *Auto-de-Fé Celebrado en la Ciudad de Logroño*, for which Moratín used the pseudonym "the batchelor Gines de Posadilla," printed at Madrid in 1820.

The best historical account of the Logroño trials is that of Gustav Henningsen, *The Witches' Advocate: Basque Witchcraft and the Spanish Inquisition (1609–1614)* (Reno, Nev., 1980).

The best account of the "Black Paintings" is now that of Priscilla E. Muller, *Goya's "Black" Paintings: Truth and Reason in Light and Liberty* (New York, 1984), with extensive and very helpful annotations, and bibliography.

Gassier has continued his extensive cataloguing of the drawings in two later works, *Francisco Goya, Drawings: The Complete Albums*, trans. James Emmons and Robert Allen (New York, 1973), and *The Drawings of Goya: The Sketches, Studies and Individual Drawings* (New York, 1975), and has produced his own illustrated monograph, *Goya, témoin de son temps* (Paris, 1983).

On the earlier eighteenth-century use of dreams to depict images and monsters of popular belief, see Diego de Torres Villaroel, *Visiones y Visitas de Torres con Don Francisco de Quevedo por la corte*, ed. Russell P. Sebold (Madrid, 1966; rpt., 1976).

There is a large literature on the persecution of witches in early modern Europe. The most recent work is that of Brian P. Levack, *The Witch–Hunt in Early Modern Europe* (New York, 1987).

THE FURTHER ADVENTURES OF DON CARLOS

A good introduction to Don Carlos in history is John Lynch, *Spain Under the Habsburgs*, Vol. 1, *Empire and Absolutism, 1519–1598* (New York, 1964), Ch. 6. More recently, see Lovett, *Early Habsburg Spain, 1517–1598*, pp. 125–126.

The myth of Don Carlos was responsibly traced by Frederick W. C. Lieder, *The Don Carlos Theme*, Harvard Studies and Notes in Philology and Literature, Vol. 12 (Cambridge, Mass., 1930), which concentrates largely on literary representation, and, more effectively and recently, by Andrée Mansau, *La création du mythe de Don Carlos* (Toulouse, 1970), some of which is summarized in her *Saint-Réal et l'humanisme cosmopolite* (Lille and Paris, 1976), an extremely valuable account, not only of the Don Carlos theme, but of many of the strands touched upon in this chapter generally. Mansau has also edited, with an introduction, the novel itself: Saint-Réal, *Don Carlos—La Conjuration des Espagnols contre la République de Venise* (Geneva, 1977).

A convenient English version of the Schiller play is that translated by Charles E. Passage, Friedrich von Schiller, *Don Carlos, Infante of Spain* (New York, 1959). On Schiller and Spanish themes, see Herbert Koch, *Schiller und Spanien* (Munich, 1973), Spanish trans. Herbert Koch and Gabriele Staubwasser de Mohorn, *Schiller y España* (Madrid, 1978).

On Verdi and the theme, there is an interesting study of the opera in Vincent Godefroy, *The Dramatic Genius of Verdi: Studies of Selected Operas*, Vol. 2 (London, 1977), but the account is best read in the study of Julian Budden, *Verdi* (London, 1985). There is a convenient English translation of the libretto of *Don Carlo* by Mary Jane Matz, *Don Carlo: Opera in Five Acts*, G. Schirmer's Collection of Opera Librettos (New York, 1979).

The best recent account of Galileo's own beliefs, as well as his dealings with the Inquisition is Stillman Drake, *Galileo* (New York, 1980); see also Jerome J. Langford, *Galileo, Science and the Church* (Ann Arbor, 1971), both with good bibliographies.

For Bruno, see Frances Yates, *Giordano Bruno and the Hermetic Tradition* (1964; rpt. Chicago, 1979). Unfortunately, there is little scholarship on Bruno's reputation before he became in the nineteenth century an early martyr of science.

For Brewster and Brougham, I have used Sir David Brewster, *The Martyrs of Science: Lives of Galileo, Tycho Brahe, and Kepler* (London, 1903).

One of the most useful surveys of Galileo's later reputation is still that of Thomas Henri Martin, *Galilée: Les droits de la science et la méthode des sciences physiques* (Paris, 1868). There is a superb general discussion about revealed religion and science in David C. Lindberg and Ronald L. Numbers, eds., *God and Nature: Historical Essays on the Encounter between Christianity and Science* (Berkeley and Los Angeles, 1986), esp. Chs. 5–9.

On the details of Galileo's later reputation I have benefitted from A. Rupert Hall, "Galileo nel XVIII sècolo," *Rivista de Filosofía* 15 (1979), 367–390; Bernard Jacqueline, "La Chiesa e Galileo nel sècolo dell'Illuminismo," in Paul Poupard, et al., eds., *Galileo Galilei: 350 Anni di Stòria (1633–1983)* (Rome, 1984), 181–195; Marie Boas Hall, "The European Reputation of Galileo's Scientific Thought," in Carlo Maccagni, ed., *Saggi sul Galileo Galilei* (Florence, 1972), 794–807. There is also the interesting book by Italo Mereu, *Stòria dell'Intolleranza in Europa* (Milan, 1979), a study of Galileo's prosecution in the context of Counter-Reformation Europe.

For the correspondence of Descartes, I have used the edition of Ch. Adam and G. Milhaud, eds., Descartes, *Correspondence* Vol. 1 (Paris, 1936), Epp. 58, 61; cf. Vol. 5 (Paris, 1951), Ep. 337. Descartes' biographer was Adrien Baillet, *Vie de M. Descartes* (Paris, 1691), who greatly emphasized the point made by Descartes in his letters to Mersenne.

The *Discours préliminaire* of the *Encyclopédie* of d'Alembert was separately edited and published by F. Picavet in 1894 (rpt. Paris, 1984); d'Alembert's comments on Galileo and Descartes are on pp. 90–91. A good guide to the topic of religion in general in the *Encyclopédie* is John Lough, *The Encyclopédie* (New York, 1971), with further references. D'Alembert's article on Copernicus is conveniently reprinted in John Lough, ed., *The Encyclopédie of Diderot and d'Alembert: Selected Articles* (Cambridge, 1969), 32–37.

Some aspects about the formation of the legend of Galileo's tribulations before the Roman Inquisition are sensibly discussed in the still valuable work of Karl von Gebler, *Galileo Galilei and the Roman Curia*, trans. Mrs. George Sturge (London, 1879), Ch. 10. The best general account is that of Eric Cochrane in *Florence in the Forgotten Centuries* (Chicago, 1973), Book 3.

The story of the records of Galileo's trial is elegantly and learnedly told in Owen Chadwick, *Catholicism and History: The Opening of The Vatican Archives* (Cambridge, 1978). The process began with Marino Marini's papally approved

Galileo e l'Inquisizióne of 1850 and included Berti's complete publication of the record in 1876. Berti also published *Copernico e le vicende del sistèma Copernicano in Itàlia*, with documents on Bruno and Galileo, in 1876. Not surprisingly, the canon of the First Vatican Council of 1870 on papal infallibility raised all of these questions again, and very vigorously. For an example, see William W. Roberts, *The Pontifical Decrees against the Doctrine of the Earth's Movement* (1870; rpt. London, 1885).

The best general study of the problem of religious belief and scientific discovery is the splendid collection edited by David C. Lindberg and Ronald L. Numbers, *God and Nature* (Berkeley and Los Angeles, 1986), particularly Chs. 4–7 and 14–15. There is ample reference to the impact of Darwin's theory in *God and Nature*, as well as to other scholarship. Particularly important for this study have been the works of James R. Moore, *The Post-Darwinian Controversies* (Cambridge, 1979), and Ronald R. Numbers, "Science and Religion," *Osiris*, second series, Vol. 1 (1985), 59–80. Also useful is Gertrude Himmelfarb, *Darwin and the Darwinian Revolution* (1962; rpt. New York, 1968).

On Draper, see Donald Fleming, *John William Draper and the Religion of Science* (Philadelphia, 1950), and on White, Glenn C. Altschuler, *Andrew Dickson White—Educator, Historian, Diplomat* (Ithaca, 1979).

On the echoes of Hermetism found by contemporaries in the work of Galileo, see now Lawrence S. Lerner and Edward A. Gosselin, "Galileo and the Specter of Bruno," *Scientific American* 255 (1986), 126–133.

THE GRAND INQUISITOR

For a text I have used Fyodor Dostoievsky, *The Brothers Karamazov*, trans. Constance Garnett, revised by Ralph E. Matlaw (New York, 1976). The additional materials included in Matlaw's edition are extremely informative. Especially important is the essay by Nathan Rosen, "Style and Structure in *The Brothers Karamazov* (The Grand Inquisitor and The Russian Monk)," originally printed in *Russian Literature Triquarterly* 1 (1971), 352–365 (Matlaw, pp. 841–851).

On early Russian interest in Spain and the Spanish method of religious "cleansing," see James H. Billington, *The Icon and the Axe: An Interpretive History of Russian Culture* (New York, 1966), 70f. The most thorough study of Dostoievsky's developing attitude toward Latin Christianity is that of Denis Dirscherl, S. J., *Dostoevsky and the Catholic Church* (Chicago, 1986).

The case for Schiller's influence on Dostoievsky's Grand Inquisitor has been made often, notably in Passage's introduction to his English translation of *Don Carlos* and by Edmund K. Kostka, *Schiller in Russian Literature* (Philadelphia, 1965). The best account of Dostoievsky's extremely subtle and free use of Schiller is that of Alexandra H. Lyngstad, *Dostoevskij and Schiller* (The Hague and Paris, 1975), esp. pp. 74–91. Lyngstad cites the important bibliography of German critical studies of Dostoievsky and Schiller as well.

Although Billington's suggestions of Russian interest in the Spanish Inquisition from the fifteenth century on are persuasive, the reversion to a "non-inquisitorial" ecclesiology is implied in Alexander V. Muller, "The Inquisitorial Network of Peter the Great," in Robert L. Nichols and Theofanis George Stavrou, eds., *Russian Orthodoxy Under the Old Regime* (Minneapolis, 1978), 142–153. It is doubtful that Dostoievsky knew of or would have been interested in the early Russian interest. His own vision of Russian Orthodoxy is utterly free of any suggestion of inquisitions or inquisitorial styles.

Chapter 9. From Myth to History (pp. 263–295)

FROM MYTH TO HISTORY

General accounts of historiography in early modern Europe do not usually pay significant attention to the subject of The Inquisition, although a number of writers discussed by Dickens and Tonkin, for example, included accounts of various inquisitions within larger historical works.

THE INQUISITORS AND OTHER CATHOLICS WRITE HISTORY

The best general account of the emergence of Catholic church historiography is that of Eric Cochrane, *Historians and Historiography in the Italian Renaissance* (Chicago, 1981), 445–478; for Baronius, see Cyriac K. Pullapilly, *Caesar Baronius: Counter-Reformation Historian* (Notre Dame, 1975).

There is no literature on Pàramo. I have used the edition of Madrid, 1598, as well as the abridgment and French translation by Morellet in 1762 and Voltaire's *Dictionnaire philosophique*, for both of which see Ch. 6.

For Sarpi, see Ch. 6 and Cochrane, pp. 172–478. I have used the edition of 1638 of his *Història della Sacra Inquisitióne composta già dal R. P. Paolo Servita: ed hora la prima volta posta in luce. Opera pia, dotta, e curiósa: A Consiglièri, Casuisti, e Politici molto necessària.*

THE DISSENTING HISTORIANS

There is no literature in English on Limborch. For his connections with Locke, see John Locke, *Epistola de Tolerantia/A Letter on Toleration*, ed., Raymond Klibansky, with Intro. by J. W. Gough (Oxford, 1968). I have used the original edition Philippi a Limborch, *Historia Inquisitionis* (Amsterdam, 1692) as well as Chandler's translation of 1731.

GALLICAN HISTORIANS AND THE INQUISITION

Gallican and Jansenist historians in late seventeenth- and eighteenth-century France were no admirers of religious toleration of the kind advocated by Bayle, Locke, and Limborch, although they were very interested in restricting the authority of Rome and they supported the Revocation of the Edict of Nantes in 1685. The publisher and location of the work of Marsollier, Du Pin, and Goujet is alleged to be "Pierre Marteau of Cologne," although this was a false imprint, widely used for marginally controversial literature during the period. On Bayle's treatise, see Walter Rex, *Essays on Pierre Bayle and Religious Controversy* (The Hague, 1965), esp. Ch. 5.

An additional account of Freemasonry and the Inquisition, particularly in Tuscany, is that of Modesto Rastrelli, *Fatti attenenti all Inquisizióne e sua istòria* (Florence, 1783), Vekene Nos. 3998–3999.

THE ADVENTURES OF JUAN ANTONIO LLORENTE

A great deal of material on Llorente, much by himself, will be found in the work of Antonio Márquez, *Juan Antonio Llorente, Noticia biográfica* (*Autobiografía*) (Madrid, 1982); Gerard Dufour, *Juan Antonio Llorente en France* (*1813–1822*) (Geneva, 1982); G. Dufour, ed., Juan Antonio Llorente, *Memoria histórica* (Paris, 1977); Antonio Márquez, *Literatura e Inquisición en España* (*1478–1834*) (Madrid, 1980). Further references in Manuel Nuñez de Arenas, *L'Espagne des lumières au romantisme*, ed. Robert Marrast (Paris, 1963), 173–176. A reprint of the English abridgment of Llorente, with an introduction by Gabriel H. Lovett, was published at Williamstown, Mass. in 1966.

On Menendez y Pelayo, see John Lynch, "Menendez Pelayo as a Historian," *Bulletin of Hispanic Studies* 33 (1956), 187–201.

HENRY CHARLES LEA

On Lea, the only biography is E. Sculley Bradley, *Henry Charles Lea: A Biography* (Philadelphia, 1931). I am presently working on a full-length biographical study entitled *Henry Charles Lea and the American Discovery of the Past*, which should appear in 1989, a portion of which may be found in Edward Peters, "*Una morada de monstruos:* Henry Charles Lea y el descubrimiento americano de la Inquisición," in Alcalá, *Inquisición española*, 518–541. There is an excellent essay by Gustav Henningsen, "The Archives and the Historiography of the Spanish Inquisition," in Henningsen and Tedeschi, *The Inquisition in Early Modern Europe*, 54–78.

Chapter 10. Materials for a Meditation (pp. 296–315)

D. H. LAWRENCE AND OTHERS REREAD DOSTOIEVSKY

Lawrence's introduction to the 1930 reprint of *The Grand Inquisitor* has been reprinted in Fyodor Dostoievsky, *The Brothers Karamozov . . . Backgrounds and Sources, Essays in Criticism*, ed. Ralph E. Matlaw (New York, 1976). Some of the twentieth-century literature discussed below is considered in Jürgen Schreiber, *Jerzy Andrzejewskis Roman 'Ciemności Kryja Ziemie' und die Darstellung der spanischen Inquisition in Werken der Fiktionalen Literatur* (Munich, 1981), pp. 58–67.

For Zamyatin, see in addition Alex M. Shane, *The Life and Works of Evgenij I. Zamjatin* (Berkeley and Los Angeles, 1968).

Andres' novella is printed in Stefan Andres, *Novellen und Erzählungen* (Munich, 1962). Of particular interest is the essay by Karl O. Nordstrand, "El Greco malt den Grossinquisitor," in *Utopia und Weltverfahrung. Stefan Andres und sein Werk im Gedächtnis seiner Freunde* (Munich, 1972, pp. 117–131). In the same volume, see the sensitive essay by Gerd Tellenbach, "Stefan Andres und die Geschichte," pp. 166–180. An abbreviated version of Nordstrand's essay is printed in Wilhelm Grosse, ed., *Stefan Andres. Ein Reader zu Person und Werk* (Trier, 1980), pp. 115–124. In the same volume, see Lena Burm, "Stefan Andres' kritische Stellungnahme zur römisch-katholischen Kirche," pp. 180–193.

The works of Koestler and Orwell are readily available. The useful material in Sonia Orwell and Ian Angus, eds., *The Collected Essays, Journalism and Letters of George Orwell*, 4 vols. (New York, 1968), should be read with Bernard Crick, *George Orwell: A Life* (New York, 1980), used as a guide.

The work of Andrzejewski is thoroughly considered in Schueiber. For the novel, see Jerzy Andrzejewski, *The Inquisitors*, trans. Konrad Syrop (Westport, 1976).

INQUISITIONS AND WITCH-HUNTS IN THE TWENTIETH CENTURY

There are a few scattered references to witch-hunts in the standard historical accounts: Robert K. Murray, *The Red Scare: A Study of National Hysteria, 1919–1920* (1955; rpt. New York, 1964); M. S. McAuliffe, *The Red Scare and the Crisis in American Liberalism, 1947–1954* (Diss. University of Maryland, 1972); Kenneth O'Reilly, *Hoover and the Un-Americans: The FBI, HUAC, and the Red Menace* (Philadelphia, 1983), all with extensive references.

The subject of anti-Catholicism in the first half of the nineteenth century in the United States is chronicled in Ray Allen Billington, *The Protestant Crusade, 1800–1860* (rpt. Chicago, 1964), and for the later period, by John Higham, *Strangers in the Land: Patterns of American Nativism, 1860–1925*. Billington's bibliography is particularly useful for tracing publications discussed in my text in detail. On American interest in Italy, see Howard R. Marraro, *American Opinion on the Unification of Italy, 1846–1861* (rpt. New York, 1969); cf. C. T. McIntire, *England against the Papacy, 1858–1861: Tories, Liberals, and the overthrow of papal temporal power during the Italian Risorgimento* (Cambridge, 1983).

On American interest in the Middle Ages, the classic work is that of Hans Rudolf Guggisberg, *Das europaische Mittelalter im amerikanischen Geschichtsdenken des 19. und des frühen 20. Jahrhunderts* (Basel and Stuttgart, 1964), and idem, *Alte und Neue Welt in historischer Perspektiv* (Bern and Frankfurt, 1973).

The 1920 National Popular Government League report has recently been reprinted: R. G. Brown, Zechariah Chaffe, Jr., et al., *Illegal Practices of the*

Department of Justice (New York, 1969). Carey McWilliams, Witch Hunt: The Revival of Heresy (Boston, 1950); Cedric Belfrage, The American Inquisition: 1945–1960 (Indianapolis and New York, 1973); Stanley Kutler, The American Inquisition: Justice and Injustice in the Cold War (New York, 1982).

On the role of American police forces, see the references in Edward Peters, Torture, Ch. 4.

The separate printing of the Laughton version of Brecht's Leben des Galilei, with an introduction by Eric Bentley, was published in New York in 1966. There are several studies of the play and memoirs of Brecht that consider some of the points I have raised above: Gerhard Szczesny, The Case against Bertolt Brecht, trans. Alexander Gode (New York, 1969) is highly critical of Brecht, but it focuses its discussion upon Brecht's use of his historical sources and is quite useful; there is a good discussion with extensive bibliography in Werner Zimmermann, Bertolt Brecht Leben des Galilei. Dramatik der Widersprüche (Paderborn, 1985). Both of the above, as well as Bentley, consider Brecht's denial of contemporary identification of the Inquisition. So does James K. Lyon, Bertolt Brecht's American Cicerone (Bonn, 1978).

Lion Feuchtwanger's Goya oder der arge Weg der Erkenntnis was published simultaneously in German (Frankfurt, 1951) and English (as This Is the Hour [New York, 1951]). On Feuchtwanger's concerns leading to his interest in witch-hunts and inquisitions, see Lothar Kahn, Insight and Action: The Life and Work of Lion Feuchtwanger (New Jersey, 1975), and Kahn, "Der arge Weg der Erkenntnis," in John M. Spalek, ed., Lion Feuchtwanger: The Man His Ideas His Work, University of Southern California Studies in Comparative Literature, Vol. 3 (Los Angeles, 1972), pp. 201–216; cf. Ludwig Maximilian Fischer, Vernunft und Fortschritt (Königstein, 1979). I am grateful to Dr. Norbert Abels of Frankfurt for suggesting that I consider Feuchtwanger.

On Arthur Miller's approach to the Salem Village trials, see the text of The Crucible and the Introduction by Miller in Arthur Miller's Collected Plays (New York, 1957), and the useful study by Benjamin Nelson, Arthur Miller: Portrait of a Playwright (New York, 1973), esp. Chs. 12 and 13.

No Praise for Folly

A number of late twentieth-century works fit into no known bibliographical category in this book, but they play a role in illustrating some further varied uses of The Inquisition in contemporary thought. Thomas Szasz, M.D., The Manufacture of Madness: A Comparative Study of the Inquisition and the Mental Health Movement (New York, 1970; rpt. 1977) employs a reductionist model of inquisitions and witch-hunts to attack the current practice of psychiatry in much the same manner as Belfrage's American Inquisition did for some aspects of American politics. Mark Graubard, Witchcraft and the Nature of Man (Lanham, Md., 1985) reverses Belfrage's identification; the victims in the Salem Village trials are now identified with the American Right, their persecutors with the Left, and Arthur Miller is excoriated for his ideologically inspired historical distortions. But the Soviet academician I. Grigulevich, *Historia de la Inquisición*, trans. M. Kuznetsov (Moscow, 1980) argues the Belfrage– McWilliams case that the inquisitions were a natural product of feudal/capitalist society.

A similarity may now be detected in a slight modification of the old anti-clerical attitude that used to mark only confessional Protestant accounts of the inquisitions. Jacques Pinglé, *L'Inquisition ou la dictature de la foi* (Paris, 1983) is an unscholarly attack on the monstrosities of Catholicism; yet John O'Brien, *The Inquisition* (New York, 1973), a Catholic account, accepts the worst of the myths of *The Inquisition* in a post–Vatican II spirit of ecumenical goodwill, indicating that the new church will never do such things again.

In a moving essay on the political sentimentality of public language, "Politics and the English Language," published in 1946, George Orwell observed, apropos the term "fascism":

> The word Fascism has now no meaning except in so far as it signifies "something not desirable." The words *democracy, socialism, freedom, patriotic, realistic, justice,* have each of them several different meanings which cannot be reconciled with each other.

Several years ago I suggested that the word *torture* could easily be added to Orwell's list. These last works indicate that the word *inquisition* could just as easily be added as well, and that the term *inquisition* has now been reduced, out of a large and specific history, to mean simply "an undesirable, illegitimate, and distasteful form of inquiry or interrogation."

Index